MARK TWAIN–HOWELLS
LETTERS

VOLUME ONE

Howells and Clemens at Stormfield in 1909. (See letter 663.)

MARK TWAIN–HOWELLS LETTERS

The Correspondence of
Samuel L. Clemens and William D. Howells
1 8 7 2 – 1 9 1 0

Edited by
Henry Nash Smith and William M. Gibson
with the assistance of
Frederick Anderson

**THE BELKNAP PRESS OF
HARVARD UNIVERSITY PRESS**
Cambridge, Massachusetts
1 9 6 0

Typography by Burton Jones

Printed and bound by The Riverside Press
Cambridge, Massachusetts, U.S.A.

Library of Congress Catalog Card Number 60-5397

CONTENTS

CONTENTS

LIST OF ILLUSTRATIONS

VOLUME ONE

LIST OF ILLUSTRATIONS

VOLUME TWO

ACKNOWLEDGMENTS

We are deeply indebted to Mrs. Clara Clemens Samossoud and the Mark Twain Estate and to Mr. William W. Howells and The Heirs of William Dean Howells for permission to publish the many letters and significant portions of other literary documents by S. L. Clemens and W. D. Howells first printed in these volumes. The editors wish to thank the Henry W. and Albert A. Berg Collection of The New York Public Library for numerous courtesies over a period of years, especially for its generosity in making possible the publication of a reliable text by allowing us to have and use photographic copies of many unpublished letters of Mark Twain owned by the Collection. We also owe a debt of gratitude to the responsible authorities for permission to consult and copy manuscripts in the Houghton Library and the Theatre Collection of Harvard University and the University of California Library, Berkeley; and to Mr. Joseph H. Twichell and the Yale University Library for permission to consult and to quote from the Joseph H. Twichell papers and the Twichell Journal. We also wish to acknowledge the great generosity of Mr. and Mrs. Samuel C. Webster and of Mr. C. Waller Barrett in allowing us to make copies of many letters and documents by Clemens and Howells in their possession.

We owe especial thanks to Miss Mildred Howells, who has graciously permitted us to include in this work the eighty-eight letters of Howells and Mark Twain which she published in her authoritative *Life in Letters of William Dean Howells,* and to quote extensively from other letters and from her editorial comment in her book.

Our work has been generously supported by grants from the Penrose Fund of the American Philosophical Society, the Committee on Research of the Graduate School of Arts and Science, New York University, and the Senate Committee on Research, University of California, Berkeley. The Library of the University of California at Berkeley has also contributed substantially to the project over a period of years.

For help in particular editorial problems we wish to thank Messrs. Howard G. Baetzhold, L. G. Crossman, Herbert Feinstein, and John D. Gordan; Miss Carolyn E. Jakeman; Messrs. Robert J. Lowenherz, Kenneth Lynn, and Walter MacKellar; Miss Shirley J. Richardson; and Messrs. Roger B. Salomon, Alan Wilde, Ernest H. Wilkins, and Howard S. Wilson. Mrs. Henry Lynn, Jr., and Mrs. Jane Sherman assisted us with skill and devotion in preparing the manuscript. Mrs. W. S. Mallory Lash and Miss Nora Brown have given us superlative editorial assistance. Although the name of Frederick Anderson appears on the title page in recognition of his work on this book at every stage of its gestation, we wish to note specially our obligation to him for preparing the Calendar. Mr. Walter Blair placed at our disposal his wide knowledge of Mark Twain's life and writings, and read portions of the manuscript. Harper & Brothers has kindly given us permission to quote at length from several works by Howells, especially *My Mark Twain;* and Doubleday & Company has been similarly liberal in allowing quotation from Miss Mildred Howells's *Life in Letters of William Dean Howells.*

Our greatest debt, the scope of which cannot be adequately measured here but which will appear again and again to the reader of these letters, is to five scholars, living and dead. We have relied heavily on the work of the late Albert B. Paine, Bernard DeVoto, and Dixon Wecter, Literary Editors of the Mark Twain Estate, who assembled, edited, and interpreted Mark Twain's writings. Messrs. George W. Arms and Frederic C. Marston, Jr., have worked for many years preparing for publication an annotated calendar of the entire Howells correspondence, to be followed by further volumes of Howells's letters, and they have made their files and their special knowledge available to us with constant generosity. Although none of these scholars bears responsibility for our mistakes, they have all none the less become our collaborators in editing the letters of Mark Twain and Howells, and we are profoundly grateful to them.

ACKNOWLEDGMENTS

We take pleasure in acknowledging the courtesy of the following libraries and collectors in giving us access to unpublished manuscript materials, chiefly letters by Howells to correspondents other than Clemens:

Abernethy Collection, Middlebury College
American Antiquarian Society
Mr. George W. Arms
Mr. C. Waller Barrett
Brotherton Library, Leeds
Columbia University Library
Library of Congress
Connecticut Historical Society, Hartford
Duke University Library
Mrs. John Goodrich
Hayes Memorial Library
Houghton Library, Harvard University
Theatre Collection, Harvard University
Historical and Philosophical Society of Ohio Library, Cincinnati
Henry E. Huntington Library
Knox College Library
Berg Collection, New York Public Library
Manuscript Division, New York Public Library
Mr. W. Hugh Peal
University of Pennsylvania Library
Princeton University Library
Mr. Joseph Rosenberg
Rutgers University Library
Howard-Tilton Memorial Library, Tulane University
University of Virginia Library
Watkinson Library, Trinity College, Hartford
Mr. and Mrs. Samuel C. Webster
Yale University Library
Mr. E. N. Zeigler

Finally, we wish to acknowledge a debt of gratitude to the persons, institutions, and publishing houses listed below for permission to quote from unpublished letters and manuscripts of the men whose names appear in parentheses in the right-hand column:

The Honorable Bailey Aldrich and Mrs. Vinton Chapin	(Thomas Bailey Aldrich)
Mrs. Charles M. Andrews	(Mrs. Charles M. Andrews)
Mr. Philip Bancroft	(Hubert Howe Bancroft)
Chatto & Windus, Ltd.	(Andrew Chatto)
Mr. Horace B. Clark	(Charles H. Clark)
Miss Elizabeth Daly	(Augustin Daly)
The Honorable Peter Freling-huysen, Jr.	(Frederick T. Frelinghuysen)
Mr. Watt P. Marchman (for the Hayes Memorial Library)	(Rutherford B. Hayes)
Mr. John Hay Whitney and Mrs. Joan Whitney Payson	(John Hay)
Mr. William W. Howells	(John M. Howells)
Doubleday & Company	(S. S. McClure)
Mr. Guy E. Shipley (for *The Churchman*)	(Marshall Mallory)
Mr. William A. Jackson (for the Houghton Library, Harvard University)	(Charles Eliot Norton)
Miss Margaret Perry	(Thomas S. Perry)
Mr. I. N. P. Stokes	(Anson P. Stokes)

INTRODUCTION

"Brander Matthews closes his review of the Clemens biography with the suggestion that Clemens's letters to me might well be published in full. I think so too; they are wonderful; and if mine were printed with them, perhaps it would not hurt" (WDH to F. A. Duneka, New York, 14 October 1912, Am. Antiq. Soc., AGM TS)

The letters of William D. Howells and Samuel L. Clemens to each other record a friendship not easily paralleled in the history of American literature for duration and intensity. The letters of Emerson and Carlyle are characterized by high thought, yet in comparison with these they are chilly. Melville's letters to Hawthorne during their brief uneven friendship are warm and supremely interesting, but they are few, and Hawthorne's letters in answer were destroyed. The abundant, richly allusive letters of Howells and Mark Twain, both humorists, are filled with laughter, gentle or raucous, shallow or profound, which may rise from a state of pure euphoria, or a vivid satirical impulse, or an inner motion of despair, or even the frustration of a too hot desire to tell in Howells's phrase the "black heart's truth." The letters also embody on occasion the extremity of grief. They tell, in fact, a full story of almost forty years, episodic, not very dramatic, yet rarely dull, and always human. For the two men themselves it was a friendship of equals, although any measurement of them would have to balance imponderables: uneven genius against critical clairvoyance, "Elizabethan breadth of parlance" against neat ironic utterance, impulsiveness against instinctive sobriety. Nevertheless, despite their contrasting circumstances — Clemens's spendthrift wealth and Howells's modest if adequate income — the friends had much in common: their childhood in Western small towns, their lack of formal education, their long careers as back-trailers in the East, their equality in personal loss and grief, and above all their professional commitment to writing as a way of life. Each respected the other as an artist of the first rank. Whatever Howells's surmise may have been concerning his own eventual place in American literature, he wanted, as he wrote Mark Twain, to "set myself before posterity as a friend who valued you aright in your own time" (letter 541). Clemens's regard for Howells's work was less self-conscious but equally wholehearted. "You are really my only author," he exclaimed as he was reading *Indian Summer* (letter 410), and it was very nearly true.

The letters tell their own story, yet it seems proper to touch upon the chief implications of the correspondence now first drawn together and printed as a whole. For one thing, the letters seem to us to complete the destruction of the once widely held belief that Howells as an editor emasculated Mark Twain's vigor of expression and partially kept him from artistic fulfillment. In so far as Howells exerted an influence on Mark Twain's writing, his influence was distinctly for the good. His pruning out of words and expressions likely to offend *Atlantic* subscribers or the mass audience which bought subscription books may seem pointless or deplorable to a modern reader, but whether his emendations of detail were helpful or harmful, they are negligible in the light of his advice to Clemens in such larger matters as consistency of tone, verisimilitude, and the need to eliminate irrelevancy and to keep burlesque from becoming mere horseplay.

A great deal of the stimulus the two friends imparted to each other resulted from their frequent visits, in Cambridge or Hartford, or later in New York. Howells early fell into the habit of reading parts of his current work aloud to Mark Twain (badly, according to that exacting critic of oral art) — a farce, or *The Undiscovered Country,* or *A Modern Instance,* for example; and just as Mark Twain coached Howells in the art of reading aloud and speaking, he must on occasion have acted the literary critic himself. Clemens read aloud to Howells or asked him to read most of his major works, in manuscript or in proof. On these visits, they talked about the germs of stories, or the development of their current projects. They chaffed each other in the company of Aldrich or Osgood or Warner or Twichell. Sometimes they sat up half the night talking of "Providence, foreknowledge, will and fate,/Fixed fate, free will, foreknowledge absolute" or arguing whether certain striking examples of "human credulity and folly" proved that the human race was damned. Because Howells was the more experienced novelist, an editor accustomed to deadlines who wrote his fiction on a schedule, Mark Twain may have profited in a literary sense more than Howells from their conversations and what he called "the usual inspiration-boom." But as Howells once said: "Your visit was a perfect ovation for us: we *never* enjoy anything so much as those visits of yours. The smoke and the Scotch and the late hours almost kill us; but we look each other in the eyes when you are gone, and say what a glorious time it was, and air the library, and begin sleeping and dieting, and longing to have you back again" (letter 141). It is the testimony of other good friends of Clemens that, like Satan in *The Mysterious Stranger,* he "worked his enchantments upon us again with that fatal music of his voice. . . . We could only listen to him, and love him. . . . He made us drunk with the joy of being with him . . ." (DE, XXVII, 18).

Some of these two- or three- or four-day visits in Hartford and Cambridge resulted in schemes which would have done credit to Colonel Beriah Sellers. The collaborative projects of the two friends usually began in moods of vaulting enthusiasm and ended in the helpless laughter which must follow absolute failure. Their first joint venture was to wander all over North Cambridge on a raw April day in 1875 — the best place, they had boasted to Elinor Howells, from which to leave for the Centennial celebration in Concord — trying without success to find transportation. They then lingered in the cold wind, and on their return tried in vain to make the skeptical Mrs. Howells accept the preposterous notion that they had attended the celebration. This failure set the pattern. It was followed by a plan to secure for the *Atlantic* a dozen stories developed by as many writers from a single plot, projected but never realized trips together to Bermuda and down the Mississippi, the compilation of a "library of humor" (which was finally published, but without Howells's name), the writing of a full-length play (*Colonel Sellers as a Scientist,* which failed), and a never-realized scheme to tour the country in a private car with a "circus" of writers who would grow rich reading from their works in public. In *My Mark Twain,* Howells reached the conclusion that "from our joint experience in failing I argue that Clemens's affection for me must have been great to enable him to condone in me the final defection which was apt to be the end of our enterprises" (p. 42).

If Mark Twain and Howells regularly came to grief in their joint undertakings, they did not fail in their proper tasks as men of letters. From the beginning to the end of his mature writing career Clemens could count on shrewd advice at nearly every stage of the production of his books, and an authoritative, thoughtful review if Howells thought well of the work — or silence if he did not. Howells, for example, noted in reading the manuscript how and where the story of *Tom Sawyer* really closed, and launched it with a review discussing Mark Twain's artistic growth. To be sure, he did not review *Adventures of Huckleberry Finn* upon its first appearance, because for the moment he was without a critical forum; but he talked over the novel apparently from its earliest beginnings, read and edited the manuscript at various stages, arranged to have part of it typed for the printer, and read the proofs. It is not strange that Charles L. Webster and Mark Twain sent him in advance three of the first twelve copies printed of the first edition. Though Clemens might have been satisfied with Edmund C. Stedman's help in editing the manuscript of *A Connecticut Yankee,* he was pleased and relieved when Howells acceded to Olivia Clemens's urgent request that he read the book in manuscript, for Clemens wished to be sure that his "blasts of opinion" against monarchy, chivalry, and the Established Church were not "so strongly worded as to repel instead of persuade" (letter 474).

Yet it was not so much Howells's advice concerning any particular book that mattered, as the constant presence and effect of his literary taste and conscience. His judgment was not infallible, as his enthusiasm for the fatuous collaborative play about Colonel Sellers proves. But in view of Mark Twain's demonstrated capacity for producing long passages of dead humor and sentimentality, one may well conclude that Howells's most important service to the greater writer consisted in warning him against excesses of burlesque and convincing him that he ought not to take himself at too cheap a valuation. The work Howells published in the *Atlantic* or — after he ceased to be editor of the magazine — praised on first reading in manuscript is mostly the precious wheat which time has winnowed out, from "A True Story" and "The Recent Carnival of Crime in Connecticut" to "Old Times on the Mississippi," *Tom Sawyer* and *Huckleberry Finn, A Connecticut Yankee,* and "Captain Stormfield's Visit to Heaven." The stories he cared less for tend to be difficult to read. The stories he rejected are chaff, with scarcely an exception. The evidence of the letters is plain. In so far as Mark Twain needed and was able to profit from advice about his writing, Howells gave him the best that America offered, well-informed, sympathetic, shrewd, professional in the best sense.

To speak more generally, these letters help to clarify the outlines of a vernacular tradition in the Gilded Age, which has exerted a powerful influence on a number of the best writers of tales and novels in the twentieth century. Howells fostered the tradition by altering the style of the *Atlantic Monthly* as a whole in the direction of colloquial freedom and ease, and by writing his own distinguished version of the style. Concerning it he carried on an amusing argument with the conservative *Atlantic* contributor, his friend Thomas W. Higginson; and the new department which he founded in the *Atlantic* in January 1877, "The Contributors' Club," is filled with fine examples of it, all unsigned but several sent in by Clemens himself. Howells's grounds for initiating or supporting this revolution in diction, tone, and manner were impressive: Emerson's theory of language in "The American Scholar" and "The Poet," Lowell's use of the New England vernacular in his "Biglow Papers," and Dante's defense of the "Illustrious Vernacular" with his use of vulgar Italian in *The Divine Comedy.* Emerson had called for an American poet speaking "the language of the street"; Whitman in his poems consciously responded to the challenge; but it was Mark Twain who made the common speech into an instrument of narrative prose having lyric and epic as well as comic potentialities. Howells was aware of the vitality and power of his friend's colloquial style, and advised him to "yarn it off as if into my sympathetic ear" when Clemens was writing the first papers of his "Old Times on the Mississippi" series. The style of these essays on piloting clearly points toward the revolutionary accomplishment of *Huckleberry Finn*.

Howells, regarded as the leading American man of letters in his time, is not now to be ranked with Clemens or with James as a novelist, yet it is not difficult to see why Clemens and others regarded him as the "foremost critic of the day." Most Americans thought of Mark Twain during his lifetime as a public entertainer and a funny man rather than as the great historical novelist of the prewar South, or the melancholy fabulist of "Captain Stormfield," or the creator of a distinctively American prose. But from the publication of his first books, as these letters show, Howells knew him to be a great writer. The letters reveal with equal clarity the qualities of mind and spirit which brought the two men together in a long and warm friendship. Despite Clemens's "wild pleasure in shocking people with his ribaldries and profanities" and the sometimes savage exaggerations into which his "fierce intensity" led him, Howells maintained that he was not only a first-rate artist but the most truthful man he had ever known, "the most serious, the most humane, the most conscientious," whose "central and final personality was something exquisite" (MMT, p. 34). The reader of this correspondence will recognize a touch of self-characterization in the general truth of the portrait.

The correspondence forms a sequence between 1872 and 1910 in which comparatively few letters appear to be missing; no serious break in the correspondence is apparent. From an early date Howells and Clemens seem to have gone to some pains to preserve each other's letters, often sending a particularly lively letter to a friend to read but always asking that it be returned. Consequently the great bulk of the correspondence is now to be found with the Howells Papers in the Houghton Library of Harvard University, the Berg Collection of the New York Public Library, and the Mark Twain Papers in the General Library of the University of California at Berkeley. A few scattered letters are in the Watkinson Library of Trinity College, the Albert B. Paine Collection of the Henry E. Huntington Library, the Rutherford B. Hayes Memorial Library in Fremont, Ohio, and the collections of Mr. Samuel C. Webster and Mr. C. Waller Barrett.

About three hundred of the total of 681 communications have been published — accurately and with very few editorial excisions by Miss Mildred Howells in her *Life in Letters of William Dean Howells,* often partially and with errors, bowdlerizations, and "corrections" by Albert B. Paine in his irreplaceable official life, *Mark Twain, A Biography,* and his edition of *Mark Twain's Letters.*

H.N.S.
W.M.G.

May 1959

NOTE ON EDITORIAL PRACTICE

The letters in this book comprise every written communication between Clemens and Howells known to the editors. (Eight rather trivial and undated notes appear in the Appendix.) Also included are a number of directly relevant letters and notes written by other members of the two families or addressed to them by the principal correspondents. We have supplied more information in footnotes and in the Appendix than is necessary for a literal comprehension of the correspondence. Our intention has been to trace the lines of connection between the letters of Clemens and Howells and their writings, published or unpublished, and to correct or supplement existing biographies of the two men wherever the implications of the correspondence make this possible. In particular, we have quoted freely from unpublished materials in the Howells and Mark Twain papers, and from obscure contemporary sources such as newpapers. We have also included several notes on bibliographical matters.

We have transcribed the letters as accurately as we were able without resorting to unconventional typography. We have not normalized punctuation or spelling, but we have normalized the placing of quotation marks, and have omitted the few irrelevant words or numerals on sheets of paper which Clemens re-used in writing to Howells. Roswell Phelps, Clemens's secretary at one time, typed eight of the letters on a machine having capital letters only. We have regularized these texts by setting them in capitals and lower case, without altering them otherwise. The text of telegrams is, of course, in the handwriting or typewriting of clerks, and here we have transcribed portions of the printed blank necessary to make the messages intelligible. We have moved sentences written at the top or in the margins of pages to the places where we believe they belong in the text, usually as postscripts, and have raised the complimentary close to the last line of the letter where this has been typographically possible. When the date line in its entirety was not too long, we have put all its elements on one line.

Words inserted above the line by the writer of a letter have been included in the text without comment. Illegible cancellations and those representing mere slips of the pen have been ignored, but legible cancellations that throw some light on the writer's choice of words or register a change in what he intended to say are included within angle brackets, thus: ⟨ ⟩. Square brackets within the text of the letters have been reserved for the very few occasions when the editors have supplied a word evidently omitted by the writer through oversight. The square brackets which Clemens sometimes used have been transcribed as parentheses.

When places of writing and dates are not indicated by Clemens and Howells, the editors according to their combined best judgment have supplied them within square brackets in the date line. If place and date are not easily inferred from the text of the letter, question marks register serious editorial doubt concerning them, or an "MS note" presents the evidence for the editors' decision. Because many of the manuscript letters are without envelopes, and because the envelopes that have been preserved cannot certainly be assigned in every case to a given letter, we have not relied on postmarks as an indication of the place of writing except in a few cases where better evidence is lacking. In particular, we have not tried to distinguish among Boston, Belmont, and Cambridge as the place of writing by Howells on *Atlantic Monthly* letterhead, but have assigned such letters uniformly to Cambridge and later to Boston as the location of the *Atlantic* office. When Howells was obviously writing on *Atlantic* letterhead from a more distant place such as a summer residence, we try to state, within brackets in the date line, the exact place where the letter was written.

The location of the original manuscripts of the letters, or of the most accurate version known to us, is set forth in the Calendar. It will be noted that for nine letters we have been compelled to rely upon transcriptions or photographic copies made many years ago by Bernard DeVoto or Dixon Wecter from manuscripts whose present location is not known.

Mr. Gibson is responsible for the text of Howells's letters, Mr.

Smith for the text of Clemens's. The editorial notes are the product of collaborative effort.

ABBREVIATIONS USED BY THE EDITORS

Persons

TBA	Thomas Bailey Aldrich
OLC	Olivia Langdon Clemens
SLC	Samuel Langhorne Clemens
EMH	Elinor Mead Howells
WCH	William Cooper Howells
WDH	William Dean Howells
JRO	James R. Osgood
JHT	Joseph H. Twichell
CDW	Charles Dudley Warner
CLW	Charles L. Webster

Books and Periodicals

AL	*American Literature*
DE	*The Writings of Mark Twain,* Definitive Edition, 37 vols., New York, 1922–25
Frear	Walter F. Frear, *Mark Twain and Hawaii,* Chicago, 1947
LinL	Mildred Howells, ed., *Life in Letters of William Dean Howells,* 2 vols., Garden City, New York, 1928
LLMT	Dixon Wecter, ed., *The Love Letters of Mark Twain,* New York, 1949
Meserve	Walter J. Meserve, Jr., "The Complete Plays of W. D. Howells," in manuscript; to be published by New York University Press in 1960.
MFMT	Clara Clemens, *My Father, Mark Twain,* New York, 1931
MLQ	*Modern Language Quarterly*
MMT	William Dean Howells, *My Mark Twain,* New York, 1910
MTA	Albert B. Paine, ed., *Mark Twain's Autobiography,* 2 vols., New York, 1924
MTB	Albert B. Paine, *Mark Twain, A Biography,* 4 vols., New York, 1912
MTBM	Samuel C. Webster, ed., *Mark Twain, Business Man,* Boston, 1946
MTE	Bernard DeVoto, ed., *Mark Twain in Eruption,* New York, 1940
MTL	Albert B. Paine, ed., *Mark Twain's Letters,* 2 vols., New York, 1917
MTMF	Dixon Wecter, ed., *Mark Twain to Mrs. Fairbanks,* San Marino, California, 1949

MTN   Albert B. Paine, ed., *Mark Twain's Notebook,* New York, 1935

MTW   Bernard DeVoto, *Mark Twain at Work,* Cambridge, Mass., 1942

NAR   *North American Review*

NEQ   *New England Quarterly*

NF   Kenneth R. Andrews, *Nook Farm,* Cambridge, Mass., 1950

NQ   *Notes and Queries*

PMLA   [Publications of the Modern Language Association of America]

PMT   Bernard DeVoto, ed., *The Portable Mark Twain,* New York, 1946

PQ   *Philological Quarterly*

WHR   *Western Humanities Review*

YMY   William Dean Howells, *Years of My Youth,* New York, 1916

Libraries and Collections

An occasional manuscript in the possession of a private person is referred to under the name of the owner, as "W. Hugh Peal."

The abbreviation "AGM TS" ("Arms-Gibson-Marston Typescript") refers to the extensive collection of typescripts of letters by and to William D. Howells prepared jointly by George W. Arms, William M. Gibson, and Frederic C. Marston, Jr.

Am. Antiq. Soc.   American Antiquarian Society, Worcester, Massachusetts

Bancroft   Bancroft Library, University of California, Berkeley

Barrett   Collection of C. Waller Barrett, New York

Berg   Henry W. and Albert A. Berg Collection, New York Public Library

Columbia   Columbia University Library

DLC   Library of Congress

Doheny   Estelle Doheny Collection, St. John's Seminary, Camarillo, California

Hayes Memorial Library   Rutherford B. Hayes Memorial Library, Fremont, Ohio

Houghton   Houghton Library, Harvard University

MTP   Mark Twain Papers, University of California Library, Berkeley

NOTE ON EDITORIAL PRACTICE

NYPL   New York Public Library
Princeton   Princeton University Library
Rosenberg   Collection of Joseph Rosenberg
Samossoud   Collection of Mrs. Clara Clemens Samossoud, Mission Beach, California
Tilton   Howard-Tilton Memorial Library, Tulane University
Yale   Yale University Library
Watkinson   Watkinson Library, Trinity College, Hartford
Webster   Collection of Samuel C. Webster, New York

Manuscripts and Typescripts in the Mark Twain Papers, University of California, Berkeley

Manuscripts are referred to according to call numbers in two series, having the forms "Paine 1" and "DV 1."

Typescripts of Clemens's notebooks are referred to according to number: "Notebook #1, TS, p. 1."

I

GAY YEARS

(1 8 6 9 – 1 8 7 4)

&

I

(1 8 6 9 – 1 8 7 4)

*"And do you remember a lunch that Keeler gave us all at
Ober's, where Clemens first appeared among us, and after Fields
told a deliriously blasphemous story about a can of peaches,
Harte fleered out that this was 'the dream of Mark's life'?
Those were gay years, and bless God, we* knew *they were at the
time!" (WDH to TBA, New York, 8 December 1901, Houghton,
AGM TS)*

William Dean Howells and Samuel Langhorne Clemens first met
in the office of James T. Fields, editor of the *Atlantic Monthly*, late
in 1869. Howells was thirty-two and Clemens was just turning thirty-
four. They were both Westerners. Clemens had come to New England
from Missouri by way of Virginia City and San Francisco, Howells
from Ohio by way of Venice, where he had been American consul,
1861–1865. Both men had served apprenticeships in small-town printing shops and newspapers, and both were now on the way to national
prominence in literature, although Clemens's fame as a comic lecturer and as author of the recent best seller *The Innocents Abroad*
was bringing him much more money than literary prestige, and
Howells's rapid rise to *de facto* editorship of the leading American
literary magazine had not yet made him conspicuous (for Fields still
held the titular editorship of the *Atlantic*). Howells's income, then
as later, was decidedly modest in comparison with that of Clemens,
for *The Innocents Abroad* had sold 12,000 copies at $3.50 within the
first month of publication and would have a sale of 67,000 copies
within a year.

On the occasion of this first meeting, Clemens had called upon
Fields to thank him for the discriminating but surprisingly favorable
anonymous review of *The Innocents Abroad* which had appeared
in the *Atlantic* for December 1869. Fields introduced the reviewer,
who turned out to be Howells. Thus began a friendship which lasted
forty-one years and was instrumental in bringing about a new era in
American letters.

In view of Howells's veneration for the established New England

3

writers — Emerson, Lowell, Longfellow, Holmes, the founders of the *Atlantic* and still its chief contributors — his Cambridge friends must have been surprised by his praise of a Western humorist's book showing little reverence for traditional culture. Indeed, it was contrary to policy for the august *Atlantic* to take any notice at all of a book published by the American Publishing Company of Hartford. For this was a subscription house — marketing its wares not through the established channels of the book trade, but by house-to-house canvassing.*

The high-pressure world of subscription publishing was quite distinct from the more dignified world of regular publishing. The principal organs of literary criticism (including the *Atlantic*) were owned by trade publishing houses, who resented the competition of the subscription publishers and were not inclined to give them the free advertising of reviews. Even the newspapers were generally hostile. But the indifference of critics and reviewers was of small concern to the subscription agents, who concentrated their efforts in small towns and rural areas. They understood that their customers did not read book reviews and were not very much concerned with literary merit; the canvasser offered instead something big and showy, filled with pictures (usually crude woodcuts) to help the unskilled reader through the text (Arthur L. Vogelback, "The Literary Reputation of Mark Twain in America, 1869–1885," unpublished dissertation, University of Chicago, 1938, pp. 42–50). Howells himself recalled later that "no book of literary quality was made to go by subscription except Mr. Clemens's books, and I think these went because the subscription public never knew what good literature they were" ("The Man of Letters as a Man of Business," *Scribner's*, October 1893, collected in *Literature and Life,* New York, 1902, p. 15).

The Innocents Abroad is a typical example of subscription bookmaking. The binding is lavishly but crudely stamped in gold. Its 651 pages, printed on cheap paper in large type, are sprinkled with 234 illustrations, which are carefully named and numbered in a list preceding the table of contents. The tailpiece is a drawing of a cigarbutt, the smoke from which spells "Finis" backwards. While some of the drawings (as of Greek or Egyptian ruins) make an effort to be imposing, others — such as the illustration accompanying Mark Twain's imaginary playbill for a Roman gladiatorial contest (p. 281) and the series of saints "by the Old Masters" (pp. 238–239) — are as broadly comic in intent as the text but a great deal poorer in technique.

---

*In the four volumes of the magazine preceding and following the issue containing Howells's review, the only other subscription book reviewed was a semiofficial campaign biography of General Ulysses S. Grant, which commanded almost automatic support from the staunchly Republican *Atlantic.*

Mark Twain himself complained in 1874 that subscription publishers used "wretched paper & vile engravings" (to TBA, Hartford, 24 March, Houghton, TS in MTP).

Nevertheless, Howells had singled out *The Innocents Abroad* for favorable notice in the *Atlantic*. The perspective of almost a century allows us to see that his act was less surprising than it may have seemed at the time. Beneath his Italianate manner, Howells was a Westerner and a humorist himself, and one of the reasons why Fields had added him to the staff of the *Atlantic* was that he seemed "alert to new developments in literature" (James C. Austin, *Fields of the Atlantic Monthly,* San Marino, 1953, p. 143). Among the most striking of these developments in the 1860's was the rise of humorists, mainly from the West, to national celebrity. James Parton, a frequent contributor to the *Atlantic* and a great admirer of the young assistant editor, insisted that the magazine needed "relief for the Emersonian, Whippletonian pieces" that had been its standard offering since its establishment in 1857. In November 1868, when Parton was visiting the Fieldses in Boston, Mrs. Fields noted in her diary: "Parton thinks it would be possible to make the 'Atlantic Monthly' far more popular. He suggests that a writer named Mark Twain be engaged, and more articles connected with life than literature" (Mrs. James T. Fields, *Memories of a Hostess,* ed. M. A. De Wolfe Howe, Boston, 1922, p. 111). Conversations of this sort must have played a part in bringing about the dramatic offer which the *Atlantic* would presently make to Bret Harte of a year's contract at the unprecedented figure of $10,000.

The review of *The Innocents Abroad* was nevertheless Howells's own affair, and for perceptive, forthright praise of an unconventional and apparently unliterary work it will bear comparison with Emerson's letter to Whitman praising *Leaves of Grass.* Though in the review Howells consistently misspelled the author's name as "Clements" — a surprising error in the accurate, many times proofread *Atlantic* — he spoke out boldly: "It is out of the bounty and abundance of his own nature that [the author] is as amusing in the execution as in the conception of his work. And it is always good-humored humor, too, that he lavishes on his reader, and even in its impudence it is charming; we do not remember where it is indulged at the cost of the weak or helpless side, or where it is insolent, with all its sauciness and irreverence." The personal tribute to the author becomes even more explicit: "As Mr. Clements writes of his experiences, we imagine he would talk of them; and very amusing talk it would be: often not at all fine in matter or manner, but full of touches of humor, — which if not delicate are nearly always easy, — and having a base of excellent sense and good feeling. There is an amount of pure human nature

5

in the book, that rarely gets into literature. . . . " Howells's conclusion is indeed handsome: "Under his *nom de plume* of Mark Twain, Mr. Clements is well known to the very large world of newspaper-readers; and this book ought to secure him something better than the uncertain standing of a popular favorite. It is no business of ours to fix his rank among the humorists California has given us, but we think he is, in an entirely different way from all the others, quite worthy of the company of the best" (December 1869, pp. 765–766).

Mark Twain was understandably grateful for this review because the *Atlantic* was the final court of appeal in literary matters on this side of the ocean. It was as highbrow as any magazine then published, yet had a substantial circulation of fifty thousand. There is now no critical medium in this country even remotely similar in status and influence to the *Atlantic* of the post-Civil War years. Clemens therefore paid his call at the *Atlantic* office, perhaps aware that the assistant editor wrote most of the reviews. Howells is definite concerning the place — "It was in the little office of James T. Fields, over the book-store of Ticknor & Fields, at 124 Tremont Street, Boston" (MMT, p. 3) — but he is somewhat vague about the date, and an exact date cannot now be established. The meeting certainly occurred later than 31 October 1869, when Clemens wrote his fiancée from Pittsburgh: "I walked all around town this morning with a young Mr. Dean, a cousin of Wm. D. Howells, editor of the *Atlantic Monthly*. He kindly offered to give me a letter of introduction to Mr. Howells, but I thanked him sincerely & declined, saying I had a sort of delicacy about using letters of introduction. . . . I prefer to be casually introduced, or to call ceremoniously with a friend . . . " (LLMT, p. 115). More precisely, the date must have been later than the middle of November 1869, when the December issue of the *Atlantic* with Howells's review appeared. (Howells was thus mistaken in speaking of "my friend of now forty-four years" in his memoir, *My Mark Twain*, written just after the death of Clemens in 1910: this would have placed their meeting in 1866.) Strong evidence that Mark Twain acted promptly to express his pleasure in the review makes later months improbable, and the record of his whereabouts and his travels in 1869, 1870, and 1871 leads unmistakably to the inference that Mark Twain first met Howells in late November or early December 1869.

A more serious difficulty arises from Howells's later statement that at this first meeting Clemens "stamped his gratitude into my memory with a story wonderfully allegorizing the situation, which the mock modesty of print forbids my repeating here" (MMT, p. 3). Albert B. Paine, writing two years after Howells, in 1912, said that Mark Twain's remark on the occasion was: "When I read that review of yours, I felt like the woman who was so glad her baby had come white" (MTB, p. 390 n). This may well be what Howells had in mind. But if it is, Howells's memory was again at fault. For the third piece in the correspondence, the surviving fragment of a letter from Mark Twain to Howells which the editors date June 1872, connects the joke not with Howells's review of *The Innocents Abroad* in December 1869, but with his review of *Roughing It,* in the *Atlantic* for June 1872.

Even though we are forced to give up part of what Howells recalled concerning this first meeting, we may still rely on his description of Clemens's very un-Bostonian costume, "a sealskin coat, with the fur out," chosen "in the satisfaction of a caprice, or the love of strong effect which he was apt to indulge through life." Howells adds, "With his crest of dense red hair and the wide sweep of his flaming mustache, Clemens was not discordantly clothed in that sealskin coat, which afterward, in spite of his own warmth in it, sent the cold chills through me when I once accompanied it down Broadway, and shared the immense publicity it won him" (MMT, p. 4).

The acquaintance thus begun did not immediately develop. Clemens had been in and out of Boston during November and December 1869, on his way to and from engagements to lecture in nearby towns (Frear, p. 424; LLMT, *passim*). But there is no evidence that he was in Boston at any time during 1870, or during the spring or summer of 1871. He married Olivia Langdon in Elmira on 2 February 1870, they settled in Buffalo, and he temporarily gave up the lecture tours that had taken him to Boston in the past.

A letter to Elisha P. Bliss, Jr., president of the American Publishing Company of Hartford and publisher of both *The Innocents Abroad* and *Roughing It,* written from Boston on 12 November 1871,* documents the development of the friendship. Clemens wrote:

> Friend Bliss —
> Please send copies of "Innocents Abroad"
> (*marked with my compliments,*) to

*The letter (in MTP) is dated only "Boston, Nov. 12." It cannot belong to 1869 or 1870, for Clemens did not meet Aldrich before 9 February 1871 (TBA to SLC, Boston, MTP). Furthermore, on 12 November 1870 Clemens was in Buffalo (SLC to JHT and Harmony Twichell, Buffalo, 12 November 1870, MTL, p. 177). Clemens lectured at Milford, Mass., on 31 October 1871, was in and out of Boston repeatedly at that time, and can be definitely located in Boston on 12 November 1871 (he wrote to Livy from Boston on that date, LLMT, p. 362). Further support for the dating of the letter in 1871 is furnished by Howells's recollection that Bret Harte was present at a luncheon given by Ralph Keeler for Howells, Aldrich, Fields, and Clemens which apparently belongs to the period of the dinners Clemens mentions to Bliss (MMT, pp. 6–7); for Harte did not come East until 1871 (*Letters of Bret Harte,* ed. Geoffrey Bret Harte, Boston, 1926, p. 11).

{ W. D. Howells, editor "Atlantic,"
{ Thos. Bailey Aldrich, editor "Every Saturday"
{ Ralph Keeler.
    Direct them all "Care J. R. Osgood & Co.
Boston."
    I promised them. We've been having a good
many dinners together.

Whatever may have happened to Howells's review copy — it may well have been cut up for the use of printers setting the long quotations in his review — the implication of this note is that with the renewal of Clemens's visits to Boston when he returned to the lecture platform after his marriage he had begun to see Howells often. How vividly Howells remembered these "good many dinners together" appears in a letter to Aldrich written thirty years later, after he had eaten an elaborate publisher's luncheon in New York City with Mark Twain: "It brought back all the lunches which we three used to eat at poor old Osgood's cost — paying, of course with an insufficient royalty more than our share of the shot. And do you remember a lunch that Keeler gave us all at Ober's, where Clemens first appeared among us, and after Fields told a deliriously blasphemous story about a can of peaches, Harte fleered out that this was 'the dream of Mark's life'? Those were gay years, and bless God, we *knew* they were at the time!" (New York, 8 December 1901, Houghton, AGM TS). More often the group numbered Osgood, Aldrich, Howells, and Clemens, and they "talked the afternoon away till well toward the winter twilight" (MMT, p. 50).

The growing intimacy evidenced by these meetings in Boston was more important at the outset to Clemens than to Howells. By the early 1870's the pattern of Howells's development was set. Reluctantly but firmly he had turned from poetry to travel books, editing, book reviewing, and his first ventures in writing novels, such as *A Chance Acquaintance* (1873). Clemens, on the other hand — partly through Howells's influence — underwent in these years a surprising transformation. The Missouri boy who had served his turn as steamboat pilot and prospector in Nevada mining camps became a naturalized New Englander. He married an exquisite young woman representing the proprieties of Eastern society, established his family in a mansion he built for them in Hartford, and began with some astonishment to take account of himself as a man of letters. Although he followed up the popular success of *The Innocents Abroad* (1869) with *Roughing It* (1872) and *The Gilded Age* (1873, in collaboration with Charles Dudley Warner), the climax of five years' association with Howells was his rise to the status of a contributor to the *Atlantic* with the publication of "A True Story" in the issue for November 1874.

1. CLEMENS TO HOWELLS (TELEGRAM)

Wooster Ohio [1] Jan 7 1872

To W D Howells   Editor Atlantic Monthly

Please telegraph the following to Bret Harte immediately at my cost W A Kendall [2] the poet writes that he is friendless & moneyless & is dying by inches as you know doctors say he must return to California & by sea wants to sail the fifteenth will you petition the steamship Company for a pass for him & sign my name & Howells & the other boys to it & forward said pass to Kendall at three twenty three Van Buren street Brooklyn I will send him fifty dollars get him some money if you can I do not know him but I know he is a good fellow and has hard luck

S L Clemens

1. Having sold his interest in the Buffalo *Express* and installed his family in a rented house in the Nook Farm community in Hartford, Clemens had set out on another lecture tour.

2. A San Francisco poet, author of *The Voice My Soul Heard* (San Francisco, 1868) and contributor with Bret Harte and Mark Twain to the *Golden Era* and the *Californian* in the 1860's. He used the pseudonym "Comet Quirls" and his work was considered daringly erotic. Either with the help Clemens tried to provide for him, or in some other fashion, he managed to get back to San Francisco, but committed suicide there in 1876 (Franklin Walker, *San Francisco's Literary Frontier,* New York, 1943, pp. 181, 225–226, 353; "A Forgotten Poet," San Francisco *Chronicle,* 14 July 1889, p. 8).

2. CLEMENS TO HOWELLS

Elmira, Mch. 18 [1872].

Friend Howells —

We are very much obliged for the book [1] — which came to-day. We bought it & read it some time ago, but we prize this copy most on account of the autograph. I would like to send you a copy of *my* book, but I can't get a copy myself, yet, because 30,000 people who have bought & paid for it have to have preference over the author.[2] But how is that for 2 months' sale? But I'm going to send you one when I get a chance. We have just arrived here on a 2 months' holiday.[3] I shove my love at you & the other Atlantics & Every Saturdays.[4]

Yr friend

Mark.

1. Probably Howells's first book-length work of fiction, *Their Wedding Journey,* serialized in the *Atlantic* July-December 1871 and published in book form 27 December (William M. Gibson and George Arms, *A Bibliography of William Dean Howells,* New York, 1948, 72-A, p. 22).

2. Mark Twain's *Roughing It,* published in February. While this book did not quite duplicate the sensational popular success of *The Innocents Abroad,* it had, as Clemens indicates, a very wide sale. On 17 May 1872 Clemens wrote to his niece Annie Moffett that he had made $25,000 from *The Innocents Abroad* but so far had received only $10,500 from *Roughing It.* "So you see," he added, "we are not nearly so rich as the papers think we are" (Elmira, Webster; TS in MTP). Nevertheless, the sale of these two books had made Mark Twain a national figure, and he can easily be forgiven his half-astonished boasting to Howells.

3. To be spent with Livy Clemens's foster sister Susan Crane and her husband Theodore at the Cranes' home, Quarry Farm, near Elmira. Summers at Quarry Farm were a normal part of the Clemenses' year as long as they lived in Hartford.

4. Members of the staffs of the two magazines, both published by James R. Osgood & Co., especially Thomas Bailey Aldrich, editor of *Every Saturday.*

3. CLEMENS TO HOWELLS

[Hartford?, ? June 1872]

Since penning the foregoing the "Atlantic" has come to hand with that most thoroughly and entirely satisfactory notice of "Roughing it," [1] and I am as uplifted and reassured by it as a

mother who has given birth to a white baby when she was awfully afraid it was going to be a mulatto. I have been afraid and
shaky all along, but now unless the N. of [Y.?] "Tribune" gives
the book a black eye, I am all right.[2]   With many thanks

Twain

MS. This fragment of a letter — apparently a postscript — is known to
the editors only in the transcription published by A. M. Broadley, an English bookdealer and collector, in his *Chats on Autographs* (New York, 1910,
p. 229).

1. Howells's review of *Roughing It* in the *Atlantic* (XXIX, 754-755,
June 1872; reprinted in MMT, pp. 113–114).

2. The New York *Tribune* had complained that *The Innocents Abroad*
sometimes exhibited "an offensive irreverence for things which other men
hold sacred" (27 August 1869, p. 6; quoted in Vogelback, "Literary Reputation of Mark Twain," p. 60). The *Tribune's* review of *Roughing
It,* which did not appear until 31 January 1873, was less stringent: it characterized the book as "one of the most racy specimens of Mark Twain's savory
pleasantries" (quoted in Vogelback, "Literary Reputation," p. 72).

4. CLEMENS TO HOWELLS

Hartford, June 15 [1872].

Friend Howells —

Could you tell me how I could get a copy of your portrait as
published in Hearth & Home?[1] I hear so much talk about it as
being among the finest works of art which have yet appeared in
that journal, that I feel a strong desire to see it. Is it suitable
for framing? I have written the publishers of H & H time &
again, but they say that the demand for the portrait immediately
exhausted the edition & now a copy cannot be had, even for the
European demand, which has now begun. Bret Harte has been
here, & says his family would not be without that portrait for
any consideration. He says his children get up in the night &
yell for it. I would give anything for a copy of that portrait to
put up in my parlor. I have Oliver Wendell Holmes's & Bret
Harte's, as published in Every Saturday, & of all the swarms that

come every day to gaze upon them none go away that are not softened & humbled & made more resigned to the will of God. If I had yours to put up alongside of them, I believe the combination would bring more souls to earnest reflection & ultimate conviction of their lost condition, than any other kind of warning would. Where in the nation *can* I get that portrait? Here are heaps of people that want it, — that *need* it. There is my uncle. *He* wants a copy. He is lying at the point of death. He has *been* lying at the point of death for two years. He wants a copy — & I want him to *have* a copy. And I want you to send a copy to the man that shot my dog. I want to see if he is dead to Every human instinct.

Now you send me that portrait. I am sending you mine, in this letter; [2] & am glad to do it, for it has been greatly admired. People who are judges of art, find in the execution a grandeur which has not been equalled in this country, & an expression which has not been approached in *any*.   Ys Truly

S. L. Clemens.

P.S. — 62,000 copies of Roughing It sold & delivered in 4 months.

1. On the cover of the issue for 30 March, which contained a sketch of Howells's life by Edward Eggleston.
2. Clemens enclosed an even more crudely executed picture of himself clipped from the Salt Lake City *Tribune*.

The extant correspondence contains no items for the period of almost fourteen months preceding Clemens's letter of 27 February 1874. The gap is apparently due to the accidental disappearance of a number of letters. But the two writers saw each other occasionally during 1873. Early in January, Howells wrote to Charles W. Stoddard: "I lunched the other night with Mark Twain, and we had some 'very pretty conversation,' as Pepys says. Yourself was among the topics" (Boston, 3 January, Huntington, AGM TS). The two men also met in Hartford: in the same month Howells wrote to Charles Dudley Warner, his *Atlantic* contributor and the Clemenses' Hartford friend and neighbor, promising another visit to the Warners in spite of the "frightful cold" he had taken at Mark Twain's house across the way (Cambridge, 5 January, Princeton, AGM TS).

Clemens must have taken special pleasure in reading the third in-stallment of Howells's *A Chance Acquaintance* in the March *Atlantic*, for Colonel Ellison, cousin of the heroine, whose favorite reading was largely Shakespeare's plays and *Don Quixote*, "had read one book of travel, namely, The Innocents Abroad, which he held to be so good a book that he need never read anything else about the coun-tries of which it treated." Almost immediately, writing his bookstore scene in *The Gilded Age*, Mark Twain returned the compliment thus:

"Presently, while [Laura Hawkins] was holding a copy of *Vene-tian Life* in her hand and running over a familiar passage here and there, the clerk said, briskly . . . :

" 'Now here is a work that we've sold a lot of. . . . *The Pirate's Doom, or the Last of the Buccaneers. . . .* '

"Laura pushed it gently aside with her hand and went on filching from *Venetian Life*" (DE, VI, 49).

On 16 May, Howells sent a copy of *A Chance Acquaintance* to Clemens inscribed, "To S. L. Clemens with ever so much friendship, W. D. Howells."

Through the rest of the year Howells was writing his first true novel, *A Foregone Conclusion,* discussing fiction in letters to James, reading Turgenev, and getting settled in his new house on Concord Avenue. Clemens, by May, had completed *The Gilded Age* in col-laboration with Warner, and had taken his family to England, where he lectured with great success on the Sandwich Islands. In November he had come back briefly to the United States and then returned to England for another lecture tour, adding a new topic, "Roughing It on the Silver Frontier." He came home in January 1874, and con-tinued lecturing in the East. In October 1873, Howells was asking Warner when Clemens would be home, and when their collaborative novel would appear (WDH to CDW, Boston, 8 October, Watkinson, AGM TS). But when he read an advance copy at the end of the year, his reaction was mixed, and he wrote Warner: "Up to the time old Hawkins dies your novel is of the greatest promise — I read it with joy — but after that it fails to assimilate the crude material with which it is fed, and becomes a confirmed dyspeptic at last. Still it is always entertaining; and it kept me up till twelve last night, though I needed sleep. I was particularly sorry to have Sellers degenerate as he did, and none of the characters quite fulfill their early promise" (WDH to CDW, Cambridge, 28 December, Watkinson, AGM TS). Howells added that he would withhold his public opinion altogether, if Warner preferred; and he did not in fact ever review the book.

5. CLEMENS TO HOWELLS

[Hartford] Feb. 27 [1874].

My Dear Howells:

I am in a sweat, & Warner is in another. I told Redpath some time ago that I would lecture in Boston on any two days he might choose, provided they were *consecutive* days — I never dreamed [of] his choosing dates during *Lent,* since that was his special horror — but all at once he telegraphs me & writes me, & hollers at me in all manner of ways that I am booked for Boston, *March* 5 of all days in the year. — & to make matters just as mixed & uncertain as possible, I can't find out to save my life whether he means to lecture me on the 6th *also* or not.

Warner's been in here swearing like a lunatic, & saying he had written you to come on the *4*th [1] — & I said, "You leatherhead, if I talk in Boston both afternoon & evening March 5, I'll have to go to Boston the *4th*" — & then he just kicked up his heels & went off cursing after a fashion I never heard of before. Now let's just leave this thing to Providence for 24 hours — you bet it will come out all right.   Ys Ever

Mark.

1. In response to the Warners' invitation to visit them in Hartford over the weekend beginning Thursday, 5 March (Hartford, 19 February, Houghton, AGM TS), Howells had answered on 25 February that he would come with Osgood rather than Elinor (Cambridge, Watkinson, AGM TS). Then on the twenty-seventh Warner asked Howells to come down on the fourth in order not to miss the fun of having the Clemenses dine with them, since Clemens had agreed to lecture in Boston on the fifth of March (Hartford, 27 February, Houghton, AGM TS).

6. CLEMENS TO HOWELLS (TELEGRAM)

Hartford Ct — 3 [March 1874].[1]

W. D. Howells.
    Editor Atlantic Mnthly —
All right come down with me Friday [2] the superior value of birds

in the hand over those that still sport in joyous freedom amid the leafy depths of their native woodland is so universally recognized that I cannot feel necessitated to enlarge upon it to one of the first minds of the age at three cents a word by telegraph

Mark

1. The date is inferred from the telegraph operator's "3" on the date line of the telegraph blank and the sense of the message in this sequence concerning the forthcoming visit.

2. Howells had proposed to Warner that he and Osgood defer their visit for a week (Boston, 28 February, Watkinson, AGM TS), but Clemens must have arranged with James Redpath for a single lecture in Boston on the evening of Thursday, 5 March. Howells's message agreeing not to defer the trip, to which this is an answer, is not extant.

7. CLEMENS TO HOWELLS (TELEGRAM)

Hartford Ct 4 [March 1874]

W. D. Howells.
    Editor Atlantic Monthly

CA.

We ought to leave Boston ten oclock Friday morning [1] therefore wont it be better to get Aldrich to defer his lunch not let him shirk out of the lunch altogether but simply defer it,[2] I arrive at Parker House tomorrow evening answer paid

S. L. Clemens

1. Howells, Elinor Howells, Osgood, and Clemens took the train together from Boston to Hartford on Friday, 6 March, and the Howellses spent the weekend as house guests of the Warners.

2. Aldrich had written Clemens on 2 March inviting him to lunch with Howells and another friend on Friday, 6 March (Cambridge, MTP).

8. CLEMENS TO HOWELLS

[Hartford] Mch. 20 [1874].

Dear Howells:
    You or Aldrich or both of you must come to Hartford to live.

15

Mr. Hall, who lives in the house next to Mrs. Stowe's (just where we drive in to go to our new house,) [1] will sell for $16,000 or $17,000. The lot is 85 feet front & 150 deep — long time & easy payments on the purchase. You can do your work just as well here as in Cambridge, can't you? Come, will one of you boys buy that house? Now say yes.

Mrs. Clemens is an invalid yet, but is getting along pretty fairly.[2] We send best regards.   Ys

Mark.

1. The Clemenses' new house on Farmington Ave., in the Nook Farm community, was not finished; they would not move into it before September. In the meantime they were renting the John Hooker house on Forest St. Howells's recent visit in Nook Farm had given him a very favorable impression of the community. On 21 March he wrote to an old Ohio friend: "It seems to me quite an ideal life. They [Warner and Mark Twain] live very near each other, in a sort of suburban grove, and their neighbors are the Stowes and Hookers, and a great many delightful people. They go in and out of each other's houses without ringing, and nobody gets more than the first syllable of his first name — they call their minister *Joe* Twichell. I staid with Warner, but of course I saw a good deal of Twain, and he's a thoroughly great fellow. His wife is a delicate little beauty, the very flower and perfume of *ladylikeness,* who simply adores him — but this leaves no word to describe his love for her" (to J. M. Comly, Cambridge, LinL, I, 187).

2. Livy, as Clemens wrote to his brother Orion on 18 March, had "barely escaped miscarriage" (Hartford, MTP).

9. CLEMENS TO HOWELLS

[Elmira] May. 10 [1874].

My Dear Howells:

I am so strongly tempted to afford you & Mrs. Howells a glimpse of my brother's last, (just received), that I can't resist.[1]

You observe that he is afraid the interest might fall in arrears, so he pays it some weeks ahead of time.

You perceive that he is still in some way connected with that infamous Tennessee land which has been our ⟨bete⟩ destruction for 40 years (see opening chapters of Gilded Age — my brother is "Lafayette Hawkins.")

The "Mr. Stotts" whom Orion refers to is his old father-in-law, aged 75; "Mollie" is Orion's wife; "Ann" is her old sister — middle-aged, & pretty ratty.

I will remark that no member of the Clemens tribe ever writes a letter without enclosing in it a newspaper scrap or two — & these scraps, never by any accident contain anything interesting.   Ys Ever

Mark.

"Marshall" is a sentimental Keokuk lawyer.

P.S. Do not fail to note the hopeful, glad-hearted, school-boy cheeriness which bubbles out of every pore of this man who has been ALWAYS a failure.

1. The letter of Orion's which Clemens sent to Howells has not survived, but numerous others written by Orion to his famous and successful brother, closely resembling the letter described here, are in MTP. Although Clemens was frequently exasperated with Orion, he supported him and his wife year after year, and on occasion wrote to him with sincere sympathy for Orion's appalling frustrations. Thus on 4 February 1874 he had consoled Orion for the collapse of a project for inventing a flying machine: "God knows yours is hard luck, & one is bound to respect & honor the way in which you bear up under it & refuse to surrender. . . . I grieve over the laying aside of the flying machine as if it were my own broken idol" (Hartford, MTP).

10. CLEMENS TO HOWELLS

Elmira, N.Y., June 21 [1874]

My Dear Howells:

I am not going to write. I have only been re-reading the Foregone Conclusion,[1] & it does seem such absolute perfection of character-drawing & withal so moving in the matter of ⟨tears⟩ pathos ⟨now, & laughter then⟩ now, humor then, & both at once

occasionally, that Mrs. Clemens wanted me to defer my smoke &
drop you our thanks — & in truth I was nothing loath.

The new baby[2] is a gaudy thing & the mother is already
sitting up.   Ys Ever

Mark.

1. The first installment of Howells's third novel, *A Foregone Conclusion,*
had just appeared in the *Atlantic* for July 1874.

2. The new baby was Clara Langdon Clemens, born 8 June — "the
great American Giantess — weighing 7 3/4 pounds, & all solid meat" (SLC
to JHT, Elmira, 11 June 1874, Yale).

11. HOWELLS TO CLEMENS

[Newport, Vermont] June 30, 1874

My dear Clemens:

It was immensely kind of you to pause in your blissful con-
sciousness of that new little girl of yours and acknowledge that
my trivial story existed. Thank Mrs. Clemens for me, and tell
[her] how glad I am that she has another girl — boys wear out
their clothes so fast; and in the present diversity of boys and
men's costumes, you cannot roll up the paternal trowsers so as
to make them fit.[1]

You think from the gay appearance of this letterhead[2] that
I'm off here enjoying myself, but this is a mistake of yours. I'm
simply caught here on my way to Quebec by a failure of con-
nections.[3] It's all right, but it's a hard Providence.

With regards to Mrs. Clemens and compliments to the young
ladies.   Yours ever

W. D. Howells.

1. John Mead Howells, or "Bua," was nearly six.

2. The letterhead of the Memphremagog House in Newport which Howells used is an extremely elaborate example of the lithographer's art.

3. Howells's father, William Cooper Howells, had been appointed American consul at Quebec in June 1874 (LinL, I, 198), and Howells was on his
way there to help him find a house and get settled (WDH to H. W. Longfellow,
Jaffrey, N.H., 11 July, W. Hugh Peal, AGM TS).

12. HOWELLS TO CLEMENS

[Jaffrey, New Hampshire] July 11, 1874

My dear Clemens:

Your letter and telegraph[1] came to our mosquitory bower whilst I was away in Canada, and I failed to see Mr. Pope here.[2] But Thursday I ran down to Boston to call on him, and I've arranged to translate the play for him.[3] As it is owing to your kindness that I'm thus placed in relations with the stage — a long-coveted opportunity — I may tell you the terms on which I make the version. He pays me $400 outright on acceptance of my version, and $100 additional when the play has run fifty nights; and $1. a night thereafter as long as it runs. When my translation is done, I'm to tell him, and he will send his check for $400 to you, and I'll submit my MS to him. If he likes it, you send me the check, if he doesn't you return it to him.

You perceive this isn't hard on Mr. Pope. The terms were my own — he would have given me $500 down, but I didn't think he ought to buy a pig in a poke, and I felt that I ought to take some risk of a failure. I liked Mr. Pope very much, and I should be glad of his acquaintance, even if there were no money in it. As it is, imagine my gratitude to you![4]

My regards to all your family.   Yours ever
W. D. Howells.

1. They have disappeared.
2. Charles P. Pope, a theatrical producer and actor whom Mark Twain had referred to Howells.
3. Ippolito Tito d'Aste's *Sanson*. (Howells's translation would be published in book form in 1889.)
4. Howells's relative poverty in comparison with Clemens's substantial income from his writing at this period is evident in his gratitude for the chance to make $500 by doing the translation.

13. CLEMENS TO HOWELLS

Elmira, July 15 [25? July 1874] [1]

My Dear Howells —

Consound my cats — as Mrs. Clemens says when roused to ferocity — I particularly hoped to get your answering telegram while I was in Hartford, so that I could meddle in the terms. If you had only required $500 down instead of $400, & had *then* tacked on the other details, it would have been entirely satisfactory to me. I couldn't really make up my mind about a price at first, standing between two personal friends — but if one or the other of you had been a stranger I would have known all about how to proceed. I came very near telegraphing you, after I got back here, to be sure & charge enough, but it seemed a sort of disloyalty to Pope to be legging for the other side all the time. But I think you made an admirable bargain. No doubt you & I both underrate the ⟨value⟩ worth of the work far enough; but that you are warrior enough to stand up & charge *any*thing above a week's board is gaudy manliness in a literary person. Our guild are so egotistically mock-modest about their own merits. — We make a wretched bargain — caressing our darling humility the while — & then when we come to think how much more we could have got, we go behind the house & curse. — By George I admire you. I suppose "consuling" is not without its uses — it breeds common sense in parties who would otherwise develop only the *un*common.

I welcome you to the dramatic field — where I myself am browsing, now. I have taken my characters in the Gilded Age & worked them up into a 5-act drama entitled "Col. Sellers." [2] I don't think much of it, as a drama, but I suppose it will do to hang Col. Sellers on, & maybe even damn him. [3] *He* will play tolerably well, in the hands of a good actor. I have leased the play to John T. Raymond, comedian, who lately played in Boston. [4]

I have just had a note from Pope, who, naturally enough, is

charmed with you & delighted with the prospect of a translation to his liking.[5]

All our tribe are tolerably well, & we hope to drag you & your tribe, & the Aldrichs down to Hartford again in the winter.   Ever Yours

Saml L. Clemens

1. Since the letter of Charles Pope to which Clemens refers here is not only dated but postmarked 20 July (MTP), Clemens's "15" must be a slip of the pen.

2. "Colonel Sellers: A Drama in Five Acts" was entered for copyright "July 1874" (amanuensis copy, Paine 163, MTP).

3. See Appendix.

4. A letter from the actor Lawrence Barrett to Clemens (Boston, 25 May 1874, MTP) declines Clemens's invitation to take the role of Colonel Sellers, but strongly recommends Raymond for the part.

5. Pope wrote from Buffalo on 20 July to "Dear Mark": "I had a lively chase after Howells. I went to New Hampshire and saw Mrs. H. — a most charming woman. He came soon after to see me at Boston. We came to terms without trouble — and I feel that he will give me a good play. I like him" (MTP).

14. CLEMENS TO HOWELLS

Elmira, Aug. 22 [1874].

Dear Howells:

I have just finished reading the Foregone Conclusion [1] to Mrs. Clemens, & we think you have even outdone yourself. I should think that this must be the daintiest, truest, most admirable workmanship that was ever put on a story. The creatures of God do not act out their natures more unerringly than yours do. If your genuine stories can die, I wonder by what right old Walter Scott's artificialities shall continue to live.

But what I originally started to write about, was the fact that I saw Pope in Buffalo, who told David Gray [2] & me that he had received his first act & that it was a most noble & altogether perfect piece of work. I was not surprised, but I *was* gratified to see that he was not a swine who trampled calmly over pearls, mistaking them for pebbles. I argue well from his appreciation.

I brought Mrs. Clemens back from her trip[3] in a dreadfully broken down condition — so by the doctor's orders we unpacked the trunks sorrowfully to lie idle here another month instead of going at once to Hartford & proceeding at once to furnish the new house which is now finished. We hate to have it go longer desolate & tenantless, but cannot help it.

By & by, if the madam gets strong again, we are hoping to have the Grays there, & your & the Aldrich households & Osgood down to engage in an orgy with them.   Ys Ever

Mark.

1. The third installment of the novel (in the *Atlantic* for September).

2. A newspaper man and poet who had been a friend of the Clemenses since their year in Buffalo (1870–71).

3. The Clemenses had been to Fredonia, N.Y., to visit Clemens's mother and his sister, Pamela (SLC to Orion Clemens, Elmira, 28 August 1874, MTP).

15. CLEMENS TO HOWELLS

Elmira, Sept. 2 [1874].

My Dear Howells:

Your telegram just rec'd. Shall await your letter.

But I made a mistake in writing you.[1] It would take too long to explain. Suffice it that I was charging about 33 per cent more than I meant to.

This disgusts me. But I send the "Fable for Old Boys & Girls" anyway. Since its price is lowered I don't know but what you might really come to like it. But hurl it back with obloquy if you don't. I can dodge.

I enclose also a "True Story" which has no humor in it. You can pay as lightly as you choose for that, if you want it, for it is rather out of my line. I have not altered the old colored woman's story except to begin it at the beginning, instead of the middle, as she did — & ⟨worked⟩ traveled both ways.

I *told* this yarn to Hay [2] & some company & they liked it. So I thought I'd *write* it.   Ys Ever

Mark.

1. Neither this letter from Clemens to Howells nor Howells's telegram in reply is extant.

2. John Hay, then on the staff of the New York *Tribune* and a friend of long standing. On 25 April 1874 he had written to Clemens: " . . . you know what is my private opinion of all the time I dont spend with you" (New York, MTP).

16. HOWELLS TO CLEMENS

[Cambridge] Sept. 2, 1874.

My dear Clemens:

I telegraphed you last night to send on your manuscript, which I'd like very much to see. Your letter came just as I was packing up to come home,[1] and I had not strength of mind enough to answer it, though it may not appear to a man of more active intellect a very heavy job to say yes or no.

As soon as I get the ms., I'll read it.

I'm extremely sorry to hear of Mrs. Clemens's relapse. Please give her my regards, and believe both of you that I was proud as Punch to hear that you liked my story. I shall yet make immortality bitter to the divine Walters — as the French would call the Waverley man.

I sent Pope his tragedy [2] last Saturday, and I hope he'll like it. I really made it hard work for myself, and I think earned my money.   Yours ever

W. D. Howells.

1. Howells and his wife had been spending the summer at Jaffrey, N.H.

2. Howells's translation of d'Aste's *Sanson*. He wrote the actor from Cambridge on 12 August that he had gone deeply into the spirit of the

play and would annotate certain passages "giving my notion of the author's conception" (Houghton).

17. HOWELLS TO CLEMENS

[Cambridge] September 8, 1874.

My dear Clemens:

I'm going to settle *your* opinion of the next installment of A Foregone Conclusion by sending back one of your contributions. Not, let me hasten to say, that I don't think they're both very good. But The Atlantic, as regards matters of religion, is just in that Good Lord, Good Devil condition when a little fable like yours wouldn't leave it a single Presbyterian, Baptist, Unitarian, Episcopalian, Methodist or Millerite *paying* subscriber — all the dead-heads would stick to it, and abuse it in the denominational newspapers. Send your fable to some truly pious concern like Scribner or Harper, and they'll extract it into all the hymnbooks. But it would ruin *us*.[1]

I've kept the True Story which I think extremely good and touching with the best and reallest kind of black talk in it.[2] Perhaps it couldn't be better than it is; but if you feel like giving it a little more circumstantiation (you didn't know there was such a word as that, did you?) on getting the proof, why, don't mind making the printers some over-running.

The fotografs[3] were most welcome, and I'm sorry that I can't send back anything but thanks. I admire the attitude and the asthma, and the whole landscape, and I've put them all three upon the mantelpiece where I can look at them whenever so disposed.

There are parts of the Fable that I think wonderfully good even for you — that touch about Sisyphus and Atlas being ancestors of the tumble-bug, did tickle me.

Pope writes back and pretends to be overjoyed with the version of Samson.

My best regards to Mrs Clemens, for whose speedy recovery I devoutly wish.   Yours ever

W. D. Howells.

1. Concerning Howells's objections, see Appendix.

2. The sketch appeared in the *Atlantic* for November 1874, the first contribution by Mark Twain to the magazine, and one of the best short pieces he ever wrote. Howells's acceptance of this, and his rejection of the other MS submitted at the same time, show him functioning as a discriminating editor and critic. The value of advice from such a man to a developing writer is evident in the fact that Mark Twain seems to have thought more highly of the "Fable" than of "A True Story." Other contemporary readers recognized the excellence of "A True Story." J. W. De Forest wrote Howells on 5 January 1875: "By the way, tell Mark Twain to try pathos now & then. His 'True Story,' — the story of the old negress, — was a really great thing, amazingly natural & humorous, & touching even to the drawing of tears" (New Haven, MTP). Howells underlined this passage and sent it on to Mark Twain on 8 January.

3. One of the three photographs Clemens had sent to Howells, a stereopticon picture, showing Clemens seated at the writing table in his hexagonal hilltop study at Quarry Farm, is in the Howells Papers (Houghton). On the back Clemens wrote: "Do you mind that attitude? It took me hours to perfect that." The reference to "asthma" is not clear. It may have to do with one of the other photographs, now lost.

18. HOWELLS TO CLEMENS

[Cambridge] September 17, 1874.

My dear Clemens:

This little story [1] delights me more and more: I wish you had about forty of 'em!

Please send the proof back suddenly. You can reject any of the proposed corrections.

Remember me to Mrs. Clemens.   Yours ever

W. D. Howells.

1. "A True Story," of which Howells is now sending proof. In 1907 Howells recalled: " 'A True Story' was but three pages long, and I remember the anxiety with which the business side of the magazine tried to compute its pecuniary value. It was finally decided to give the author twenty dollars a page, a rate unexampled in our modest history. I believe Mr. Clemens has since been offered a thousand dollars a thousand words, but I have never regretted that we paid him so handsomely for his first contribution.

I myself felt that we were throwing in the highest recognition of his writing as literature, along with a sum we could ill afford; but the late Mr. Houghton, who had then become owner and paymaster, had no such reflection to please him in the headlong outlay. He had always believed that Mark Twain was literature, and it was his zeal and courage which justified me in asking for more and more contributions from him, though at a lower rate" ("Recollections of an Atlantic Editorship," *Atlantic C*, 601, November 1907).

19. CLEMENS TO HOWELLS

[Hartford] Sept. 20 [1874].

My Dear Howells:

All right, my boy, send proof sheets *here*.[1] I amend dialect stuff by talking & talking & *talking* it till it sounds right — & I had difficulty with this negro talk because a negro sometimes (rarely) says "goin'" & sometimes "gwyne", & they make just such discrepancies in other words — & when you come to reproduce them on paper they look as if the variation resulted from the writer's carelessness. But I want to work at the proofs & get the dialect as nearly right as possible.

We are in part of the new house. Goodness knows when we'll get in the rest of it — full of workmen yet.

I worked a month at my play, & launched it in New York last Wednesday.[2] I believe it will go. The newspapers have been complimentary. It is simply a *setting* for the one character, Col. Sellers — as a *play* I guess it will not bear a critical assault in force.

The Warners are as charming as ever. They go shortly to the devil for a year — (which is but a poetical way of saying they are going to afflict themselves with the unsurpassable ⟨hell?⟩ (bad word) of *travel* for a spell.) I believe they mean to go & see you, first — so they mean to start from heaven ⟨to hell?⟩ to the other place; not from Earth. How is that? I think that is no slouch of a compliment — kind of a dim religious light about it. I enjoy that sort of thing.

Do tell Aldrich that he has made Mrs. Clemens (neè Langdon) the happiest & proudest woman in the land by digging up & glorifying her ancestor Governor Langdon of Portsmouth.[3] I think she would let Aldrich walk off with anything in the house, now, but the cubs. But don't you know, *I* don't feel so grateful about it; for I have no ancestor but an Injun, & he was not a chief. I shall have this old swell flung at my head often enough, I promise you. Now if Aldrich will only resurrect a villainous fictitious portrait of the Governor that will let him down a peg or two in the Madam's estimation (I would not mind his being a trifle drunk,) so that I can hang him again — this time where he will keep peace in a family & tone down vanity — I shall be under lasting obligations to him.

Ys Ever

Mark.

1. Clemens is replying to Howells's reference to proofs of "A True Story" in his letter of 8 September, which had been sent to Elmira. The Clemenses had returned to Hartford on 19 September (SLC to Orion Clemens Hartford, 21 September 1874, MTP), and Clemens had not yet received the letter of 17 September, which, with a set of proof sheets, had also been sent to Elmira.

2. That is, on 16 September, at the Park Theatre. Mark Twain had evidently made some last-minute revisions of the script, and then, as he wrote to Orion, he and Livy stopped over in New York on the way home from Elmira while he "staid on the stage 2 to 4 hours several days in succession showing them how I thought the speeches ought to be uttered. The consequence was, the play went right through without a hitch on the very first night. They are better actors than I am, but of course I wanted the play played *my* way unless my way was radically wrong" (Hartford, 21 September 1874, MTP).

3. John Langdon (1741–1819), soldier in the American Revolution, member of Congress, and Governor of New Hampshire 1805–1809, 1810–1812. Aldrich had devoted a couple of paragraphs to the Langdon house, and to the man who built it, in an article on Portsmouth entitled "An Old Town by the Sea" in *Harper's Monthly* for October 1874.

II

A SUBTILE HUMORIST

(1 8 7 4 – 1 8 7 5)

II

(1 8 7 4 – 1 8 7 5)

"Here is the fine humor . . . ; here is the burlesque, that seems such plain and simple fun at first, doubling and turning upon itself till you wonder why Mr. Clemens has ever been left out of the list of our subtile humorists; . . . here is the incorruptible right-mindedness that always warms the heart to this wit" (WDH in the Atlantic, December 1875)

The success of Mark Twain's "A True Story" led Howells to ask him again and again for further contributions to the *Atlantic.* The editor's persistence was rewarded with the seven installments of "Old Times on the Mississippi," for which he persuaded the publisher of the magazine to pay at a higher rate than was allowed any other contributor. Despite the chronic half-invalidism of both men's wives, the Howellses paid a brief visit to the Clemenses in Hartford in March 1875, and the Clemenses returned the visit in the autumn. When Howells heard that Clemens was writing *The Adventures of Tom Sawyer,* he suggested it should also be serialized in the *Atlantic,* but upon reading the manuscript he recognized it as a story for boys (" . . . altogether the best boy's story I ever read") and thus not appropriate for a literary magazine. Clemens's financial returns from the dramatization of *The Gilded Age* aroused Howells's interest in writing for the stage (and perhaps led him to cast such sketches as "The Parlor Car" in dramatic form). Nevertheless, he wisely declined Clemens's proposal that he should make a dramatic version of *Tom Sawyer.* He had completed an international novel, *A Foregone Conclusion,* and was at work on *Private Theatricals.* Clemens was immensely gratified by Howells's laudatory review of his *Sketches, New and Old* (1875) in the *Atlantic,* which he described as "the recognized critical Court of Last Resort in this country. . . . "

3 1

20. HOWELLS TO CLEMENS

[Cambridge] Sept. 30, 1874.

My dear Clemens:

Couldn't you send me some such story as that colored one,[1] for our Jan'y number — that is, within a month? — I'm glad to see that even President Grant recognized the excellence of the Sellers character in your play.[2] — What a good time we *did* have with the Warners! [3]

With regards to Mrs. Clemens,   Yours ever

W. D. Howells.

1. "A True Story."

2. On 28 September, President Grant, attending a performance of the play, "invited Mr. Raymond into his dressing room and complimented him on his performance of *Col. Sellers*" (New York *Sun,* 29 September 1874, p. 1).

3. Charles Dudley Warner and his wife had visited the Howellses before they sailed for Europe and the Near East late in September (WDH to CDW, Cambridge, 28, 30 September 1874, LinL, I, 193–194).

21. HOWELLS TO CLEMENS

[Cambridge] Oct. 5, 1874

My dear Clemens:

Do you know C. W. Stoddard's address? I want to pay him for an article, and I suppose he wont want any coy delays in the matter.[1]

Are you going to give me another of those little stories?

Yours ever

W. D. Howells.

1. Charles Warren Stoddard, of San Francisco, had contributed to the *Atlantic* "A Prodigal in Buskins" (July 1874), "Over the Foot-Lights" (August 1874), and "Behind the Scenes" (to be published in the November issue). The last of these is probably the article to which Howells refers.

Stoddard had acted as Mark Twain's secretary during his English lecture tour of 1873. Howells would write an introductory letter to his *South-Sea Idyls* when the 1873 edition was reprinted in 1892.

22. CLEMENS TO HOWELLS

Hartford, Oct. 24 [1874].

My Dear Howells:

I have delayed thus long, hoping I might do something for the January number, & Mrs. Clemens has diligently persecuted me day by day with urgings to go to work & do that something, but it's no use — I find I can't. We are in such a state of weary & endless confusion that my head won't "go." So I give it up.

⟨Say,⟩ I sent you the St. Louis Republican's enthusiastic review of Samson forwarded to me by Pope.[1] Of course Pope sent one to you, but perhaps he didn't italicise the most significant feature, & so I did it myself (the repeated calls before the curtain) — though now it occurs to me that you would naturally notice that very particularly without any of my assistance.

But now why don't you invent a play yourself? It would pay you, say $30 a night in New York & $20 everywhere else. That, I remember, is what Daly was to pay Bret Harte (this was 3 years ago) — & he was to ⟨advance⟩ pay him one or two thousand dollars, besides, on the delivery of the MS. Daly has the most superb company of actors in America — they would almost do justice to even a play written by you. Shan't I drop Daly a line & hint to him that it isn't likely you would want to bother with a play but that possibly you *might* if persuasively tackled?[2] Shan't I?

Ys Ever

Mark.

With Mrs. Clemens & Twichells' warm regards.

1. Pope had opened in Howells's version at the Olympic Theatre, St. Louis, on 5 October, with considerable success. He toured with it during the season 1874–75 and it became one of his stand-bys in his later years on the stage (A. H. Quinn, *History of the American Drama from the Civil*

War to the Present Day, New York, 1936, I, 68). Tomasso Salvini, who had played d'Aste's drama in the original Italian in the United States in 1874, used Howells's translation on his farewell tour in 1889–90. During the season 1894–95, J. Walter Kennedy acted in Howells's version in Philadelphia, New York, and Chicago (Meserve).

2. John Augustin Daly, the celebrated actor, drama critic, and theatrical manager, had produced an unsuccessful extravaganza entitled *Roughing It* in 1873 which drew a small fraction of its material from the book and mentioned Mark Twain in its playbill (photostat in MTP). On 8 August 1874 he had asked Mark Twain to do "something for my company & my theatre," adding, "I think I could put you on the road to a good thing . . ." (New York, MTP). Mark Twain replied on 29 October that he was not able to write a play at that time, and suggested that Daly approach Howells (Joseph F. Daly, *The Life of Augustin Daly*, New York, 1917, p. 147). On 4 November, Daly thanked Mark Twain for the suggestion. "I do wish," he said, "our leading writers would try their hands at play writing now & then: I am ready to help them with the *mechanics* of the work & ready to *produce* the efforts whenever they are offered to me" (New York, MTP). On 8 November, Howells replied to Daly's request for a play that he had an idea he would sketch out and submit for criticism (WDH to WCH, Cambridge, 8 November, Houghton).

23. CLEMENS TO HOWELLS

Home [Hartford], 24th [October 1874].

Later ——— P.M.

My Dear Howells:

I shall not stop the letter I wrote 2 hours ago, because it has the suggestion about the play — but I take back the remark that I can't write for the Jan. number. For Twichell & I have had a long walk in the woods & I got to telling him about old Mississippi days of steamboating glory & grandeur as I saw them (during 5 years) *from the pilot house.* He said "What a virgin subject to hurl into a magazine!" I hadn't thought of that before.[1] Would you like a series of papers to run through 3 months or 6 or 9? — or about 4 months, say? [2]   Yrs Ever

Mark.

If you can't print the enclosed poem — you must be sure to

send it back to me.[3] Seems good for a child of 17 — though I am no judge of poetry — it is as much as I can do to write it.

1. Mark Twain must mean that he had not thought of using his experiences piloting on the Mississippi as material for magazine articles. He had long intended to write a book about the River, if not necessarily about this precise subject. As early as January 1866, he had written to his mother and sister from San Francisco that he was planning a book of "about three hundred pages," of which "the last hundred will have to be written in St. Louis, because the materials for them can only be got there" (20 January 1866 [misdated 1865], MTP). Just after he had finished *Roughing It,* he had written to Livy: ". . . when I come to write the Mississippi book, *then* look out! I will spend 2 months on the river & take notes, & I bet you I will make a standard work" (Bennington, Vt., 27 November 1871, LLMT, p. 166).

2. "Old Times on the Mississippi," serialized in the *Atlantic* in 1875, was expanded into *Life on the Mississippi* (1883).

3. The poem has disappeared.

24. CLEMENS TO HOWELLS

[Hartford] Oct. 29 [1874].

Dear Howells —

All right — I'll presently sail in — but you must be sure to mention me in the advertisements or I shall be as uppish & airish as any third-rate actor whose name is not made loud enough in the bills.[1]

I think likely I will write the first No. tomorrow.

I wish Pope would *stay* north, where the material for success is in its strength: i.e. population & cash.　　Ys Ever

Mark

1. Howells's evidently favorable reply to the suggestion of a series of articles about piloting on the Mississippi is not extant. But the theme must have appealed to him powerfully. As a boy he had traveled on the Ohio with his Dean uncles, who were pilots of the *New England* and the *New England No. 2* (YMY, p. 30).

25. CLEMENS TO HOWELLS (TELEGRAM)

Webster, Mass. [13 November 1874]

We arrive by rail at about 7 o'clock, the first of a series of grand annual pedestrian tours from Hartford to Boston to be performed by us will take place *next year*. [1]

1. The pedestrian excursion of Clemens and Twichell from Hartford to Boston, which began on the morning of 12 November, had been announced in the newspapers by the publication of this telegram to James Redpath, manager of Clemens's lecture tours: "Hartford, Nov. 9 Dear Redpath: — Rev. J. H. Twichell and I expect to start at 8 o'clock Thursday morning, to walk to Boston in 24 hours — or more. We shall telegraph Young's Hotel for rooms for Saturday night, in order to allow for a low average of pedestrianism. Yours, S. L. Clemens" (clipping in Twichell Journal, 17 November, Yale). They had set out along the old Boston stage road, reaching Westford, Conn. (a distance of twenty-eight miles) the first day. Although Clemens was very lame next morning, they made the six miles to North Ashford before they gave up and decided to take the train. Clemens's telegram to Howells was sent from Webster, the first station beyond New Boston, where they boarded the train. At the same time he telegraphed Redpath: "We have made thirty-five miles in less than five days. This demonstrates the thing can be done. Shall now finish by rail. Did you have any bets on us?" (Twichell Journal, 17 November, Yale). That Mark Twain was already a national celebrity is indicated by the fact that, as he recalled in his Autobiographical Dictation (12 September 1908, p. 18, MTP), "the Associated press had informed the country about our start," and sent out a bulletin next day announcing that the pedestrians were expected to reach Boston by nightfall.

26. HOWELLS TO CLEMENS (TELEGRAM)

[Cambridge, 13 November 1874]

You and Twichell come right out to 37 Concord Avenue Cambridge near observatory party waiting for you.

W. D. Howells

MS. The telegram was addressed to Clemens at Young's Hotel, Boston. The two travelers reached Howells's house about nine o'clock and found a party there which included Miss Longfellow, Miss Rose Hawthorne, John Fiske, and Larkin G. Mead and his wife. Howells wrote his father two days later: "I never saw a more used-up, hungrier man than Clemens. It was something fearful to see him eat escalloped oysters" (Cambridge, Houghton). After Clemens's death, Howells still found the memory of him on this occasion vivid: "I can see him now as he stood up in the midst of our friends, with his head thrown back, and in his hand a dish of those escalloped oysters . . . exulting in the tale of adventure, which had abounded in the most original characters and amusing incidents . . ." (MMT, p. 45). Next day, Saturday, Clemens gave a supper for Howells, Aldrich, Osgood, and Mead — "a rare good time," Twichell noted in his Journal, "which I enjoyed to the full. Heard lots of bright good talk." Monday they heard a lecture by Professor Edward S. Morse at the Radical Club at eleven in the morning. "To Howells at 2 o'clock to lunch — disgracefully tardy — a most delightful afternoon." In the late afternoon Howells took them to call on Lowell, where the talk was mostly about Henry Ward Beecher, and accompanied them as far as the Harvard Memorial Hall. "Then back to Boston and by the 9 o'clock train to Hartford, after, on some accounts the most pleasant experience of my life" (Twichell Journal, 17 November 1874, Yale). Twichell's newspaper clippings which complete the entry suggest that the newspapers made as much of Mark Twain's failure as of his original boast — a result he doubtless foresaw.

27. CLEMENS TO OLIVIA L. CLEMENS [1]

Boston, Nov. 16, 1935 [1874].

Dear Livy:

You observe I still call this beloved old place by the name it had when I was young. *Limerick!* It is enough to make a body sick.

The gentlemen-in-waiting stare to see me sit here *telegraphing* this letter to you, & no doubt they are smiling in their sleeves. But *let* them! The slow old fashions are good enough for me, thank God, & I will none other. When I see one of these modern fools sit absorbed, holding the end of a telegraph wire in his hand, & reflect that a thousand miles away there is another fool hitched to the other end of it, it makes me frantic with rage; & then am I more implacably fixed & resolved than ever, to continue taking twenty minutes to telegraph you what

I might communicate in ten seconds by the new way if I would so debase myself. And when I see a whole silent, solemn drawing-room full of idiots sitting with their hands on each other's foreheads "communing," I tug the white hairs from my head & curse till my asthma brings me the blessed relief of suffocation. In our old day such a gathering talked pure drivel & "rot," mostly, but better that, a thousand times, than these dreary conversational funerals that oppress our spirits in this mad generation.

It is sixty years since I was here before. I walked hither, then, with my precious old friend. It seems incredible, now, that we did it in two days, but such is my recollection. I no longer mention that we walked back in a single day, it makes me so furious to see doubt in the face of the hearer. Men were *men* in those old times. Think of one of the puerile organisms in this effeminate age attempting such a feat.

My air-ship was delayed by a collision with a fellow from China loaded with the usual cargo of jabbering, copper-colored missionaries, & so I was nearly an hour on my journey. But by the goodness of God thirteen of the missionaries were crippled & several killed, so I was content to lose the time. I love to lose time, anyway, because it brings soothing reminiscences of the creeping railroad days of old, now lost to us forever.

Our game was neatly played, & successfully. — None expected us, of course. You should have seen the guards at the ducal palace stare when I said, "Announce his grace the Archbishop of Dublin & the Rt. Hon. the Earl of Hartford." Arrived within, we were all eyes to see the Duke of Cambridge & his Duchess, wondering if we might remember their faces, & they ours. In a moment, they came tottering in; he, ⟨stooped &⟩ bent & withered & bald; she blooming with wholesome old age. He peered through his glasses a moment, then screeched in a reedy voice: "Come to my arms! Away with titles — I'll know ye by no names but Twain & Twichell!" Then fell he on our necks & jammed his trumpet in his ear, the which we filled with shoutings to this effect: "God bless you, old Howells, what is left of you!"

We *talked* late that night — none of your silent idiot "communings" for ⟨we⟩ us of the olden time. We rolled a stream of ancient anecdotes over our tongues & drank till the lord Archbishop grew so mellow in the mellow past that Dublin ceased to be Dublin to him & resumed its sweeter forgotten name of New York. In truth he almost got back into his ancient religion, too, good Jesuit as he has always been since O'Mulligan the First established that faith in the Empire.

And we canvassed everybody. Bailey Aldrich, Marquis of Ponkapog,[2] came in, got nobly drunk, & told us all about how poor Osgood lost his earldom & was hanged for conspiring against the Second Emperor — but he didn't mention how near he himself came to being hanged, too, for engaging in the same enterprise. He was as chaffy as he was sixty years ago, too, & swore the Archbishop & I never walked to Boston — but there was never a day that Ponkapog wouldn't lie, so be it by the grace of God he got the opportunity. —

The Lord High Admiral came in, a hale gentleman close upon seventy & bronzed by the suns & storms of many climes & scarred with the wounds got in many battles, & I told him how I had seen him sit in a high chair & eat fruit & cakes & answer to the name of Johnny.[3] His granddaughter (the eldest) is but lately married to the youngest of the Grand Dukes, & so who knows but a day may come when the blood of the Howells's may reign in the land? I must not forget to say, while I think of it, that your new false teeth are done, my dear, & your wig. Keep your head well bundled with a shawl till the latter comes, & so cheat your persecuting neuralgias & rheumatisms. Would you believe it? — the Duchess of Cambridge is deafer than you — deafer than her husband. They call her to breakfast with a park of artillery; & usually when it thunders she looks up expectantly & says "Come in." But she has become subdued & gentle with age & never destroys the furniture, now, except when uncommonly vexed. God knows, my dear, it would be a happy thing if you & old Lady Harmony[4] would imitate this spirit. But indeed the older you grow the less secure becomes the furniture. When *I* throw chairs through the window I have a sufficient reason to back it. But you — you are but a creature of passion.

The monument to the author of "Gloverson & His Silent Partners"[5] is finished. It is the stateliest & the costliest ever erected to the memory of any man. This noble classic has now been translated into all the languages of the earth & is adored by all nations & known to all creatures. Yet I have conversed as familiarly with the author of it as I do with my own great-grandchildren.

I wish you could see old Cambridge & Ponkapog. I love them as dearly as ever, but privately, my dear, they are not much improvement on idiots. It is melancholy to hear them jabber over the same pointless anecdotes three & four times of an evening, forgetting that they had jabbered them over three or four times the evening before. Ponkapog still writes poetry, but the old-time fire has mostly gone out of it. — Perhaps his best effort of late years is this:

> "O soul, soul, soul of mine!
> Soul, soul, soul of thine!
> Thy soul, my soul, two souls entwine,
> And sing thy lauds in crystal wine!"

This he goes about repeating to everybody, daily & nightly, insomuch that he is become a sore affliction to all that know him.

But I must desist. There are drafts here, everywhere & my gout is something frightful. My left foot hath resemblance to a snuff-bladder. God be with you.   Hartford.

These to Lady Hartford, in the earldom of Hartford, in the upper portion of the city of Dublin.

1. In his letter to Howells of 25 November 1874 Clemens says: "Oh, that letter wasn't written to my wife, but to *you*." In the Autobiographical Dictation for 16 July 1908, Clemens says again that the letter was written "To my wife ostensibly, but really to Mr. Howells" (MTE, p. 1). Howells's letter of 23 November indicates that Clemens had sent him a copy of it immediately upon his return to Hartford.

2. Aldrich is named Marquis of Ponkapog after the town twelve miles

south of Boston where he had recently taken up his residence after leaving the editorship of *Every Saturday*.

3. The Lord High Admiral was, of course, Howells's son John Mead Howells, then six years old.

4. Lady Harmony was Mrs. Twichell.

5. The author of this very Dickensian novel, laid in San Francisco (Boston, cop. 1868), was Ralph Keeler, former cabin boy on Great Lakes steamers, banjo-player for blackface minstrel shows, and vagabond who had written travel sketches for the *Atlantic* and was something of a mascot of Boston literary people.

28. CLEMENS TO HOWELLS

Home [Hartford], Nov. 17 [1874].

My Dear Howells:

We *must* apologize again for our shameless delay in getting out to lunch.[1] If Mrs. Howells will forgive & forget, we will always be strictly on time henceforth.

Mrs. Clemens gets upon the verge of swearing & goes tearing around in an unseemly fury when I enlarge upon the delightful time we had in Boston & she not there to have her share. I think she will be mighty sure to be along when we go again. I have tried hard to reproduce Mrs. Howells to her, & have probably not made a shining success of it.[2] Jo & I had so much to talk about that the train got here before we were expecting that event.

With the kindest regards to all the Howells household,

Ys Ever

Mark.

1. "We" refers to Clemens and Twichell (who is the "Jo" mentioned later). The luncheon took place on Monday, 16 November. The guests arrived late after having attended a meeting of the Radical Club in Boston.

2. This reference to Mrs. Howells suggests that Clemens met her for the first time on this visit.

[Hartford?, 17 or 18 or 19 November? 1874?]

Dear Howells —

Cut it, scarify it, reject it — handle it with entire freedom.

Ys Ever

Mark.

It will make 4 1/2 or 5 pages. Is that too long? Suppose we publish only every other month — that is best, isn't it?

MS. The dating of this note, together with certain other matters of chronology for the week following Clemens's and Twichell's return to Hartford, is conjectural. Twichell's Journal establishes the fact that the two friends reached home at midnight of Monday, 16 November. At some time within the next few days Mark Twain sent to Howells the letter from Limerick and the MS of the first installment of "Old Times on the Mississippi." Howells's letter of 23 November indicates that both documents arrived in Cambridge on Friday, 20 November, possibly under separate covers.

[Cambridge] November 23, 1874.

Dear Clemens:

The deliberation with which I respond to your letters of Friday is but a faint token of the delight that their coming gave me. I hope you're going to let me keep the letter from Limerick: at any rate I'm going to keep it till I've showed it round — especially to Aldrich and Osgood. I quite agree with Twichell about its deliciousness. (You not like Lamb! When the L. in your name stands for Lamb, and you know very well that you were christened Charles, and afterwards changed it to Solomon, for a joke.) Mrs. Howells is simply absurd about it, and thinks it better than the most tragical mirth in A Foreg. Conc.

The piece about the Mississippi is capital — it almost made

the water in our ice-pitcher muddy as I read it, and I hope to send you a proof directly. I don't think I shall meddle much with it even in the way of suggestion. The sketch of the low-lived little town was so good, that I could have wished ever so much more of it; and perhaps the tearful watchman's story might have been abridged — tho this may seem different in print. I want the sketches, if you can make them, *every month.*

Don't say another word about being late at lunch. I hope we know how to forgive a deadly injury, — especially when we know what is going to happen to the person when he dies.

Mrs. Howells thanks you ever so much for the fotografs. We both admire the babies, who seem to have behaved uncommonly well under fire of the fotografer, and to have come out seriously charming. We think they and the house the prettiest in the world. Give our best regards to Mrs. Clemens and the Twichells.

Your visit was an inexpressible pleasure. We hope for that great day when you shall bring your wife.   Yours ever

W. D. Howells.

31. HOWELLS TO CLEMENS

[Cambridge] November 24, 1874

Dear Clemens:

The only thing I'm doubtful of is the night watchman's story.[1] It doesn't seem so natural and probable as the rest of the sketch — seems made-up, on your part.

Please show it to Twitchell, and let me have the proof again as soon as you can.[2]   Yours ever

W. D. H.

1. In the MS of the first installment of "Old Times on the Mississippi."
2. Howells was evidently eager to get Mark Twain's contribution into the January number of the *Atlantic.* It was logical to begin a series with the first number of a new volume, and Howells always worked to make the January issues strong. Although he had acknowledged receipt of the MS only on Monday, 23 November (and although the MS itself can

43

hardly have reached the editor before Friday, 20 November), Howells has rushed it through the composing room and is able to enclose a proof on Tuesday, 24 November.

32. CLEMENS TO HOWELLS

Hartford, Nov. 25 [1874].

My Dear Howells:

Your amendment was good. As soon as I saw the watchman in print I perceived that he was lame & artificial. I wrote him up twice before sending him to you, but couldn't get Mrs. Clemens to approve of him at all. Dam the watchman [1] — as Twichell's ostler [2] would say — & as Mrs. Clemens *thinks,* though she seldom expresses a thought of that nature — never, indeed, unless strongly moved.

Oh, that letter wasn't written to my wife, but to *you.* Twichell only saw it because he knew I would naturally write you when I got home & he asked me not to mail the note when written, until he could inspect it, because he would be a party concerned.

No, I detest Lamb — even the modern addition of mint sauce does not beguile me. I am named after more obscure but nobler beings.

You Atlantic people spell well enough, & you plainly improve one's grammar, but you don't divide good. [3]

I am seriously afraid to appear in print often — newspapers soon get to lying in wait for me to blackguard me. [4] You think it over & you will see that it will doubtless be better for all of us that I don't infuriate the "critics" to frequently.

With kindest regards to Mrs. Howells & the children —

Ys Ever

Mark.

1. Although the reference to Howells's "amendment" might be taken to mean that the editor had deleted the watchman's story, it remained (possibly in shortened form) in the installment of "Old Times on the Mississippi" published in the January 1875 *Atlantic,* and eventually in the

fifth chapter of *Life on the Mississippi* (DE, XII, 41–43). With his pre-posterous claim to be the son of an English nobleman, the watchman is a literary ancestor of the Duke and the King in *Huckleberry Finn.*

2. Clemens and Twichell, on their pedestrian tour, had encountered in a tavern at Westford, Conn., "a sublimely profane hostler" (according to Twichell's Journal, 17 November 1874, Yale), who delighted Clemens so much by his innocent oaths in the presence of an incognito clergyman that he wrote out a description of the incident (probably in the 1880's; the sketch is published in MTE, pp. 366-372).

3. In criticizing the way in which the typesetter for the Riverside Press, which printed the *Atlantic,* "divided" (that is, syllabified words at the ends of lines), Clemens the former compositor was judging a shop which ranked as one of the best in the country.

4. For decades Clemens held to the belief that in the early stages of his career the newspapers had been consistently hostile to him. Not long before his death he said in his *Autobiography* (II, 69–70) that a reviewer of *The Gilded Age* in the New York *Daily Graphic* in 1873 had charged that Mark Twain had used his reputation "to play a swindle upon the public" by allowing his name to be signed to the book merely in order to "float" it. This charge of "dishonest conduct," he said, was copied from the *Graphic* by "all the critics of America, one after the other." Like other recollections preserved in the *Autobiography,* this one seems exaggerated. Arthur L. Vogelback's study of contemporary newspaper comment ("The Literary Reputation of Mark Twain") indicates that the canard was not so widely disseminated as Clemens believed, but there was some basis for his assertion. The Chicago *Tribune* quoted from the St. Louis *Democrat* on 5 April 1874 (p. 10) the following item — which the *Democrat* may well have picked up from the *Graphic:* "The secret is out. It is confidently asserted that *The Gilded Age* is a gigantic practical joke. It is declared that, wishing to test the credulity of the public, these two notorious wits [Mark Twain and Charles Dudley Warner] had the book prepared by several obscure newspaper local reporters. The covenant was solemnly made that the joke was to be kept a profound secret till 300,000 copies of the work were sold . . ." (quoted in Vogelback, "Literary Reputation," p. 80).

33. CLEMENS TO HOWELLS

[Hartford] Dec. 2 [1874].

Dear Howells:

Mrs. Clemens is so afraid I will litter up your house with photographs of myself, that at her earnest request I suggest that if I have sent you any others before this, you destroy them. But I consider this fresh picture quite a bully one — or rather, Mrs. Clemens does, the expression being hers.

With kindest regards to you all,   Ys Ever

S. L. C.

34. HOWELLS TO CLEMENS

[Cambridge] Dec. 3, 1874

My dear Clemens:

The fotograf is a wonderful success, and Mrs. Howells and I are exultantly grateful. We've got it framed to match Warner's, and it turns its eagle-eye away from me towards Boston, on my study mantel-piece. Apparently it is looking for Twichell, and I hope it will soon see him coming.[1] (Read this poetic passage to him — that he may not forget the picture he promised us.) By even post with this, I expect to send my book[2] to Mrs. Clemens with the hope that she will accept it. Please tell her that her liking it as it went through the magazine was a great comfort and pleasure to me.

We had a curious sort of fish-symposium yesterday in a little wooden house that hangs amphibiously on to the side of the South Boston Bridge, and belongs to a Boat Club that hasn't got any boat. The dinner was given by Underwood ("Lord of Himself,")[3] and Osgood. Aldrich was there, and we had a good time that asked nothing but to be crowned by the presence of you and Twichell. — I hope you're getting ready the second paper of reminiscences, for we've announced it for February. If I might put in my jaw at this point, I should say, stick to actual fact and character in the thing, and give things in *detail*. *All* that belongs with old river life is novel and is now mostly historical. Don't write *at* any supposed Atlantic audience, but yarn it off as if into my sympathetic ear. Don't be afraid of rests or pieces of dead color. I fancied a sort of hurried and anxious air in the first.   Yours ever

W. D. Howells.

1. Clemens took the photograph of Twichell to Howells when he went to Boston on 15 December to attend the *Atlantic* contributors' dinner. Howells acknowledged the gift thus, to Twichell: "In spite of your proud command, we *have* framed you, and now from above the dining room clock, you confront the *other* Washington on the opposite wall. Below you on the right is Twain, on the left Warner (that serpent of old Nile, who wont write to me), and I can fancy myself in Hartford when I look at you" (Cambridge, 19 December, Twichell Journal, Yale).

2. *A Foregone Conclusion,* published that day.

3. Francis H. Underwood, Boston lawyer and one of the founders of the *Atlantic,* had recently published a Kentucky novel *Lord of Himself,* which Howells had reviewed in the September issue of the magazine.

35. CLEMENS TO HOWELLS

[Hartford] Dec. 3. 1874

My Dear Howells:

Let us change the heading to *"Piloting* on the Miss in the Old Times" — or to *"Steamboating* on the M in the Old Times" — or to *"Personal* Old Times on the Missi." — We could change it for Feb. if now too late for Jan. —

I suggest it because the present heading is too pretentious, too broad & general. It seems to command me to deliver a Second Book of Revelation to the world, & cover all the Old Times the Misssissiipi (dang that word, it is worse than type or Egypt) ever saw — whereas here I have finished Article No. III & am about to start on No. 4 and yet I have spoken of nothing but of Piloting as a science so far; and I doubt if I ever get beyond that portion of my subject. And I don't care to. Any muggins can write about Old Times on the Miss. of 500 different kinds, but I am the only man alive that can scribble about the piloting of that day — and no man ever has tried to scribble about it yet. Its newness pleases me all the time — and it is about the only new subject I know of. If I were to write fifty articles they would all be about pilots and piloting — therefore let's get the word Piloting into the heading. There's a sort of freshness about that, too.   Ys ever,

Mark.

MS. At the head of the letter is an endorsement in Howells's hand: "From Mark Twain. W. D. H."

36. HOWELLS TO CLEMENS

[Cambridge] December 4, 1874.

Dear Clemens:

All right; Piloting it shall be; and I think it will be well to give a different title to each of the papers.[1] Glad you're getting on so well with them. I hope you can soon send us some copy.

Yours truly ever,

W. D. Howells.

1. Despite Howells's apparent concurrence in the suggestion made by Mark Twain in his letter of 3 December, all seven installments of the series appeared in the *Atlantic* under the title, "Old Times on the Mississippi." In his "Recollections of an Atlantic Editorship," thirty-one years later, Howells wrote: "We counted largely on [Mark Twain's] popularity to increase our circulation when we began to print the piloting papers; but with one leading journal in New York republishing them as quickly as they appeared, and another in St. Louis supplying the demand of the Mississippi Valley, and another off in San Francisco offering them to his old public on the Pacific slope, the sales of the *Atlantic Monthly* were not advanced a single copy, so far as we could make out. Those were the simple days when the magazines did not guard their copyright as they do now; advance copies were sent to the great newspapers, which helped their readers to the plums, poetic and prosaic, before the magazine could reach the newsstands, and so relieved them of the necessity of buying it" (*Atlantic*, C, 601, November 1907).

37. OLIVIA L. CLEMENS TO HOWELLS

Hartford Dec. 6th 1874

Very many thanks, Mr Howells, for the copy of "A Foregone Conclusion" which reached me yesterday.

Mr Clemens and I have thoroughly enjoyed the story each month as it came to us in the Atlantic.

I wanted Mr Clemens to write you when we had finished the last chapters, that if you would come and study closely our home life, you would find here a woman who was able to maintain the "operatic pitch" without encouragement.[1] I don't know why he was unwilling to do it, I am sure it would have increased your sense of his manly dignity.

We are looking forward with very pleasant anticipations to the time when you and Mrs Howells will visit us. We hope to be entirely settled by Christmas and after that we shall be anxious to see you here, and show you our babies and our new home.

Please give my kind regards to Mrs Howells.

Yours sincerely

Livy L. Clemens

1. The passage to which Livy Clemens alludes is in the last chapter of *A Foregone Conclusion*: "People are never equal to the romance of their youth in after life, except by fits, and Ferris [Henry Ferris, a young American painter] especially could not keep himself at what he called the operatic pitch of their [i.e., his and Florida Vervain's] brief betrothal and the early days of their marriage. With his help, or even his encouragement, his wife might have been able to maintain it. She had a gift for idealizing him, at least. . . ."

38. CLEMENS TO HOWELLS

Htfd, Dec. 8 [1874].

My Dear Howells:

It isn't the Atlantic audience that distresses me; for *it* is the only audience that I sit down before in perfect serenity (for the simple reason that it don't require a "humorist" to paint himself stripèd & stand on his head every fifteen minutes.) The trouble was, that I was only bent on "working up an atmosphere" & that is to me a most fidgety & irksome thing sometimes. I avoid it, usually, but in this case it was absolutely necessary, else every reader would be applying the atmosphere of his own river or sea experiences, & *that* ⟨would spoil everything⟩ shirt wouldn't fit, you know.

49

I could have sent this Article 2 a week ago, or more, but I couldn't bring myself to the drudgery of revising & correcting it. I have been at that tedious work 3 hours, now, & by *George* but I am glad it is over.

Say — I am as prompt as a clock, if I only know the *day* a thing is wanted — otherwise I am a natural procrastinaturalist. — Tell me what day & date you want Nos. 3 & 4, & I will tackle & revise them & they'll be there to the minute. —

I could wind up with No. 4, but there are some things more, which I am powerfully moved to write. Which is natural enough, since I am a person who would quit authorizing in a minute to go to piloting, if the madam would stand it.[1] I would rather sink a steamboat than eat, any time.

My wife was afraid to write you — so I said with simplicity, "*I* will give you the language — & ideas." Through the infinite grace of God there has not been such another insurrection in the family before as followed this. However, the letter was written, & promptly, too — whereas, heretofore she has *remained* afraid to do such things.

With kind regards to Mrs. Howells,   Yrs Ever

Mark.

1. This declaration of Mark Twain is quoted by Van Wyck Brooks in *The Ordeal of Mark Twain* (New York, 1920, pp. 27-28) in support of the view that "as a pilot he had experienced the full flow of the creative life as he had not experienced it in literature . . . that he had, in fact, found himself in his career as a pilot and lost himself with that career." Mr. Brooks quotes other statements of similar import. But Mark Twain made equally strong assertions to the opposite effect. For example, he wrote to his sister Pamela from Esmeralda, Nev., in 1862: "I never have *once* thought of returning home to go on the river again, and I never expect to do any more piloting at any price" (15 August, MTL, p. 85). Similarly, in the year of his death, he wrote: "To me, the most important feature of my life is its literary feature," and he asserted that he had been committed to a career in literature from the moment he was apprenticed to a printer at the age of fourteen ("The Turning-Point of my Life," DE, XXVI, 130–131). The present letter was written when Mark Twain was under the spell of writing about his piloting days; if anything, it testifies to the boundless satisfaction he found in the act of composition.

A SUBTILE HUMORIST (1874–1875)

39. CLEMENS TO HOWELLS

HARTFORD, DEC. 9, 1874.

MY DEAR HOWELLS:

I WANT TO ADD A SHORT PARAGRAPH TO ARTICLE NO. 1,[1] WHEN THE PROOF COMES. MERELY A LINE OR TWO, HOWEVER.

I DONT KNOW WHETHER I AM OGING TO MAKE THIS TYPE-WRITING MACHINE GO OR NTO, : THAT LAST WORD WAS INTENDRED FOR N-N*OT:* BUT I GUESS I SHALL MAKE SOME SORT OF A SUCC SS OF IT BEFORE I RUN IT VERY LO G. I AM SO THICK-FINGERED THAT I MISS THE KEYS.

YOU NEEDNT A SWER THIS; I AM ONLY PRACTICING TO GET THREE :*ANOTHER SLIP-UP THERE:* ONLY PRACTICI?NG TO GET THE HANG OF THE THING. I NOTICE I MISS FIRE & GET IN A GOOD MANY UNNECESSARY LETTERS & PUNCTUATION MARKS. I AM SIMPLY USING YOU FOR A TAR-GET TO BANG AT.BLAME MY CATS BUT THIS THING REQUIRES GENIUS IN ORDER TO WORK IT JUST RIGHT.   YOURS EVER,

MARK.

MS. The letter was written on a typewriter which had only capital letters. The marks of punctuation represented here by colons consist of three dots one above another in the original letter.

1. An error, explained in Clemens's next letter.

40. HOWELLS TO CLEMENS

[Cambridge] Dec. 11, 1874.

My dear Clemens:

Don't you dare to refuse that invitation to the Atlantic dinner for Tuesday evening. For fear you *mayn't* have got it, I'll just say that it was from the publishers, and asked you to meet Emerson, Aldrich, and all "those boys" at the Parker House at 6 o'clock, Tuesday, Dec. 15. *Come!*

— This instalment [1] is capital. I've just been reading it aloud to Mrs. Howells, who could rival Mrs. Clemens in her ignorance of Western steamboating, and she has enjoyed it every word — but the profane words. These she thinks could be better taken for granted; and in fact I think the sagacious reader could infer them.[2]

I have your printed letter of yesterday. Fire away; and when you get tired of the machine, lend it to me.

With our united regards to Mrs. Clemens,

Yours ever
W. D. Howells.

1. The second of "Old Times on the Mississippi."
2. In objecting to profanity in the MS Howells and his wife align themselves with Livy, whose attitude is described in Clemens's letter of 14 December.

41. CLEMENS TO HOWELLS

Hartford, Dec. 11 [1874].

My Dear Howells:

Mrs. Clemens is distressed to think you could believe she could receive that book & not have the grace to sit down & write you thanking you for it. — (She really believes that you think I wrote her note.) I tell her, never mind, she shall have the credit of writing some of *my* letters, but that don't seem to cover the difficulty.

Here I have been waiting to add two or three lines to article No. 1 when the proof should come, wholly forgetting that the proof *has* come & gone again, long ago! However, it is no matter; but I do wish I had thought about it sooner.

Mrs. Clemens was not ⟨much⟩ wholly pleased with No. 1 — which I had not time to re-write. Now she disapproves of a considerable portion of No. 4, so I shall lick it into shape before I tackle No. 5.

I have the madam's permission to treat myself to a holiday

next Tuesday, the 15th, & so I mean to be at that Atlantic dinner.[1] Mrs. Clemens would go with me to Boston, but her mother is to arrive here that night.

With kindest remembrances to Mrs. Howells —

Yrs Ever

Clemens

1. The first of four dinners for "a few of the contributors" to be given by H. O. Houghton & Co., who had recently taken over the *Atlantic* when the firm of James R. Osgood & Co. failed. Mark Twain's inclusion in the inner circle of *Atlantic* contributors (there were only twenty-eight persons at the dinner), when he had published only two pieces in the magazine ("A True Story" and the first installment of "Old Times on the Mississippi," which had appeared just before the dinner in the January 1875 number), tends to refute Howells's recollection (MMT, p. 47) that he "seemed not to hit the favor of our community of scribes and scholars, as Bret Harte had done, when he came on from California. . . . " It was even more striking that Clemens was asked to speak in an after-dinner program whose Bostonian character was authenticated by the recital of an occasional poem by Dr. Holmes. Mark Twain responded to the toast, "The President of the United States and the Female Contributors of the *Atlantic*." "Professing to be staggered by the greatness of the subject, he asked permission, with the utmost apparent solicitude, to attack it in sections. He thereupon began to talk on quite other matters. . . . The dinner he pronounced 'nice,' in fact 'really good,' 'an admirable dinner,' 'quite as good as he would have had if he had stayed at home!' " (Arthur Gilman, "Atlantic Dinners and Diners," *Atlantic,* C, 651, November 1907).

42. CLEMENS TO HOWELLS

Hartford, Sunday [13 December 1874].

My Dear Howells:

I want you to ask Mrs. Howells to let you stay all night at the Parker House & tell lies & have an improving time, & take breakfast with me in the morning.[1] I will have a good room for you, & a fire. Can't you tell her it always makes you sick to go home late at night, or something like that? That sort of thing rouses Mrs Clemens's sympathies, easily; the only trouble is to *keep* them up. Twichell & I talked till 2 or 3 in the morning, the night we supped at your house & it restored his health on account of his being drooping for some time & made him much more robuster than what he was before. Will Mrs. Howells let you?   Ys Ever

                                                               S. L. C.

1. The proposal is for a visit after the *Atlantic* dinner on 15 December.

43. CLEMENS TO HOWELLS

[Hartford, 14 December 1874]

HARTFORD, MONDAY. MY DEAR HOWELLS:
MRS. CLEMENS RECEIVED THE MAIL THIS MOR ING, & THE NEXT MINUTE SHE LIT INTO THE STUDY WITH DANGER IN HER EYE & THIS DEMAND ON HER TONGUE: WHERE IS THE PROFANITY MR. HOWELLS SPEAKS OF? THEN I HAD TO MISERABLY CONFESS THAT I HAD LEFT IT OUT WHEN READING THE MSS. TO HER. NOTHING BUT ALMOST INSPIRED LYING GOT ME OUT OF THIS SCRAPE WITH MY SCALP. DOES YOUR WIFE GIVE YOU RATS, LIKE THIS, WHEN YOU GO A LITTLE ONE-SIDED? [1]

I GUESS I SHALL HAVE TO AFFLICT YOU WITH THE MACHINE BEFORE LONG; IT IS MOST TOO TEARI G ON THE MIND FOR   YOURS, EVER,
                                                               MARK.

MS. This letter is typed on the typewriter which made its appearance with Clemens's letter of 9 December.
1. Livy was serious in her intention of deleting profanity from her husband's writings, but his description of her has a tone of comic exaggeration rather than of remorse or frustration.

44. CLEMENS TO HOWELLS

Hartford, Dec. 18 [1874].

My Dear Howells:

I left No. 3 [1] in my eldest's [2] reach, & it may have gone to the postman & it likewise may have gone into the fire. I confess

Clemens in 1874. (See letter 34.)

Olivia L. Clemens in 1873.

Howells in 1877. From a steel engraving
by J. J. Cade.

Howells in Venice in the early
1860's.

Elinor M. Howells before her marriage. From
a drawing by her brother, Larkin G. Mead,
1861 or 1862.

to a dread that the latter is the case & that that stack of MS. will have to be written over again. If so, O for the return of the lamented Herod!

You & Aldrich have made one woman deeply & sincerely grateful — Mrs. Clemens. For months — I may even say years — she has shown an unaccountable animosity toward my neck-tie, even getting up in the night to take it with the tongs & blackguard it — sometimes also going so far as to threaten it.

When I said you & Aldrich had given me two *new* neck-ties, & that they were in a paper in my overcoat pocket, she was in a fever of happiness until she found I was going to frame them; then all the venom in her nature gathered itself together, — insomuch that I, being near to a door, went without, perceiving danger.

Now I wear one of the new neck-ties, nothing being sacred in Mrs. Clemens's eyes that can be perverted to a gaud that shall make the person of her husband more alluring than it was aforetime.[3]

Jo Twichell was the delightedest old boy I ever saw, when he read the words you had written in that book.[4] He & I went to the Concert of the Yale students last night & had a good time.

Mrs. Clemens dreads our going to New Orleans, but I tell her she'll have to give her consent this time.[5]

With kindest regards unto ye both —　　　　Ys Ever
　　　　　　　　　　　　　　　　　　　　　　　　S. L. Clemens

P.S. — John Hay of his own free will & accord, volunteers me a letter which is so gratifying in its nature that I am obliged to copy it for you to read. I was born & reared at Hannibal, & John Hay at Warsaw, 40 miles higher up, on the river (one of the Keokuk packet ports):

"Dear Clemens — I have just read with delight your article in the Atlantic. It is perfect — no more nor less. I don't see how you do it. I knew all that, every word of it — passed as much time on the levee as you ever did, knew the same crowd & saw the same scenes, — but I could not have remembered one word of it all. You have the two greatest gifts of the writer, memory & imagination. I congratulate you." [6]

Now isn't that outspoken & hearty, & just like that splendid John Hay?

S. L. C.

1. The third installment of "Old Times on the Mississippi."

2. Susy (Olivia Susan), born 19 March 1872.

3. The flavor of the passage suggests Mark Twain's reading in older English literature, which was to find expression in *The Prince and the Pauper* (1882) and *A Connecticut Yankee* (1889).

4. Clemens brought back from the *Atlantic* dinner a copy of *A Foregone Conclusion* inscribed to Twichell.

5. The trip to New Orleans was possibly a scheme developed in conversation with Howells during Mark Twain's recent visit to Boston, and was of course to be made for gathering material for the "Mississippi book."

6. The letter from Hay (New York, 16 December 1874), quoted by Clemens with only minor typographical changes, is in MTP.

45. HOWELLS TO CLEMENS

[Cambridge] Dec. 19, 1874.

Dear Clemens:

Your No. 3 is safe among the dead-heads in my drawer, so you can dismiss all fears but those of publication. It's very interesting, and quite a revelation in its way; for the brute public, it would have been better if it had ended with some sort of incident. Perhaps you could still contrive one. — I rejoice as much as you do in Hay's letter — or should, if I didn't like your papers so much as to be jealous of every other admirer. What business has *Hay*, I should like to know, praising a favorite of mine? It's interfering.

Now that Mrs. Clemens has bowed her neck to the yoke, Mrs. Howells has sprung back from it with astonishing vigor and is saying that I ought not to go to New Orleans without her. I suppose it will end by our looking at N. O. on the map; but I don't give it up yet, and don't *you*. We will keep this project alive if [it] takes all winter.

— Here are $3 to pay for Aldrich's board and lodging at the Parker House. He was *my* guest for bed and breakfast, and I didn't mean to palm him off on you, who had calculated merely to pay my expenses.[1] If you paid for his dinner, you did it at your own risk.

Honesty is the best policy, but it is not the cheapest.

Yours ever

W. D. Howells.

I'm glad Twichell was pleased. My love to him.

1. On 20 December, Howells wrote to his father: "After the dinner, Aldrich and I staid all night with Clemens at the Parker House, and sat up talking it over till two o'clock in the morning" (Cambridge, LinL, I, 199).

46. HOWELLS TO CLEMENS

[Cambridge] Jan. 10, 1875.

My dear Clemens:

Here's your No. II, and I'll undertake to say for the publishers that you shall make any arrangement for simultaneity[1] in England that you like; only you won't be able to simultane with the January and February numbers. I'll send you two proofs of the III.[2]

— I declare, it's too bad of you to send me that Toronto letter, and the accompanying taunt.[3] Here I am, painfully ⟨lawfully⟩ clawing a few tattered dollars together from a colossal work of the imagination,[4] and you from a few paltry compilations of facts are able to roll in wealth. It is too bad, and enough to drive one to serious literature at once. I daren't show that letter to Mrs. Howells, who already thinks meanly of my talent ⟨when⟩ since she's heard what you've made by your play.

And speaking of Mrs. Howells brings me to New Orleans, — or rather it doesn't. Far back in the dark ages of last summer, Mrs. Howells and I talked of going off somewhere to a milder climate next March, and we said Bethlehem, Pa., by way of settling something. But when I thought of meeting you at the Atlantic dinner, I said, "I'll propose to Clemens to take Mrs. Clemens, and I'll take you, and we'll all go to New Orleans together."

She frantically approved; and then you couldn't take Mrs. Clemens, you said, and I said, never mind, you and I will go, and you with yr accustomed amiability said, yes. Well, now: Mrs. Howells would let me go, and if I went, I know I should solemnly promise to take her to Bethlehem some time in March. But you see, I wouldn't take her, when it came to the pinch. I would sneak out of it, saying that I hadn't the time or the money — which would be perfectly true. I can't do both these things, so, without referring the matter to her, I must be a man for once in my life, and say No, when I'd inexpressibly rather say Yes. Forgive my having led you on to fix a time; I never thought it would come to that, I supposed you would die, or something. I'm really more sorry and ashamed than I can make it appear.

Yours ever,

W. D. Howells.

1. Simultaneous serial publication.

2. The roman numerals refer to installments of "Old Times on the Mississippi."

3. Evidently a report on royalties from Mark Twain's play *Colonel Sellers,* which John T. Raymond had taken on tour after a highly successful run of 115 nights in New York. Later that month Clemens said the play was yielding him "from five hundred to a thousand dollars a week," and the same amount for Raymond (SLC to Robert Watt, Hartford, 26 January 1875, Berg, TS in MTP).

4. *A Foregone Conclusion,* published a month earlier.

47. CLEMENS TO HOWELLS

Hartford Jan. 12 [1875].

My Dear Howells:

We *mustn't* give up the New Orleans trip. Mrs. Clemens would gladly go if her strength would permit, but can't Mrs. Howells go anyway? I think she would find it very pleasant. I *know* she would. We can *put off* New Orleans until March 1st, & then that would do in place of Bethlehem. You just persuade her.

We are expecting the furniture for one of the guest rooms in a few days. When it comes can't you & Mrs. Howells run down here for 3 or 4 days & have a talk about this matter? We would go to Boston but for the fact that we are not foot-free now; at least *she* ain't, on account of having to see to little odds & ends of settling every day or so — nothing of much consequence, but just enough to make her presence in a manner necessary; so she begs & I beg that the Howellses will come to *us* in place of our attempting to get to Boston. Now *do* try to come.

Ys Ever

Mark.

I know how we can make our expenses going to N.O., but you'd just lose money going to Beth.

48. HOWELLS TO CLEMENS

[Cambridge] Jan. 12, 1875

Dear Clemens:

This number [1] is extraordinarily good. I've just been reading it to my wife, who's delighted with it.

W. D. H.

1. An installment of "Old Times on the Mississippi," probably the third (which was to appear in the March number of the *Atlantic*).

49. CLEMENS TO HOWELLS

Hartford, 15th [January 1875]

My Dear Howells:

I am very glad you like it; & glad, too, that there wasn't any profanity in it, since you read it to Mrs. Howells; though I have noticed that a little judicious profanity helps out an otherwise ineffectual sketch or poem remarkably. I attribute the feebleness of many of Tupper's [1] noblest efforts to the lack of this element.

59

You said once that you wanted a snapper put on to the end of this No. 3, but I judge you have concluded to leave it as it is — which is doubtless best, for it is already plenty long enough.

Upon second thought, it is too much trouble to make a whole lot of corrections over again in the duplicate proof in order to "simultane" with Temple Bar, & so I'm not going to do it. I have already broken my promise twice to Mr. Bentley,[2] & the penalty for a third infraction cannot increase my calamities much hereafter, & besides it may chance to be wholly overlooked amid the multitude of my sins. So you needn't bother about sending me the duplicate proofs.

Susie is croupy, but today we believe it isn't going to be serious.   Ys Ever

Mark.

P.S. I mail you, either in this or another envelop, No. 4 — which I have just added a snapper to it.[3] True story, too.

1. Martin Farquhar Tupper (1810–1889), author of the immensely popular *Proverbial Philosophy*. This book would appear on the parlor table in the Grangerfords' house in *Huckleberry Finn*.

2. Richard Bentley (1828–1895) was editor of *Temple Bar*, a London magazine. The promise is explained in a letter of Clemens to Bentley (Hartford, 26 April 1876, Barrett): "You remember a visit which Joaquin Miller & I paid you once [this must have been in 1873]. You asked me then to send you advance sheets of such sketches as I might write for magazines here, & I always purposed doing it, but continually forgot it."

3. The "snapper" was the story of the sleep-walking pilot who takes his boat through a most hazardous stretch of the river at night. An observer comments: ". . . if he can do such . . . piloting when he is sound asleep, what couldn't he do if he was dead!" (*Atlantic*, XXXV, 452, April 1875).

50. HOWELLS TO CLEMENS

[Cambridge] Jan'y 24, 1875.

My dear Clemens:

I'm working against time at present,[1] so as to be able to get off *somewhere* in March, and I can't spare 3 or 4 days to the delight of going to Hartford — I really can't and mustn't. It's lovely of you and Mrs. Clemens to ask us, and we consider that visit put down to our credit on your books.

About New Orleans, I can't tell. Mrs. Howells is behaving very handsomely about it, and so am I; but the probabilities are that as she would not like to go to N.O. under the circumstances, I shall go to Bethlehem, though she *says*, in the noblest way, "Well, *go* to New Orleans, if you want to so *much*." (You know the tone.) I suppose it will do, if I let you know sometime about the middle of February?

You're doing the science of piloting splendidly. Every word's interesting. And don't you drop the series till you've got every bit of anecdote and reminiscence into it.   Ever yours

W. D. H.

1. On this same day Howells wrote his father that he was stalled on his history of Venice (Cambridge, 24 January 1875, Houghton).

51. CLEMENS TO HOWELLS

[Hartford?, January? 1875]

P.S. — Look here! Yes, it will do to let me know by the middle of February, & then I do hope you will decide to make the steamboat trip. Of course you mustn't go if Mrs. Howells's desires should remain in any degree against it, for that would impair your enjoyment of it too much, & hers likewise — but I will live in the hope that Providence will develop an interest in this expedition, & if that once occurs the thing will clip right along to the entire satisfaction of all parties concerned. You mark my words.

S. L. C.

MS. Only the postscript of this letter has survived. The sheet bears the number "5" in Clemens's hand.

52. CLEMENS TO HOWELLS

Hartford, Jan. 26 [1875].

My Dear Howells:

When Mrs. Clemens read your letter she said: "Well, then, *wherever* they go, in March, the direction will be southward & so they must give us a visit on the way." I do not know what sort of control you may be under, but when my wife speaks as positively as that, I am not in the habit of talking back & getting into trouble. Situated as I am, I would not be able to understand, now, how you could pass by this town without feeling that you were running a wanton risk & doing a daredevil thing. I consider it settled that you are to come in March, & I would be sincerely sorry to learn that you & Mrs. Howells feel differently about it.

The piloting material has been uncovering itself by degrees, until it has exposed such a huge hoard to my view that a whole book will be required to contain it if I use it. So I have agreed to write the book for Bliss. I won't be able to run the articles in the Atlantic later than the September number, for the reason that a subscription book issued in the fall has a much larger sale than if issued at any other season of the year.[1] It is funny when I reflect that when I originally wrote you & proposed to do from 6 to 9 articles for the magazine, the vague thought in my mind was that 6 might exhaust the material & 9 would be pretty sure to do it. Or rather it *seems* to me that that was my thought, — can't tell at this distance. But in truth 9 chapters don't now seem to more than open up the subject fairly & start the yarn to wagging.

I've been sick abed several days, for the first time in 21 years. How little confirmed invalids appreciate their advantages. I was able to read the English edition of the Greville Memoirs [2] through without interruption, take my meals in bed, neglect all business without a pang, & smoke 18 cigars a day. I try not to look back upon these 21 years with a feeling of resentment, & yet the partialities of Providence do seem to me to be slathered around (as one may say) without that gravity & attention to detail which the real importance of the matter would seem to suggest. However, there are so many things to attend to & look after in a universe so unnecessarily large as this one, that after all, the real wonder is that more people are not overlooked than are.

I have just received some pictures of the Madam — not astonishingly good, but I can get her to a gallery only once in 4 years, & so am pretty glad to have any at all. I am sure you said you wanted one, & promised us Mrs. Howells's & the children's, too — so I venture to enclose one [3] & look for the fulfillment of your oath. I'm afraid to send one to Aldrich lest he'll be dreading another deluge! [4]   Yrs Ever

Mark.

1. The last installment of "Old Times on the Mississippi" appeared in the *Atlantic* for August, but the book — expanded to twice the length of the magazine series — was not to be completed until 1883, when it was published as *Life on the Mississippi*.

2. The first series of the *Memoirs* of Charles Cavendish Fulke Greville (1794–1865), clerk to the Privy Council, was published in London in 1874. The subtitle of the volume is, "A Journal of the Reigns of King George IV and King William IV."

3. The photograph of Livy has disappeared.

4. Clemens refers to a practical joke he had recently played on Aldrich by sending one photograph of himself a day for two weeks and on New Year's Day, twenty in twenty separate covers (Ferris Greenslet, *The Life of Thomas Bailey Aldrich*, Boston, 1908, pp. 112–117).

53. CLEMENS TO ELINOR M. HOWELLS

[Hartford, February? 1875]

Dear Mrs. Howells:

Mrs. Clemens is delighted to get the pictures,[1] & so am I. I can perceive, in the group, that Mr Howells is feeling as I so often feel, viz: "Well no doubt I *am* in the wrong, though I do not know where or how or why — but anyway it will be safest to look meek, & walk circumspectly for a while, & not *discuss* the thing." And you look exactly as Mrs. Clemens does just after she has said, "Indeed I do not *wonder* that you can frame no reply: for you know only too well that your conduct admits of no excuse, palliation or argument — *none!*"

I shall just delight in that group on account of the good old human domestic spirit that pervades it — bother these family groups that put on a state aspect to get their pictures taken in.

We want a heliotype made of *our* eldest daughter. How soft & rich & lovely the picture is. Mr. Howells must tell me how to proceed in the matter.　　　Truly Yours

Saml L. Clemens.

P.S. The physician has commanded that Mrs. Clemens lie abed to-day — so she begs you will excuse her deputing me to deliver her thanks for the pictures.

1. The photographs of the Howells family have disappeared.

54. CLEMENS TO HOWELLS

[Hartford, February? 1875]

My Dear Howells:

Two weeks ago I was writing several anecdotes about Strother Wiley's[1] delicious impertinences to steamboat captains (to go in No. 6 or 7) & wondering if he were still alive & if we might have the good luck to go to New Orleans with him (he is brim full of river reminiscences,) & behold he turns up in a letter to me from St Louis yesterday. You can con his happy orthography & then consign him to the waste basket.[2]

Ys Ever

Mark.

MS. This letter begins on p. 3 of Clemens's letter to Mrs. Howells, immediately under the signature.

1. Although Strother Wiley is not mentioned in "Old Times on the Mississippi," a "Stephen W." who is extremely impertinent to steamboat

captains figures in both the sixth and seventh installments (Chapters XIV and XVII of *Life on the Mississippi*).

2. The letter from Wiley is not extant.

55. CLEMENS TO HOWELLS

Hartford, Feb. 10 [1875].

My Dear Howells:

Your praises of my literature gave me the solidest gratification; but I never did have the fullest confidence in my critical penetration, & now your verdict on Stoddard[1] has knocked what little I *did* have, gally-west! *I* didn't enjoy his *gush,* but I thought a lot of his similes were ever so vivid & good. But it's just my luck; every time I go into convulsions of admiration over a picture & want to buy it right away before I've lost the chance, some wretch who really understands art comes along & damns it. But I don't mind. I would rather have my ignorance than another man's knowledge, because I have got so much more *of* it.

Mind you try *hard,* on the 15th, to say you will go to New Orleans. If Mrs. Howells will consent to go, too, I will make a pleasant young lady neighbor of ours go also, so she can have respectable as well as talented company.

I send you No. 5[2] to-day. I have written & re-written the first half of it three different times, yesterday & to-day, & at last Mrs. Clemens says it will do. I never saw a woman so hard to please about things she don't know anything about.

Ys Ever

Mark.

1. Clemens had clipped one of Charles W. Stoddard's articles about San Marco from a New York paper and had sent it to Howells, judging it "good literature" (SLC to Stoddard, Hartford, 1 February 1875, MTL, pp. 248–249). In a letter which is missing, Howells apparently praised Mark Twain's current writing, and damned Stoddard's San Marco piece.

2. The fifth installment of "Old Times on the Mississippi," which was to appear in the *Atlantic* for May 1875.

56. HOWELLS TO CLEMENS

Cambridge, Feb'y 16, 1875.

My dear Clemens:

I can't manage the trip, this winter. It's too bad, after talking it up, and getting you into the notion but it's quite beyond my range. I've been under the weather and on half-work the whole winter, so that I don't feel as if I had earned my salary, and I oughtn't to take three weeks or a month out for a pleasure-trip on the chance of making it up *some*how. I'm all the more bound because I shouldn't be questioned about it. At Bethlehem, I can keep writing something. Now, be as merciful as possible in your thoughts of me; I'll explain more fully when I see you at Hartford early in March.

I'm delighted that you entered so thoroughly into the spirit of our family group. It shows Mrs. Howells and me in our true relations of domination and subjection. But don't you think I've made a very successful stagger at looking knowing, and as if I just gave way to humor her? And doesn't Winny [1] look as the oldest daughter always does? And isn't it in character for Pilla [2] not to have any eyes, and for Bua [3] to run to lower lip?

— The heliotypes are $5 a *hundred*. You send your negative to Osgood, and he heliotypes you, and takes the sum out of your copyright.

— Wiley's letter is delightful. But my Uncle Sam can beat him in spelling. "I could of done it" — that's his style. No. 5 is first-rate. Yours ever

W. D. H.

We're both sorry about Mrs. Clemens. Isn't our visit going to be an affliction?

1. Winifred Howells, born in 1863.
2. Mildred Howells, born in 1872.
3. John Mead Howells, born in 1868.

57. CLEMENS TO HOWELLS

[Hartford] Feb. 20 [1875].

My Dear Howells:

After all, I find I cannot go to Boston. And what grieves me as much, is, that I have to give up the river trip, too.

So I'll trim up & finish 2 or 3 more river sketches for the magazine (if you still think you want them), & then buckle in on another book for Bliss,[1] finish it the end of May, & then either make the river trip or drop it indefinitely. I give up the river trip, *now,* because I find our mother[2] cannot remain here with my wife, but must return to her own home & finish her building enterprise — namely, her house.

We are looking forward with the pleasantest anticipations to your visit, & we want you to give us just as many days as you can. We shall be utterly out of company, & you can choose your own rooms, & change & take *ours* if they don't suit.

Yrs Ever

Mark.

1. Almost certainly *Tom Sawyer*, which had been begun the previous year and which would be finished by 5 July 1875 (MTW, pp. 3–4).
2. Mrs. Jervis Langdon, Livy's mother.

58. HOWELLS TO CLEMENS

[Cambridge] Feb. 28, 1875.

My dear Clemens:

Your giving up that river-trip has been such a blow to me that I have not been able to write until now.

Mrs. Howells and I expect to appear at Hartford on Thursday, March 11, to afflict you very briefly. As Mrs. H. and Mrs. Clemens are both tearing invalids, don't you think it would be better not to give that ball *this* visit? Let us have just a nice sit-down, quiet time. Of course if the date named wont do, you can temporize: we're unsuspecting people. I want you to give me all the Pilot experiences you can in conscience. It'll help your book to have had them talked about beforehand. I know that our pay is small, comparatively.[1]

We missed you dreadfully at the dinner,[2] the other day, where we had a beautiful time.   Yours ever

W. D. Howells.

Mrs. H. expects to go on to N.Y. the Saturday after her arrival in Hartford.

1. Although the *Atlantic* had offered Bret Harte ten thousand dollars for twelve contributions in 1871, such a rate of payment was exceptional if not unique. Mark Twain was correct in his statement to Charles W. Stoddard that the twenty dollars per page he received from the *Atlantic* for the "Old Times on the Mississippi" series was a higher rate than the magazine was paying any of its other contributors (Hartford, 1 February 1875, MTL, p. 248; see letter 18, note 1).

2. Of the Nautilus Club, on 24 February. James R. Osgood had invited Clemens in a letter of 16 February (Boston, MTP), saying, "It will be Aldrich's last public appearance before crossing the Atlantic."

59. CLEMENS TO HOWELLS

[Hartford] Mch. 1 [1875].

My Dear Howells:

Now you shall find us the most reasonable people in the world. We had thought of precipitating upon you George Warner [1] & wife [2] one day; Twichell & his jewel of a wife another day, & Chas. Perkins [3] & wife another. Only those — simply members of our family, they are. But I'll close the door against them all — which will "fix" all of the lot except Twichell, who will no more hesitate to climb in at the back window than *nothing*.

And you shall go to bed when you please, get up when you please, talk when you please, read when you please. Mrs. Howells may even go to New York Saturday if she feels that she must, but if some gentle, unannoying coaxing can beguile her into putting that off a few days, we shall be more than glad, for I do wish she & Mrs. Clemens could have a good square chance to get acquainted with each other. But first & last & all the time, we want you to feel untrameled & wholly free from restraint, here.

The date suits — *all* dates suit.   Yrs Evr

Mark

1. Brother of Charles Dudley Warner, and agent for the American Emigrant Co., which arranged for the settlement of European immigrants on lands in Iowa.

2. Elizabeth ("Lilly") Warner, niece of John Hooker, the founder of the Nook Farm community. She was a close friend of Livy Clemens.

3. A lawyer, one of the Clemenses' friends in Nook Farm, who sometimes acted as Clemens's business agent.

60. CLEMENS TO HOWELLS

[Hartford, 2 or 9 March 1875]

Howells, didn't I *tell* you that this Jo Twichell couldn't be kept out? He was going to exchange with some New Jersey preacher Sunday the 14th, till he heard that you are coming. Now if you *can* manage to stay here Sunday & several days after, it would be so splendid of you. Meantime, you see, the *weather* would settle, & then Mrs. Howells could travel so much more comfortably.   Ys Evr

Mark

MS. This is an endorsement upon a note from Twichell to Clemens, dated "Tuesday morning," which reads in part: "I wish you would find out, if you can, whether the Howellses, or Howells, will be here over Sunday. I wouldn't miss being here myself, if they were to be, for a good deal."

61. HOWELLS TO CLEMENS

[Cambridge] March 15, 1875.

My dear Clemens:

Your own feelings will give you no clew to our enjoyment of the little visit we made you.[1] There never was anything more unalloyed in the way of pleasure — I was even spared the pang of bidding the ladies goodbye.

I'm sorry you're not coming up to the Aldrich lunch,[2] to which I found myself invited. — Don't say anything to anybody about the Longfellow book [3] till you hear from me.

Yours ever,

W. D. Howells.

1. Howells and his wife arrived in Hartford on Thursday, 11 March; Howells returned to Cambridge on Saturday the thirteenth; and Elinor Howells went on to New York, where Howells was to join her with the children, in a week or ten days, for their trip to Bethlehem, Pa. Howells reported to his father: "We had a really charming visit, not marred by anything. The Clemenses are whole-souled hosts, with inextinguishable money, and a palace of a house, to which, by the way I really prefer ours, — and we met all the pleasant people whose acquaintance I made last year, except the [Charles Dudley] Warners, who are now up the Nile" (Cambridge, 14 March 1875, Houghton).

2. Presumably another farewell party; Aldrich and his wife sailed for Europe before the end of March (Greenslet, *Life,* p. 117).

3. Longfellow had had his poem "Morituri Salutamus," which he was to deliver at the Bowdoin Commencement, set up in "large clear type," and Howells knew of the existence of proofs or, possibly, a few privately printed copies (information from Andrew R. Hilen, Jr.; W. Sloane Kennedy, *Henry W. Longfellow,* Cambridge, 1882, pp. 107–108). The poet's enormous prestige is revealed in the importance Howells attaches to this information.

62. CLEMENS TO HOWELLS

[Hartford] Tuesday [16 March 1875].

My Dear Howells:

Well, all that was necessary to make that visit perfect was to know that you & Mrs. Howells enjoyed it. Sunday morning Mrs. Clemens said, "Nothing could have been added to that visit to make it more charming, except *days*." [1] And presently she said she felt fresher & stronger than usual — & I was able to say "You look it" — which was the case. My most secret reason for not going to the Aldrich lunch was that I had got intellectual friction enough out of your visit to be able to go to work Monday. Which turned out to be correct — I wrote 4000 words yesterday.

To-day I am proposing to bang away again.

I'll remember & not divulge the Longfellow matter.

I found it was the wet-nurse who had drank 200 bottles of the 252 — so I have been making an awful row in the servants' quarters, this morning, & clearing the atmosphere. My beer will be respected, now, I hope, for I do not wish to resort to bloodshed.[2]

Old Twichell dropped in Saturday night in the hope that you had remained over. I guess that same hope moved him to cancel his "exchange."

Jolly times to you all & the Aldrichs — & the kindest remembrances from us to Mrs Howells.　　　Ys Ever

Mark

1. To her mother, Livy had written on 14 March (Hartford, Jervis Langdon, TS in MTP): "Mr and Mrs Howells came Thursday noon, and left us yesterday (Saturday) noon — We had an exceedingly pleasant time with them — Thursday I invited Mr and Mrs Perkins, and Mannix — Mr and Mrs Twichell and Mr and Mrs G. Warner to dine with them — We had a good time — Friday evening we were invited to Mr Perkins — Mrs Howells is not a bit like Mrs Aldrich. She is exceedingly simple in her dress. . . . She is *exceedingly* bright — very intellectual — sensible and nice. I liked her — She is almost common in her dress. . . . Thought the house was the most delightful one that she was ever in — we had a very satisfactory visit and hope that it will be often repeated." Twichell noted in his Journal that he and his wife had enjoyed "a most delightful evening with some of the best people in the world" and that their children had behaved well when they took them over the next morning "to let the Howellses see them" (11, 12 March, Yale). Lilly Warner wrote her husband: "The Howells went yester. noon, & we ran over to say goodbye. Such friendly folk as they are. I feel as if I knew them well . . ." (Hartford, 14 March 1875, MTP).

2. The wet nurse with a taste for beer, a Rabelaisian character of almost mythical powers, is fully described in Mark Twain's unpublished "A Family Sketch" (undated, but written after 8 May 1897; copy in MTP). Her name was McLaughlin. She was fifth in a series (and last — Clara was almost nine months old). She was "a wonder, a portent . . . apparently Irish, with a powerful strain of Egyptian in her." Mark Twain continued, "There was never any wet-nurse like that one — the unique, the sublime, the unapproachable! She stood six feet in her stockings, she was perfect in form and contour, raven-haired, dark as an Indian, stately, carrying her head like an empress. . . . She was as healthy as iron, she had the appetite of a crocodile, the stomach of a cellar, and the digestion of a quartz-mill. Scorning the adamantine law that a wet-nurse must partake of delicate things only, she devoured anything and everything she could get her hands on, shoveling into her person fiendish combinations of fresh pork, lemon pie, boiled cabbage, ice cream, green apples, pickled tripe, raw turnips, and washing the cargo down with freshets of coffee, tea, brandy, whisky, . . . — anything that was liquid; she smoked pipes, cigars, cigarettes, she whooped like a Pawnee and swore like a demon; and then she would go up stairs loaded as described and perfectly delight the baby with a banquet of which [*sic*] ought to have killed it at thirty yards, but which only made it happy and fat and boozy."

63. HOWELLS TO CLEMENS

[Cambridge] April 14, 1875.

My dear Clemens:

Here is the united prayer of Mrs. Howells and myself that, when you come up to attend the Lexington Centennial,[1] you and Mrs. Clemens come to our house, which though humble will receive you with open doors and a cordial welcome. I don't know that I need add anything except that I "mean business." Tell us what day and hour to expect you. We got home from Bethlehem yesterday after a most satisfactory fortnight of unbroken spring weather.

I telegraphed this afternoon for your sixth installment[2] of Atlantic copy. Yours ever

W. D. Howells.

1. Commemorating the battle, 19 April 1775.

2. Of "Old Times on the Mississippi"; it was to appear in the June number. Howells's telegram has not survived.

64. HOWELLS TO CLEMENS

[Cambridge] April 22, 1875

My dear Clemens:

Send back this proof[1] as soon as possible, for we're getting short for time — please.

I thought you'd like to see this letter. Mr. Fawcette wrote The Pillars of Hercules in the January of 1874. I'd like his letter again.[2]

You left your fur cap, which I propose to keep as a hostage.

I hope you've made Twichell envious of our Centennial. — Mrs. Howells joins me in regards to the Clemens family.

Yours ever
W. D. Howells.

1 Presumably of the sixth installment of "Old Times on the Mississippi."

2. The letter (from W. L. Fawcette to Howells) has not been found. The article in the *Atlantic* is entitled "The History of the Two Pillars."

65. CLEMENS TO HOWELLS

[Hartford] Apl. 23 [1875].

My Dear Howells:

I've got Mrs. Clemens's picture before me, & hope I shall not forget to send it with this.

Jo Twichell preached morning & evening here last Sunday; took midnight train for Boston; got an early breakfast & started by rail at 7.30 AM for Concord; swelled around there until 1 P.M., seeing everything;[1] then traveled *on top* of a train to Lexington; saw everything there; traveled on top of a train to Boston, (with hundreds in company) deluged with dust, smoke & cinders; yelled & hurrahed all the way like a schoolboy; lay flat down to dodge numerous bridges, & sailed into the depot, howling with excitement & as black as a chimney sweep; got to Young's Hotel at 7. P.M.; sat down in reading-room & immediately fell asleep; was promptly awakened by a porter who supposed he was drunk; wandered around an hour & a half; then took 9 PM train, sat down in smoking car & remembered nothing more until awakened by conductor as the train came into Hartford at 1.30 AM. Hopped up in the morning & hived his Chinaman (buried one of the Chinese students).[2] Thinks he had simply a glorious time — & wouldn't have missed the Centennial for the world. He would have run out to see us a moment at Cambridge,[3] but was too dirty. I wouldn't have wanted him there — his appaling energy would have been an insufferable reproach to mild adventurers like you & me.

Some of the things Joe saw were inexpressibly funny — pity but he could talk on paper as he does with his mouth.

Well, he is welcome to the good time he had — I had a deal better one. My narrative has made Mrs. Clemens wish she could have been there. — When I think over what a splendid good sociable time I had in your house I feel ever so thankful to the wise providence that thwarted our several ably-planned & ingenious attempts to get to Lexington. I am coming again before long, & then she shall be of the party.

Now you said that you & Mrs. Howells could run down here nearly any Saturday. Very well then, let us call it next Saturday, for a "starter." Can you do that? By that time it will really be spring & you won't freeze. The birds are already out; a small one paid us a visit yesterday. We entertained it & let it go again, Susie protesting.

The spring laziness is already upon me — insomuch that the spirit begins to move me to cease from Mississippi articles & everything else & give myself over to idleness until we go to New Orleans. I have one article already finished, but somehow it dont seem as proper a chapter to close with as the one already in your hands. I hope to get in a mood & rattle off a *good* one to finish with — but just now all my moods are lazy ones.

Winnie's literature sings through me yet! Surely that child has one of these "future's" before her.[4]

Now try to come — will you?

With the warmest regards of the two of us —

Ys Ever

S. L. Clemens

1. That is, the Centennial ceremonies.

2. The Chinese Educational Mission, directed by Twichell's friend, Yung Wing, which supervised the education of Chinese students in the United States, had its headquarters in Hartford.

3. Clemens had accepted the invitation conveyed in Howells's letter of 14 April. Howells included a long reminiscence of the adventure in MMT (pp. 39–41). Clemens described it thus to Dean Sage: "Howells and I fooled around all day, never got to the Centennial at all, though we made forty idiotic attempts to accomplish it. As our failures multiplied . . . I kept observing to myself that he was a 'dam fool.' I learned afterwards that he was clandestinely making the same remark about me all the time — and if you could have heard his wife ridicule us when we got home, you would have judged each of us 'in his rude untutored way' had approximated the truth" (Hartford, 22 April, Mrs. Meredith Hare, TS in MTP). Although they had special invitations, with passage provided from Boston, they decided to take a train from Cambridge instead. But the train proved to be so crowded they could not get on. No other means of transportation could be found, even though Clemens ran down the street in pursuit of a tallyho with cheering students on top. The raw April weather finally drove the two friends back to Howells's house and a warm hearth-fire. They had agreed they would pretend to Mrs. Howells they had actually been to Lexington and back, but to Clemens's delight she instantly saw through the deception. Clemens recalled this incident with pleasure not long before his death, thirty-five years later (MMT, p. 41).

4. Winifred Howells, then eleven years old, had shown a talent for poetry from early childhood.

66. OLIVIA L. CLEMENS TO ELINOR M. HOWELLS

[Hartford, 23 April 1875]

My dear Mrs Howells

Don't dream for one instant that my not getting a letter

from you kept me from Boston. I am too anxious to go to let such a thing as that keep me. A wet nurse that is tractable and good when I am in the house but who gets drunk when I go away, together with other irresponsible doings by this same nurse when I am not present, lead me to feel that I had better stay closely with my baby until she is weaned, which will not be until next October.

I do wish you and Mr Howells would come down for the next Sunday after this reaches you, ⟨which I suppose would not be next Sunday⟩. *Do come* if possible, remember that I am tied now and cannot go to Cambridge. Mr Clemens did have such a good time with you and Mr Howells, he evidently has no regret that he did not get to the centenial. I was driven nearly distracted by his long account of Mr Howells and his wanderings. I would keep asking if they ever got there, ⟨but⟩ he would never answer but made me listen to a very minute account of every thing that they did. At last I found them back where they started from.

If you find misspelled words in this note, you will remember my infirmity and not hold me responsible.

Hoping you and Mr Howells will come and with kind regards to him.   I am affectionately yours

Livy L. Clemens

Friday Evening

MS. Although Howells many years later, reading the letters over before lending them to A. B. Paine, wrote "1876" at the top of this letter, it was clearly written immediately after the Centennial and seconds Mark Twain's invitation of the same day.

67. CLEMENS TO HOWELLS

[Hartford] Apl. 24 [1875].

My Dear Howells:

An actor named D. H. Harkins [1] has been here to ask me to put upon paper a 5-act play which he has been mapping out in his mind for 3 or 4 years. He sat down & told me his plot all through, in a clear, bright way, & I was a deal taken with it; but it is a line of characters whose fine shading & ⟨systematic?⟩ artistic development require an abler hand than mine; so I easily perceived that I must not make the attempt. But I like the man, & thought there was a good deal of stuff in him; & therefore I wanted his play to be written, & by a capable hand, too. So I suggested you, & said I would write & see if you would be willing to undertake it. If you like the idea, he will call upon you in the course of two or three weeks & describe his plot & his characters. Then if it don't strike you favorably, of course you can simply decline; but it seems to me well worth while that you should hear what he has to say. You could also "average" him while he talks, & judge whether he could play your priest [2] — though I doubt if any man can do that justice.

Shan't I write him & say he may call? If you wish to communicate directly with him instead, his address is "Marchmont Manor, Westchester Co., N.Y."

Do you know, the chill of that 19th of April seems to be in my bones yet? I am inert & drowsy all the time. That was villainous weather for a couple of wandering children to be out in.   Ys Ever

Mark.

1. A leading man and stage manager with Augustin Daly's company.

2. The reference to "your priest" indicates that Clemens has in mind Howells's dramatization of his novel *A Foregone Conclusion*. The previous autumn, when Daly had asked Clemens to do a play for him, Clemens had pleaded lack of time and had suggested that Daly approach Howells. Daly had done so, and on 14 November 1874 Howells had replied: "I have long had the notion of a play, which I have now briefly exposed to Mr. Clemens, and which he thinks will do." The play would be "rather tragical," but it would also be "in some parts such a light affair that many people would never know how deeply they ought to have been moved by it" (Cambridge, quoted in Daly, *Life of Augustin Daly*, p. 148). Howells's dramatization of his novel was not produced, however, until 18 November 1886, when Alexander Salvini played the part of the priest, Don Ippolito, at the Madison Square Theatre (Quinn, *History of the American Drama from the Civil War to the Present Day*, I, 74).

68. CLEMENS TO HOWELLS

[Hartford, 25 or 26 April 1875]

My Dear Howells:

Good for Fawcett! The idea of a Mississippi pilot writing profound essays upon so imposing a subject as Ancient Oriental Trade! [1] I think I'll ring that into a chapter, for the honor of the craft. All the boys had brains, & plenty of them — but they mostly lacked education & the literary faculty.

We are ashamed to find that we gave you & Mrs. Howells a villainously hard bed to sleep on in the mahogany room. The bed is not built for that room yet, & we did not know the abandoned character of the temporary one. When you come next Saturday we'll put you in a bed you'll like better.

Yrs Ever

Mark.

I've written you twice since I got home — directed simply to W D Howells, Cambridge.

1. Clemens must be referring to the letter from W. L. Fawcette mentioned by Howells on 22 April. Fawcette's article "Old-Time Oriental Trade" appeared in the *Atlantic* for October 1876.

69. HOWELLS TO CLEMENS

[Cambridge] April 27, 1875

My dear Clemens:

As soon as I get fairly launched in my story [1] again, I shall be glad to come to Hartford, but I must start before I can stop. Mrs. Howells was pleased to be included by you and Mrs. Clemens in the arrangement I had made for myself alone when I planned those little informal Saturday runs to Hartford, but she says she can't join me on the first three or four. — I don't wonder you found that bed hard: we got all the sleep out of it, and left it a mere husk or skeleton of the luxurious couch it had been. We shall not ask for anything better when we come again.

Thank you for thinking of me for Mr. Harkins's play. I should certainly like to talk with him, for I believe I could write a play in that way — by having an actor give me his notion.

— Now, Clemens, it really hurts me, since you seemed to wish me so much to go with you to New Orleans, to say that I can't. It would be the ruin of my summer's work, and though I think something literary might come of it for me, I haven't the courage to borrow any more of the future, when I'm already in debt to it. You are very good, and I'm touched and flattered that you want my company so much as to be willing to pay vastly more for it than it's worth.[2]

We did both of us have a glorious time when you were here, and we long for another visit. There seems to be a slight disparity of statement between Mrs. Clemens and yourself as to her coming with you soon, but we hope you wont mind each other, but come.

— It was like Twichell to have the sort of Centennial he had. It shows what can be done by drifting with the current, instead of opposing it with energy and genius, as we did. Mrs. Howells was charmed with your account of Twichell's performance, and Mrs. Clemens's report of your own attempted mystification. I hope you did [not] betray the fact of my pitiable terror in returning uncentennialed to the bosom of my family?

Yours ever
W. D. Howells.

1. "Private Theatricals," to be serialized in the *Atlantic* November 1875–May 1876.

2. In a letter now lost, or in conversation, Clemens must have offered to pay Howells's expenses on the New Orleans trip they had been talking about. Two years later he made such an offer to Howells for a trip to Bermuda (letter 152); and in 1878 he paid the expenses of Twichell for the European trip described in *A Tramp Abroad*.

[Cambridge] May 4, 1875.

Dear Clemens:

The "father" referred to in this letter [1] is my dear old Uncle Alec who has been palsied for fifteen years, and now has your papers read to him as he lies in the bed from which he'll never rise again. I sent him the Ms. of the first paper. I should like to hear him talk of you.

I don't believe I thanked you on the part of Mrs. Howells for your wife's beautiful fotograf, *though Mrs. Howells believes I did, thank heaven!* I do so now. We greatly prized the gift of it, and sent it to the bank-note engraving brother-in-law,[2] who says it would make the basest counterfeit pass.

I have seen Raymond, and I've done some shouting over him for the next Atlantic.[3] The play is *good*. Go and see it through. — Don't forget to send me your seventh paper.[4] —We unite in regards to both of you.   Ever yours

W. D. Howells.

1. To Howells from C. J. Dean dated Pittsburgh, 1 May 1875, of which the relevant paragraph is as follows: "Father desires me to write to you and thank you for your kind remembrance of him in sending him the manuscript of Mark Twain's 'Old Times on the Mississippi.' He has read his articles on this subject with a keen appreciation. It vividly recalls an experience in his life about which he is never tired talking. He has unanimously resolved that Mark is the 'Prince of Wits' the 'King of Jesters.' Father and Uncle William and the boys have some hearty laughs over the 'cub-pilot's' adventures all of which they appreciate and enjoy as we 'land-lubbers' do not. We have not seen his fifth article yet but I suppose it will be copied into some of our papers before long" (MTP).

2. Augustus D. Shepard, brother-in-law of Elinor Howells, who lived in Plainfield, N.J. He was trustee of the American Bank Note Co. of New York.

3. Howells discussed John T. Raymond's acting in the role of Colonel Sellers in an article on "Drama" in the *Atlantic* for June 1875 (reprinted in MMT, pp. 115–119). He welcomed Raymond to "the group of realistic actors whom we shall be slow to believe less fine than the finest who have

charmed the theatre-going world." Like Sothern as Lord Dundreary and Jefferson in *Rip Van Winkle,* Howells declared, Raymond "does not merely represent; he becomes, he impersonates, the character he plays" (p. 115).

4. The last installment of "Old Times on the Mississippi," to appear in the *Atlantic* for August.

71. CLEMENS TO HOWELLS

[Hartford] May 7 [1875].

My Dear Howells:

I'm glad to have the letter from your uncle. There's something charming about the lonely sublimity of being the prophet of a hitherto unsung race. There are so many prophets for the other guilds & races & religions that no one of them can become signally conspicuous, but I haven't any rivals; my people have got to take me or go prophetless. If I live a year, I will make one more attempt to go down the river, for I ⟨shall will⟩ shall have lived in vain if I go silent out of the world and thus lengthen the list of the "lost arts." Confidentially, I'm "laying" for a monument.

Good! I'm glad you are shouting for Raymond; & if I were there I would look through the MS & see if there was a crevice where you might casually remark that Raymond has not taken a vague suggestion from the novel & by his genius created a fine original character from it, but has simply faithfully reproduced the Sellers that is in the book. For this fellow had the impudence to tell me in Boston (he got it from the newspapers) that the above was the state of the case — whereas the truth is that the finer points in Sellers's character are a trifle above Raymond's level.

Of course you do not need to say any of this at all, for no doubt it would have an ungracious look; & I think I am rather small potatoes myself for caring two cents ⟨whether⟩ if the world *does* hail Raymond as the gifted creator of Sellers. The actual truth is, that *nobody* created Sellers — I simply put him on paper as I found him in life (he is a relative of mine [1] — but *not* my brother) & any scrub of a newspaper reporter could have done the same thing.[2]

Shall I write Mr. D H Harkins the actor, or have you done so?

I wish Clarence King would put his Pike County people [3] on

MS. This letter is incomplete; an undetermined number of pages is missing at the end.

1. In the *Autobiography* (I, 89) Mark Twain says that his mother's favorite cousin, James Lampton, "figures in the *Gilded Age* as Colonel Sellers. . . ."

2. This extravagant assertion is evidence of Mark Twain's failure to recognize how artful and complex his own technique as a writer was.

3. Characters in King's "Wayside Pikes" in the *Atlantic* for November 1871. The sketch belonged to a series of eight which appeared in the magazine March–December 1871 and were collected into book form under the title *Mountaineering in the Sierra Nevada* in 1872.

72. HOWELLS TO CLEMENS

[Cambridge] May 10, 1875.

My dear old fellow —

It's 'most time — *quite* time — for your seventh number: send what you've got; I know it's good.

Here's what I said of Raymond, and by instinct I reduced his laurels to the true proportions. If I'd only known of his pretending to invent Sellers — to do anything but put *your* Sellers on the stage, I'd have made the point so sharp that neither he nor any newspaper friend could miss it. He hasn't added a solitary idea to the character. But he does play it wonderfully — and that's glory enough for him. — Observe the neat parting stab.[1]

I wish you'd write Harkins — just a line to say I'd like to talk with him.   Yours ever

W. D. Howells

1. The parting stab in Howells's review of Raymond's performance is as follows: "Sellers is not a mere glare of absurdity; you do not want to be

laughing at him *all* the time; and Mr. Raymond might trust the sympathy of his audience in showing all the tenderness of the man's heart. We are loath to believe that he is not himself equal to showing it" (*Atlantic*, XXXV, 751, June 1875).

73. CLEMENS TO HOWELLS

[Hartford] May 12 [1875].

My Dear Howells:

All right, I'll send the No.[1] along, & alter it in the proof if I find it needs it.

I've written Harkins.

That's a superb notice for the play. Raymond put that "Well I won't" in & I can't get him to take it out.[2] Your closing stab will reach his vitals, for the reason that he *can't* do a pathetic thing — he isn't man enough.

He writes to-day asking me to *give him the rest of this season* in consideration of what he has done for ⟨me & my rep⟩ my pocket & my reputation! And he fits the language & the manner to the *thing* — i.e. groveling appeal for charity.

His letter would make a dog blush. But I guess there is some villainy under it somewhere.

I believe it *will* be lovely weather here one of these days — & then you've got to dig out & come.

Your criticism of the play says *exactly* what I want. It glorifies Sellers & shows that the play would be simply worthless without him. And you see, the thing I want to do when the proper opportunity offers, is to pile that play onto the thief Densmore's shoulders![3] But for Raymond, I'd have done it in the beginning.

In a hurry to catch the postman,   Ys Ever

Mark.

1. The last installment of "Old Times on the Mississippi."

2. Clemens's reference to Raymond's addition to the play confirms Howells's guess: "Only one point we must except, and we suspect it is not the author's lapse; that is where the colonel borrows ten dollars of Clay

Hawkins, and being asked not to mention the return of it, stops on his way out and with a glance of low cunning at the audience says, 'Well, I won't!' This is thoroughly false and bad, and the stupid laugh it raises ought to make Mr. Raymond ashamed" (*Atlantic,* XXXV, 750).

3. The not entirely clear circumstances of Clemens's relations with Densmore are described in the Appendix. What he means here is that he considers the play a very poor affair aside from the character of Colonel Sellers, which is derived from the novel, and he eventually means to make clear to the public that Densmore is responsible for whatever in the play differs from the novel. He has refrained from taking this step because Raymond insists the drawing power of the play would be diminished if it were known to be a joint production.

74. HOWELLS TO CLEMENS

[Cambridge] May 20, 1875

My dear Clemens:

This is capital [1] — I shall hate to have you stop! — but there's one paragraph (marked ?d) which I'd leave out because it seems lugged in, a little. I don't know but it would be well to omit *all* that about sea-songs. But use your own taste. Maybe it wouldnt.

Glad you liked the Raymond criticism so well.

Yours ever

W. D. Howells.

Please return *soon.*[2]

1. Once again, the last installment of "Old Times on the Mississippi," which would appear in the August issue of the *Atlantic.*

2. Howells's request to have the proof returned soon was probably due to his eagerness to finish his work on the August number before he left Cambridge for the summer.

75. CLEMENS TO HOWELLS

[Hartford] Saturday May 22 [1875].

My Dear Howells:

I have scratched out all about the songs — as you suggest, it was best.[1]

You may not approve the last paragraph of the postscript which I have added,[2] but it seems necessary because otherwise I either seem to have stopped in the middle of my subject at the editor's request, or else regularly "petered out." But No. 6 closes the series first-rate with the death of piloting, & needs no postscript. Therefore I would suggest that you leave out this No. 7 entirely & let the articles end with the June No. On the whole I should think that would be the neatest thing to do. I retire with dignity, then, instead of awkwardly.

There is a world of river stuff to write about, but I find it won't cut up into chapters, worth a cent. It needs to run right along, with no breaks but imaginary ones.

Bret Harte was here the other day to rent a house. Haven't heard how he succeeded.

Can't you & Mrs. Howells run down next Saturday? I wish you'd try. Things are blooming now. We've tried hard to get to Cambridge, but ever so many things have interfered.

Yrs Ever

Clemens

1. Mark Twain omitted all reference to sea songs, but retained brief references to river songs — Negro stevedores chanting "De Las' Sack," deck hands singing in a group around the windlass as the steamboat leaves the landing, and the crew singing on the forecastle at nightfall in the glare of the torch-baskets.

2. Apparently the four-page anecdote which concludes the seventh installment (retained as the conclusion of Chapter XVII in *Life on the Mississippi,* DE, XII, 159–162). Stephen, a pilot, is described as a genius at inventing pretexts for not paying back money he has borrowed from his friends. The last paragraph, containing a comic allusion to heaven which Mark Twain may have thought would offend *Atlantic* readers, appears as he wrote it.

76. CLEMENS TO HOWELLS

Hartford, June 7 [1875].

My Dear Howells:

By all means come! Be sure to come! You speak in the first person singular number; do double it, if within the possibilities,

& bring Mrs. Howells with you. Take the fast train which leaves Boston about ten o'clock & here you are at luncheon almost before you think you've started! Mrs. Howells will feel hardly any fatigue.

I'll have the letter shipped to Warner.[1]

⟨Bless me, I understood you to say you *had* announced me for August — & so I have carried the nightmare of having to re-chew that odious chapter, ever since! If you haven't announced it *much,* couldn't you just let on that you didn't mean it? I am proposing to take hold of the thing to-day or tomorrow — but it is *so* hard to pump up a new interest in what one has written once & dismissed from his mind.⟩

I think that that music is lovely. Mr. Potter[2] was here when it came, & he sat down at the piano & played & sang it — & his is a noble voice. Next I want to get Rev. Mr. Parker[3] here & have him sing it for me.

I *am* a splendid ass! Upon referring to your former letter I perceive that you ask me to telegraph, so that you can stop the announcement of the August number. I am unutterably stupid. Now I will go ahead & finish the article without another wriggle.

I am ever so grateful to you & to Mr. Booth[4] for that music. Mr. Potter liked it exceedingly, & sang it several times. He spoke as if he knew Mr. Booth — which is very likely, for Potter is a composer of music, himself.

For two days the weather has been swelling around, threatening big things, but I could put the result in a tin dipper & not crowd it.   Ys Ever

                                                    Clemens

1. At least one letter from Howells to Clemens is missing from the series at this point. The reference to shipping a letter to Warner cannot be explained on the basis of surviving documents.

2. Probably Edward T. Potter of New York, architect of Mark Twain's house in Hartford.

3. Probably Edwin Pond Parker, a Congregational minister of Hartford.

4. Francis Boott (1813–1904), whose name Clemens misspells as Booth, a Cambridge composer and one of Howells's Italianate acquaintances. The music was Boott's song entitled "No More" (letter 81, below). Howells may already have been thinking of another new feature which

John Hay in 1871.

Bret Harte in 1871.

Charles L. Webster in 1875.

John T. Raymond in Colonel
Sellers, first produced in 1874.

Howells in 1886. From a wood engraving by R. Staudenbaur.

The house Howells built in 1873 at 37 Concord Avenue, Cambridge.

The study in Howells's house on Concord Avenue, Cambridge.

would appear in the *Atlantic* in 1877, a series of original poems set to music by such Boston and Cambridge composers as Boott, J. K. Paine, and Dudley Buck (WDH to J. R. Lowell, Townsend Harbor, Mass., 8 August 1876, Houghton, AGM TS). It was Boott who served as the "model" for Gilbert Osmond, and his daughter Lizzie for Pansy Osmond, in James's *Portrait of a Lady* (Leon Edel, ed., *Portrait of a Lady*, Boston, 1956, p. xiv), and Boott's son-in-law Frank Duveneck figures as Englehart, the artist and art teacher in Howells's *Indian Summer*.

77. HOWELLS TO CLEMENS (POSTCARD)

[Cambridge, 10? June 1875]

Dear Clemens:

I shall not be able to start conveniently till Saturday afternoon, on the three o'clock train. I'm sorry that I must come alone. The rest is not well enough.   Yours

W. D. H.

MS. The postmark is dated 10 June.

78. CLEMENS TO HOWELLS

Hartford June 21 [1875].

My Dear Howells:

O, the visit was just jolly![1] It couldn't be improved on. And after the reputation we gained on Lexington Centennial Day it would have been a pity to become commonplace again by catching trains & being on time like the general scum of the earth. Since the walk to Boston Twichell & I invariably descend in the public estimation when discovered in a vehicle of any kind.

Thank you ever so much for the praises you give the story.[2] I am going to take into serious consideration all you have said, & then make up my mind by & by. Since there is no plot to the thing, it is likely to follow its own drift, & so is as likely to

87

drift into manhood as anywhere — I won't interpose. If I only had the Mississippi book written, I would surely venture this story in the Atlantic. But I'll see — I'll think the whole thing over.

I don't think Bliss wants that type-writer, because he don't send for it. I'll sell it to you for the twelve dollars I've got to pay him for his saddle — or I'll gladly send it to you for nothing if you choose (for, ⟨plainly⟩ to be honest, I think $12 *is* too much for it.) Anyway, I'll send it.

Mrs. Clemens is sick abed & likely to remain so some days, poor thing. I'm just going to her, now.   Yrs Ever

Clemens

1. Howells spent Saturday evening, 12 June, and Sunday with Clemens in Hartford. He wrote to his father that he had "a beaming visit, of course, and did a month's laughing" (Cambridge, 20 June 1875, Houghton). Twichell joined them on Saturday evening and they heard him preach Sunday morning. Twichell noted in his Journal (12, 13 June, Yale) that he had "quite a talk on religious subjects" with Howells, who seemed "very humble and earnest, and vastly loveable."

2. *The Adventures of Tom Sawyer.* On 5 July Mark Twain would write to Howells that he had finished it. The book was copyrighted on 21 July 1875 by title page only; copies were not filed in Washington until 2 January 1877. This letter indicates that Howells may have advised Mark Twain to let Tom Sawyer "drift into manhood."

79. HOWELLS TO CLEMENS (POSTCARD)

[Cambridge, 23? June 1875]

Please send the machine, and if I cannot afford to receive it for nothing, I will pay the extortionate sum you name.

W. D. H.

MS. The postmark is dated 23 June.

80. CLEMENS TO HOWELLS

[Hartford] June 25 [1875].

My Dear Howells:

I told Patrick [1] to get some carpenters & box the machine & send it to you — & found that Bliss had sent for the machine & carried it off. I have been *talking* to you & *writing* to you as if you were present when I traded the machine to Bliss for a twelve-dollar saddle worth $25 (cheating him outrageously, of course — but conscience got the upper hand again & I told him before I left the premises that I'd pay for the saddle if he didn't like the machine — on condition that he donate said machine to a charity) — but now I began to suspect that you never had heard that conversation; which suspicion Dan,[2] who *was* present, confirms, & says it was Joaquin Miller that was with us, & not you. And that is perfectly true. I remember it now, perfectly well, though I have had the impression all this time that it was you. This was a little over *five weeks* ago — so I had long ago concluded that Bliss didn't want the machine & *did* want the saddle — wherefore I jumped at the chance of shoving the machine off onto you, saddle or no saddle so I got the blamed thing out of my sight.

The saddle hangs on Tara's [3] walls down below in the stable & the machine is at Bliss's, grimly pursuing its appointed mission, slowly & implacably rotting away another man's chances for salvation.

I have sent Bliss word *not* to donate it to a charity (though it *is* a pity to fool away a chance to do a charity an ill turn), but to let me know when he has got his dose, because I've got another candidate for damnation. You just wait a couple of weeks & if you don't see the Type-Writer come tilting along toward Cambridge with the raging hell of an unsatisfied appetite in its eye, I lose my guess.

Don't you be mad about this blunder, Howells — it only comes of a bad memory & the stupidity which is inseparable from true genius. Nothing intentionally criminal in it.

Mrs. Clemens is still sick abed but getting along very promisingly & satisfactorily.

One of these days let's run down to Washington for a day. I've a moment's business with the President [4] — haven't you?

Yrs Ever

Mark.

1. Patrick McAleer, the coachman, who entered the Clemenses' employ shortly after their marriage, in 1870, remained with them until the Hartford house was closed in 1891, and returned to Clemens's service after Livy's death.

2. Probably Dan Slote, Mark Twain's cabin mate on the *Quaker City* excursion, who was at this time a partner in Slote, Woodman & Co., New York, manufacturers of "Mark Twain's Scrapbook."

3. Tara was a pony; Mark Twain is, of course, parodying Thomas Moore, from whom the name was presumably taken in the first place.

4. Probably a lobbying mission for international copyright legislation. The topic is first mentioned explicitly in this correspondence in letter 88, below.

81. HOWELLS TO CLEMENS

[Cambridge] July 3, 1875

Dear Clemens:

I care nothing about that type-writer personally, but I'm sorry for you, because I had about made up my mind to let you give it me. You may never have another opportunity to do me a charity.

Sorry to hear that Mrs. Clemens is poorly. I hope she is better by this time.

Mr. Boott, who wrote that No More music, says he is much pleased at your notion of giving it to Miss Kellogg [1] to sing. He would like to know, I suppose, how she likes it.

You must be thinking well of the notion of giving us that story. I really feel very much interested in your making that your chief work; you wont have such another chance; don't waste it on a *boy,* and don't hurry the writing for the sake of making a book. Take your time, and deliberately advertise it by Atlantic publication.[2] Mr. Houghton has his back up, and says he would like to catch any newspaper copying it.[3]

Yours ever,

W. D. Howells.

I have seen Barrett.[4] His *plot* was a series of *stage-situations*, which no mortal ingenuity could harness together. But I think I shall write him a play. He offers me $50 a night for 50 nights; then $3000 down; then $50 a night, on.

1. Clara Louise Kellogg (1842–1916), a soprano who had toured the country in various operatic roles 1868–1872. In 1913 she was to publish *Memoirs of an American Prima Donna.*

2. The passage is obscure. One possible interpretation of it is that Howells is urging Mark Twain to carry the adventures of Tom Sawyer into the hero's mature years, and to serialize the story in the *Atlantic,* though he may mean, "Don't waste your story on a juvenile audience."

3. Howells means to assure Mark Twain that Henry O. Houghton, publisher of the *Atlantic,* could prosecute any newspaper reprinting installments of the book.

4. Lawrence Barrett, an actor of moderate renown, author of a biography of Edwin Forrest. In 1877 he bought the acting rights to Howells's *A Counterfeit Presentment* (see letter 154).

82. CLEMENS TO HOWELLS

[Hartford] July 5 [1875].

My Dear Howells:

I have finished the story [1] & didn't take the chap beyond boyhood. I believe it would be fatal to do it in any shape but autobiographically — like Gil Blas. I perhaps made a mistake in not writing it in the first person. If I went on, now, & took him into manhood, he would just be like all the one-horse men in literature & the reader would conceive a hearty contempt for him. It is *not* a boy's book, at all. It will only be read by adults. It is only written for adults.

Moreover, the book is plenty long enough, as it stands. It is about 900 pages of MS., & may be 1000 when I shall have

9 1

finished "working up" vague places; so it would make from 130 to 150 pages of the Atlantic — about what the Foregone Conclusion made, isn't it?

I would dearly like to see it in the Atlantic, but I doubt if it would pay the publishers to buy the privilege, or me to sell it. Bret Harte has sold his novel [2] (same size as mine, I should say) to Scribner's Monthly for $6,500 (publication to begin in September, I think,) & he gets a royalty of 7½ percent from Bliss in book form afterward. He gets a royalty of ten percent on it in England (issued in serial numbers) & the same royalty on it in book form afterward, & is to receive an advance payment of five hundred pounds the day the first No. of the serial appears. If I could do as well, here & there, with mine, it might possibly pay me, but I seriously doubt it — though it is likely I could do better in England than Bret, who is not widely known there.

You see I take a vile, mercenary view of things — but then my household expenses are something almost ghastly.

By & by I shall take a boy of twelve & run him on through life (in the first person) but not Tom Sawyer — he would not be a good character for it.[3]

I wish you would promise to read the MS of Tom Sawyer some time, & see if you don't really decide that I am right in closing with him as a boy — & point out the most glaring defects for me. It is a tremendous favor to ask, & I expect you to refuse, & would be ashamed to expect you to do otherwise. But the thing has been so many months in my mind that it seems a relief to snake it out. I don't know any other person whose judgment I could venture to take fully & entirely. Don't hesitate about saying no, for I know how your time is taxed, & I would have honest need to blush if you said yes.[4]

Osgood & I are "going for" the puppy Gill on infringement of trademark.[5] To win one or two suits of this kind will set literary folks on a firmer bottom. The N.Y. Tribune doesn't own the world — I wish Osgood would sue it for stealing Holmes's poem.[6] Wouldn't it be gorgeous to sue Whitelaw Read [7] for *petty larceny*? I will promise to go into court & swear I think him capable of stealing pea-nuts from a blind pedlar.

Mrs. C. grows stronger. Susie is down with a fever. Kindest regards to you all.   Yrs Ever

Clemens

1. *The Adventures of Tom Sawyer.*

2. *Gabriel Conroy,* which was to begin running serially in *Scribner's Monthly* in November 1875. The tone of Mark Twain's account of Harte's royalty arrangements seems a little competitive. Since Bliss was to publish *Gabriel Conroy* after it was serialized, the two writers were placed in a suggestive relation to one another.

3. This idea was the germ of *Huckleberry Finn.* It is significant that the technical problem of point-of-view was present to Mark Twain from the first.

4. Howells did read the MS of *Tom Sawyer,* but several months later (letter 98).

5. Mark Twain's "An Encounter with an Interviewer" (DE, XIX, 378–383) had been included in an anthology entitled *Lotos Leaves* (pp. 27–32), edited by John Brougham and John Elderkin, and published in Boston by William F. Gill & Co. late in 1874 (with the title-page date 1875). It cannot now be determined whether the sketch had been previously published, but from the correspondence cited below it appears that Gill had Mark Twain's permission. In July 1875, the sketch was included in Volume I, *Burlesque,* of *The Treasure Trove Series,* "Edited by R. H. Stoddard. Compiled by W. S. Walsh" (pp. 177–184), also published by Gill. On 3 July, James R. Osgood wrote to Howells: "In spite of all, our friend Gill has used your name on the back of his book between 'Praed' and 'Poe.' Do you propose to stand it, or will you join your publisher in stopping it? I have written to Mark Twain, whose name is also there" (Boston, Houghton). No selection from Howells appears in this volume, but Gill presumably meant to list authors to be included in later volumes as well. Threatened legal action against Gill led to his dropping the names of Howells and Mark Twain from the list of twenty-five stamped on the spine, after some copies of the first volume had been bound. (SLC to Elisha Bliss, Hartford, February 1875; SLC to William F. Gill, Hartford, 31 May 1875, Barrett; SLC to JRO, Hartford, 13 July 1875; SLC to Gill, Hartford, 8 June 1875; SLC to JRO, Hartford, 20 July, 23 July 1875; SLC to JRO, Newport, R.I., 16 [August] 1875: TSS in MTP). On 25 January 1876 Mark Twain wrote to Osgood: " . . . the lawyer says Gill has taken my *nom de plume* out of the book although he has left the article in it. Of course this destroys the possibility of my suing him for violating trade-mark, & I don't wish to sue him for anything else" (Hartford, Harvard Theatre Collection, TS in MTP).

6. Oliver Wendell Holmes's "Grandmother's Story of Bunker Hill Battle," first published by James R. Osgood & Co. as a sixteen-page pamphlet in

1875. "On page 1 is the following note: 'As this poem is written expressly for this [Bunker Hill] Memorial and not intended for publication elsewhere, the Publishers request that it be not copied or reprinted' " (George B. Ives, *A Bibliography of Oliver Wendell Holmes,* Boston, 1907, p. 31). The entire poem was, nevertheless, reprinted in the New York *Tribune* on 4 June 1875 (p. 8).

7. Editor of the *Tribune.* The correct spelling is "Reid."

83. HOWELLS TO CLEMENS

[Cambridge] July 6, 1875

Dear Clemens:

Send on your Ms. when it's ready. You've no idea what I may ask you to do for *me* some day. I'm sorry that you can't do it for the Atlantic, but I succumb. Perhaps you'll do Boy No. 2 [1] for us.

Here's some more music from Mr. Boott which he thought might suit Miss Kellogg better than No More.

I count it a pleasure and privilege to read your story. There!

I'm very glad Mrs. Clemens is better, and very sorry for poor little Susy. Yours ever

W. D. Howells.

1. The twelve-year-old mentioned in Clemens's letter of 5 July.

84. HOWELLS TO CLEMENS

[Cambridge] July 8, 1875.

Dear Clemens:

I can't. I say it with tears in my eyes, for I *do* have such good times with you.[1] And what grieves me more is that we shall not be in Cambridge from Aug. 1 till Oct. 1. We go into the Country at Shirley Village, Mass., on the 1st prox., and stay there till mid-September, when we hope to go to Quebec, for the rest of that month. But all this needn't prevent your running up with Mrs. Clemens in October, when we shall be as glad to see you as possible.

Meantime, don't forget to let me see that Ms., as you promised.   Yours ever

W. D. Howells.

1. A letter inviting Howells to pay another visit to Hartford is evidently missing from the series.

85. CLEMENS TO HOWELLS

[Hartford] July 13 [1875].

My Dear Howells:

Just as soon as you consented I realized all the atrocity of my request, & straightway blushed & weakened. I telegraphed my theatrical agent to come here & carry off the MS [1] & copy it.

But I will glad[l]y send it to you if you will do as follows: dramatize it if you perceive that you can, & take, for your remuneration, half of the first $6,000 which I receive for its representation on the stage. You could alter the plot entirely, if you chose. I would help in the work, most cheerfully, after you had arranged the plot. I have my eye upon two young girls who can play "Tom" & "Huck." I believe a good deal of a drama can be made of it. — Come — can't you tackle this in the odd hours of your vacation? — or later, if you prefer?

I do wish you could come down once more before your holiday. I'd give anything!

Twichell heard from. Has caught his first 20-pounder.[2]

I'm looking for the music along, but it hasn't arrived yet.

Mrs. Clemens is doing *tolerably* well, only. Susie well again.

Yrs Ever

Mark

1. Of *Tom Sawyer*.
2. Twichell was fishing on the Restigouche River in Canada.

86. HOWELLS TO CLEMENS

[Cambridge] July 19, 1875.

My dear Clemens:

It's very pleasant to have you propose my working in any sort of concert with you; and if the $3000 were no temptation, it *is* a temptation to think of trying to do you a favor. But I couldn't do it, and if I could, it wouldn't be a favor to dramatize your story. In fact I don't see how anybody can do that but yourself. I could never find the time, for one thing. My story [1] is coming into the daylight, but when I get it done — say Sept. 14, — I'm going off to Quebec on a two weeks' *rest*, and then I'm going to tackle a play of my own, which is asking to be written.[2] Besides all this, I couldn't enter into the spirit of another man's work sufficiently to do the thing you propose.

— I'm going up to Shirley [3] tomorrow to see if the last touches have been put to the preparation of our quarters there, and my wife will probably follow on Thursday. Her health has been most wretched all summer, and we earnestly hope for benefit from this change. We are both very sorry to hear your half-hearted report of Mrs. Clemens. Newport,[4] I should think would do her good. You'll find my friend Col. Waring,[5] a capital fellow, and most usefully learned in everything a stranger wants to ask about Newport.   Yours ever

                                                    W. D. Howells.

1. "Private Theatricals," to be published in the *Atlantic* November 1875–May 1876.

2. Probably "The Parlor Car," the "farce or vaudeville of strictly American circumstances" which Howells had mentioned to Augustin Daly on 14 November 1874 (Daly, *Life of Augustin Daly,* p. 148). It would be published in the *Atlantic* for September 1876.

3. The Shaker community in Massachusetts where the Howellses spent the summers of 1875 and 1876. The Shakers' customs, their fine craftsmanship, and their ideal of social living fascinated Howells, as his "A Shaker Village" (*Atlantic,* June 1876) and his Shaker novels attest.

4. The Clemenses went to Bateman's Point, Newport, at the end of July

(SLC to Pamela Clemens Moffett, Hartford, 23 July 1875, MTP) and were there as late as 16 August (SLC to JRO, Bateman's Point, Newport, 16 August 1875, MTP).

5. George Edwin Waring, a sanitary engineer who contributed occasionally to the *Atlantic*.

87. HOWELLS TO CLEMENS

Shirley Village, Mass.,
August 16, 1875

My dear Clemens:

They put your name to this proof[1] on their own responsibility, guessing the authorship from the handwriting.

We are very happy here in our humble country sojourn, and I only hope that the gilded haunts of fashion at Newport may be doing Mrs. Clemens as much [good] as this air has done Mrs. Howells, who has gained an ounce and a half since she came, and would easily turn the scale at 65 pounds. We should like to stay here till October, but our landlord and landlady (who have both been divorced from former partners) are profiting of the occasion to separate.[2] This *may* oblige us to leave.

— I like Gondour greatly, and wish we could keep your name. Send me some more accounts of the same country.

Yours ever

W. D. Howells.

Please return this in the enclosed envelope — *not* to me.

1. Of "The Curious Republic of Gondour." It was to be published anonymously in the *Atlantic* for October 1875.
2. Howells later used in *A Modern Instance* some of his observations concerning these devotees of divorce.

88. HOWELLS TO CLEMENS

[Chesterfield, N.H.] Sept. 11, 1875

My dear Clemens:

In comment on Charles Reade's letters[1] (I wish the man

wasn't such a gas-bag), don't you want to air your notions of copyright in the Atlantic? Also,'can't you promise us [for] the next year, half a doz[en] papers — sketches or essays — on almost anything under the sun?

Your Cu. Rep. of Gon. moves that eminent political economist Mrs. Howells, to as much admiration as it did me.

I hope you're all well. It's ages since I heard from you. My wife joins me in regards to Mrs. Clemens and yourself.

Yours ever

W. D. Howells.

Address me at
Prospect House
Chesterfield
N.H.

1. Thirteen letters by Charles Reade to the *Pall Mall Gazette* (London) on problems of international copyright had recently been reprinted in the New York *Tribune* (19 June; 17, 21, 24 July; 7, 10, 14, 21, 25 August; 4, 11, 14, 25 September 1875). The letters were collected under the title "The Rights and Wrongs of Authors" in Reade's *Readiana* (Boston [1899], pp. 169–305).

89. CLEMENS TO HOWELLS

Hartford Sept 14 [1875].

My dear Howells:

I question if I can write this note intelligibly, for Susie is in the study with me & requires pretty constant attention.

I did think of writing upon copyright (without signature), but concluded that the most effectual method of carrying out my views will be to get all authors signatures to my petition & then go to Washington & besiege Congress myself, (appearing simply as agent for bigger men.) This is of course the best way — & to make it effectual, no literature must let the cat out of the bag beforehand.

As to other articles, I can venture to promise that during

the year I will write "some articles" not specifying *when* or the number or subject of them. — I had better not try to be more definite.

Have told Bliss to send my volume of Sketches[1] to you before any one else (it is in press now). I think it is an exceedingly handsome book. I destroyed a mass of sketches, & now heartily wish I had destroyed some more of them — but it is too late to grieve now.

I wish you & Mrs Howells were here. It is exceedingly pleasant weather. Mrs Clemens & I join in love to you both.

Ever Yrs
S. L. Clemens

Susie's patience is exhausted!

1. *Mark Twain's Sketches, New and Old*, published by Elisha Bliss's American Publishing Co. of Hartford. It was made up principally of pieces which had appeared in the *Galaxy* and the Buffalo *Express*, but it also included Mark Twain's first contribution to the *Atlantic*, "A True Story."

90. CLEMENS TO HOWELLS

Hartford, Sept. 18 [1875].

My Dear Howells:

My plan is this — You are to get Mr. Lowell & Mr. Longfellow to be the first signers of my copyright petition; you must sign it yourself & get Mr. Whittier to do likewise. Then Holmes will sign — he said he would if he didn't have to stand at the head. Then I'm fixed. I will then put a gentlemanly chap under wages & send him personally to every author of distinction in the country & corral the rest of the signatures. Then I'll have the whole thing lithographed (about a thousand copies) & move upon the President & Congress *in person*, but in the subordinate capacity of a party who is merely the agent of better & wiser men — men whom the country cannot venture to laugh at.

I will ask the President to recommend the thing in his message (& if he should ask me to ʻsit down & frame the paragraph for him I should blush — but still I would frame it.)

Next I would get a prime leader in Congress; I would also see that votes enough to carry the measure were privately secured before the bill was offered. This I would try through my leader & my friends there.

And *then* if Europe chose to go on stealing from us, we would say with noble enthusiasm, "American law-makers *do steal* — but not from foreign authors, not from foreign authors!"

You see, what I want to drive into the ⟨public⟩ Congressional mind is the simple fact that the moral law is, "*Thou shalt not steal*" — no matter what Europe may do.

I swear I can't see any use in robbing European authors for the benefit of American booksellers, anyway.

If we can ever get this thing through Congress, we can try making copyright *perpetual,* some day. There would be no sort of use in it, since only one book in a hundred millions outlives the present copyright term — no sort of use except that the writer of that one book have his *rights* — which is something.

If we only had some God in the country's laws, instead of being in such a sweat to get Him into the Constitution, it would be better all around.

The only man who ever signed my petition with alacrity, & said that the fact that a thing was *right* was all-sufficient, was Rev. Dr. Bushnell.[1]

I have lost my old petition, (which was brief) but will draft & enclose another — not in the *words* it ought to be, but in the *substance.* I want Mr. Lowell to furnish the words (& the ideas too,) if he will do it.

Say — Redpath [2] *beseeches* me to lecture in Boston in November — telegraphs that Beecher's [3] & Nast's [4] withdrawal has put him in the tightest kind of a place. So I guess I'll do that old "Roughing It" lecture over again in November & repeat it 2 or 3 times in New York while I am at it.[5]

Can I take a carriage after the lecture & go out & stay with you that night provided you find at that distant time that it will not inconvenience you? Is Aldrich home yet?

With love to you all —   Yrs Ever

S. L. C.

To the Hon. the Senate & House of Representatives in Congress assembled:

Whereas, There being no provision in the Christian code of morals which justifies robbery in retaliation for robbery, but the moral law being simply *"Thou* shalt not steal," no matter what thy neighbor may do — and

Whereas, In violation of this principle the United States has legalized the robbery of foreign authors by ⟨American publishers⟩ refusing to them the benefit of copyright & —

Whereas, There being nothing in the Christian code of morals which justifies a man in requiring that another man shall promise to stop stealing from him before he will consent to stop stealing from said other man —

Therefore, We, your petitioners, American authors & artists, do pray your honorable body to grant unto all foreign authors & artists full & free copyright in the United States (upon the same terms which we ourselves enjoy); & that you do this not as an act of grace or charity, but as their *right;* & furthermore that you do this without hampering the deed with any provision requiring a like justice at the hands of foreign governments toward American authors & artists. We petition thus, as being the *only* ⟨persons⟩ craftsmen in our country legitimately concerned in the matter.

Believing that the infusing the spirit of God into our laws will be something better than the empty honor of putting His name in the Constitution, we will ever pray, etc.

Signed.

1. Horace Bushnell, "the Emerson of Hartford" (NF, p. 29).
2. James Redpath, founder of the Boston Lyceum Bureau.
3. Henry Ward Beecher. The six-months' trial of Theodore Tilton's suit against him for damages on account of Beecher's alienation of the affec-

tions of his wife had ended in a hung jury on 2 July 1874. Despite the "vindication" of Beecher by an extralegal cónference at his Plymouth Church in Brooklyn in 1874, public opinion had turned against him, and he was well advised in canceling his lecture tour for the season 1875–76 (Robert Shaplen, *Free Love and Heavenly Sinners*, New York, 1954, pp. 185–260).

4. Thomas Nast, the cartoonist, who was to become a lifelong friend of Mark Twain.

5. The *Roughing It* lecture had been delivered first in England in the winter of 1873–74.

91. HOWELLS TO CLEMENS

Prospect House, Chesterfield, N. H. Sept. 21, 1875.

Dear Clemens:

You will be beautifully welcome at my house in November, or any other month of the year. Of course let us know in time, and Mrs. Howells and I will come to the lecture and drive out to Cambridge with you. This is none of your Lexington Centennial swindles [1] — I mean business.

As soon as I get finally home — in about a fortnight — I'll see those venerable men about the petition for International Justice and Decency in copyright. I expect to go down to Cambridge perhaps to-morrow, and return Saturday night, preparatory to a short visit to my father at Quebec.[2] Then, please the pigs, I shall stick to Cambridge for *one* while. I can't tell you how sick I am of enjoying myself — that's what it is called.

Mrs. Howells joins me in affectionate remembrances to both of you. 　　　　　　　　　　　　　　　Ever yours

W. D. Howells.

1. See letter 65.
2. Howells's father was United States consul at Quebec.

92. CLEMENS TO HOWELLS

Hartford, Sept. 22 [and 27 Sept. 1875]

My Dear Howells:

I'm not going to lecture this year, after all. I've subterfuged myself out of it. I can *not* lecture. I loathe it. But we are coming to see you by and by, anyway. (27TH) I told Bliss to send you advance sheets of my Sketch volume — which I suppose he has done. The book will be published in a week or ten days. I saw the first copy yesterday — & about the first thing I ran across was an extract from "Hospital Days" (page 199) — an entirely gratuitous addition by Mr. Bliss to neatly fill out a page.[1] I have ordered it *out,* instanter.

Lord, what colds my wife & I have got!

MS. The bottom of p. 2 of this letter has been cut off.
1. See Appendix.

93. CLEMENS TO HOWELLS

[Hartford?] Oct. 4/75.

My Dear Howells:

We had a royal good time at your house,[1] & have had a royal good time ever since, talking about it, both privately & with the neighbors. Mrs. Clemens's bodily strength came up handsomely under that cheery respite from household & nursery cares. ⟨I don't doubt that Mrs. Howe⟩ I do hope that Mrs. Howells's didn't go correspondingly down, under the added burden to *her* cares & responsibilities. Of course I didn't expect to get through without committing some crimes & hearing of them afterwards, so I have taken the inevitable lashings & been able to hum a tune while the punishment went on. I "caught it" for letting Mrs Howells bother & bother about her coffee when it was "a good deal better than we get at home." I "caught it" for interrupting Mrs. C. at the last moment & losing her the opportunity to urge you not to forget to send her that MS [2] when the printers are done with it. — I caught it once more for personating that drunken Col. James. I caught it ⟨like everything for confessing, with contrition⟩ for mentioning that Mr. Longfellow's picture was slightly damaged; & when, after a lull in the storm, I confessed, shame-facedly, that I had privately suggested to you that we hadn't any *frames* & that if you wouldn't mind hinting to Mr. Houghton, &c., &c., &c., the madam was simply speechless for the space of a minute. Then she said:

"How *could* you, Youth! The idea of sending Mr. Howells, with his sensitive nature, upon such a repulsive er — "

"Oh, *Howells* won't mind it! You don't know Howells. Howells is a man who — "

She was gone. But George [3] was the first person she stumbled on in the hall, so she took it out of George. I was glad of that, because it saved the babies.

You will judge, by the enclosed [4] (as I do,) that Miss Kellogg never got that song of Mr. Boott's which I mailed to her. (Mr. Bull [5] was the very party who urged me to send it to her; he saw her a week after I mailed it, & she never mentioned the fact to him.) When she comes here I will drink four bottles of lager & then sing it for her — for I never can get any ease or expression into music without a good backing of inspiration. She will admire that song, then.

What do you mean? Relieve a screed that is too light and rollicking, by adding some more of the same sort to its company? If you had a patient who was already suffering with the colic, would it help matters any to drive a nail in his foot & give him the lockjaw? — No, no, that wouldn't mend ⟨matters⟩ the thing. I will wager that the editor-instinct in you is the right one. So don't you have any false delicacy about obeying its suggestion. I will put the article in the New York Times — Sunday edition — & let it boom along on its grievous mission & carry sleepless nights & suffering to a thousand households.[6] Don't you allow yourself one *bit* of discomfort about this.

Booah's [7] idea of the wasteful magnificence of the Greeks is delicious! Pity but you could ingeniously draw him out, on the whole subject, & thus build an article upon A Boy's Comments Upon Homer.

I've got another rattling good character for my novel! That great work is mulling itself into shape gradually. — [8] (All of the above ruthlessly condemned by the Head Chief of the Clemens tribe.)

Mrs. Clemens sends love to Mrs. Howells — meantime she is diligently laying up material for a letter to her.　　　Yrs Ever

Mark

1. The visit of Clemens and Livy to the Howellses in Cambridge, Livy's first, cannot be dated precisely.

2. Probably the MS of Howells's review of *Sketches, New and Old,* which was to appear in the *Atlantic* for December. Howells's letter of 19 October suggests that Livy's intense interest in the review led him to submit it to Clemens even before it was set.

3. George Griffin, the remarkable Negro man-of-all-work for the Clemens household who, as Mark Twain said, "came to wash some windows, and remained half a generation" ("Family Sketch," p. 4, TS in MTP).

4. Presumably a letter, now lost, from Clara Kellogg to Clemens.

5. The Norwegian violinist Ole Bull, who had married an American woman in 1870 and had recently established his residence in Cambridge.

6. The article under discussion here was probably "A Literary Nightmare" (eventually published in the *Atlantic* for February 1876, and reprinted as the title piece of *Punch, Brothers, Punch! and Other Sketches* in 1878; DE, XIX, 335–342). Mark Twain was capitalizing upon a literary craze for doggerel verse begun by Isaac Bromley of the New York *Tribune* and Noah Brooks of the *Times,* who created a jingle based upon a notice in a horsecar of the Fourth Ave. line reading, "The conductor, when he receives a fare, will immediately punch in the presence of the passenger," etc. (*Scribner's Monthly,* XI, 910–912, April 1876; MTB, pp. 555–556; New York *Times,* 8 August 1915, Section I, p. 12).

7. John Howells, then seven years old.

8. A cancellation occurs at this point which is more than half a page long. The following words can be deciphered in it: "Those [?] graded foetuses one sees in bottles of alcohol in anatomical [?] museums. . . . I can look back over my row of bottles, now, & discover that it has already developed from a rather inferior frog into a perceptible though libelous suggestion of a child. I hope to add a bottle a day, now, right along." This extended metaphor refers to the novel which is under way. Unfortunately,

there is no way of determining which novel is in question. *Huckleberry Finn* was not begun before 1876.

94. HOWELLS TO CLEMENS

[Cambridge] Oct. 19, 1875.

My dear Clemens:

The poor fellow who wrote this notice [1] thinks I had better show it to you before I put it in type. He says he's afraid it's awful rot; but he hopes you may look mercifully on it. Please return it to me (with objections) at once. You can imagine the difficulty of noticing a book of short sketches; it's like noticing a library.

I spoke to Longfellow about the international copyright petition. He will gladly sign it — if it doesn't entail any cares upon him. I'll see Lowell soon.

How much will Bliss take for your type-writer *now?*

Yours ever

W. D. H.

1. Howells's review of *Sketches, New and Old.* He says, accurately, that "A True Story" is "by far the most perfect piece of work in the book . . . a study of character as true as life itself, strong, tender, and most movingly pathetic in its perfect fidelity to the tragic fact." He also refers with approval to Mark Twain's ironic "petition to Congress asking that all property shall be held during the period of forty-two years, or for just so long as an author is permitted to claim copyright in his book" (*Atlantic,* XXXVI, 749, December 1875).

95. CLEMENS TO HOWELLS

Hartford Oct 19 [1875]

My Dear Howells:

That is a perfectly superb notice. You can easily believe that nothing ever gratified me so much before. The newspaper praises bestowed upon the Innocents Abroad were large & generous, but I hadn't *confidence* in the critical judgment of the parties who furnished them. *You* know how that is, yourself, from reading the newspaper notices of your own books. They gratify a body, but they always leave a small pang behind in the shape of a fear that the critic's good words could not safely be depended upon as *authority*. Yours is the recognized critical Court of Last Resort in this country; from its decision there is no appeal; & so, to have gained this decree of yours before I am forty years old, I regard as a thing to be right down proud of. Mrs. Clemens says, "Tell him *I* am just as grateful to him as I can be." (It *sounds* as if she were grateful to you for heroically trampling the truth under foot in order to praise me — but in reality it means that she is grateful to you for being bold to utter a truth which she fully believes all competent people know, but which none has heretofore been brave enough to utter.) [1] You see, the thing that gravels her is that I am so persistently glorified as a mere buffoon, as if that entirely covered my case — which she denies with venom.

The other day Mrs Clemens was planning a visit to you, & so I am waiting, with a pleasurable hope, for the result of her deliberations. We are expecting visitors every day, now, from New York; & afterward some are to come from Elmira. I judge that we shall then be free to go Boston-ward. I should be just delighted; because we could visit in comfort, ⟨because⟩ since we shouldn't have to do any shopping — did it all in New York last week, & a tremendous pull it was, too.

Mrs. C. said the other day, "We will go to Cambridge if we have to walk; for I don't believe we can ever get the Howellses to come here again until we have been there." [2] I was gratified to see that there was *one* string anyway, that could snake her to Cambridge. But I will do her the justice to say that she is always wanting to go to Cambridge, independent of the selfish desire to get a visit out of you by it. I want her to get started, now, before children's diseases get fashionable again, because they always play such hob with visiting arrangements.

With our love to you all Yrs Ever

S. L. Clemens

P.S. I shall change this pen, by & by, for one that will write regular & not emphasize so indiscriminately.[3]

1. Livy's gratitude was due in part to Howells's assertion of "a growing seriousness of meaning in the apparently unmoralized drolling" of a *"subtile* humorist" (*Atlantic,* XXXVI, 749, December 1875).

2. The only hypothesis that makes this statement intelligible is that after the visit of the Clemenses to Cambridge which occurred before 4 October, the Howellses had made an unrecorded visit to the Clemenses in Hartford after their return from Quebec about 14 October (WDH to CDW, Cambridge, 24 October, Watkinson, AGM TS).

3. The handwriting of the letter shows great variation in the width of the pen strokes.

96. CLEMENS TO HOWELLS

[Hartford] Oct. 27 [1875]

Say, boss, do you want this[1] to lighten up your old freight-train with? I suppose you won't, but then it won't take you long to say so. — I do not enclose stamps for re-mailing because I have hardly enough to see me through the day, & neither is there a shinplaster in the house.

I shall run up to you very early in November[2] — the madam, too, if she is strong enough — & go with you to see some of the literary big guns about the copyright project. Shall want to abide with you 3 or 4 days.

Mrs. Clemens is dejected, despondent, discouraged. She gets up at 9, & by 11 is clear broken down & tired out. If this were May in place of October I would have her on board a Cunard steamer inside of 48 hours.   Yrs Ever

Mark.

P.S. Mrs. Howells's letter has just come & Mrs. Perkins[3] & I have almost persuaded Mrs Clemens to go right off tomorrow to Cambridge & leave the children here. Mrs. Perkins says she will visit them every day & look after them. Mrs. C. has gone with Mrs. P. to luncheon, & I do hope they'll come to the right decision in this matter — in which case I will telegraph you.

1. An unidentified MS apparently offered as a companion piece for "A Literary Nightmare" (letter 93).

2. Clemens's high-spirited letter of a week earlier to Aldrich, welcoming him home from Europe, is actually addressed equally to Howells: "I am waiting for Osgood to invite us all to dinner; at which time I shall be glad to advance to Boston & renew, etc. I would suggest, through you, that he invite Howells too. It would not be wise to leave Howells out, for he occupies a very influential position & is a man who would not hesitate to destroy a book of yours or mine if we seemed to connive at any prandial slights in his case. Gill the publisher is a nice person, too; but Howells has privately tried, without success, to get him to put his 'Private Theatricals' into the 'Treasure Found & Gobbled Series' — & so there may be bad blood between them. I perceive that this 'Private Theatricals' is going to lift Howells a trifle too high in the public estimation. Could you give it a black eye in an article? I could get it inserted in the Hartford papers" (Hartford, 20 October, photostat in MTP).

3. Mary Beecher Perkins, wife of Thomas C. Perkins and sister of Harriet Beecher Stowe (NF, p. 17).

97. HOWELLS TO CLEMENS

[Cambridge] Nov. 5, 1875

My dear Clemens:

The type-writer came Wednesday night, and is already beginning to have its effect on me. Of course it doesn't work: if I can persuade some of the letters to get up against the ribbon they wont get down again without digital assistance. The treadle refuses to have any part or parcel in the performance; and *I* don't know how to get the roller to turn with the paper. Nevertheless, I have begun several letters to *My d ar lemans,* as it prefers to spell your respected name, and I don't despair yet of sending you something in its beautiful hand writing — after I've had a man out from the agent's to put it in order. It's fascinating, in the meantime, and it wastes my time like an old friend.

Don't vex yourself to provide a companion piece for the Literary Nightmare, though if you've anything ready, send it along.[1] But it will do magnificently as it is. I've been reading it over, with joy.

I hope to get at the story [2] on Sunday.　　Yours ever

W. D. Howells.

MS. At the head of the letter is pasted a clipping from the New York *Sun* (1 November 1875) which reads as follows:

"This is the latest addition to the streetcar poetry. It applies, of course, to the bobtail cars:

> When the passenger wishes to leave the cair,
> He must ring the bell with modest air,
> Must bow to the gentlemanly drivair
> And say, 'Beg pardon, excuse me sair,
> But really, I'd like to get out of this cair.'
> Then the driver will turn with a terrible glare,
> And shout at the wretched passenjair;
> 'A blank of a place to stop this hair
> Machine, on this grade; you hold on there,'
> And clammy and cold grows the passenjair,
> And he wilts like a blighted cucumbair."

Bobtail cars had a driver but no conductor.

1. Howells has apparently rejected the MS submitted on 27 October as a companion piece for "A Literary Nightmare."

2. *Tom Sawyer.*

98. HOWELLS TO CLEMENS

[Cambridge] Nov. 21, 1875.

Dear Clemens:

Here is the Literary Nightmare,[1] which I'm going to put into the January, and want back by the return mail. I couldn't give it up.

— I finished reading Tom Sawyer a week ago, sitting up till one A.M., to get to the end, simply because it was impossible to leave off. It's altogether the best boy's story I ever read. It will be an immense success. But I think you ought to treat it explicitly *as* a boy's story. Grown-ups will enjoy it just as much if you do; and if you should put it forth as a study of boy character from the grown-up point of view, you'd give the wrong key to it.[2] I have made some corrections and suggestions in faltering pencil, which you'll have to look for.[3] They're almost all in the first third. When you fairly swing off, you had better be let alone. — The adventures are enchanting. I wish *I* had been on that island. The treasure-hunting, the loss in the cave — it's all exciting and splendid. I shouldn't think of publishing this story serially. Give me a hint when it's to be out, and I'll start the sheep to jumping in the right places.

— I don't seem to think I like the last chapter.[4] I believe I would cut that.

— Mrs. H. has Mrs. C.'s letter to answer. In the meantime she sends love, and I will send the Ms. of my notice some time this week — it's at the printers'. How shall I return the book MS?   Yours ever

W. D. Howells.

Took down Roughing It, last night, and made a fool of myself over it, as usual.

1. That is, proof sheets of the article.

2. The implication is that to publish the novel serially in the *Atlantic* would be inevitably to "put it forth as a study of boy character from the grown-up point of view." The sequence of events leading to Howells's tribute, in this well-known letter, to Mark Twain's lovely image of Hannibal was this: Clemens had talked with Howells about *Tom Sawyer* in June. The exchange of letters of 3 and 5 July reveals that Howells wanted the story for the *Atlantic,* but Mark Twain felt he could not afford to accept what the *Atlantic* could pay for it. Nevertheless, Clemens wished Howells to read and edit it. With a twinge of conscience, he proposed that Howells collaborate with him in dramatizing the novel. Howells refused but urged Clemens to send it on for him to read. According to Clemens's letter of 13 July, he had sent the MS to be copied. Howells received the amanuensis copy at an undetermined date apparently not long before he wrote to Clemens on 5 November. (This copy, now in the State Capitol of Missouri at Jefferson City, contains marginal comments in Howells's handwriting.) He began to read and edit the MS on Sunday, 7 November, and finished it on the night of Sunday, 14 November.

3. Howells's comments on the MS are discussed in note 3 to letter 103.

4. Bernard DeVoto suggests (MTW, p. 11) that this chapter was one in which "*Adventures of Huckleberry Finn* began prematurely." The opening section of *Huckleberry Finn* certainly deals with "Huck's life at the

Widow's" — as Mark Twain summarizes the matter of the last chapter in letter 99.

99. CLEMENS TO HOWELLS

Hartford, Nov. 23/75.

My Dear Howells:

Herewith is the proof.[1] In spite of myself, how awkwardly I do jumble words together; & how often I do use three words where one would answer — a thing I am always trying to guard against. I shall become as slovenly a writer as Charles Francis Adams if I don't look out. (That is said in jest; because of course I do not seriously fear getting so bad as that. I never shall drop so far toward his & Bret Harte's level as to catch myself saying "It ⟨might⟩ must have been wiser to have believed that he ⟨could⟩ might have accomplished it if he could have felt that he would have been supported by those who should have &c., &c., &c.,")[2] The reference to Bret Harte reminds me that I often accuse him of being a deliberate imitator of Dickens; & this in turn reminds me that I have charged unconscious plagiarism upon Charley Warner; & *this* in turn reminds me that I have been delighting my soul for two weeks over a bran new & ingenious way of beginning a novel — & behold, all at once it flashes upon me that *Charley Warner* originated the idea 3 years ago & told me about it! Aha! So much for self-righteousness! I am well repaid. Here are 108 pages of MS, new & clean, lying disgraced in the waste paper basket, & I am beginning the novel over again in an unstolen way. I would not wonder if I am the worst literary thief in the world, without knowing it.

It is glorious news that you like Tom Sawyer so well. I mean to see to it that your review of it shall have plenty of time to appear before the other notices. Mrs. Clemens decides with you that the book should issue as a book for boys, pure & simple — & so do I. It is surely the correct idea. As to that last chapter, I think of just leaving it off & adding nothing in its place. Something told me that the book was done when I got to that point — & so the strong temptation to put Huck's life at the widow's into detail instead of generalizing it in a paragraph, was resisted. Just send Sawyer to me by Express — I enclose money for it.[3] If it should get lost it will be no great matter.[4]

Company interfered last night, & so "Private Theatricals" goes over till this evening, to be read aloud.[5] Mrs. Clemens is mad, but the story will take *that* all out. This is going to be a splendid winter night for fireside reading, anyway.

I am almost at a dead stand-still with my new story, on account of the misery of having to do it all over again.

We-all send love to you-all.   Yrs Ever

Mark.

1. Of "A Literary Nightmare."

2. The reference to the style of Charles Francis Adams, Jr., is probably suggested by an article by him in the *Atlantic* for November 1875.

3. Thirty-five years later Howells remembered (no doubt mistakenly) that Clemens retrieved the MS in person. "I went with him to the horse-car station in Harvard Square, as my frequent wont was," Howells wrote in MMT (pp. 47–48), "to put him aboard a car with his MS. in his hand, stayed and reassured, so far as I counted, concerning it."

4. Clemens is indifferent to the risk of loss of the MS in transit because he has another copy of it.

5. This story by Howells was serialized in the *Atlantic* November 1875–May 1876. One of his least known novels, it is yet one of his liveliest and most dramatic in portraying a cold-hearted charming flirt. Because of it, the Springfield *Republican* spoke of Howells's "well-known contempt of women" (WDH to CDW, Cambridge, 5 January 1876, Watkinson, AGM TS), and Fanny Kemble wrote, "Mrs. Farrell is terrific — do for pity's sake give her the small pox — she deserves it . . . " (LinL, I, 205, 20 December 1875). It was not brought out as a book until 1921, after Howells's death, under the title *Mrs. Farrell, a Novel*: Howells may just possibly have been threatened with suit by the couple who ran the Mountain Farm where he had stayed, and who considered they had been caricatured in the novel (Edwin H. Cady, *The Road to Realism*, Syracuse, 1956, p. 192).

III

I WISH I HAD BEEN on THAT ISLAND

(1 8 7 6)

III

(1 8 7 6)

"I have made some corrections and suggestions in faltering pen-
cil, which you'll have to look for. They're almost all in the
first third. When you fairly swing off, you had better be let
alone. — The adventures are enchanting. I wish I had been on
that island" (WDH to SLC, Cambridge, 21 November 1875,
MTP)

Profiting by Howells's "pencil marks scattered all along" in the
manuscript of *Tom Sawyer,* Clemens made his final revision of the
book and the American Publishing Company began production of
it early in 1876. Although various confusions and mishaps delayed
publication until the end of the year, Howells's review, from proof
sheets, appeared in the May issue of the *Atlantic* — an anomaly
for which Clemens apologized and Howells easily forgave him. The
two friends discussed at length their plan for a series of stories to be
written by twelve authors using the same plot, but nothing came of
the project. During the Presidential campaign of 1876 Howells wrote
a biography of Rutherford B. Hayes, who was his wife's cousin, and
Clemens spoke at a Republican rally in Hartford. They were agonized
by the months of uncertainty concerning the outcome of the election and exulted in Hayes's final victory. On 9 August, Clemens had
finished the first four hundred manuscript pages of "Huck Finn's
Autobiography," which he liked "only tolerably well." He reported
with more enthusiasm that he had agreed to collaborate with Bret
Harte in writing a play laid in a California mining camp, to be
called *Ah Sin.* Although household cares usually kept Elinor Howells
and Livy Clemens at home, the two husbands managed to visit back
and forth. In March 1876 Howells brought his six-year-old son John
for a week end in Hartford, and, in May, Clemens invited the
Howellses and Aldriches to join him and his friend Joseph Twichell
in a box at the disastrous performance of Anna Dickinson's *A Crown of*
Thorns, or Ann Boleyn in Boston.

[Cambridge] Jan. 4, 1876,

Yes, my dear old fellow, on Scrofulous Humor or any other comic subject,[1] except Theology which I'm now reserving for our holy land contributor C. D. W.[2] I would be mighty glad, as you know well enough, to have something from you every month.

— We were both — Mrs. Howells and I — getting up a bad state of feeling towards you both, because you hadn't made any sign of existence for so long, when your jumping-frog came luridly hopping along, and looking as if he had just got out of a pond of H. fire.[3] Now we are all right again, and we join in best wishes for your continued health and prosperity. — How does the novel?[4] The more I think over your boy-book[5] the more I like it. — Is it true that you're going to Europe in the spring?

Yours ever,

W. D. Howells

1. Evidently an answer to a question in a letter from Clemens now lost.
2. Charles Dudley Warner, still abroad on a trip to the Near East, contributed to the *Atlantic* during 1875 and 1876 six articles about his travels.
3. Clemens had apparently sent Howells a copy of his first book, *The Celebrated Jumping Frog of Calaveras County, and Other Sketches* (1867), which had a bright maroon binding with the picture of a frog stamped in gold on the cover.
4. Not now identifiable.
5. *Tom Sawyer.*

Hartford Jan 11./76

My Dear Howells —

Indeed we haven't forgotten the Howellses, nor scared up a grudge of any kind against them; but the fact is I was under the doctor's hands for four weeks on a stretch, & have been disabled from working for a week or so beside. I thought I was well, about ten days ago, so I sent for a short-hand writer & dictated answers to a bushel or so of letters that had been accumulating during my illness. Getting everything ship-shape & cleared up, I went to work next day upon an Atlantic article,[1] which ought to be worth the $20 per page (which is the price they usually pay for my work I believe) for although it is only 70 pages MS (less than 2 days work, counting by bulk,) I have spent 3 more days trimming, altering & working at it. I shall put in one more day's polishing on it, & then read it before our Club, which is to meet at our house Monday evening the 24th inst.[2] I think it will bring out considerable discussion among the gentlemen of the Club — though the title of the article will not give them much notion of what is to follow — this title being "The *Facts* Concerning the Recent Carnival of Crime in Connecticut" — which reminds me that today's Tribune says there will be a *start*ling article in the CURRENT Atlantic, in which a being which is *tangible but invisible* will figure [3] — exactly the case with the sketch of mine which I am talking about! However, mine can lie unpublished a year or two as well as not — though I wish that contributor of yours had not interfered, with his coincidence of heroes.

But what I am coming at, is this: won't you & Mrs. Howells come down Saturday the 22d, ⟨meet a gang⟩ & remain to the Club on Monday night? We always have a ratling good time at the Club, & we do want you to come, ever so much. Will you? Now say you will. Mrs. Clemens & I are persuading ourselves that you twain *will* come.

My volume of Sketches [4] is doing very well, considering the times; received my quarterly statement today from Bliss, by which I perceive that 20,000 copies have been sold. — or rather, 20,000 had been sold 3 weeks ago; a lot more by this time, no doubt.

I am on the sick list again — & was, day before yesterday — but on the whole I'm getting along.   Yrs Ever

Mark.

1. "The Facts Concerning the Recent Carnival of Crime in Connecticut," which would be published in the June 1876 issue (DE, XIX, 302–325).

2. The Monday Evening Club had been founded in 1869 by Horace Bushnell, Charles S. Henry, and James H. Trumbull. Mark Twain was invited to join in 1871, even before he established his residence in Hartford. Twichell, Warner, and Charles E. Perkins were members. The club met every two weeks except during the summer to hear and to discuss a paper read by a member on a subject of his choice. Mark Twain had read his first paper (on "The License of the Press") 31 March 1873, and his second (on "Universal Suffrage") 15 February 1875. He read "The Facts Concerning the Recent Carnival of Crime" to the Club on 24 January 1876 (*The List of Members of the Monday Evening Club Together with the Record of Papers Read at Their Meetings 1869–1954 with an Introduction by the Fourth Secretary of the Club* [Howell Cheney], Hartford, 1954). Twichell noted that Mark Twain's paper was "very finely written — serious in its intent though vastly funny and splendidly, brilliantly read" (Twichell Journal, 24 January 1876, Yale).

3. Charles A. De Kay's "Manmat'ha" (February 1876).

4. *Mark Twain's Sketches, New and Old.*

102. HOWELLS TO CLEMENS

Cambridge, Jan. 16, 1876.

My dear Clemens:

I'm ever so sorry to hear of your sickness, which seems a thing altogether out of character with you, and hardly fair on a man who has made so many other people feel well. How do you pretend to justify it? — I wish Mrs. Howells and I *could* go down to Hartford next Saturday; I'd had a sneaking desire for an invitation some time; but now when it comes, and I haven't disgraced myself by hinting for it, why we're neither of us in a position to accept it. We've invited Ward the sculptor [1] to visit us, and he's half accepted, and may accept the other half, and come at a day's notice. Besides, as I printed my story [2] along, I found that I had to reconstruct the last three numbers almost entirely, and to *write* them all over. This has almost killed me, and I haven't finished the work yet, and I couldn't leave home on any account till it is done. Thanks and heartfelt regrets from both of us.

Our contributor's story is a very good one, as I think you'll say when you read it, but I don't believe it'll interfere with anything you're doing. At any rate, I want you to make me judge in the matter, and send me your MS. as soon as you can.

Mrs. Howells joins me in regards to both of you.

Ever yours

W. D. Howells.

I'm glad to hear that the Sketches have done so well. Get Bliss to hurry out Tom Sawyer. That boy is going to make a prodigious hit.

1. John Quincy Adams Ward (1830–1910), whom Howells had known since they had talked about painting and sculpture together in Columbus in the winter of 1860–61 (YMY, pp. 215–216).

2. "Private Theatricals," then being serialized in the *Atlantic.*

103. CLEMENS TO HOWELLS

Hartford, Jan 18/76

My Dear Howells:

Thanks, & ever so many, for the good opinion of Tom Sawyer. Williams[1] has made about 200 rattling pictures for it — some of them very dainty. Poor devil, what a genius he has, & how he does murder it with rum.[2] He takes a book of mine, & without suggestion from anybody builds no end of pictures just from his reading of it.

There [never] was a man in the world so grateful to another as I was to you day before yesterday, when I sat down (in still rather wretched health) to set myself to the dreary & hateful task of making final revision of Tom Sawyer, & discovered, upon opening the package of MS that your pencil marks were scattered all along. This was splendid, & swept away all labor. Instead of *reading* the MS, I simply hunted out the pencil marks & made the emendations which they suggested. I reduced the boy-battle to a curt paragraph; I finally concluded to cut the Sunday-school speech down to the first two sentences, (leaving no suggestion of satire, since the book is to be for boys & girls; I tamed the various obscenities until I judged that [they] no longer carried offense.[3] So, at a single sitting I began & finished a revision which I had supposed would occupy 3 or 4 days & leave me mentally & physically fagged out at the end. I was careful not to inflict the MS upon you until I had thoroughly & painstakingly revised it. Therefore, the only faults left were those that would discover themselves to others, not me — & these you had pointed out.

There was one expression which perhaps you overlooked. When Huck is complaining to Tom of the rigorous system in vogue at the widow's, he says the servants harass him with all manner of compulsory decencies, & he winds up by saying, "and they comb me all to hell." (No exclamation point.) Long ago, when I read that to Mrs. Clemens, she made no comment; another time I created occasion to read that chapter to her aunt & her mother (both sensitive & loyal subjects of the kingdom of heaven, so to speak,) & *they* let it pass. I was glad, for it was the most natural remark in the world for that boy to make (& he had been allowed few privileges of speech in the book); when I saw that you, too, had let it go without protest, I was glad, & afraid, too — afraid you hadn't observed it. Did you? And did you question the propriety of it? Since the book is now professedly & confessedly a boy's & girl's book, that dern word bothers me some nights, but it never did until I had ceased to regard the volume as being for adults.[4]

Don't bother to answer *now*, (for you've writing enough to do without allowing me to add to the burden,) but tell me when you see me again.

Which we do hope will be next Saturday or Sunday or Monday. Couldn't you come now & mull over the alterations which you are going to make in your MS, & make them after you [go] back? Wouldn't it *assist* the work, if you dropped out of harness & routine for a day or two & have that sort of revivification which comes of a holiday-forgetfulness of the workshop? I can always work after I've been to your house; & if you will come to mine, now, & hear the club toot their various horns over the exasperating metaphysical question which I mean to lay before them in the disguise of a literary extravaganza, it would just brace you up like a cordial. As for Ward, you [can] fix it easily with him for the next week.

(I feel sort of mean, trying to persuade a man to put down a critical piece of work at a critical time, but yet I am honest in thinking it would not hurt the work nor impair your interest in it to come, under the circumstances.) Mrs. Clemens says, "Maybe the Howellses could come *Monday* if they cannot come Saturday; ask them; it is worth trying." Well, how's that? *Could* you? It would be splendid if you could. Drop me a postal card — I should have a twinge of conscience if I forced you to write a letter, (I am honest about that,) — & if you find you can't make out to come, tell me that you bodies will come the *next* Saturday if the thing be possible, & stay over Sunday.

Yrs Ever

Mark.

1. True W. Williams, who had drawn illustrations for *The Innocents Abroad* and for *Sketches, New and Old,* and would be called upon later to contribute a few illustrations for *A Tramp Abroad.*

2. On 3 October 1871, Orion Clemens, then employed by the American Publishing Co. in Hartford, wrote to his wife that he had seen Williams "climbing a lamp post, and offering to go to the top, for the amusement of some loafers in front of Tim Dooley's saloon" (Hartford, MTP).

3. Bernard DeVoto summarizes Howells's comments as follows: He suggested shortening the sham fight at the end of Chapter III and Mr. Walters's speech in Sunday school in Chapter IV. He questioned a number of words and phrases, including a few mild "obscenities" that Mark Twain mentions here. He found the description of the poodle who sat down on the pinchbug and sailed up the aisle "with his tail shut down like a hasp" to be "awfully good but a little too dirty," and Mark Twain omitted the reference to the tail. The most important revision recommended by Howells was a shortening of the incident of Becky Thatcher's looking at the anatomy textbook from the teacher's desk in Chapter XX (MTW, pp. 12–14).

4. This distinction should be kept in mind in evaluating Howells's and Clemens's revisions.

104. HOWELLS TO CLEMENS

[Cambridge] Jan. 19, 1875.[1]

My dear Clemens:

There is one chance in a thousand that I may run down alone on Saturday afternoon; Mrs. Howells is quite out of the question, and I'd rather come some time soon when you haven't your Club. I confess that I'd like awfully to go now, but an interruption would be disastrous to my work: I'm not confused about it; I have a perfectly clear vision of what I want to do, and I only need the time to do it.

As to the point in your book: I'd have that swearing out in an instant.[2] I suppose I didn't notice it because the locution was so familiar to my Western sense, and so exactly the thing that Huck would say. But it wont do for the children.

My love is longer than I can make my letter. Don't expect me, but —   Yours ever

W. D. Howells.

1. An oversight for 1876.
2. The reading "they comb me all to hell" in the MS became, in the published version, "they comb me all to thunder" (Chapter XXXV).

105. HOWELLS TO CLEMENS

[Cambridge] Jan. 27, 1876.

My dear Clemens:

I shall not be able to come down to Hartford this Saturday, but I am getting the better of my literary misery, and you may depend upon seeing me very soon.

In the meantime I must tell you what an immense success the Literary Nightmare is, though you know already. It took here instantly. The day the number[1] came out, I dined at

Ernest Longfellow's,[2] and before I got into the parlor, I heard him and Tom Appleton [3] urging each other to punch with care. They said the Longfellow ladies all had it by heart, and last night at the Fieldses [4] they told me that Boston was simply devastated by it. And everybody appreciates and enjoys the way you have set the thing. In my own family it is simply a nuisance. John clacks it off at mealtime till boxed into silence, and then Pilla starts up with, "Punch, *brullers,* punch with care!" I hear of its raging similarly in families all along this street, and of course Harvard is full of it.

When are you going to send me that paper you read before your Club? Let me see it even if you don't want to publish it.

Yours ever

W. D. Howells.

1. The *Atlantic* for February 1876.
2. An artist, the son of the poet.
3. Thomas Gold Appleton (1812–1884), brother-in-law of Henry Wadsworth Longfellow, author, artist, founder of the Boston Literary Club, and a noted diner-out and wit of Brahmin Boston. In *The Autocrat of the Breakfast Table* Holmes attributes to him the epigram, "Good Americans, when they die, go to Paris" (VI).
4. James T. Fields, the publisher, and his wife, a celebrated hostess.

106. CLEMENS TO HOWELLS (POSTCARD)

Hartford 26th [February 1876]

Good! I'll be at the station about 2.30, P.M., March 3d, to fetch you.[1] We are all sorry Mrs. Howells cannot come with you. That sideboard which you & I ordered in Boston leaves there to-day. I've got a project for a summer's holiday with you if you can go. I've written a little short Atlantic article,[2] but I don't believe you'll dare to print it. However, I'll send it for inspection by & by.

S. L. C.

1. The letter or telegram of Howells to which Clemens replies is missing.
2. Not now identifiable.

107. HOWELLS TO CLEMENS

[Cambridge] March 5, 1876.

My dear Clemens:

My wife has your wife's very kind letter,[1] for which she sends her love, and bids me say with tears that she is a thousand times grateful, but that it's quite impossible for her to leave home at this time. She will hold the invitation *in terrorem* over Mrs. Clemens, and that in the meantime your hospitality may not go defrauded she lets me ask if I may bring Bua with me. He wont make you any trouble I can promise, and he can sleep with me, so that his habitual nightmare must not disturb the other slumberers. May I?   Yours ever

W. D. Howells.

1. Livy Clemens's letter of invitation has not survived.

108. HOWELLS TO CLEMENS (POSTCARD)

[Cambridge, 6 or 7 March 1876]

Your telegraph received (in my absence, with the usual terror.)

John and I expect to leave Boston at 3 o'clock Saturday afternoon, and reach Hartford at 7.

W. D. H.

MS. The card bears no postmark, as if it had been enclosed in an envelope instead of being mailed in the normal fashion. But the date is almost certainly 6 or 7 March, when Clemens would have received Howells's letter of 5 March and would have telegraphed approval of the idea of bringing Howells's son along.

109. HOWELLS TO CLEMENS

[Cambridge, 13 March 1876]

Dear Clemens:

Here's the letter about copyright, which please return.

Bua and I did have a *good* time,[1] and he has flourished your princely hospitality and orient pearl over Winny at a pitiless rate.[2]

The "great globe," etc., is in the Tempest, Scene I, Act 4., Prospero speaking.

Best regards and Mrs. Howells's love to the ladies.

Yours ever

W. D. H.

1. John and his father spent Saturday evening and Sunday, 11 and 12 March, with the Clemenses (WDH to TBA, Cambridge, 21 March 1876, LinL, I, 219).

2. Howells wrote to his father: "I took John with me, and as his mother had prepared his mind for the splendors of the Twain mansion, he came to everything with the most exalted fairy-palace expectations. He found some red soap in the bathroom. 'Why, they've even got their soap painted!' says he; and the next morning when he found the black serving-man getting ready for breakfast, he came and woke me. 'Better get up, papa. The *slave* is setting the table.' I suppose he thought Clemens could have that darkey's head off whenever he liked. He was delightful through the whole visit" (Cambridge, 19 March 1876, Houghton). Thirty-two years later John Howells became the architect for Mark Twain's last house, "Stormfield," at Redding, Conn.

110. HOWELLS TO CLEMENS (POSTCARD)

[Cambridge, 20 March 1876]

Dear Clemens:

I have the proof of Tom Sawyer. Now send me the *title* of the book in full, *quick.*[1]

W. D. H.

MS. The date is inferred from the postmark.
1. Howells was writing a review of *Tom Sawyer* from proof sheets.

111. HOWELLS TO CLEMENS

[Cambridge] April 2, 1876.

My dear Clemens:

Mr. Boott wishes me to send you this song [1] which he has set in a key suitable for your voice. I know he would be vastly gratified to get some direct acknowledgment from you. [2]

Yours ever

W. D. Howells.

1. Not now identifiable.
2. On 3 April, Clemens wrote to Boott (in care of Howells) thanking him for the song, and on 15 April, Boott acknowledged the note (Cambridge, MTP).

112. CLEMENS TO HOWELLS

[Hartford] Apl. 3 [1876].

My Dear Howells:

It is a splendid notice, & will embolden weak-kneed journalistic admirers to speak out, & will modify or shut up the unfriendly. To "fear God & dread the Sunday school" [1] exactly describes that old feeling which I used to have but I couldn't have formulated it. I want to enclose one of the illustrations in this letter, if I do not forget it. Of course the book is to be elaborately illustrated, & I think that many of the pictures are considerably above the American average, in conception if not in execution.

I do not re-enclose your review [2] to you, for you have evidently read & corrected it, & so I judge you do not need it.

About two days after the Atlantic issues I mean to begin to send books to principal journals & magazines.

I read that "Carnival of Crime" proof in New York when worn & witless & so left some things unamended which I might possibly have altered had I been at home. For instance "I shall always address you in your own s-n-i-v-e-l-ing d-r-a-w-l — baby." I saw that you objected to something there, but I did not understand what. Was it that it was too personal? — Should the language have been altered? — or the hyphens taken out? Won't you please fix it the way it ought to be, altering the language as you choose, only making it bitter & contemptuous? [3]

"Deuced" was not strong enough; so I met you half way with "devilish." [4]

Mrs. Clemens has returned from New York with dreadful sore throat, & bones racked with rheumatism. She keeps her bed. *"Aloha nui!"* [5] as the Kanakas say

Mark.

1. Quoted from Howells's review of *Tom Sawyer* (which would appear in the *Atlantic,* XXXVII, 621, May 1876).

2. The proof sheets.

3. The passage remains unaltered in both the *Atlantic* text and that of the reprinting of the sketch in *Tom Sawyer Abroad, Tom Sawyer Detective, and Other Stories* (1896).

4. The hideous dwarf who represents the author's conscience opens his conversation with the remark, "Seems to me it's devilish odd weather for this time of year." If "deuced" is not strong enough and "devilish" a halfway compromise, the original epithet was probably "damned."

5. An entry in Clemens's notebook for 1866, while he was in Hawaii, reads: "Aloha, Love, Nui, great" (Notebook #5, TS, p. 6nn., MTP).

113. CLEMENS TO HOWELLS

[Hartford] Apl 22/76.

My Dear Howells:

You'll see per enclosed slip [1] that I appear for the first time on the stage next Wednesday. You & Mrs. H. come down & you shall skip in free.

I wrote my skeleton novelette [2] yesterday & to-day. It will make a little under 12 pages.

Please tell Aldrich I've got a photographer engaged, & tri-weekly issue is about to begin. Show him the canvassing specimens & beseech him to subscribe.[3]   Ever Yrs

S L C

1. Presumably a playbill for an amateur production of *The Loan of a Lover* (a play that had held the boards for forty years) on 26 April 1876. Mark Twain played the role of Peter Spyk, having rewritten the part so as to "change the language *&* the character" (SLC to Augustin Daly, Hartford, 4 May 1876, in Daly, *Life of Augustin Daly*, p. 146). There was apparently a second performance on 27 April. On 2 May, Augustin Daly wrote: "My dear Twain, Why don't you come down here & play 'Peter Spyk' some Saturday night for one of my 'Benefit' occasions. Would you — will you — ?" and on 6 May: "My invitation was seriously & earnestly meant — and I am ready to repeat it whenever you are willing to let me. Not for one night but for many" (New York, MTP).

2. Probably during the week end of 11 March, in Hartford, Clemens and Howells had agreed to collaborate in devising a plot which would be submitted to twelve writers, each of whom "was to write a story, using the same plot, 'blindfolded' as to what the others had written" (MTL, pp. 275–276). A "skeleton" would logically be an outline; but Clemens's statement that his MS would run to a little under twelve *Atlantic* pages (that is, to perhaps 9000 words) suggests that he had actually written out the story which he, as one of the twelve hypothetical participants, was supposed to develop from the common plot. On 2 April, Howells wrote Aldrich: "I send also a scheme of Mark Twain's which we shall carry out if we can get any one to help. That is he and I will write a story on the proposed basis, if you and two or three others will do so" (Cambridge, Houghton). Clemens was still actively interested in this scheme eight years later — he proposed it to Richard Watson Gilder, editor of the *Century* magazine, and to George W. Cable in 1884 (Harry R. Warfel, "George W. Cable Amends a Mark Twain Plot," AL, VI, 328–331, November 1934). But nothing tangible came of it, and his story was never published. It is entitled "A Murder, a Mystery, and a Marriage," and is about 8600 words long (a photographic copy of a privately printed version of it is in MTP). It is a preposterous tale of stereotyped and incredible intrigue having only two points of interest: the setting is "a remote and out-of-the-way village in south-western Missouri," not unlike the St. Petersburg of *Tom Sawyer* and *Huckleberry Finn* although it is not on the Mississippi; and one of the principal characters, Jean Mercier, a Frenchman fluent in many languages, arrives in the neighborhood by falling from a balloon which disappears before he is discovered.

The circumstances of this mysterious arrival and the character of Mercier are faintly suggestive of the depiction of Satan in one of the early versions (the "Print-shop Version") of *The Mysterious Stranger.*

3. Howells's letter of 28 April indicates that Clemens had sent photographs of himself and his daughters. Clemens apparently wished to remind Aldrich of the occasion in December 1874–January 1875 when he had deluged Aldrich with photographs of himself.

114. HOWELLS TO CLEMENS

[Cambridge] April 24, 1876.

My dear Clemens:

I send you this letter [1] as a matter of form. Our people leave the whole thing to you, and don't presume to say what you will do with your property. They will return [any] answer you may make to Mr. Moore.

I hope you're all well. We are, and send regards.

Yours ever

W. D. Howells.

1. A letter to H. O. Houghton from Frank Moore (New York, 21 April 1876, MTP), stating: "I have collected all the Horse Car Poetry & am to print it in the Record of the Year, and I want to print Mark Twains article from the Atlantic." The *Record of the Year* was a short-lived monthly magazine published in New York by G.W. Carleton & Co. Moore was editor.

115. CLEMENS TO HOWELLS

Hartford, Apl. 26 [1876]

My Dear Howells:

Thanks for the slips [1] & thanks for giving me the place of honor. [2]

Bliss made a failure in the matter of getting Tom Sawyer ready on time — the engravers assisting, as usual. I went down to see how *much* of a delay there was going to be, & found that the man had not even put a canvasser on or issued an advertisement yet — in fact that the *electrotypes* would not all be done for a month! But of course the main trouble was the fact that no canvassing had been done — because a subscription harvest is *before* publication, (not *after,* when people have discovered how bad one's book is).

Well, yesterday I put in the Courant[3] an editorial paragraph stating that Tom Sawyer is "ready to issue, but publication is put off in order to secure English copyright by simultaneous publication there & here. The English edition is unavoidably delayed."

You see, part of that is true. Very well. When I observed that my Sketches had dropped from a sale of 6 or 7000 a month down to 1200 a month, I said *"this* ain't no time to be publishing books; therefore, let Tom lay still till autumn, Mr. Bliss, & make a holiday book of him to beguile the young people withal."

Howells, you must forgive me, if I seem to have made the Atlantic any wrong.[4] I — but I'll talk to you about it & show you that it was one of those cases where "the best laid schemes of mice & men, &c."

I shall print items occasionally still further delaying Tom, till I ease him down to autumn without shock to the waiting world.

As to that "Literary Nightmare" proposition, I'm obliged to withhold consent, for what seems a good reason — to wit: a single page of horse-car poetry is all that the average reader can stand, without nausea; now, to stack together *all* of it that has been written, & then add to it my article would be to enrage & disgust each & every reader & win the deathless enmity of the lot.

Even if that reason were insufficient, there would still be a sufficient reason left, in the fact that Mr. Carleton seems to be the publisher of the magazine in which it is proposed to publish this horse-car matter. — Carleton insulted me in Feb, 1867;[5] & so when the day arrives that sees me doing him a civility, I shall feel that I am ready for Paradise, since my list of possible and impossible forgivenesses will then be complete.

Mrs. Clemens says my version of the blindfold novelette "A Murder & a Marriage" is "good." Pretty strong language — for her. However, it is not original. God said the same of another Creation.

The Fieldses are coming down to the play [6] tomorrow & they promise to try to get you & Mrs. Howells to come, too, but I hope you'll do nothing of the kind if it will inconvenience you, for I ain't going to play either striking bad enough or well enough to make the journey pay you.

My wife & I think of going to Boston May 7th to see Anna Dickinson's *debut* on the 8th.[7] If I find we can go, I'll try to get a stage box, & then you & Mrs. Howells must come to Parker's & go with us to the crucifixion. (Is that spelt right? — some how it doesn't *look* right.)

With our very kindest regards to the whole family,

Yrs Ever

Mark.

Mrs. Clemens heard a visiting Vermont gentleman quote Johnny's remark about the "slave" getting breakfast ready last night.

1. Proof sheets of "The Facts Concerning the Recent Carnival of Crime."

2. The article was to lead off the *Atlantic* for June.

3. The Hartford *Courant*, owned and edited by Clemens's friends Joseph R. Hawley and Charles Dudley Warner.

4. By allowing Howells's review of *Tom Sawyer* to appear so long before the book was to be published.

5. George W. Carleton, Artemus Ward's publisher, had rejected *The Celebrated Jumping Frog* volume before it was published by Charles H. Webb in 1867. The rejection itself or Carleton's manner in making it is probably the insult to which Clemens refers. On 23 April 1867 he wrote to his friend Charles W. Stoddard that Bret Harte "is publishing with a Son of a Bitch who will swindle him, & he may print that opinion if he chooses, with my name signed to it. I don't know how his book [*Condensed Novels. And Other Papers,* G.W. Carleton & Co., New York, 1867] is coming on — we of Bohemia keep away from Carleton's" (New York, TS in Bancroft). Mark Twain told A. B. Paine that many years later, when he and Carleton met by chance in Switzerland, the publisher told him, "My chief claim to immortality is the distinction of having declined your first book" (MTB, p. 308).

6. *The Loan of a Lover.*

7. Anna E. Dickinson (1842–1932) was a celebrated reformer and lecturer on abolition and woman's rights whom Clemens had known since they were both on James Redpath's list of lecturers in 1868–69. Miss Dickinson had now determined to become an actress and a playwright. She made her theatrical debut at the Eagle Theatre, New York, on 4 April 1876 in the title role of her own play, *A Crown of Thorns, or Ann Boleyn*. The play was a resounding failure. In 1882 she appeared in New York in the role of Hamlet, but gave this up after a week, and returned briefly to the role of Ann Boleyn (Odell, *Annals*, X, 261–262).

116. HOWELLS TO CLEMENS

[Cambridge] April 28, 1876.

Dear Clemens:

The pictures of the infants are lovely in the eyes of all of us, and yours is firstrate. Thanks for them; we're ever so glad of them.

Never mind about Tom Sawyer. I rather like the fun of the thing;[1] besides I know I shall do you an injury some day, and I want a grievance to square accounts with.

Mrs. Howells and I accept with joy the possible seats in your possible box, and if we never get them, we'll *try* to be just as grateful.

Aldrich was here to-day, and we talked over the Blindfold Novelette business. But we've neither of us begun ours. Can't you send me yours?   Yours ever

W. D.H.

Sorry not to see you act. Did you get the Queen of Hearts?[2] We send regards to Mrs. Clemens, whom [we] are glad to think of seeing soon.

1. The anomaly of reviewing a book long before its publication.

2. Immediately after his notice of *Tom Sawyer* in the *Atlantic* for May 1876, Howells published an enthusiastic review of a play by James B. Greenough, professor of Latin at Harvard, entitled, *The Queen of Hearts. A Dramatic Fantasia. For Private Theatricals* (Cambridge, 1875). Howells had seen the play in an amateur production at Henry W. Longfellow's

house a year earlier (WDH to WCH, Cambridge, 9 January, Houghton). In view of the fact that Mark Twain was very fond of amateur theatricals, and was still fresh from his triumph on 26–27 April in *The Loan of a Lover,* it seems probable he had asked Howells to send him the review copy of the play.

117. CLEMENS TO HOWELLS

[Hartford] Monday afternoon [1 May 1876]

My dear Howells:

Here is the "Blindfold Novelettes." You will see that I have altered it as we contemplated. The most prominent features in the story being the Murder & the Marriage, the one name will aptly fit all the versions. Then the thing will read thus in the headings:

"A Murder & a Marriage. Story No. 1, (or 2, or 3, &c) — Mr. Harte's Version of it."

You could add to this screed of mine an editorial bracket to this effect. — (*over*)

"Messrs. Howells, Trowbridge,[1] &c., have agreed to furnish versions of this story, but it is also desirable that any who please shall furnish versions of it also, whether the writers be of literary fame or not. The MSS offered will be judged upon their merits & accepted or declined accordingly. The stories should be only 8 or 10 Atlantic pages long. — *Ed. Atlantic.*"

Something of that sort, you know, to keep people from imagining that because my name is attached to the proposition, the thing is merely intended for a joke.

Bliss promises me those sheets [2] Friday night.

Great love to you all.   Yrs Ever

Mark.

P.S. I enclose the "Conscience" article.[3] —Please correct it mercilessly.

1. John T. Trowbridge, a popular novelist and a frequent contributor to the *Atlantic.*

2. Proofs of *Tom Sawyer*.

3. Proofs of "The Facts Concerning the Recent Carnival of Crime in Connecticut."

118. CLEMENS TO HOWELLS

[Hartford] May 4 [1876].

My Dear Howells:

I shall reach Boston on Monday the 8th either at 4.30 P.M. or 6 P.M., (*Which is best?*) & go straight to Parker's.[1] If you & Mrs. Howells cannot be there by half past 4, I'll not plan to arrive till the later train-time (6), because I don't want to be there alone — even a minute. *Still,* Joe Twichell will doubtless go with me (forgot that,) — is going to try hard to. Mrs. Clemens has given up going, because Susie is just recovering from about the savagest assault of diphtheria a child ever *did* recover from, & therefore will not be entirely her healthy self again by the 8th.

Would you & Mrs. Howells like to invite Mr. & Mrs. Aldrich? I have a large proscenium box [2] — plenty of room. Use your own pleasure about it — I mainly (that is honest,) suggest it because I am seeking to make matters pleasant for you & Mrs. Howells. I invited Twichell because I thought I knew you'd like that. I want you to fix it so that you & the madam can remain in Boston all night; for I leave next day & we can't have a *talk,* other wise. I am going to get two rooms & a parlor; & would like to know what you decide about the Aldrich's so as to know whether to apply for an additional bedroom or not.

Don't dine that evening, for I shall arrive dinnerless & need your help.

I'll bring my Blindfold Novelette, but shan't exhibit it unless you exhibit yours. You would simply go to work & write a novelette that would make mine sick. Because you would know all about where my weak points lay. No, Sir, I'm one of these old wary birds!

Don't bother to write a letter — 3 lines on a postal card is all that I can permit from a busy man.   Yrs Ever

                                                         Mark

P.S. — Good! You'll (over) not have to feel any call to mention that debut in the Atlantic — they've made me pay the grand cash for my box! — a thing which most managers would be too worldly-wise to do, with journalistic folks. But I'm most honestly glad, for I'd rather pay three prices, any time, than to have my tongue half paralyzed with a dead-head ticket.

Hang that Anna Dickinson, a body never can depend upon her debuts! She has made five or six false starts already. If she fails to debut this time, I will never bet on her again.

1. The Parker House.
2. Twichell, the Aldriches, and the Howellses shared Clemens's box for Anna Dickinson's appearance in Boston (WDH to TBA, Cambridge, 5 May 1876, Houghton, AGM TS).

119. HOWELLS TO CLEMENS

[Cambridge] May 5, 1876.

My dear Clemens:

I have sent your invitation to Aldrich, and we Howellses — if Mrs. Howells is well — will meet you at Parkers at 5 o'clock. *I* expect to be there anyway. Delighted to see you and Twichell.

I'm glad you had to pay for the box, for now I shall feel free to hiss.[1]   Yours ever

                                                         W. D. H.

I didn't ask A to the dinner.

1. Howells reported to Augustin Daly after the performance: "It was sorrowfully bad, the acting, and the heaps of cut flowers for the funeral only made the gloom heavier" (Cambridge, 9 May 1876, quoted in Daly, *Life of Augustin Daly*, p. 233).

120. CLEMENS TO HOWELLS

[Hartford] Sunday [8? or 15? May 1876].

P.S. Dean Sage[1] has been visiting Twichell, & left this sketch for him & me to read & forward to you. I read it aloud to Mrs. Clemens & both of us were charmed with it; not because we care 2 cents about hunting & fishing, but because this man's admirable gift in narrative-writing seems able to make any narrative of his irresistible. He has an artlessness, an absence of self-consciousness, a ditto of striving after effect, & a pauseless canter, that ⟨cause⟩ make the reader forget the writer & become *himself* the actor in the adventures. And here is a curious thing: Dean Sage's happiest "surprises" are his simply-stated *failures*, after having worked ⟨up his theme⟩ up one's expectancy to a point where you are holding your breath for the climax, & you suppose you of course know what that climax is going to be. But instead of said climax, Sage gives you the quiet, simple TRUTH, & goes on about his business, cheerful, content, unafflicted by his defeat — even almost unconscious of it. The idea of making so fine a picture as that of that buck, & so breathless a situation; then *missing* him, & then going right on to tell what the hunting-dogs did & how hunting dogs *do* under this, that, & other circumstances! — & never a hint that the writer was aware of having missed a climax as well as the buck. The simplicity, the frozen truth, the homely phraseology — no use talking, this is the best & the happiest narrative-talent that has tackled pen since Thoreau.

Read it. I think you'll use it; but still you may not.[2] In the latter case return it to Sage, whose address is at the bottom of his note accompanying this.

Say — if Daly produces your little play[3] within the next 30 days, let's go down (without letting Daly or any one know) & slip quietly into the theatre with the general herd & see it. After 30 days I go to Elmira, 1,000,000 miles from New York.

Mark.

MS. The letter to which this postscript belongs has been lost.

1. A Yale classmate and close friend of Twichell, now a wholesale dealer in lumber. He lived in Brooklyn.

2. Howells refused the essay, finding that it lacked the charm of Sage's former paper "though our friend Clemens likes it quite as well" (WDH to Dean Sage, Cambridge, 6 June 1876, Arms, AGM TS).

3. "The Parlor Car" (first published in the *Atlantic* for September 1876, and issued as a book the same year). The play was not brought to the professional stage, but like the many one-act farces and comedies by Howells which succeeded it, "The Parlor Car" was popular in private theatricals.

121. CLEMENS TO HOWELLS

[Hartford] Friday Night [? May 1876].

My Dear Howells:

We have just finished the Shaker article [1] & Mrs. C has gone to bed. The sketch is so full of pathos; I mean all through — in every sentence, I should say; for even the humorous sentences are filmed about with the haze of pathos. I so envy those people, & am so unaccountably sorry for them, too, somehow. The parted lovers; the visit of the little child — these stand out strongly; & I looked for the hoarded bit of embroidery that one of the sisters kept for secret worship (you told me about it once) but you left it out.[2] You had to do it, of course, but it was a pity.

It was pleasant to know that one of the brethren had heard me & not damned me — I was pleased with that.[3]

Well, my enjoyment of the article was rounded & complete, when I caught you in a bit of bad English construction! "They had also some of them read Mr. Bret &c." You'd have made *me* say, "Some of them had also read &c." [4]

Aha!   Yrs Ever

Mark

1. "A Shaker Village," published in the *Atlantic* for June 1876. This issue would have reached the Clemenses around the middle of May, and the circumstance provides a clue to the probable date of the letter.

2. Clemens's memory of Howells's telling him about "the hoarded

bit of embroidery" suggests the extent to which the two writers discussed their work with each other.

3. "Certain things they would think indecorous rather than wicked," Howells wrote, "and I do not suppose a Shaker would go twice to the opera bouffe; but such an entertainment as a lecture by our right-hearted humorist, Mark Twain, had been attended by one of the brethren not only without self-reproach, but with great enjoyment" (*Atlantic,* XXXVII, 709).

4. Fortunately, Howells did not concur in Mark Twain's rather school-marmish objection to the sentence about Bret Harte. He left the passage unchanged when the article was reprinted in *Three Villages* (Boston, 1884, pp. 108–109).

122. HOWELLS TO CLEMENS

[Cambridge] June 8, 1876

My dear Clemens:

Your last letter came just as I was hurrying off to Philadelphia, and I hadn't time to do it half justice. One thing was your kind offer to go down to New York with me to see my small play. It has not yet been given, and I have not heard from Daly anything about it. I have heard from others however that he promises rashly; and I dare say it's quite likely that on second thought he doesn't find the play desirable. Small blame to him, in any case. I shall quietly pass it down to posterity in the September Atlantic.

I have written a mighty long account of the Centennial in the July number,[1] and I shall now hammer away at my comedy.[2] We go into the country for the summer, next week, and I'm to run up to the farm this morning to see that everything's in order.

— I have sent Sage's paper back to him. Everything you say of it is true, and yet it somehow fell too far below the other paper[3] in freshness and character. I hope he wont be discouraged about sending me other things.

Let us hear from each other now and then during the summer, and drop me a line to say just when you're going to

Elmira. Mrs. Howells salutes Mrs. Clemens from the habitual sick-bed.   Yours ever

W. D. Howells.

P.S. What about your novel? Or is it two of them?[4] If it's two, why can't you let us print one in The Atlantic next year?

1. "A Sennight of the Centennial" (XXXVIII, 92–107).
2. "Out of the Question" (to be published in the *Atlantic*, February-April 1877, and as a book, the same year).
3. Sage's "Ten Days' Sport on Salmon Rivers" (*Atlantic*, August 1875).
4. In his letter of 9 August, Mark Twain says he put aside his "double-barreled novel" (which cannot be identified) a month ago, and began a book we can recognize as *Huckleberry Finn*.

123. HOWELLS TO CLEMENS (POSTCARD)

[Cambridge, 13 June 1876][1]

No, I'm going to Philadelphia the 3d. I wish I were, but can't.[2] — I wrote you a long letter a week since. Didn't you get it? — We go into the country this week: Shirley Village, Mass.

W. D. H.

1. The date is inferred from the postmark.
2. In a communication now lost Mark Twain apparently asked Howells whether he was planning to attend the Congress of Authors arranged for 1 July in connection with the Philadelphia Centennial. The Congress had been announced as a gathering of "American historians and men of letters generally," who were to "prepare memoirs of the great men of our revolutionary period" (James D. McCabe, *The Illustrated History of the Centennial Exhibition*, Philadelphia, 1876, p. 743). Mark Twain was listed among the authors expected to attend (New York *Herald*, 1 July 1876, p. 6), and although as late as 8 June he was undecided about going to Philadelphia (SLC to "Dear Sir," Hartford, 1876 [misdated 1877 in the published version], *Twainian,* February 1944, p. 5), he almost certainly did attend (SLC to Mrs. Abel W. Fairbanks, Hartford, 1 September 1876, MTMF, p. 202). His dignified eight-hundred-word eulogy of Francis Lightfoot Lee was published as one of a series of the tributes prepared by members of the Congress of Authors, in *Pennsylvania Magazine*, I (1877), No. 3, pp. 343–347. (See also George H. Brownell, "Mark Twain's Tribute to

Francis Lightfoot Lee," *Twainian,* November 1943, pp. 1–3; Milo M. Quaife, "George in Historyland," *Twainian,* January 1944, pp. 5–6.) Howells's visit on 3 July must have been for the purpose of attending the elaborate ceremonies on 4 July commemorating the signing of the Declaration of Independence.

124. HOWELLS TO CLEMENS

[Townsend Harbor, Mass.] Aug. 5, 1876.

My dear Clemens:

I wrote you a long and affectionate letter just before you left Hartford, and you replied with a postal card; on which instantly forgetting all the past kindnesses between us, I dropped you. You may not have known it but I did. Now I find I can't very well get on without hearing from you, and I wish you would give me your news — what you are doing, thinking, saying. We went first to our Shaker place in Shirley Village, but that proved a wonderful failure, and ten days ago we came away to this place — Townsend Harbor, Mass., — where we find ourselves in the utmost clover, and where we propose to stay till November. — I've just finished my comedy, "Out of the Question," [1] with a fair degree of satisfaction, and now I'm about to begin a campaign life of Hayes,[2] which Mr. Houghton wants to publish. (You know I wrote the Life of Lincoln which elected him.) I expect that it will sell; at any rate I like the *man,* and shall like doing it. Gen. Hayes is Mrs. Howells's cousin, and *she* thinks that any one who votes for Tilden will go to the Bad Place.

What are you doing with your double-barrel novel? Now that books are so dreadfully dead,[3] why don't you think of selling it to the Atlantic for next year? Mr. Houghton wants me to ask you to name a price, and he promises to prosecute anybody who copies it.

My wife joins me in cordial regards to Mrs. Clemens.

Yours ever

W. D. Howells.

1. It would appear in the *Atlantic,* February–April 1877.

2. The biography was turned out on schedule and published on 15 September 1876 (Gibson and Arms, *Howells Bibliography,* 76-C, p. 26).

3. Presumably because of the continued effects of the Panic of 1873.

125. CLEMENS TO HOWELLS

Elmira, Aug. 9 [1876].

My Dear Howells:

I was just about to write you, when your letter came — & not on one of those obscene postal cards, either, but reverently, upon paper.

I shall read that biography, though the letter of acceptance [1] was amply sufficient to corral my vote without any further knowledge of the man. Which reminds me that a campaign club in Jersey City wrote a few days ago & invited me to be present at the raising of a Tilden & Hendricks flag there & take the stand & give them some "counsel." Well, I could not go, but gave them counsel & advice by letter, & in the kindliest terms as to the raising of the flag — advised them "not to raise it."

Get your book out quick, for this is a momentous time. If Tilden is elected I think the entire country will go pretty straight to Mrs. Howells's bad place.

I am infringing on your patent — I started a record of our children's sayings, last night.[2] Which reminds me that last week I sent down & got Susie a vast pair of shoes of a most villainous pattern, for I discovered that her feet were being twisted & cramped out of shape by a smaller & prettier article. She did not complain, but looked degraded & injured. At night her mamma gave her the usual admonition when she was about to say her prayers — to-wit:

"Now, Susie — think about God."

"Mamma, I can't, with these shoes."

The farm is perfectly delightful, this season. It is as quiet & peaceful as a South-sea island. Some of the sun-sets which we have witnessed from this commanding eminence were marvelous.

One evening a rainbow spanned an entire range of hills with its mighty arch, & from a black hub resting upon the hill-top in the exact centre, *black* rays diverged upward in perfect regularity to the rainbow's arch & created a very strongly defined & altogether the most majestic, magnificent, & startling half-sunk wagon wheel you can imagine. After that, a world of tumbling & prodigious clouds came drifting up out of the west & took to themselves a wonderfully rich & brilliant *green* color — the decided green of new spring foliage. Close by them we saw the intense blue of the skies, through rents in the cloud-rack, & away off in another quarter were drifting clouds of a delicate pink color. In one place hung a pall of dense black clouds, like compacted pitch-smoke. And the stupendous wagon wheel was still in the supremacy of its unspeakable grandeur. So you see, the colors present in the sky at one & the same time were blue, green, pink, black, & the vari-colored splendors of the rainbow. All strong & decided colors, too. I don't know whether this wierd & astounding spectacle most suggested heaven, or hell. The wonder with its constant, stately, & always surprising changes, lasted upwards of two hours, & we all stood on the top of the hill by my study till the final miracle was complete & the greatest day ended that we ever saw.

Our farmer, who is a grave man, watched that spectacle to the end, & then observed that it was "dam funny."

The double-barreled novel lies torpid. I found I could not go on with it. The chapters I had written were still too new & familiar to me. I may take it up next winter, but cannot tell yet. I waited & waited, to see if my interest in it would not revive, but gave it up a month ago & began another boys' book — more to be at work than anything else. I have written 400 pages on it — therefore it is very nearly half done. It is Huck Finn's Autobiography. I like it only tolerably well, as far as I have got, & may possibly pigeonhole or burn the MS when it is done.[3]

So the comedy is done, & with a "fair degree of satisfaction." That rejoices me, & makes me mad, too — for *I* can't plan a comedy, & what have you done that God should be so good to you? I have racked myself baldheaded trying to plan a comedy-harness for some promising characters of mine to work in, & had to give it up. It is a noble lot of blooded stock & worth no end of money, but they must stand in the stable & be profitless. I want to be present when the comedy is produced, & help enjoy the success. —

Warner's book [4] is mighty readable, I think. Love to Ye's.

Ys Ever

Mark.

Mrs. Clemens sends her love & warm regards to the two of you respectively. That is what I understood her to mean.

You better give that campaign book to Bliss — but *don't* tell Houghton I suggested it. It's my sentiments, though.

1. Hayes's letter accepting the Republican nomination, dated 7 August 1876, pledges the candidate to a single term as President in order to eliminate all temptation to use patronage as a means to re-election; advocates civil service reform, resumption of specie payments, protection of the public schools against sectarian interference, and enforcement of the recent amendments to the Constitution; and promises a "policy which will wipe out forever the distinction between North and South" (Charles R. Williams, *The Life of Rutherford Birchard Hayes*, 2 vols., Boston, 1914, I, 460–462).

2. "A Record of Small Foolishnesses," the journal in which Clemens recorded the remarks of his daughters over a period of some nine years. The unpublished MS is now in the possession of Clifton Waller Barrett of New York; there is a typescript in MTP.

3. Fortunately, when he broke off at this first stage in the writing of *Huckleberry Finn*, Mark Twain did not burn his MS but put it aside to take it up again in 1879 or 1880 and then to finish it in 1883 (Walter Blair, "When Was *Huckleberry Finn* Written?" AL, XXX, 1–25, March 1958).

4. *My Winter on the Nile, among the Mummies and Moslems,* published in 1876 by the American Publishing Co.

126. HOWELLS TO CLEMENS

[Townsend Harbor, Mass.] Aug. 20, 1876.

My dear Clemens:

Why don't you come out with a letter, or speech, or something, for Hayes? I honestly believe that there isn't another man in the country who could help him so much as you. Do think the matter seriously over.

I'm making an enormous quantity of copy in a very brief time,[1] and my love is longer than my letter can be. Mrs. Howells and I delighted in that speech of Susie's — it was charming; and I must tell you one of Bua's in return. I'm sorry to say that he picked up at Shirley the habit of profane swearing, of which he broke himself with many tears and groans. The other night, here, he had nightmares, and I went to him as usual. He wanted, of course, to make conversation, so as to prolong the interview, and asked if I thought his B.D. (bad dream) came from something he'd eaten for supper. I said I thought not. "Then do you suppose it was something the matter with the *prayers?*" (He prays before going to sleep for 15 minutes, lying with his hands folded like the effigy of a crusader.) "I *told* him (the Almighty) that I hadn't *sworn* that day"!   Yours ever

W. D. Howells.

1. The campaign biography of Hayes. As Howells boasts in his letter of 8 September, he wrote it in twenty-two days.

127. CLEMENS TO HOWELLS

Elmira, Aug. 23 [1876].

My Dear Howells:

I am glad you think I could do Hayes any good, for I have been wanting to write a letter or make a speech to that end. I'll be careful not to do either, however, until the opportunity comes in a natural, justifiable & unlugged way; & shall not then do anything unless I've got it all digested & worded just right. In which case I *might* do some good — in any other I should do harm. When a humorist ventures upon the grave concerns of life he must do his job better than another man or he works harm to his cause.

Very greatly did we enjoy the suggestion in Johnny's remark that the Almighty had hardly dealt fairly by him — & the apparent conviction that a day void of profanity was necessarily void of sin justly punishable by nightmare.

We think that both of our children are developing whooping-cough — which is unfortunate, for it is getting pretty cold here, now, & we want to get away homeward Sept. 5.

The farce [1] is wonderfully bright & delicious, & *must* make a hit. You read it to me, & it was mighty good; I read it last night & it was better; I read it aloud to the household this morning & it was better than ever. So it would be worth going a long way to see it well played; for without any question an actor of genius always adds a subtle something to any man's work that none but the writer knew was there before. Even if *he* knew it. I have heard of readers convulsing audiences with my "Aurelia's Unfortunate Young Man." [2] If there is anything really funny in the piece, the author is not aware of it.

All right — advertise me for the new volume. I send you herewith a sketch [3] which will make 3 1/2 pages of the Atlantic. If you like it & accept it, you must get it into the *December* No., (Nov. 15, ain't it?) because I shall read it in public in Boston the 13th & 14th of Nov.[4] If it went in a month earlier it would be too old for me to read *except* as old matter; & if it went in a month later it would be too old for the Atlantic — do you see? And if you wish to use it, will you set it up *now*, & send me 3 proofs? — one to correct for Atlantic, one to send to Temple Bar (shall I tell them to use it not earlier than their November No?) & one to use in practising for my Boston readings.

We must get up a less elaborate & a much better skeleton-plan for the Blindfold Novels & make a success of that idea. David Gray [5] spent Sunday here & said we could but little comprehend what a rattling stir that thing would make in the country. He thought it would make a mighty strike. So do I. But with only 8 pages to tell the tale in, the plot must be less elaborate, doubtless. What do you think?

When we exchange visits I'll show you an unfinished sketch

of Elizabeth's time [6] which shook David Gray's system up pretty exhaustively.   Ys Ever

Mark.

1. "The Parlor Car," in the *Atlantic* for September.

2. A sketch by Mark Twain published first in the San Francisco *Californian* on 22 October 1864 under the title "Whereas." It was reprinted in *The Celebrated Jumping Frog of Calaveras County, and Other Sketches* (1867) and again in *Sketches, New and Old* (1875) under the title which Mark Twain uses here (DE, VII, 305–309).

3. "The Canvasser's Tale," which appeared in the *Atlantic* for December 1876, as he stipulated (DE, XIX, 369–377).

4. Clemens had agreed to give a series of readings in James Redpath's lyceum series. During November 1876 he appeared on the same program with several musicians in Brooklyn and Providence as well as in Boston. But he did not, after all, read "The Canvasser's Tale" in Boston. His readings there (at the Music Hall on 21 November and at the Chelsea Academy of Music on 23 November) consisted of "The Experiences of the McWilliamses with the Membranous Croup" and "My Late Senatorial Secretaryship" from *Sketches, New and Old,* and "An Encounter with an Interviewer," which had appeared in *Lotos Leaves* in 1875 (Boston *Transcript,* 18 November 1876, p. 6; 22 November, p. 5).

5. Editor of the Buffalo *Courier.*

6. The celebrated exercise in ribaldry, *1601. Conversation, As It Was by the Social Fireside, in the Time of the Tudors,* privately printed in 1880 and often subsequently, but never officially published.

128. HOWELLS TO CLEMENS

Cambridge, Sept. 8, 1876.

My dear Clemens:

Of course I was glad to get the little paper,[1] and I'll print it in December. I fancied I traced its origin to that story of the cave-collector,[2] but I didn't enjoy it the less on that account, nor think it the less yours. It came to me at Townsend Harbor, just as I was leaving for Cambridge, and when I got to Cambridge I was seized with dysentery. I had to keep at work on my Hayes book, all the time, and you can imagine that other things went out of my mind. I beg your pardon for the delay.

I finished the book yesterday, having written it in twenty-two days, and read for it as I wrote. It was a terrible pull. They expect to publish it on Monday,[3] and of course I'll send you a copy at once.

Do you intend to speak or write any politics? I hope you do, though I recognize the difficulties you speak of. I may as well own that it was I who set the National Committee at you.

I'm to be here till Tuesday. Remember me to Mrs. Clemens, who I know likes the Parlor Car though she didn't say so. Think of my being accused of drawing illogical women! It's too bad. — How I wish I could see you!   Yours evermore

                                                      W. D. Howells.

1. "The Canvasser's Tale," about a man who collects echoes.
2. The allusion is obscure.
3. Hurd & Houghton brought out Howells's campaign biography of Hayes between 11 and 15 September. It shows the marks of haste, is decidedly inferior to the 1860 life of Lincoln, and sold fewer than three thousand copies; but it earned him great influence in the White House — which he used sparingly and discreetly. He could have had an ambassadorship.

129. HOWELLS TO CLEMENS

                                    [Cambridge] Sept. 10, 1876.

Dear Clemens:

Here is a very curious story which was given my sister.[1] She passed it over to me, and it struck me as being just in your line. See if you can't make something of it.

Yes, we *must* try the Blindfold Novelettes for next year. It'll be a great feature, I believe. Send me any modification of plot that occurs to you.   Yours ever

                                                      W. D. Howells.

1. Very probably Anne Thomas Howells, herself a writer. In brief, the story was this. At the death of an aged farmer in a New England country town, wealthy Boston relatives had sent the coffin, with a silver plate, for the old man's burial. But the elderly sexton of the village could not bring himself to bury the precious silver. When the widow indignantly rejected his proposal to remove it before interment, he took it upon himself to remove the plate after everyone had left the burial ground, and finally hid it in the old sounding board over the pulpit. Years later, workmen remodeling the church building as a school came across the plate, and it was given to a grandson from the city. The grandson's family, unhappy with this *memento mori* in their midst, then sent the plate to an uncle in the West who was something of an antiquarian. The uncle, in turn, greatly shocked, sent his father's coffin plate back to the home village in New England, and the by now ancient sexton buried the silver plate in the old man's grave where it belonged. Howells seems to have thought that the chance to satirize Yankee parsimony or the opportunity for graveyard humor would interest Clemens.

130. CLEMENS TO HOWELLS

[Hartford] Sept. 14 [1876].

My Dear Howells:

Yes, the collection of caves was the origin of it. I changed it to echoes because these being invisible & intangible, constituted a still more absurd species of property, & yet a man could really own an echo, & sell it, too, for a high figure — such an echo as that at the villa Simonetti, two miles from Milan,[1] for instance. My first purpose was to have the man make a collection of caves & *afterwards* of echoes, but perceived that the element of absurdity & impracticability was so nearly identical as to amount to a repetition of an idea.

I am reading & enjoying the biography. It is a marvelous thing that you read for it & wrote it in such a little bit of a time, let alone conduct a dysentery at the same time — when I have that disease, even mildly, I can write absolutely nothing. Warner had a good & appreciative review of the book in yesterday's paper.[2] He put down everything else to attend to that. I like W. better & better, every day.[3] I have had prejudices & dislikes, there, but I think they have worn themselves out, now. I believe Mrs. Clemens is as blindly fond of him as she is of you — which is a great argument with me, because her instincts in the perception of worth are always truer than mine.

I will not & do not believe that there is a possibility of Hayes's defeat, but I want the victory to be sweeping. Every little helps. Now haven't you somebody handy who can make a ten-cent book, to be given away, of this nature, to-wit: A miniature volume, with a page the size of a postage stamp, with this title-page: "What Mr. Tilden has done for His Country." And put in it paragraphs like this:

"In October, 1862 I contributed $7,000 toward the public revenues for the patriotic purpose of prosecuting the war against rebellion."

Put into the little volume all the services which Tilden has unselfishly rendered his country — you see the book should be sized according to the material his career is able to furnish.

Then make this pygmy book fast, with a string — or tack it inside the cover, of a 12 or 24 or 8vo (according to materials,) to bear this title-page: "What Mr. Tilden has done for Himself." This book should be paragraphed thus:

"In October, 1862, I raised my right hand, & kissed a book, & for this service allowed myself $20,000 or $30,000 of government money, my time being valuable & this compensation not seeming to me exorbitant."

And so forth & so on. Read the enclosed slip from the Courant.[4] Such a book, issued 2 or 3 weeks before election, might help, some. It is a book that anybody can write, with a campaign file of the N.Y. Times to get his material from. I would write it myself if I had the time & the materials, though I would of course question the wisdom and also the propriety of putting my name to such a piece of work.

It seems odd to find myself interested in an election. I never was before. And I can't seem to get over my repugnance to reading or thinking about politics, yet. But in truth I care little about any party's politics — the man behind it is the important thing.

You may well know that Mrs. Clemens liked the Parlor Car — enjoyed it ever so much, & was indignant at you all through, & kept exploding into rages at you for ⟨drawing such⟩ pretending that such a woman ever existed — closing each & every explosion with "But it is just what such a woman would do" — "It is just what such a woman would say." They all voted the Parlor Car perfection — except me. I said they wouldn't have been allowed to court & quarrel there so long, uninterrupted; but at each critical moment the odious train-boy would come in & pile foul literature all over them four or five inches deep, & the lover would turn his head aside & curse — & presently that train-boy would be back again (as on all those western roads) to take up the literature & leave prize candy.

Of course the thing is perfect, in the magazine, without the train-boy; but I was thinking of the stage & the groundlings. If the dainty touches went over their heads, the train-boy, & other possible interruptions would fetch them every time. Would it mar the flow of the thing too much to insert that devil? I thought it over a couple of hours & concluded it wouldn't, & that he ought to be in for the sake of the groundlings (& to get new copyright on the piece.) —

And it seemed to me that now that the fourth act is so successfully written, why not go ahead & write the 3 preceding acts? And then after it is finished, let me put into it a low-comedy character (the girl's or the lover's father or uncle) & gobble a big pecuniary interest in your work for myself. Do not let this generous proposition disturb your rest — but *do* write the other 3 acts, & then it will be valuable to managers. And don't go & sell it to anybody, like Harte, but keep it for yourself.

Harte's play [5] can be doctored till it will be entirely acceptable & then it will clear a great sum every year. I am out of all patience with Harte for selling it. The play entertained me hugely, even in its present crude state.

That is a good story of your sister's, but I don't think I could make it go except in one fashion — by taking the idea & applying it in some other way, as I did with the caves, & do with pretty much everything. There are few stories that have anything superlatively good in them except the *idea*, — & that is always bettered by transplanting.

But Aldrich has genius enough to get over that difficulty. The man that wrote Marjorie Daw would make an admirable thing of the perplexities of these people, I should think.

I was going to enclose it, for Aldrich, but I think I won't, yet. I'll wait. By & by the story will grab hold of me, maybe.

Pardon the length of this. Love to you all.

Ys Ever

Mark.

1. Described in *The Innocents Abroad* (DE, I, 195–196).

2. "Howells's Life of Hayes. A Capital Biography of a Strong Man," Hartford *Courant,* 12 September 1876, p. 1.

3. The Warners had returned in July from almost two years of travel in Europe and the Near East, and the Clemenses had renewed their association with their neighbors upon their return to Hartford from Elmira on 11 September.

4. The clipping is not extant.

5. *Two Men of Sandy Bar,* which was first produced at the Union Square Theatre, New York, on 28 August 1876, and ran until 30 September (T. Allston Brown, *A History of the New York Stage,* 3 vols., New York, 1903, III, 155). Clemens probably saw it when he passed through New York en route from Elmira to Hartford.

131. CLEMENS TO HOWELLS

[Hartford, 21 September 1876]

Look here, Howells, it is going to be time, now, pretty soon, for some of Grant's blacklegs to retire from the consulships & render them into the hands of stainless literary incapables — of whom Stoddard [1] is one of which.

Now I'll be fair with you. I'll tell you what I will do. If you will sit down & be the first office-seeker in the field, & write a letter & ask Gov. Hayes to replace, with Stoddard, the first blackguard he catches in a consulship after the fourth of next March, I will agree to support my brother *myself,* all through the administration; otherwise I will throw him upon the government — as he did with himself in Mr. Lincoln's time. My brother has the strongest possible claims upon Gov. Hayes, too; because it was my brother's sagacious desertion of the republican party three months ago (he is simply hell on political sagacity, as St Chrysostom would say) that made Mr. Tilden's coming defeat so inflexibly & implacably & absolutely certain. I can always tell which party's funeral is appointed if I can find out how my brother has made up his mind to vote. For some inscrutable reason God never allows him to vote right. (I believe I told you once about my brother's religious gymnastics? Well, I have some late news under that head: he is getting stuck after the Mohammedan plan of salvation, now.)

Poor, sweet, pure-hearted, good-intentioned, impotent Stoddard, I have known him 12 years, now, & in all that time he has never been fit for anything but a consul. When I was at the Langham Hotel in London [2] I hired him for 3 months, at $15 a week & board & lodging, to sit up nights with me & dissipate. At the end of the time he wouldn't take a cent. I had to finally smuggle it to him through Dolby [3] after leaving England. Stoddard's got no worldly sense. He is just the stuff for a consul. Don't you think so? Now *you* ought to know, you know. You ought to know about these things. Now you pitch in & leg for him. Get a quiet consulship *created,* at Terra del Fuego, if there shouldn't be a vacancy.

You are to answer my interminable letters only with postal cards, you understand. I write long, because I'm idle.

Ys Ever

Mark.

1. Charles Warren Stoddard (1843–1909), a rather neurasthenic minor poet, had grown up in San Francisco, where Clemens had met him in the 1860's, probably in the office of the *Golden Era.* In the spring of 1876 he had set out on an extended tour of Egypt and Asia Minor which he was financing precariously by free-lance correspondence for newspapers.

2. During the winter of 1873–74.

3. George Dolby, the manager of Mark Twain's lecture tour in England in 1873–74.

[Pepperell,[1] Mass., 22 September 1876]

All right. C. W. S.[2] shall be inspector of consulates. He's in too good repair for a resident consul. Epilepsy or softening of the brain is requisite: a game arm will not do.[3] He should be bedridden, if he wishes a consulate-general. I have a long letter to write you from Cambridge.   Yours

W. D. H.

1. A town in northern Massachusetts a few miles from Townsend Harbor, where the Howellses were spending the latter part of their summer.
2. Charles Warren Stoddard.
3. In 1874 Stoddard had suffered a badly broken arm when his horse fell with him during a night ride in the Campagna (Stoddard to SLC, Venice, 24 February 1875, MTP).

[Cambridge] Oct. 8, 1876.

My dear Clemens:

I think with you that the notion of the Blindfold Novelettes oughtn't to be dropped. The difficulty is to get people to write them. You would do it and so would I, but Aldrich is doubtful. Do you think Warner would do one? If I could scrape up four or five authors, I'd be all right. If you'll simplify the skeleton of the story, and send me your new plot, I'll try again. I know the thing would be a great card for the magazine, and the owners are crazy over it.

— I wrote you that I would leg like a centipede for C. W. Stoddard, whose virtue-ward-leaning frailties I love and admire. But it would be well to get David Gray to make interest with Tilden, wouldn't [it], too? Nobody knows what is going to happen. The only certainty is that the Life of Hayes hasn't sold

2000 copies. There's success for you. It makes *me* despair of the Republic, I can tell you. And the bills continue to come in with unabated fierceness.

— Mrs. Howells and I in our own political eclipse, still rejoice in your effulgence. Your speech [1] was civil service reform in a nutshell. You are the only Republican orator quoted without distinction of party by all the newspapers,[2] and I wish you could have gone largely into the canvass. Lowell was delighted with your hit at plumbers. — In a few days I'll send you the proof of your too-small contribution for December.[3] Couldn't you let me have something for January?   Yours ever

W. D. Howells.

1. See Appendix.

2. The speech, short as it was, clearly followed the line of the reformers who made up the left wing of Hayes's supporters, and it naturally irritated journals committed to party regularity and orthodoxy. The Boston *Transcript* said that "somebody should have led him [Clemens] from the platform by the ear," and added: "A political speech setting out with a richly and racily illuminated catalogue of all the sins charged upon the party in power could hardly have been what the average Connecticut partisan was looking for, even from Mark Twain" (3 October 1876, p. 4). But the Chicago *Tribune* (7 October 1876, quoted in Vogelback, "Literary Reputation," p. 13) said that Mark Twain was "received with much favor" by his audience.

3. "The Canvasser's Tale."

134. HOWELLS TO CLEMENS

[Cambridge] Oct. 10, 1876.

My dear Clemens:

We begin our Contributors' Club in January. Do send me at least a ¶, spitting your spite at somebody or something. Write it as if it were a passage from a private letter.[1]

Yours ever

W. D. Howells.

1. Mark Twain's anonymous paragraph in the first Contributors' Club of the *Atlantic* (XXXIX, 108, January 1877), one of many new fea-

tures in the magazine during Howells's editorship, took for a text Anna Dickinson's second attempt on the stage. His point was that "genius itself succeeds only by arduous self-training," and he predicted, accurately, her failure. It would serve, he concluded, as a "knock-down hint to the effect that to do a thing you must learn how; and that to play on the fiddle it is not merely necessary to take a bow and fiddle with it."

135. CLEMENS TO HOWELLS

Hartford, Oct. 11 [1876].

My Dear Howells:

I don't believe I am going to be able to do anything for Jany. No. We shall see.

I have put in this whole day clearing off a fortnight's accumulating correspondence — have just sent the result to the post-box — an arm-full of letters. Think of a whole day wasted in such exasperating folly. It is enough to make a man say dern.

Now I propose to take it out of *you*. I will sit here & write to you till I drop.

In the first place you will have to do me a favor — for I don't somehow feel like trusting anybody else. It is a secret, to be known to nobody but you (of course I comprehend that Mrs. Howells is part of you) that Bret Harte came up here the other day & asked me to help him write a play & divide the swag, & I agreed. I am to put in Scotty Briggs (see Buck Fanshaw's Funeral, in Roughing It), & he is to put in a Chinaman (a wonderfully funny creature, as Bret presents him — for 5 minutes — in his Sandy Bar play.[1]) This Chinaman is to be *the* character of the play, & both of us will work on him & develop him. Bret is to draw a plot, & I am to do the same; we shall use the best of the two, or gouge from both & build a third. My plot is built — finished it yesterday — six days' work, 8 or 9 hours a day, & has nearly killed me.

Now the favor I ask of you is that you will have the words

157

"Ah Sin, a Drama," printed in the middle of a note-paper page, & send the same to me, with bill. We don't want anybody to know that we are building this play. I can't get this title-page printed here without having to lie so much that the thought of it is disagreeable to one reared as I have been. And yet the *title* of the play must be *printed* — the rest of the application for copyright is allowable in penmanship.

Of course I haven't had time to even glance at Mr. Boot's music, but I'm going to. I met Miss Kellogg the other day, & she was vastly cordial, but I'm done offering music to any villain that yawps on a stage, be he male or female.

To have such a sweat as I had with that woman over that piece of music is a sufficiency of that sort of thing. Kellogg says she's coming to our house the first chance she gets; then I'll let her sing this piece; & if she likes it & wants it & *says* so, like a man, she shall have it; but I ain't going to give her any more chances to act the son of a gun with Mr. Boott & me. I wish you'd tell Mr. Boott I like this song ever so much — because I know I shall like it.

We have got the very best gang of servants in America, now. When George [2] first came he was one of the most religious of men. He had but one fault — young George Washington's. But I have trained him; & now it fairly breaks Mrs. Clemens's heart to hear George stand at that front door & lie to the un-welcome visitor. But your time is valuable; I must not dwell upon these things.

I am mighty sorry that book does not sell better; but don't you worry about Hayes.

He is as bound to go to the White House as Tilden is to go to the devil when the last trump blows. I don't worry the least in the world, since my brother went over to the enemy. If you knew him as well as I do you would have confidence in him. His instinct to do the wrong thing is absolutely unerring.

But I must not dwell upon these things. I'll ask Warner & Harte if they'll do Blindfold Novelettes. Some time I'll simplify that plot. All it needs is that the hanging & the marriage shall not be appointed for the same day. I got over that difficulty, but it required too much MS to reconcile the thing — so the movement of the story was clogged.

I came near agreeing to make political speeches with our candidate for Governor the 16th & 23d inst., but I had to give up the idea, for Harte & I will be here at work then. (Of course the printers *would* leave off the word "gas-" from "pipe" in my remark about the plumbers,[3] thus marring the music & clearness of the sentence.)

But I will not dwell upon these things. Will you send me 3 proofs of my December article?[4] Corrected ones.

Yrs Ever

Mark.

Reply only with postal card. You've got writing enough to do without my burdening you.

I'll try to contribute to the Contributors' Club — you leave out our names, don't you?

"Reflect" is exactly the right word in the Echo article.[5] Scientists use no other in such places.

Please send me a couple more copies. *Corrected* copies, I mean. I couldn't read all that hogwash over again.

Check for $1,616.16 has just arrived — my clear profit on Raymond's first week in Philadelphia.[6] Write a drama, Howells.

1. *Two Men of Sandy Bar*, first produced on 28 August 1876.

2. George Griffin, the Clemenses' Negro butler and Admirable Crichton.

3. In the newspaper report of his speech. See Appendix.

4. "The Canvasser's Tale."

5. Again, "The Canvasser's Tale." The passage in question concerns a collector of echoes who, having bought one of two hills that together provide "the king echo of the universe," finds that a rival collector has bought the other, and in spite cuts down his hill so that "there would be nothing to reflect [his rival's] echo" (DE, XIX, 374).

6. John T. Raymond was producing and acting in Mark Twain's play *Colonel Sellers.*

159

136. CLEMENS TO HOWELLS

Hartford, Oct. 12 [1876].

My Dear Howells:

I see where the trouble lies. The various authors dislike trotting in procession behind me. I vaguely thought of that in the beginning, but did not give it its just importance. We must have a new deal.[1] The Blindfold Novelettes must be suggested anonymously. Warner says, let this anonymous person say his uncle has died & left him all his property — this property consisting of nothing in the world but the skeleton of a novel; he does not like to waste it, yet cannot utilize it himself because he can't write novels; he therefore begs writers to fill up the skeleton for him — in which way he hopes to get 6 or 8 novels in place of one, & thus become wealthy.

Now *I* would suggest that Aldrich devise the skeleton-plan, for it needs an ingenious head to contrive a plot which shall be prettily complicated & yet well fitted for lucid & interesting development in the brief compass of 10 Atlantic pages. My plot was awkward & overloaded with tough requirements.

Warner will fill up the skeleton — for one. No doubt Harte will; will ask him. Won't Mr. Holmes? Won't Henry James?[2] Won't Mr. Lowell, & some more of the big literary fish?

If we could ring in one or two towering names beside your own, we wouldn't have to beg the lesser fry very hard. Holmes, Howells, Harte, James, Aldrich, Warner, Trobridge, Twain — now there's a good & godly gang — team, I mean — everything's a team, now. —

If we fail to connect, here, I'll start it anonymously in Temple Bar & see if I can't get the English Authors to do it up handsomely. It would make a stunning book to sell on railway trains. But I believe we can make it go, here, with the proposition to come ano[n]ymously & Aldrich to construct the plot.

Yrs Ever

Mark.

1. This letter gives the phrase back to Mark Twain from Henry James, who, as Henry Seidel Canby has observed, caused his Lady Aurora to say in *The Princess Casamassima*, "Possibly you don't know that I am one of those who believe that a great new deal is destined to take place and that it can't make things worse than they are" (*Turn West, Turn East*, Boston, 1951, p. 180). James's use of the phrase (in the *Atlantic* in 1886) preceded by nearly three years Mark Twain's use of it in *A Connecticut Yankee*, where Franklin D. Roosevelt found it.

2. It is interesting that as early as 1876 Clemens includes Henry James so casually beside Holmes and Lowell in a list of "big literary fish." At this time James had published only two novels of consequence — *Roderick Hudson* and *The American*. Both had been serialized in the *Atlantic* under Howells's editorship, and Howells had no doubt brought to bear on Clemens the force of his unceasing efforts to persuade readers of James's merits. But Clemens wavered in the faith. After *The Bostonians* had been serialized in the *Century* along with *The Rise of Silas Lapham* and chapters from *Huckleberry Finn*, Clemens wrote to Howells that he "would rather be damned to John Bunyan's heaven" than read it (21 July 1885). Yet many years later, Clemens remarked of a French work on Joan of Arc: "If a master — say Henry James — should translate it I think it would live forever" (SLC to T. Douglas Murray, London, 31 January 1900, MTP; the letter was possibly never mailed).

137. HOWELLS TO CLEMENS

[Cambridge] October 18, 1876.

My dear Clemens:

I have been putting the Atlantic people up to a little enterprise, which I think will be a pretty thing, and I appeal to you with all the generosity of a man who knows he is asking a favor, to share in the impending prosperity. I have persuaded them to attempt a series of reprints of one-number stories from the Atlantic, with a page like the enclosed, to which they will fit an elegant cover and make the most stylish little book ever published in this country.[1]

Now why can't you let us start the Atlantic Series with your Carnival of Crime? It is a thing apart from your other writings, and wouldn't in the course of nature be collected into a volume of sketches for some years. This publication wouldn't hurt the volume, and it would put money in your purse, besides starting the Series brilliantly. Don't consent for my sake — you're capable of it! — but if you *can* consent with comfort and confidence, do it. — The print will be lifted and backed a little on the page so as to give a deep bottom and side margin, as in the Elzevirs.[2] We mean to make something exquisite. — I sent you the Ah-Sin titles some days ago. I shall be curious to know the outcome of your undertaking. I think Harte has acted crazily about the criticism of his play, but he's been shamefully decried and abused. Of course no man knows till he's tried how absurdly he'll act, but I wish Harte had not been tried.

> Yours ever
>
> W. D. Howells.

1. For whatever reason, Howells's project did not thrive, although Mark Twain did bring out a 32mo edition of *A True Story and the Recent Carnival of Crime* through James R. Osgood & Co. in September 1877. Howells's idea may, however, have resulted in the later Riverside Aldine Series, where the print was "lifted and backed a little on the page so as to give a deep bottom and side margin" and the composition and format were fine.

2. Howells must be referring to the books printed by the famous seventeenth-century family of Dutch printers.

138. CLEMENS TO HOWELLS (TELEGRAM)

> Hartford Ct Nov. 8th [1876]

To W. D. Howells
37 Concord Ave

I love to steal a while away[1] from every cumbering care and while returns come in today lift up my voice & swear[2]

> Plymouth Collection[3]

1. Concerning the author of the hymn "I Love to Steal a While Away," see letter 287, note 4.

2. Clemens is anxious about the election returns, which seem favorable to Tilden. Thirty years later, in his Autobiographical Dictation, he recalled that Bret Harte was visiting him at this time, and that he was astonished at Harte's indifference to the outcome of the election. Howells wrote to his father later in the month that Clemens was "the most comfortable Republican I have met in a long while; hereabouts, you know, they are a very lukewarm brotherhood" (Cambridge, 26 November 1876, Houghton). By 1907 Clemens had reversed his attitude toward the election, but he recalled that in 1876 he was "excited away up to the election limit, for that vast political conflagration was blazing at white heat which was presently to end in one of the Republican party's most cold-blooded swindles of the American people, the stealing of the presidential chair from Mr. Tilden, who had been elected, and the conferring of it upon Mr. Hayes, who had been defeated" (MTE, pp. 286–287).

3. The hymnbook published for the use of Henry Ward Beecher's Plymouth Church in Brooklyn.

139. CLEMENS TO HOWELLS (TELEGRAM)

Hartford Ct Nov 9th 1876

To W. D. Howells
  37 Concord Ave

Praise God from whom all blessings flow praise him all creatures here below praise him above ye heavenly host praise Father Son & Holy Ghost, The congregation will rise & sing [1]

Mark

1. The election returns look better for Hayes.

140. CLEMENS TO HOWELLS

[Hartford] Sunday Morning [26 Nov. 1876]

My Dear Howells:

All gone to church. Dean Sage is trying to persuade Twichell to travel in Europe 3 or 4 months with him.

163

The sideboard is perfectly satisfactory to Mrs. Clemens, & it will be ordered at once.

I was passing down Franklin street Friday morning, seeking Osgood's, when I stumbled upon a place (D P Ives & Co) where I hopped in to buy a trifle which I saw in the window — & when I emerged, 50 minutes later, I had drawn 5 checks on my bank. My, but they had a world of pretty things there. Time & again I got within 15 feet of the front door, & then saw something more which we couldn't do without.

Mrs. C. hopes Mr. Millett [1] can come — so do I.

We dined with the Warners yesterday eve., & the Twichells dropped in. Of course Warner hadn't any grudge against you — I told you that. I read Winnie's letter & poem — & they were received with great & honest applause. I return the letter herewith, according to promise.

"Hess" [2] (as the baby calls her) is at church — hence I write by mine own hand. Mrs. Clemens sends a lot of cordial messages to you two ⟨which I am beginning to believe, but I⟩ & I my grateful remembrances of a jolly good time at your home.

Saml. L C

It is no harm to put these words into wise old Omar-Khèyam's mouth, for he would have said them if he had thought of it.[3]

---

1. Frank Millet, artist and newspaper correspondent, whom the Clemenses wished to engage to do a portrait of Clemens. As Howells states in his letter of 30 November, Millet was on the point of setting out to report the Russo-Turkish War for the New York *Herald* and the London *Daily News* (LinL, I, 229), but he came to Hartford and painted the portrait before his departure (MTB, p. 583). The friendship thus begun lasted many years. At the time of his death on the *Titanic* in 1912 Millet was head of the American Academy at Rome (MTB, p. 1442).

2. Fanny C. Hesse, Clemens's secretary. She left his employ in 1877 ("A Record of Small Foolishnesses," TS, p. 9, MTP).

3. This allusion cannot be explained.

I WISH I HAD BEEN ON THAT ISLAND (1876)

[Cambridge] Nov. 30, 1876.

My dear Clemens:

Here is Millet's letter, received to-day. His terms are reasonable, certainly; but he seems bound to go.[1] I don't know when he means to come back. Perhaps you may think [it] worth while to write him. — There are two pictures for sale by that painter — Eugene Benson [2] — who did the oriental scene over Appleton's mantelpiece. I'll see them, and write you of them.

— You ought to write something better than that about Helen's Babbies.[3] You use expressions there that would lose us all our book-club circulation. Do attack the folly systematically and analytically — write what you said at dinner the other day about it.

— I am still looking up the spot-ivy business. I'm going to see Dr. Gray [4] about it, and get a bit of true spot to send you. — I doubt *both* the present specimens.

Your visit was a perfect ovation for us: we *never* enjoy anything so much as those visits of yours. The smoke and the Scotch and the late hours almost kill us; but we look each other in the eyes when [you] are gone, and say what a glorious time it was, and air the library, and begin sleeping and dieting, and longing to have you back again.[5] I hope the play [6] didn't suffer any hurt from your absence. Mrs. Howells, whom you talked to most about it, thinks it's going to be tremendously funny, and I liked all you told me of it.   Yours ever

W. D. Howells.

1. See note 1 to letter 140.
2. An American genre and figure painter.
3. A sentimental novel by John Habberton, published in 1876, which Mark Twain found peculiarly offensive. What seems to have disturbed him most in the book was the supposedly comic baby talk of two small boys being supervised by their bachelor uncle while their parents were on vacation.

4. Presumably Asa Gray, of Harvard, the eminent botanist.

5. Clemens had appeared in public readings on Redpath's lyceum circuit on 21 and 23 November (see note 4 to letter 127). Howells wrote of Clemens's visits during this period in MMT (p. 38): "Fully half our meetings were at my house in Cambridge, where he made himself as much at home as in Hartford. He would come ostensibly to stay at the Parker House, in Boston, and take a room, where he would light the gas and leave it burning, after dressing, while he drove out to Cambridge and stayed two or three days with us. Once, I suppose it was after a lecture, he came in evening dress and passed twenty-four hours with us in that guise, wearing an overcoat to hide it when we went out for a walk. Sometimes he wore the slippers which he preferred to shoes at home, and if it was muddy, as it was wont to be in Cambridge, he would put a pair of rubbers over them for our rambles. He liked the lawlessness and our delight in allowing it, and he rejoiced in the confession of his hostess, after we had once almost worn ourselves out in our pleasure with his intense talk, with the stories and the laughing, that his coming almost killed her, but it was worth it."

6. The collaborative undertaking of Mark Twain and Bret Harte, *Ah Sin.* Harte was staying in the Clemens house much of the time while the two men worked on the play (Isabella Beecher Hooker Diary, pp. 193–195 [entry for 1 December 1876], Connecticut Historical Society, TS in MTP).

142. HOWELLS TO CLEMENS

[Cambridge, 4 December 1876]

"What answer?" as our friend Miss Dickinson [1] would say.

MS. An endorsement on a two-page letter to Howells on the letterhead of *Belford's Monthly Magazine,* Toronto, dated 29 November 1876 and signed "Belford Bros.," asking whether arrangement can be made to publish Mark Twain's future contributions to the *Atlantic.* "We would be willing to pay liberaly for the right to publish them in the magazine," assert Belford Bros., "although the law allows us *to pirate* them." Howells's envelope is postmarked 4 December.

1. Anna E. Dickinson had published a novel about miscegenation entitled *What Answer?* in 1868 and Howells had reviewed it in the *Atlantic* for January 1869. See also note 7 to letter 115.

143. CLEMENS TO HOWELLS (POSTCARD)

[Hartford, 5 December 1876]

If there is another magazine in Toronto (or Montreal) I want to *give* it advanced sheets.[1] — Belford Bros., the miserable thieves couldn't buy a sentence from me for any money. *Is* there another magazine — I earnestly want to give advanced sheets to it. Tell me if there is.

S. L. C.

1. Clemens has in mind a general policy for the future. "The Canvasser's Tale" had already appeared in the December *Atlantic,* and except for an unsigned paragraph in the Contributors' Club for January, he had no other piece scheduled for publication in the magazine.

IV

GIVE ME YOUR PLAIN, SQUARE ADVICE

(1877–1879)

IV

(1877–1879)

"I have rung in that fragrant account of the Limberger cheese & the coffin-box full of guns. Had I better leave that out? Give me your plain, square advice, for I propose to follow it" (SLC to WDH, Munich, 30 January 1879, Houghton)

During 1877 *Ah Sin* failed in New York but Lawrence Barrett was able to keep his dramatization of Howells's *A Counterfeit Presentment* going for some thirty performances on the road, and Howells had the pleasure of hearing the play applauded in Boston. In May, Clemens and Twichell made the trip to Bermuda which Clemens described for the *Atlantic* in four installments of "Some Rambling Notes of an Idle Excursion." Not discouraged by the failure of *Ah Sin*, Clemens wrote a play called "Cap'n Simon Wheeler, The Amateur Detective," also intended for "the kitchen & stable" rather than the drawing room, which was fortunately never produced. His eagerness to reach a popular audience in the theatre was due in part to his need for money: as early as 1875 he had remarked to Howells, "my household expenses are something almost ghastly." The decision of the Clemenses to carry out a long-discussed plan of making an extended visit to Europe in order to escape the expenses and the social distractions of their life in Hartford was possibly hastened by what Howells called the "hideous mistake" of Clemens's comic speech at the Whittier Birthday Dinner in December 1877. The entire family, with Livy's friend Clara Spaulding and the German nursemaid Rosina Hay, sailed for Hamburg in April 1878, and proceeded by easy stages to Heidelberg. In August, Joseph Twichell joined Clemens for a month of leisurely travel through Germany, Switzerland, and France. The Clemenses then spent six weeks in Italy and established themselves for the winter in Munich, where Clemens struggled with the writing of *A Tramp Abroad*. They returned to the United States by way of Paris and London, landing in New York on 3 September and proceeding directly to Elmira. During the absence of the Clemenses, Howells supervised the build-

171

ing of his house in Belmont, continued his editing of the series of memoirs (of Gibbon, Marmontel, and others) he was preparing for Osgood, and completed *The Lady of the Aroostook,* which Clemens praised in the highest terms for its "truth to life."

144. CLEMENS TO HOWELLS

Hartford, Feb. 22 [1877]

My Dear Howells:

Here's a shout for Hayes! The fact is I was afraid to shout by telegraph last Sunday, I have been fooled so often.[1] I hope he will put Lt. Col. Richard Irwin Dodge (Author of "The Great Plains & their Inhabitants") at the head of the Indian Department.[2] *There's* a man who knows all about Indians, & yet has some humanity in him — (knowledge of Indians, & humanity, are seldom found in the same individual). Come! — it is high time we were fixing up this cabinet, my boy.

Look here — send postal to say you & the madam will be here 2^d or 3^d of March[3] — do, now, please. The play[4] is done. We are plotting out another one.   Yrs Ever

Mark.

P.S. — I suppose you got our letter[5] about the March visit a week or two ago?

1. Clemens's impulse to rejoice on Sunday, 18 February, was probably due to the fact that on Saturday the Hayes delegates to the electoral college were declared elected in Louisiana (Boston *Transcript,* 17 February 1877, p. 2) and most Southern Democrats in Congress decided to abandon the filibuster which had been delaying completion of the electoral count in the Hayes-Tilden imbroglio (Boston *Transcript,* 17 February 1877, p. 1). Further votes, speeches, and conversations in and out of Congress made the defection of the Southerners and the victory of Hayes more and more unmistakable during the next few days. By Thursday, when this letter was written, Hayes's advisers had decided the crisis was past (C. Vann Woodward, *Reunion and Reaction. The Compromise of 1877 and the End of Reconstruction,* Boston, 1951, pp. 177–182).

2. Although Howells sent this letter on to Hayes (Lyon N. Richardson, "Men of Letters and the Hayes Administration," NEQ, XV, 128, March

1942), Dodge was not appointed Commissioner of Indian Affairs.

3. Howells visited Hartford during March (WDH to CDW, Cambridge, 1 April 1877, Watkinson, LinL, I, 232) but the exact date is uncertain.

4. *Ah Sin,* written in collaboration with Bret Harte.

5. Not extant.

145. CLEMENS TO HOWELLS

[Hartford] Friday, AM [late March? 1877].

My Dear Howells:

Been reading Out of the ? aloud to the family & have just finished it. All hands bewitched with it. It is wonderful dialogue. It didn't seem wonderful (for *you*) when you read it to me. I think you have a gift or faculty of disguising the merit of your productions when you read them aloud. I *know* it, in fact. The Parlor Car was as much as 25 times better, in print, than it was when you read it to me.

My lawsuit is done.[1] The villain got only $300 out of me instead of $10,000, & his lawyer got *that.* My lawyer's bill & some little items, added to the $300 only swelled my expense to $800 — so I got off admirably well.

I began Orion's autobiography[2] yesterday & am charmed with the work. I have started him at 18, printer's apprentice, soft & sappy, full of fine intentions & shifting religions & not aware that he is a shining ass. Like Tom Sawyer he will stop where I start him, no doubt — 20, 21 or along there; can't tell; am driving along without plot, plan, or purpose — & enjoying it.

I had such a good time, at your house, but with a biting conscience all the time for stopping your wheels.

Yrs Ever

Mark.

(It was about the Switzerland matter.)[3]

All we Clemenses send warmest regards to all you Howellses.

MS. The date of this letter is established reasonably well by the reference to Howells's "Out of the Question," which ran serially in the

Atlantic February–April 1877. The play was published in book form on 25 April, but Clemens is probably referring to the last installment, which would have reached Hartford shortly after 15 March.

1. See Appendix.

2. The MS, untitled but called by Albert B. Paine "Autobiography of a Damned Fool," is in MTP (DV 310). It runs to 114 pp., with 9 pp. of notes. The story of course embodies many themes and incidents from Mark Twain's memories of Hannibal, and occasional hints of *Huckleberry Finn*, such as: "Listens to the printer-tramp & is charmed. Goes on a months expedition in summer with him, delivering temperance lectures & sermons & spreeing on the proceeds. 'BURNING SHAME' " (p. 9 of notes).

3. The postscript is intended to explain a long illegible cancellation. Clemens approached Longfellow and, through him, Lowell, in an effort to secure the appointment of Howells as United States minister to Switzerland (Henry W. Longfellow to SLC, Cambridge, 12 June 1877, MTP), despite the fact that when Horatio S. Noyes, Mrs. Howells's uncle and first cousin of President Hayes, sent Hayes a memorandum requesting that Howells might be "remembered in the distribution of the minor foreign appointments," Howells himself had written to W. K. Rogers, Hayes's secretary, asking that Noyes's memorandum be destroyed (Cambridge, 13 March 1877, LinL, I, 231–232). On 22 April, Howells wrote to his father: "You see the Swiss mission has been given to a Mr. Schneider of Chicago. I suppose I might have had it if I had tried for it, but I don't regret that the faint annoying hope that it might be offered in such a way as to make acceptance possible, is gone" (Cambridge, Houghton). George Schneider declined the appointment, and Nicholas Fish served as chargé d'affaires to Switzerland 1877–1881.

146. CLEMENS TO HOWELLS

[Hartford] Apr. 19 [1877].

My Dear Howells:

Many thanks. I was not intending to intrude on the President, but I shall certainly go now & present your letter [1] if there is a reception while I am in Washington — & of course there will be, as I shall be there a week or more.[2] I am mighty sorry you can't go.[3] Mrs. Howells ought to go now & not put it off — invitations from Presidents are so kind of seldom, you know.

Ys Ever

Mark.

1. A letter of introduction to President Hayes, who was Elinor Howells's cousin.

2. Clemens intended to go to Washington for the opening of *Ah Sin*.

3. The Howellses had refused an invitation to come to the White House for a visit. They consented to stay with the Hayeses only near the end of the President's term, when it was clear that he was retiring from office (Cady, *The Road to Realism*, p. 179).

147. CLEMENS TO HOWELLS

Baltimore, Apl. 27 [1877] (On the
stage of Ford's Theatre, 11
in the morning.

My Dear Howells —

I am needed every moment during these daily rehearsals,[1] but I *must* steal a second to wish you were here at this instant. There's a combat going on, of the most furious & earnest nature, between two men in every-day clothes, who rave & roar & fell each other with imaginary chairs & shoot each other with imaginary pistols & *pretend* to fall & die in agony & be thrown into the Stanislaus river — & by George all the other actors & actresses sit within 6 feet of them & calmly converse about the reasonable price of board in Baltimore!   Ys Ever

Mark.

1. *Ah Sin* was rehearsed in Baltimore for its opening at the National Theatre in Washington on 7 May.

148. CLEMENS TO HOWELLS

Baltimore May 1/76 [1]

My Dear Howells: Found I was not absolutely needed in Washington, so I only staid 24 hours, & am on my way home, now.[2] I called at the White House & got admission to Col.

Rodgers,[3] because I wanted to inquire what was the right hour to go & infest the President. It was my luck to strike the place in the dead waste & middle of the day, the very busiest time. I perceived that Mr. Rodgers took me for George Francis Train [4] & had made up his mind not to let me get at the President; so at the end of half an hour I took my letter of introduction from the table & went away. It was a great pity all round, & a loss to the nation, for I was brim full of the Eastern question.[5] I didn't get to see the President or the Chief Magistrate either, though I had a sort of glimpse of a lady at a window who resembled her portraits.   Yrs Ever

                                                        Mark

1. The date "76" is a slip of the pen.
2. Clemens was returning home because of an attack of bronchitis.
3. William K. Rogers, at one time Hayes's law partner, now his private secretary.
4. A well-known eccentric given to speeches, press interviews, and uninhibited behavior. He was imprisoned many times for various offenses, once on the charge that a journal he edited under the title the *Train Ligue* was obscene (Arthur L. Vogelback, "Mark Twain and the Fight for Control of the *Tribune*," AL, XXVI, 380 n, November 1954).
5. The crisis in the Balkans arising from the disintegration of the Turkish empire in Europe. Revolts had broken out in Bosnia and Herzegovinia which would lead to the Russo-Turkish War of 1877–78.

149. CLEMENS TO HOWELLS

                                        [Hartford, 5? May 1877]

Here is as pathetic a conjunction, Howells, as ever was: this forced hilarity & this broken-hearted face.[1]

2 1/2 years civil "practice" has yielded him just *one* case. He will try criminal law,[2] now, poor fellow.

                                                        Mark

MS. Clemens's note is an endorsement on a letter to him from his brother Orion (Keokuk, Iowa, 2 May 1877, MTP).

1. Orion began: "I enclose a picture of the leech that draws the blood that Col. Sellers makes."

2. Opposite Orion's statement that he hopes to "get Judge Newman at the August term to appoint me to assist in defending some scoundrel for misdemeanor or felony (*the latter penitentiary, the former under that degree*) . . . " Clemens writes in the margin: "the legal instinct to explain."

150. HOWELLS TO CLEMENS

[Cambridge] May 9, 1877.

My dear Clemens:

I was extremely vexed at the result of your attempt to see the President who would, I know, like to have seen you. If you and I had *both* been there, our combined skill would no doubt have procured us to be expelled from the White House by Fred Douglass.[1] But the thing seems to have been a tolerably complete failure as it was. "Try to *do* a G — d — man a G — d — kindness" — and you know how it turns out.

Your brother's letter has been a joy forever to Mrs. H. and me — and what a good kind face the poor old fellow has. I 'most hate to send it back.

I'm very glad to see by the papers that your play[2] started off well. You must have had an awful time working over it in Baltimore. I wish I could have been with you.

We all send regards to your household.   Yours ever
W. D. Howells.

1. United States Marshal for the District of Columbia (LinL, I, 234). Clemens called him "a personal friend" in January 1881, when he wrote President-elect Garfield asking that Douglass be retained in his position (Hartford, 12 January, MTL, p. 394).

2. *Ah Sin*, with Charles T. Parsloe in the title role, was well received on opening night (7 May, at the National Theatre, Washington). There were curtain calls after each act, and the house cheered a letter from Mark Twain explaining his absence which Parsloe read after the final curtain.

151. HOWELLS TO CLEMENS

[Cambridge] May 15, 1877.

My dear Clemens:

My translator in Switzerland [1] is an American woman, who, having turned A Foregone Conclusion into Italian, now fails to find a publisher for it.

I shouldn't at all know how to go about verifying the intentions, much less the existence of your correspondent. I wish I *could* be of use.

— I suppose you're going to sea for your health. [2] You're an enviable man to be able to go. I know *one* set of shaky nerves that can't.

Good bye and good luck.   Yours ever

W. D. Howells.

1. A letter from Clemens inquiring about Howells's translator in Switzerland has been lost. He had received a proposal for a French translation of *Tom Sawyer* dated 22 February 1877 from one L. J. Bribant [?] (Neuchâtel, MTP).

2. The lost letter must have announced Clemens's intention of making a trip to Bermuda with Joe Twichell, and, as Clemens's letter of 29 May indicates, must have invited Howells to go also at Clemens's expense.

152. CLEMENS TO HOWELLS

[Hartford] May 29 [1877].

Confound you, Joe Twichell & I roamed about Bermuda [1] day & night & never ceased to gabble & enjoy. — About half the talk was — "It is a burning shame that Howells isn't here;" "Nobody could get at the very meat & marrow of this pervading charm & deliciousness like Howells;" "How Howells would revel in the quaintness, & the simplicity of this people & the Sabbath repose of this land!" "What an imperishable sketch Howells would make of Capt. West the whaler, & Capt. Hope with the patient, pathetic face, wanderer in all the oceans for 43 years, lucky in none; coming home defeated once more, now, minus his ship — resigned, uncomplaining, being used to this;" "What a rattling chapter Howells would make out of the small boy Alfred, with his alert eye & military brevity & exactness of speech; & out of the old landlady; & her sacred onions; & her daughter; & the visiting clergyman; & the ancient pianos of Hamilton & the venerable music in vogue there — & forty other things which we shall leave untouched or touch but lightly upon, we not being worthy;" "*Dam* Howells for not being here!" (this usually from me, not Twichell.)

O, your insufferable pride, which will have a fall some day! If you had gone with us & let me pay the $50 which the trip, & the board & the various nick-nacks & mementoes would cost, I would have picked up enough droppings from your conversation to pay me 500 per cent profit in the way of the *several* magazine articles which I could have written, whereas I can now write only one or two[2] & am therefore largely out of pocket by your proud ways. Ponder these things. Lord, what a perfectly bewitching excursion it was! I traveled under an assumed name & was never molested with a polite attention from *any* body. Love to you all.   Yrs Ever

                                                                    Mark.

1. They sailed from New York on 16 May, arrived in Bermuda on 19 May, and sailed for New York on 24 May.

2. Clemens wrote four papers about the trip to Bermuda under the general title, "Some Rambling Notes of an Idle Excursion." They were published in the *Atlantic* (October 1877–January 1878; DE, XIX, 242–301). Of the topics mentioned in the letter, the old whaleship master, the young waiter Alfred, and the venerable pianos of Hamilton figure in the published notes.

A letter of 3 June from Clemens to Aldrich is addressed with transparent indirection to Howells as well. Clemens says that he intends to write a book "similar to your new one in the Atlantic . . . though I have not heard what the nature of that one is. Immoral, I suppose." He continues: "Well, you are right. Such books sell best, Howells says. Howells says he is going to make his next book indelicate. He says he thinks there is money in it. He says there is a large class of the young, in schools & seminaries who — but you let him tell you. He has ciphered it all down to a demonstration" (Hartford, Abernethy Library, Middlebury, Vt., TS in MTP).

153. CLEMENS TO HOWELLS

[Hartford] June 6/77.

My Dear Howells:

No sir, I wasn't blackguarding you for delaying to answer. Exactly the reverse. My letter was hardly out of my hand till I was saying, "There, it is gone, & I have forgotten to say, 'This needs no answer' — so I have gone & laid one more burden upon a man whose guards were in the water already — will never neglect that P.S. again." The debt was discharged when you sent the Hammond pamphlet [1] — & I so considered it. I took that to *be* your answer.

Autobiog's? [2] I didn't know there *were* any but old Franklin's & Benvenuto Cellini's. But if I should think of any I will mention them with pleasure.

I am more delighted about Barrett & the play than I can express.[3] I hope you get good terms out of him, & have drawn your contract from the standpoint that he is the blackest-livered scoundrel on earth. That is the standpoint of our contract with Parsloe,[4] who is a mighty good fellow & as gentle as a lamb.

Blast a man who lets on that he is going to buy a man's house, & then doesn't do it.[5] — However, there is a hell. That thought calms me even in my bitterest moments.

I have written two Numbers of my "Random Notes of an Idle Excursion" (you see that does not indicate whither the ship is bound & therefore the reader can't be saying "Why all this introduction — are we never coming to Bermuda?") The reader never discovers whither the ship *is* bound, until the last paragraph of the Second number informs him. It begins to look as if this Excursion may string out to 4 or 6 Numbers. Will re-read & correct & forward 1 & 2 when I get to Elmira. (We leave for there to-day.)

180

Now if you should print these things, couldn't you set them up 2 or 3 months before you are going to use them, so that I can have duplicate proofs & simultane with Temple Bar? [6]

The love of our crowd to yours.   Yrs Ever

Mark.

1. Not now identifiable.

2. Howells was planning his series of "Choice Autobiographies" which James R. Osgood & Co. and Houghton, Osgood & Co. would publish late in 1877 and early in 1878. The series eventually included the autobiographies of the Princess Sophia Wilhelmina of Prussia, Lord Herbert of Cherbury, Thomas Ellwood, Alfieri, Goldoni, Gibbon, and Marmontel.

3. The actor-manager-producer Lawrence Barrett was interested in Howells's comedy, *A Counterfeit Presentment*, which was to be serialized in the *Atlantic* from August through October 1877, and first produced in Cincinnati on 11 October.

4. Charles T. Parsloe, the actor who had played in *Ah Sin* briefly in May, and would take the play to New York at the end of July.

5. In the letter (now lost) to which Clemens is replying, Howells had evidently reported that his neighbor John Fiske, who he had hoped would buy the house at 37 Concord Ave., Cambridge, had decided to build rather than buy (WDH to Moncure D. Conway, Cambridge, 5 June 1877, Columbia, AGM TS).

6. The London magazine published by George Bentley.

154. HOWELLS TO CLEMENS

[Conanicut, R. I.] June 9, 1877.

My dear Clemens:

Send on I and III [1] as soon as they are ready, and I will have them put in type at once. If it is quite the same to you I would rather begin printing them in the October number. This, considering that the printers now have the August copy, is not so late as it seems. But let me know if you have any prejudices or preferences in the matter.

The wretch who sold you that type-writer has not yet come to a cruel death. In the meantime he offers me $20.00 for it. I never could regard it as more than a loan, so I ask you whether I shall sell it at that price, or pass it along to you at Elmira.

Barrett offered me $25 a night for the play anywhere outside of New York, and $50 a night there, and I agreed. Perhaps I could have made better terms, but to tell you the truth I was so knocked down by his taking the play that I couldn't summon all my rapacity to my aid on the instant. Of course I have been suffering for it ever since.

We have come down (by a sympathetic simultaneity with you,[2] on the 6th) to this island of Conanicut, near Newport, and are in a white fog that carries desolation to the soul. Our address is P.O. Box 160, Newport. I know now why you wished to kill your landlord and fellow boarders when in this region.[3] If Providence ever lets me get back to live in my own house, I don't *think* I'll leave it for a while. — I don't dare to tell Mrs. Howells how low I feel. She chipperly joins me in love to you all.

Yours ever
W. D. Howells.

I think your plan for the sketches capital.

1. Installments of "Some Rambling Notes of an Idle Excursion." "III" must be a slip of the pen for "II."

2. Howells means that he and his family left Cambridge for the seashore just as the Clemenses were leaving Hartford for their usual summer at Quarry Farm near Elmira.

3. The Clemenses had spent a couple of weeks at Bateman's Point, near Newport, in August 1875.

155. CLEMENS TO HOWELLS

The Farm, Elmira, June 14 [1877].

My Dear Howells:

Good for you. There are no better terms than those you got, except an equal division of profits — & the latter method costs a body $2000 a year for an agent's salary & expenses & is more wear & tear & trouble than keeping hotel.[1]

Yes, October suits me for these sketches. Shall send you the first two numbers tomorrow. I revised them to-day, & began No. 3. Isn't there some Montreal magazine I can sell or give them to, & thus beat Belford Bros., thieves, of Toronto? [2]

Sell the type-writer for $20? Yes. Do not lose this opportunity of swindling that reptile. I didn't lend you that thing; I *gave* it to you because you had been doing me some offense or other, & there seemed no other way to avenge myself; but I am placable now & am willing to take $10, you to take the other ten for commission, bother, express-expenses &c. Let us compromise on that.[3]

We had to remain at Mother's in Elmira [4] until yesterday, to let our youngest [5] have a run of fever & get back her strength. But we are housed here on top of the hill, now, where it is always cool, & still, & reposeful & bewitching.

The love of we'uns unto you'uns Yrs Ever

             Mark

1. Over a period of years Clemens had employed an agent to tour with John T. Raymond in order to make sure the actor correctly reported income and expenses in connection with *Colonel Sellers.*

2. Taking advantage of the ambiguous state of the law of international copyright, Belford Bros. had published unauthorized editions of the "Old Times on the Mississippi" papers in the *Atlantic* and of *Tom Sawyer,* and had sold copies both in Canada and in the United States (Andrew D. Chatto to Moncure D. Conway, London, 15 November 1876, MTP). Orion Clemens had stopped the sale of the Canadian edition of *Tom Sawyer* in Keokuk by threatening booksellers with legal proceedings, acting in this instance as an agent for the American Publishing Co. (Orion Clemens to Elisha Bliss, Jr., Keokuk, 1 February 1877, MTP). In 1876 the Belfords had established a magazine, *Belford's Monthly,* and Clemens feared they would now republish his articles from the *Atlantic* without authorization. Concerning the arrangement which he eventually made for publication in Canada of the "Rambling Notes," see note 5 to letter 164.

3. In a sketch published in *Harper's Weekly* in 1905 (18 March; collected under the title "The First Writing Machines," DE, XXIV, 227–228), Mark Twain said this first typewriter he bought "was full of caprices, full of defects — devilish ones. It had as many immoralities as the machine of to-day has virtues. After a year or two I found that it was degrading my character, so I thought I would give it to Howells. He was reluctant, for he was suspicious of novelties and unfriendly toward them, and he remains so to this day. But I persuaded him. He had great confidence in me, and I

got him to believe things about the machine that I did not believe myself. He took it home to Boston, and my morals began to improve, but his have never recovered." Mark Twain added, "He kept it six months, and then returned it to me. I gave it away twice after that, but it wouldn't stay; it came back." Clemens ended by giving the machine to Patrick McAleer, who traded it for a sidesaddle which he could not use.

4. The house of Mrs. Jervis Langdon, Livy's mother.

5. Clara, born in 1874.

156. CLEMENS TO HOWELLS

Elmira, June 27 [1877]

My Dear Howells:

If you should not like the first 2 chapters, send them to me & begin with Chap. 3 — or *Part* 3, I believe you call these things in the magazine. I have finished No. 4, which closes the series, & will mail it tomorrow if I think of it. I like this one, I liked the preceding one (already mailed to you some time ago) but I had my doubts about 1 & 2. Do not hesitate to squelch them, even with derision & insult.

To-day I am deep in a comedy [1] which I began this morning — principal character, that old detective — I skeletoned the first act & *wrote* the second, to-day; & am dog-tired, now. Fifty-four close pages of MS in 7 hours. Once I wrote 55 pages at a sitting — that was on the opening chapters of the Gilded Age novel. — When I cool down, an hour from now, I shall go to zero, I judge.

When does Barrett open in your piece [2] in N.Y (or Boston). I calculate to be there.   Ys Ever

Mark.

1. "Cap'n Simon Wheeler, The Amateur Detective."

2. *A Counterfeit Presentment,* which would open in Cincinnati on 11 October.

GIVE ME YOUR PLAIN ADVICE (1877–1879)

[Conanicut, R. I.] June 30, 1877.

Dear Clemens:

I have just simmered down to-day after nearly two weeks of arduous journeying and junketing. First I went to Quebec to my sister's wedding,[1] which was a very pleasant affair, and then I got back to Cambridge in time for the President's visit to Boston,[2] and then in Newport. Nothing can give you an adequate notion of the cordiality of his welcome, and you would have liked to see how *perfectly* he did his part. I was with his suite a great deal, breakfasted with him and met him at the Mayor's dinner.

My feeling was that on every occasion he was far the simplest and greatest man (except Longfellow and Emerson) present. — His son Webb and the young ladies of the party expressed their great regret at the failure of your attempt to see him in Washington. W. said his father would have been so glad to meet you, and the family would have been pleased to have you call at the White House. — Mrs. Howells kept your two letters about B. H. for me. I think *now* there is no danger of the national calamity [3] you feared, and I don't believe there ever was much. So I understood from W. H.[4]

I've just been reading aloud to my wife your Bermuda papers. That they're delightfully entertaining goes without saying; but we also found that you gave us the only realizing sense of Bermuda that we've ever had. I know that they will be a great success. — The fog has cleared off, and we're in raptures with Conanicut. Would that we could bring your hill-top to our shore! — That joke you put into Twichell's mouth advising you to make the most of a place that was *like* Heaven,[5] about killed us.   Yours ever

                                                    W. D. Howells.

1. Howells's sister Anne married Antoine Léonard Achille Fréchette, translator in the Canadian House of Commons, on 20 June.

2. On 26–28 June 1877 (Boston *Transcript,* 26 June 1877, p. 1; 28 June, p. 1).

3. The appointment of Bret Harte to a consulship. The bad feeling between Clemens and Harte, which had arisen while they were collaborating on the play *Ah Sin* during the autumn and winter of 1876, had been brought to a head by a letter Harte wrote to Clemens on 1 March 1877 (New York, TS in MTP). In it Harte accuses Clemens of being in some way to blame for Harte's financial misunderstanding with Elisha Bliss of the American Publishing Co. about advances and royalties on *Gabriel Conroy,* complains that Clemens had refused to lend him money when he needed it, declines with elaborate irony Clemens's offer to pay Harte "$25 per week and board" while they should collaborate on another play, and implies that Clemens has been "marring" *Ah Sin* by alterations. As a final thrust Harte added a postscript: "I have kept a copy of this letter." On the back of the last page Clemens wrote: "I have read two pages of this ineffable idiocy — it is all I can stand of it. S. L. C." In June 1877, Howells agreed with Clemens sufficiently to send on the "two letters about B. H." to Hayes. But remembering Harte's charm when he first came East from California and his present reform after a long decline into borrowing and drinking, Howells would recommend him for a consular position to the President a year later, glossing over none of Harte's past (LinL, I, 251–252). Howells's one condition was that his letter should be returned to him. He would help Harte if he could — but he would not risk his friendship with Clemens for Harte's sake.

4. Hayes's son Webb.

5. The joke is in Part III of the published text of "Some Rambling Notes": "We went ashore and found a novelty of a pleasant nature: there were no hackmen, hacks, or omnibuses on the pier or about it anywhere, and nobody offered his services to us, or molested us in any way. I said it was like being in heaven. The Reverend rebukingly and rather pointedly advised me to make the most of it, then" (DE, XIX, 272).

158. CLEMENS TO HOWELLS

Elmira, July 4 [–6 July 1877].

My Dear Howells —

It is *splendid* of you to say those pleasant things. But I am still plagued with doubts about Parts I & II.[1] If *you* have any, don't print. If otherwise, please make some cold villain like Lathrop[2] read & pass sentence on them. Mind, *I* thought they were good at first — it was the *second* reading that accomplished its hellish purpose on *me*. Put them up for a new verdict. Part IV has lain in my pigeon-hole a good while, & when I put it there I had a Christian's confidence in 4 aces in it; & you *can* ⟨bet⟩ be sure it will skip toward Conanticut tomorrow before any fatal fresh reading makes me draw my bet.

I've piled up 151 MS pages on my comedy. The first, second & fourth acts are done, & done to my satisfaction, too. — Tomorrow & next day will finish the 3d act & the play. I have not written less than 30 pages any day since I began. Never had so much fun over anything in my life — never such consuming interest & delight. (But Lord bless you the second reading will fetch it!)

And just think! — I had Sol Smith Russell [3] in my mind's eye for the old detective's part, & hang it he has gone off pottering with Oliver Optic, or else the papers lie.

I read everything about the President's doings there with exultation. He looms up grand & fine, like the old-time national benefactors of history. Well, it's a long time since we've had anybody to feel proud of & have confidence in. I mean to take my fill now while the meal's hot & the appetite ravenous.

I wish that old ass of a private secretary hadn't taken me for George Francis Train. If ignorance were a means of grace I wouldn't trade that gorilla's chances for the Archbishop of Canterbury's.

I shall call on the President again, by & by. I shall go in my war paint; & if I am obstructed, the nation will have the unusual spectacle of a private secretary with a pen over one ear & a tomahawk over the other.

I read the entire Atlantic this time. Wonderful number. Mrs. Rose Terry Cooke's story [4] was a ten-strike. I wish she would write 12 old-time New England tales a year.

Good-times to you all! Mind if you don't run here for a few days you will go ⟨to⟩ ⟨hell⟩ hence without having had a foreglimpse of heaven.

Mark.

P.S — 2 days later, being July 6 —
My play is finished; 4-Act comedy, with 14 characters; con-

ceived, plotted out, written & completed in 6 1/2 working days of 6 1/2 hours each; just a fraction under 250 MS pages besides the pages that were torn up & the few pages of odds & ends of notes, such as one sets down in the midst of his work for future reference; it is an average of 5 Atlantic pages each day. *I* think it was a prodigious dash of work; I'm the tiredest man in America. My old fool detective pervades the piece from beginning to end — always on hand & busy.

I go to New York Monday (St James Hotel,) & take MS with me. Shall visit theatres for a week or ten days & see if I can find a man who can play the detective as well as Sol Smith Russell could doubtless have done it — though I never have seen *him*. If the play's a success it is worth $50,000 or more — if it fails it is worth nothing — & yet even the worst of failures can't rob me of the 6 1/2 days of booming pleasure I have had in writing it.

Mark

I *meant* it for a comedy — but it is only a long farce. Wish you'd come to New York & go to theatres.

1. Of "Some Rambling Notes of an Idle Excursion."

2. George Parsons Lathrop, associate editor of the *Atlantic*.

3. A celebrated comic impersonator, equally at home in variety or in theatrical burlesque (Odell, *Annals,* X, 75–76). Russell wrote to Clemens from New York on 27 August saying: "Both Mr. Daly and Harry Wall have spoken to me of your new play 'Clues' Mr. Daly thinking the star part will suit me advised this letter," but a second letter from him on 28 August implies that he would have to leave town before he could meet Mark Twain for a conversation about the play (MTP).

4. "Freedom Wheeler's Controversy with Providence," in the July *Atlantic.*

159. CLEMENS TO HOWELLS

Elmira
Wednesday PM [11 July 1877].

My Dear Howells:

It's finished. I was misled by hurried mis-paging. There were ten pages of notes, & over 300 pages of MS when the play was done.[1] Did it in 42 hours, by the clock; 40 pages of the Atlantic — but then of course it's very "fat." Those are the figures, but I don't believe them myself, because the thing's impossible.

But let that pass. All day long, & every day, since I finished (in the rough), I have been diligently, altering, amending, re-writing, cutting down.[2] I finished finally to-day. Can't think of anything else in the way of an improvement. I thought I would stick to it while the interest was hot — & I am mighty glad I did. A week from now it will be frozen — then, revising would be drudgery. (You see I learned something from the fatal blunder of putting Ah Sin aside before it was finished.)

She's all right, now. She reads in 2 hours & 20 minutes & will play not longer than 2 3/4 hours. Nineteen characters; 3 acts; ⟨(I doubled one.) (I redu) (I bunched 2 into 1.)

To-morrow I will draw up an exhaustive synopsis to insert in the printed title-page for copyrighting,[3] & then on Friday or Saturday I go to New York to remain a week or ten days & lay for an actor. Wish you could run down there & have a holiday. 'Twould be fun.

My wife won't have Balaam Ass;[4] therefore I call the piece "Cap'n Simon Wheeler, The Amateur Detective."

Yrs

Mark.

1. The MS of "Cap'n Simon Wheeler, The Amateur Detective" (DV 321, MTP) runs to 292 sheets of text, many with verso additions.

2. The MS does indeed show much more cancellation and revision than Clemens's MSS usually do. The title was deposited in the copyright office on 20 July 1877. The play is quite phenomenally bad; this may account for the fact that it was never produced or published. Less than two years later Clemens was himself describing it as "dreadfully witless & flat" (letter 195). Simon Wheeler will be recalled as the "good-natured, garrulous" old man in the ghost town of Angel's Camp who tells the story of the Jumping Frog. His characterization here, like that of Colonel Sellers in the later play *Colonel Sellers as a Scientist*, seems to owe something also to Clemens's conception of his brother Orion. There is a MS called "Simon Wheeler, Detective" in the Berg Collection, a rewriting of the play in narrative form, which also was never published. Some bits of plot and situation from the

Simon Wheeler material were eventually used in *Huckleberry Finn* and in *Tom Sawyer, Detective* (1896).

3. In MTP there is a photostatic copy of a printed broadside containing about 2500 words summarizing the plot of the play, with occasional passages of quoted dialogue.

4. Mark Twain's original intention to call the play "Balaam Ass" is not mentioned in any other surviving document.

160. HOWELLS TO CLEMENS

[Conanicut, R. I., 12 July 1877]

No. 4 of your Notes of an I. Ex. is glorious. I nearly killed Mrs. Howells with it. — I want to see that comedy! Why not run on here with it from N.Y. next week?

July 12   W. D. Howells

MS. An endorsement on a letter from Birchard A. Hayes (eldest son of the President) to Elinor Howells (Washington, 9 July 1877, MTP) reading in part as follows: "A few days ago Webb received a letter from Laura Mitchell [Hayes's favorite niece, cousin of Elinor Howells], enclosing two letters from Mark Twain to Mr. Howells on the appointment of Bret Harte to some consulship. Father has read the letters and directs me to tell you there is no danger of his appointment. Father will keep the letters with his autograph letters." The letters of Clemens about Bret Harte are not with the bulk of Hayes's papers in the Hayes Memorial Library, nor are they in the Library of Congress.

161. HOWELLS TO CLEMENS

[Conanicut, R. I.] Aug. 2, 1877.

Dear Clemens:

This is first-rate.[1] I hope they've sent you duplicate proofs[2] for simultaning?

I got your invitation to see Ah Sin with you, and if it had been

The Amateur Detective, I think you would have had me on your hands. I'm very curious to read that play. Haven't you a duplicate that you could send me?

Why don't you run up from New York, and see a fellow? There are six ferryboats a day from Newport to Jamestown, on Conanicut.   Yours ever

W. D. Howells.

1. An installment of "Some Rambling Notes."
2. Of earlier installments.

162. CLEMENS TO HOWELLS

Elmira, Aug. 3 [1877].

My Dear Howells:

I have mailed one set of the slips to London, & told Bentley you would print Sept. 15 in October Atlantic, & he must not print earlier in Temple Bar.¹ Have I got the dates & things right?

I am powerful glad to see that No. 1 reads a nation sight better in print than it did in MS. I told Bentley we'd send him the slips each time 6 weeks before day of publication. We can do that, can't we? Two months ahead would be still better I suppose, but *I* don't know.

"Ah Sin" went a-booming at the Fifth Avenue.² The reception of Col. Sellers was calm compared to it. If Bret Harte had suppressed his name (it didn't occur to me to suggest it) the play would have received as great applause in the papers as it did in the Theatre. x The criticisms were just;³ the criticisms of the great New York dailies are always just, ⟨always⟩ intelligent, & ⟨always⟩ square & honest — notwithstanding by a blunder which nobody was seriously to blame for I was made to say exactly the opposite of this in a ⟨Baltimore paper⟩ newspaper some time ago. Never said it at all, & moreover I never thought it. I could not publicly correct it before the play appeared in New York, because that would look as if I had really said that thing & then was moved by fears for my pocket & my reputation to take it back. But I can correct it now, & shall do it; for now my motives cannot be impugned. When I began this letter it had not occurred to me to use you in this connection, but it occurs to me now. Your opinion & mine, uttered a year ago, & repeated more than once since, that the candor & ability of the New York critics were beyond question, is a matter which makes it proper enough that I should speak through you at this time. Therefore if you will print this paragraph somewhere, it may remove the impression that I say unjust things which I do not think, merely for the pleasure of talking.

There, now. Can't you say —

"In a letter to Mr. Howells of the Atlantic Monthly, Mark Twain describes the reception of the new comedy "Ah Sin," & then goes on to say:" &c

Beginning at the x with the words, "The criticisms were just."

Will you cut that paragraph out of this letter & precede it with the remarks suggested (or with better ones,) & send it to the Globe or some other paper? You can't do me a bigger favor; & yet IF IT IS IN THE LEAST DISAGREEABLE, YOU MUSTN'T THINK OF IT. But let me know, right away, for I want to correct this thing before it grows stale again. I explained myself to only one critic (the World) — the consequence was a noble notice of the play. This one called on me, else I shouldn't have explained myself to *him*.

Mrs. Clemens says, *"Don't* ask that of Mr. Howells — it *will* be disagreeable to him." I hadn't thought it, but I will bet two to one on the correctness of her instinct. We shall see.[4]

I have been putting in a deal of hard work on that play in New York, & have left hardly a foot-print of Harte in it anywhere. But it is full of incurable defects: to-wit, Harte's deliberate thefts & plagiarisms, & my own unconscious ones. I don't believe Harte ever had an idea that he came by honestly. He is the most abandoned thief that defiles the earth.

My old Plunkett family seemed wonderfully coarse & vulgar on the stage, but it was because they were played in such an

outrageously & inexcusably coarse way. The Chinaman is killingly funny. I don't know when I have enjoyed anything as
much as I did him. The people say there isn't enough of him
in the piece. — That's a triumph — there'll never be any *more*
of him in it.

John Brougham [5] said, "Read the list of things which the
critics have condemned in the piece, & you have unassailable
proof that the play contains all the requirements of success & a
long life."

That is true. Nearly every time the audience roared I knew
it was over something that would be condemned in the morning
(justly, too) but must be left in — for low comedies are written
for the drawing-room, the kitchen & the stable, & if you cut out
the kitchen & the stable the drawing-room can't support the
play by itself.

There was as much money in the house the first 2 nights as
in the first 10 of Sellers. Haven't heard from the third — I came
away.   Yrs Ever

                                                        Mark.

1. Although Clemens mailed duplicate proofs of the first two installments of "Some Rambling Notes" to George Bentley, editor of *Temple
Bar* (London), the "Notes" were not serialized in that magazine. Moncure
D. Conway, the American Unitarian minister then living in England who
was enthusiastically acting as a volunteer literary agent for Clemens, had
arranged for Chatto & Windus to bring out the English edition of *Tom
Sawyer*. As early as 16 November 1876 he had urged Clemens to "write an
article for Chatto's excellent magazine — 'Belgravia' " (London, MTP). Now,
apparently, he exercised his authority as literary agent in asking Bentley to
send the proofs of the first two installments of the "Notes" to Chatto, who
acknowledged their receipt, together with proofs of a third installment sent
direct, in a letter to Clemens dated 25 October 1877 (London, MTP). The
"Notes" were published in *Belgravia* October 1877–January 1878. Chatto
liked the articles very much: he regretted that Clemens "brought them to a
close so soon," and hoped that the writer would "let us have something else
every month" (Andrew Chatto to SLC, London, 3 November 1877, MTP).

2. The play had opened at Daly's Fifth Avenue Theatre in New York
on Tuesday, 31 July, with much fanfare, including a graceful curtain speech
by Mark Twain (Daly, *Life of Augustin Daly*, pp. 234–236). But the play
did not prove popular despite Mark Twain's rewriting of the end of the

second act, and after five weeks Parsloe took it on the road (Charles T. Parsloe to SLC, New York, 10 August 1877; Maze Edwards to SLC, New York, "Tuesday" [1877], MTP). Parsloe reported to Clemens that John T. Raymond considered it "the worst play he *ever saw*," but Parsloe had a higher opinion of it himself (New York, 5 August 1877, MTP). One consequence of this production was a further estrangement between Clemens and Harte, who complained that he "was forgotten" by Clemens and Parsloe: they sent him no news of its reception or its financial success (Daly, *Life of Augustin Daly,* p. 236).

3. Clippings of reviews are preserved in Mark Twain's scrapbook, 1869–1878 (MTP). While the New York *World* said the characters in the play spoke the language of real life instead of the stilted language of books, and gave a flatteringly detailed summary of the plot, the other papers were caustic in condemning the low tone and coarse dialogue of the play *(Herald),* the sluggish and "inartificial" development of the plot *(Tribune),* and the absence of characterization *(Sun).* The *Times,* however, said the play was "capitally acted," and found an air of freshness and "the charm of local color" in it; the *Tribune* found the dialogue "sparkling with wit"; and the *Sun,* while declaring that "as a piece of dramatic work the play is beneath criticism," conceded that "as an entertainment it is laughable and lively, owing to the clever manner in which it is played."

4. This paragraph is written in the margin.

5. A veteran actor and playright, active in the New York theatre since 1842.

163. CLEMENS TO HOWELLS

Elmira, Aug. 25 [–27]/77

My Dear Howellses:

I thought I ought to make a sort of record of it for future reference; the pleasantest way to do that would be to write it to somebody; BUT that somebody would let it leak into print, & that we wish to avoid. The Howellses would be safe — so let us tell the Howellses about it.

Day before yesterday was a fine summer day away up here on the summit. Aunt Marsh & Cousin May Marsh were here visiting Susie Crane & Livy at our farm house. By & by mother Langdon came up the hill in the "high carriage" with Nora the nurse &

little Jervis (Charley Langdon's little boy) — Timothy the coach-man driving. Behind these came Charley's wife & little girl in the buggy, with the new, young, spry gray horse — a high-stepper. Theodore Crane arrived a little later.

The Bay [1] & Susie were on hand with their nurse, Rosa.[2] I was on hand, too. Susie Crane's trio of colored servants ditto — these being Josie, housemaid; Aunty Cord, cook, aged 62, tur-baned, very tall, very broad, very fine every way (see her portrait in "A True Story Just as I Heard It" in my Sketches); Chocklate (the laundress,) (as the Bay calls her — she can't say Charlotte), still taller, still more majestic of proportions, turbaned, very black, straight as an Indian — age, 24. Then there was the farm-er's wife (colored) & her little girl, Susie.

Wasn't it a good audience to get up an excitement before? Good excitable, inflammable ⟨combustible⟩ material?

Lewis was still down town, three miles away, with his two-horse wagon, to get a load of manure. Lewis is the farmer (colored.) He is of mighty frame & muscle, stocky, stooping, un-gainly, has a good manly face & a clear eye. Age about 45 — & the most picturesque of men, when he sits in his fluttering work-day rags, humped forward into a bunch, with his aged slouch hat mashed down over his ears & neck. It is a spectacle to make the broken-hearted smile.

Lewis has worked mighty hard & remained mighty poor. At the end of each whole year's toil he can't show a gain of fifty dollars. He had borrowed money of the Cranes till he owed them $700 — & he being conscientious & honest, imagine what it was to him to have to carry this stubborn, hopeless load year in & year out.

Well, sunset came, & Ida the young & comely (Charley Langdon's wife) & her little Julia & the nurse Nora, drove out at the gate behind the new gray horse & started down the long hill — the high carriage receiving its load under the porte cochère. Ida was seen to turn her face toward us across the fence & intervening lawn — Theodore waved good bye to her, for he did not know that her sign was a speechless appeal for help.

The next moment Livy said, "Ida's driving too fast down

hill!" She followed it with a sort of scream, "Her horse is running away!"

We could see two hundred yards down that descent. The buggy seemed to fly. It would strike obstructions & apparently spring the height of a man from the ground.

Theodore & I left the shrieking crowd behind & ran down the hill bareheaded & shouting. A neighbor appeared at his gate — a tenth of a second too late! — the buggy vanished past him like a thought. My last glimpse showed it for one instant, far down the descent, springing high in the air out of a cloud of dust, & then it disappeared. As I flew down the road, my impulse was to shut my eyes as I turned them to the right or left, & so delay for a moment the ghastly spectacle of mutilation & death I was expecting.

I ran on & on, still spared this spectacle, but saying to myself "I shall see it at the turn of the road; they never can pass that turn alive." When I came in sight of that turn I saw two wagons there bunched together — one of them full of people. I said, "Just so — they are staring petrified at the remains."

But when I got amongst that bunch, there sat Ida in her buggy & nobody hurt, not even the horse or the vehicle. OVER Ida was pale but serene. As I came tearing down she smiled back over her shoulder at me & [I] said, "Well, you're alive yet, *aren't* you?" OVER AGAIN [3] A miracle had been performed — nothing less.

You see, Lewis, — the prodigious, humped upon his front seat, had been toiling up, on his load of manure; he saw the frantic horse plunging down the hill toward him, on a full gallop, throwing his heels as high as a man's head at every jump. So Lewis turned his team diagonally across the road just at the "turn," thus making a V with the fence — the running horse could not escape that but must enter it. Then Lewis sprang to the ground & stood in this V. He gathered his vast strength, and with a perfect Creedmoor aim [4] he siezed the gray horse's bit as he plunged by & fetched him up standing!

It was down hill, mind you; ten feet *further* down hill neither Lewis nor any other man could have saved them, for they would have been on the abrupt "turn," then. But how this miracle was ever accomplished at all, by human strength, generalship & accuracy, is clear beyond my comprehension — & grows more so the more I go & examine the ground & try to believe it was actually done. I know one thing, well; if Lewis had missed his aim he would have been killed on the spot in the trap he had made for himself, & we should have found the rest of the remains away down at the bottom of the steep ravine.

Ten minutes later Theodore & I arrived opposite the house, with the servants straggling after us, & shouted to the distracted group on the porch, "Everybody safe!"

Believe it? Why how *could* they? They knew the road perfectly. We might as well have said it to people who had seen their friends go over Niagara.

However, we convinced them; & then, instead of saying something, or going on crying, they grew very still — words could not express it, I suppose.

Nobody could do anything that night, or sleep, either; but there was a deal of moving talk, with long pauses between — pictures of that flying carriage, these pauses represented — this picture intruded itself all the time & disjointed the talk.

But yesterday evening late, when Lewis arrived from down town he found his supper spread, & some presents of books there, with very complimentary writings on the fly-leaves, & certain very complimentary letters, & more or less greenbacks of dignified denomination pinned to these letters & fly-leaves, — & one said, among other things, (signed by The Cranes) "We cancel $400 of your indebtedness to us," &c &c.

(The end whereof is not yet, of course, for Charley Langdon is west & will arrive ignorant of all these things to-day.)

The supper-room had been kept locked & imposingly secret & mysterious until Lewis should arrive; but around that part of the house were gathered Lewis's wife & child, Chocklate, Josie, Aunty Cord & our Rosa, canvassing things & waiting impatiently. They were all on hand when the ⟨avalanche came⟩ curtain rose.

Now Aunty Cord is a violent Methodist & Lewis an ⟨fanatic⟩ implacable Dunker-Baptist. These two are inveterate religious disputants. The revealments having been made, Aunty Cord said with effusion —

"*Now* let folks go on saying there ain't no God! Lewis, the Lord sent you there to stop that horse."

Says Lewis —

"Then who sent the *horse* there in sich a shape?"

But I want to call your attention to one thing. When Lewis arrived the other evening, after saving those lives by a feat which I think is the most marvelous of any I can call to mind — when he arrived, hunched up on his manure wagon & as grotesquely picturesque as usual, everybody wanted to go & see how he looked. — They came back & said he was beautiful. It was *so*, too — & yet he would have *photographed* exactly as he would have done any day these past 7 years that he has occupied this farm.

Aug. 27.

P.S. — Our little romance in real life is happily & satisfactorily completed. Charley has come, listened, acted — & now John T. Lewis has ceased to consider himself as belonging to that class called "the poor."

It has been known, during some years, that it was Lewis's purpose to buy a thirty-dollar silver watch some day, if he ever got where he could afford it. To-day Ida has given him a new, sumptuous gold Swiss stem-winding stop-watch; & if any scoffer shall say "Behold this thing is out of character," there is an inscription within, which will silence him; for it will teach him that this wearer aggrandizes the watch, not the watch the wearer.

I was asked, beforehand, if this would be a wise gift, & I said "Yes, the very wisest of all; I know the colored race, & I know that in Lewis's eyes this fine toy will throw the other more valuable testimonials far away into the shade. If he lived in England, the Humane Society would give him a gold medal as costly as this watch, & nobody would say 'It is out of character.'

If Lewis chose to wear a town clock, who would become it better?"

Lewis has sound common sense, & is not going to be spoiled. — The instant he found himself possessed of money, he forgot himself in a plan to make his old father comfortable, who is wretchedly poor & lives down in Maryland. His next act, on the spot, was the proffer to the Cranes of the $300 of his remaining indebtedness to them. This was put off by them to the indefinite future, for he is not going to be allowed to pay that at all, though he doesn't know it.

A letter of acknowledgment from Lewis contains a sentence which raises it to the dignity of literature:

"But I beg to say, humbly, that inasmuch as divine providence saw fit to use me as a instrument for the saving of those presshious lives, the honner conferd upon me was greater than the feat performed."

That is well said.   Yrs Ever

Mark.[5]

1. Clara Clemens.

2. Rosina Hay, the German nursemaid who had worked for the Clemenses since March 1874.

3. This passage is written on the back of the page.

4. Creedmoor, on Long Island, was the site of the target range of the National Rifle Association.

5. Clemens sent an almost verbatim copy of this letter, bearing the same date, to his friend Dr. John Brown of Edinburgh, author of *Rab and his Friends* (Berg, TS in MTP).

164. CLEMENS TO HOWELLS

Elmira, Aug. 29 [1877].

My Dear Howells:

Just got your letter last night. No, dern that article,[1] it made me cry when I read it in proof, it was so oppressively & ostentatiously poor. Skim your eye over it again & you will think as I do. If Isaac & the prophets of Baal can be doctored gently & made permissible, it will redeem the thing; but if it can't, let's burn

199

all of the article except the tail-end of it [2] & use that as an introduction to the *next* article — as I suggested in my letter to you
of day before yesterday. (I had this proof from Cambridge before yours came.)

Boucicault [3] says my new play is ever so much better than
Ah Sin; says the Amateur detective is a bully character, too. An
actor [4] is chawing over the play in New York, to see if the old
Detective is suited to his abilities. Haven't heard from him yet.

If you've got that paragraph by you yet, & if in your judgment it would be good to publish it, & if you *absolute*ly would
not mind doing it, then I think I'd like to have you do it — or
else put some other words in my mouth that will be properer, &
publish *them*. But mind, don't think of it for a moment if it is
distasteful — & doubtless it is. I value your judgment more than
my own, as to the wisdom of saying anything at all in this matter. To say nothing leaves me in an injurious position — &
yet maybe I might do better to speak to the men themselves
when I go to New York. This was my latest idea, & it looked
wise.

We *expect* to leave here for home Sept. 4, reaching there
the 8th — but we may be delayed a week.

I wish I knew whether the "house" will send the "advance"
sheets to the "Canadian Monthly" or whether I am to do it.[5]
Do you know? It is perfectly easy for me to do it, but no need
of both of us doing it.

Curious thing. I read passages from my play, & a full synopsis,
to Boucicault, who was re-writing a play which he wrote & laid
aside 3 or 4 years ago. (My detective is about that age, you
know). Then he read a passage from his play, where a *real* detective does some things that are as idiotic as some of my old
Wheeler's performances. Showed me the passages, & behold, *his*
man's name is Wheeler! However, his Wheeler is not a prominent
character, so we'll not alter the names. My Wheeler's name is
taken from the old Jumping Frog sketch.

I am re-reading Ticknor's diary,[6] & am charmed with it;
though I still say he *refers* to too many good things when he
could just as well have *told* them. — Think of the man traveling

8 days in convoy & familiar intercourse with a band of outlaws through the mountain fastnesses of Spain — he the fourth stranger they had encountered in thirty years — & compressing this priceless experience into a single colorless paragraph of his diary! They spun yarns to this unworthy devil, too.

I wrote you a very long letter a day or two ago, but Susie Crane wanted to make a copy of it to keep, so it has not gone yet. It may go to-day, possibly.

We unite in warm regards to you & yourn.

Yrs Ever

Mark

1. The second installment of "Some Rambling Notes."

2. Captain "Hurricane" Jones's tale of Isaac and the prophets of Baal (DE, XIX, 264–267) as Mark Twain heard it from Twichell (CDW to WDH, Hartford, 19 October, Houghton) was left in the published text. The Captain himself, like Captain Ned Blakely in *Roughing It,* owes a great deal to an actual skipper — Edgar Wakeman, commander of the steamer *America* in which Mark Twain traveled from San Francisco to Nicaragua on his way to New York in 1866. Captains Jones and Blakely are both literary ancestors of the Captain Stormfield who, many years later, would make a memorable visit to heaven.

3. Dion Boucicault, Irish-born actor and playwright who became one of the most conspicuous theatrical personalities of the late nineteenth century in New York.

4. Probably Sol Smith Russell (Russell to SLC, New York, 28 August 1877, MTP).

5. Clemens had undertaken to find a publishing outlet in Canada that would enable him to forestall Belford Bros. He had asked the opinion of Henry O. Houghton, publisher of the *Atlantic,* concerning the *Canadian Monthly,* published by Hart & Rawlinson of Toronto, and upon receiving Houghton's assurance that it was "a first class journal," had asked to have duplicate proofs of the series sent to that magazine (Henry O. Houghton to SLC, New York, 9 August 1877; Hart & Rawlinson to H.O. Houghton & Co., Toronto, 27 August 1877; Hurd & Houghton ["per W. S. S."] to SLC, Cambridge, 30 August 1877, MTP). "Some Rambling Notes" appeared in the *Canadian Monthly,* October 1877–January 1878, with the statement: "Published from advance sheets by arrangement with the author and his American publishers." Clemens probably offered the articles to the *Canadian Monthly* without charge. The device prevented Belford Bros. from pirating them; but the strategy could not be repeated because in June 1878, the *Canadian Monthly* was taken over by the Belfords and merged with *Belford's*

Monthly in a magazine called *Rose-Belford's Canadian Monthly and National Review* — which in turn ceased publication in June 1882.

6. The *Life, Letters and Journals of George Ticknor*, published by Osgood in 1876.

165. HOWELLS TO CLEMENS

[Cambridge] Sept. 17, 1877.

Dear Clemens:

Decidedly don't let those fellows [1] have that story about the captain. They'd be sure to slap it into print.

I have to see Mrs. Howells and talk over the whens of our visit to the Warners before I can fix a time for seeing you. I'm quite as eager to see the new play as you are to show it.

Can't I use that story in the Club about your Elmira life-preserver? [2] As you tell it, I think it's one of the most impressive things I've ever read. I feel myself quite a beast for not thanking you at once for my private copy of it.

Yours ever

W. D. Howells

I don't know where I've put that ¶ of yours that you wanted me to father for the press.[3] But if I were you, I'd let my new play answer the censures of the old.

1. Clemens's reply (letter 166) indicates that "those fellows" were members of a San Francisco club — but the club cannot now be identified.

2. John T. Lewis, described in letter 163.

3. Part of Clemens's letter of 3 August. When Howells professes to have mislaid the letter, he may well be adopting a polite evasion, in the belief that an author is bound to appear in a bad light if he enters into public discussion with his critics.

166. CLEMENS TO HOWELLS

Hartford Sept. 19 [1877].

My Dear Howells:

All right — shan't send anything to that San Frisco club.

I don't really see how the story of the runaway horse could

read well with the little details of names & places & things left out. *They* are the true life of all narrative. It wouldn't quite do to print them at this time.[1] We'll talk about it when you come. Delicacy — a sad, sad false delicacy — robs literature of the two best things among its belongings: Family-circle narratives & obscene stories. But no matter; in that better world which I trust we are all going to I have the hope & belief that they will not be denied us. ¶. — Say — Twichell & I had an adventure at sea, 4 1/2 months ago, which I did not put in my Bermuda articles, because there was not enough *to* it. But the press dispatches bring the sequel to-day, & now there's plenty to it. A sailless, mastless, chartless, compassless, grubless old condemned tub that has been drifting helpless about the ocean for 4 months & a half, begging bread & water like any other tramp, flying a signal of distress permanently, & with 13 innocent, marveling, chuckle-headed Bermuda niggers on board taking a Pleasure Excursion! Our ship fed the poor devils on the 25th of last May, far out at sea & left them to bullyrag their way to New York — & now they ain't as near New York as they were then by 250 miles! They have drifted south & west 750 miles & are *still* drifting south in the relentless Gulf Stream! What a delicious magazine chapter it would make — but I had to deny myself. I had to come right out in the papers at once,[2] with my details, so as to try to raise the government's sympathy sufficiently to have better succor sent them than the cutter Colfax, which went a little way in search of them the other day & then struck a fog & gave it up.

If the President were in Washington I would telegraph him.[3]

When I hear that the "Jonas Smith" has been found again, I mean to send for one of those darkies to come to Hartford & give me his adventures for an Atlantic article.

Likely you will see my to-day's article in the newspapers.

Ys Ever

Mark.

The revenue cutter Colfax went after the Jonas Smith thinking there was mutiny or other crime on board. It occurs to me now that since there is only mere suffering & misery & nobody to punish, it ceases to be a matter which (a republican form of) government will feel authorized to interfere in further. Dam a republican form of government.

I am not the author of this noble obituary — though deceased was a relative.[4]

1. Mark Twain later used the incident as the basis for a passage in a long but unfinished and unpublished fictional narrative called "The Adam Monument" (DV 309a, TS, pp. 171ff., MTP).

2. With a long letter to the Hartford *Courant* dated 19 September (including a quotation from Clemens's notebook entry for 25 May 1877, when the steamer *Bermuda* on which he and Twichell were returning to New York encountered the *Jonas Smith* at sea).

3. In MTP are three additional documents bearing on the *Jonas Smith* incident: 1) the undated text of a telegram to President Hayes, written in pencil in Clemens's hand, asking him to "order the Cutter Colfax to search again"; 2) the text of a telegram received from the President, also in Clemens's hand, dated Chattanooga, Tenn., 20 September 1877, asking Clemens to communicate with the Secretary of the Treasury; and 3) a letter to Clemens signed by Secretary John Sherman, dated in Washington, 22 September, in reply to a letter of Clemens's dated 20 September, conveying the information that on 16 September the commander of the revenue cutter *Colfax* had boarded "the Schooner 'Jonas Smith,' Christian, Master, from Boston for Savannah, cargo ice, 35 days out, and found nothing unusual in her condition." Since the schooner "did not appear to need assistance, it was deemed unnecessary to send out the 'Colfax' again." One can only conclude that Clemens was misled concerning the "Pleasure Excursion."

4. This sentence was written by Clemens beside the following clipping from a newspaper pasted in the middle of the first page of the letter:
"Obituary.
"Mary Langdon passed from earth to heaven at 6:00 A.M. Sept. 12th, 1877. Her maiden name was Lee. She was born near Poughkeepsie, Dutchess county, N.Y., July 20, 1790. Her husband Mr. Amos Langdon died in March, 1867. They had moved from Dutchess county to Newfield, Tompkins county in 1831, and in 1838 to a place now well known as Langdon hill, near Breesport, Chemung county, N.Y. For more than forty years she had been a most worthy and devoted member of the M.E. Church. Her home for quite a number of years has been with her daughter, Mrs. Ulysses Breese; and it was from their filial care and elegant residence at West Junction that she exchanged earth for Heaven. It was also there that the funeral services were held on the 13th, and from thence the precious remains were borne to the 'Scotch burial ground' in Erin, accompanied by numerous relatives and friends. Peace to her memory and blessings on her posterity.
ERIN, Sept. 13, 1877."

GIVE ME YOUR PLAIN ADVICE (1877–1879)

167. HOWELLS TO CLEMENS (POSTCARD)

[Cambridge, 14 October 1877]

Barrett has given my play twice in Cincinnati with what he calls grand success: the first time to a fair house; the second to a house in which every seat was sold.[1]

W. D. H.

1. Except for Howells's adaptation of a Spanish tragedy, *Yorick's Love,* *A Counterfeit Presentment* was his greatest stage success. Lawrence Barrett had presented the comedy at the Grand Opera House in Cincinnati on 11 and 12 October. The critics of the Cincinnati *Gazette* and *Commercial* gave it long and enthusiastic reviews (WDH to Whelply, Cambridge, 17 October 1877, Hist. and Phil. Soc. of Ohio, AGM TS), and when Barrett took the play to Cleveland, the reviewers of the *Herald* and *Leader* were equally delighted. John Hay, Mrs. A. W. Fairbanks, and Constance F. Woolson all wrote Howells privately of its success (WDH to WCH, 28 October, Houghton; WDH to JRO, 28 October, Rutgers, AGM TS; WDH to Barrett, 14 November, Princeton, AGM TS; all written from Cambridge). Despite successful performances in Franklyn and Pittsburgh, Pa., Barrett soon came to feel that the play needed more action to hold popular audiences, and he therefore asked Howells to add new incidents and new characters to the play. Howells instead wrote a new act, "Dissolving Views," for insertion between the second and third acts of the original play, telling Barrett when he sent the new section that he had worked toward "comedy of *character*" and had developed Barrett's part as the hero, Bartlett (Cambridge, 14 November, Princeton, AGM TS; Meserve). Barrett's tour continued with a triumph in Indianapolis, and though he was distrustful of the new act he found that the expanded play went well in Detroit and Chicago and St. Louis. Both author and actor-manager were greatly pleased because they now had a full-length play (Barrett to JRO, 13 December, Harvard Theatre Collection, as quoted in Meserve). After at least one performance in Canada, on his way East, Barrett persuaded Howells at the end of the year to go out to Worcester, Mass., where, Howells wrote to Warner, "I saw it . . . and thought better of it than I should like to own" (Cambridge, 28 December, Watkinson, AGM TS).

168. CLEMENS TO HOWELLS

[Hartford] Oct. 15 [1877]

My Dear Howells — I am *entirely* glad, a hundred times over! I saw the item in the papers 2 days ago & was going to send jubilations, but I was afraid of the confounded after-claps that come later, sometimes & spoil everything. But a house full of *money,* & so soon as the second night, is one of those Scripture truths that lay all doubts on the shelf. I'm mighty glad — there's no two ways about that.

I've got some good news too — (but keep it to yourself for the present) — "Ah Sin" is a most abject & incurable failure! It will leave the stage permanently within a week, & then I shall be a cheerful being again. I'm sorry for poor Parsloe, but for nobody else concerned.   Ys Ever

Mark.

P.S. When you come, remind me to show you my "Undertaker's Tale" [1] — & tell me what is the trouble with it.

1. "The Undertaker's Tale" (DV 312, MS of 36 pp., MTP) is the story of a Mr. Cadaver's tribulations when no one dies for a time in a New England village, and his eventual prosperity and happiness when cholera strikes "in its most malignant form." The tale involves a love affair between the undertaker's daughter and an ambitious young gravedigger, and a town miser who holds the inevitable mortgage upon Cadaver's home. The opinion of the unresponsive audience at Quarry Farm, to whom Clemens first read it aloud, must have been confirmed by Howells, analytically. The story was never published.

169. HOWELLS TO CLEMENS

[Cambridge] Oct. 31, 1877

My dear Clemens:

The glimpse I had of you last week [1] was such an aggravation that I almost wish I hadn't seen you at all. I want a good old three-dayser, next time. — This number of the Bermudas is delicious. But you can't put a health-officer's heart on a fork in The Atlantic Monthly.[2] None of our readers ever heard of such a thing. I sent you duplicates some days ago for simultaning. Please return me this proof.

I've thought somewhat about your amateur detective, since I came home. It seems to me that he ought to be as like Capt. Wakeman as you can make him. Why not fairly and squarely retire an old sea-dog, and let him [take] to detecting in the ennui of the country? This is what you first tho't of doing, and I don't believe you can think of anything better. I want the story for The Atlantic.[3]

Our love to all your family. Sorry you wont be at the lunch, to-morrow.[4] Yours ever

W. D. Howells.

1. The Howellses had gone down to Hartford for dinner with the Warners on 26 October, and on to Mark Twain's house to attend a neighborhood reception for Yung Wing and his wife (Twichell Journal, 26 October, Yale). A visitors' book of the Clemens household contains this inscription: "'Not last, but least.' W. D. Howells. Oct. 26, 1877" (MTP).

2. In Mark Twain's MS the last paragraph of the last installment of "Some Rambling Notes" denounced a health officer of the Port of New York who had compelled the steamer *Bermuda* to lie at anchor overnight in order to undergo an entirely perfunctory "inspection" next morning. The text in the *Atlantic* for January 1878 reads: "For a great ship to lie idle all night is a most costly loss of time; for her passengers to have to do the same thing works to them the same damage, with the addition of an amount of exasperation and bitterness of soul that the spectacle of that health-offi. . . . . could hardly sweeten." Mark Twain added in a footnote: "When the proofs of this article came to me I saw that The Atlantic had condemned the words which occupied the place where is now a vacancy. I can invent no figure worthy to stand in the shoes of the lurid colossus which a too decent respect for the opinions of mankind has thus ruthlessly banished from his due and rightful pedestal in the world's literature. Let the blank remain a blank; and let it suggest to the reader that he has sustained a precious loss which can never be made good to him. M. T." In the text of *Punch, Brothers, Punch!* published in 1878, the words are still omitted, though Mark Twain's note of explanation no longer appears. By 1882, in the text of *The Stolen White Elephant*, he either restored the original wording, or altered the figure of the health officer's "heart on a fork" thus: ". . . with the

addition of an amount of exasperation and bitterness of soul that the spectacle of that health officer's ashes on a shovel could hardly sweeten."

3. See letter 159, note 2.

4. Replying from Cambridge to James R. Osgood's invitation to lunch, Howells told Osgood that Warner would come, "but Clemens, who said you were the best publisher who ever breathed, and that you could have everything he owned, . . . could not" (28 October, Rutgers, AGM TS).

170. CLEMENS TO HOWELLS

[Hartford, 1 November 1877]

My Dear Howells —

I don't know whether this is old or new. Joe Twichell got it from a Cleveland clergyman, who said it was very recent. If you print it, put it where I have marked it in the proof, & send a proof of it to Canada & forward one to me for London. If it is too powerful, squelch it & let me have the MS again.[1]

Some Simsbury ass printed the story of Daniel in the Lion's Den yesterday in the Hartford Times,[2] & did it so wretchedly & nastily & witlessly that I suppose the whole nation of Helen's Baby's admirers will welcome it as a very inspiration of humor & read & copy it everywhere.[3]

Your visit was entirely too short. I do hope you will all be able to make a long one when you come in December. We'll make Johnny & Winnie enjoy it.

This tribe sends loving regards to yours.

Mrs. Gilman has fitful glimmerings of reason, in which she straightway plunges into schemes for paying the swindled creditors, & is soon a frantic maniac again.[4]

Ys Ever

Mark.

MS. The date is established by the reference to the publication of the piece about Daniel in the lions' den in the Hartford *Times* "yesterday" ("Ending Mark Twain's 'Captain's Story,' in His Trip to Bermuda, No. II," Hartford *Times,* 31 October 1877, p. [1]).

1. The MS cannot be identified.

2. One Frank Jewett, dating his communication Simsbury, 29 October 1877, wrote to the Hartford *Times* (31 October 1877, p. [1]) concerning Captain "Hurricane" Jones's version of the story of Isaac and the prophets of Baal in the second installment of Mark Twain's "Some Rambling Notes of an Idle Excursion" in the *Atlantic* for November 1877 (DE, XIX, 264–267). Jewett said that on 3 April 1843 Captain Jones related to a passenger his version of the story of Daniel. Daniel's enemies, according to Captain Jones, got the King drunk and persuaded him to issue an order that Daniel should be thrown to the lions. When the King sobered up he regretted his action, but such orders were unchangeable. With great ingenuity he fed the lions horses, calves, and sheep until they were full. Then Daniel was cast into the den. Next morning, "Thar he spied Dan, as cool as a glass of iced punch, a-settin' on the quarter-deck of a dead veal, whittling a shingle."

3. In John Habberton's widely popular novel, *Helen's Babies* (1876), the bachelor hero is forced to listen to Bible stories retold in childish prattle by the young nephews whom he has undertaken to care for in the absence of their parents.

4. Clemens seems to have remembered incorrectly the name of a Mrs. Chapman who figures often in Twichell's Journal (Yale). On 11 February 1877 her husband, James L. Chapman, a cashier in the Farmers & Mechanics Bank of Hartford and a deacon in Twichell's church, was arrested for embezzlement. On 11 March, Twichell writes: "Visited Mrs. J L C. Her face was the picture of woe and sorrow and her voice the sound of grief and despair. Yet she must live for her children." After the death of Mrs. Chapman's son Louis, Twichell wrote on 23 September 1877 that she was "like stone, nor did she find how to weep for several days."

171. HOWELLS TO CLEMENS

[Cambridge] November 23, 1877.

My dear Clemens:

Didn't you once read me some passages out of an idiot novel called Allen Bay? I send a notice *of* the author written, I think, *by* the author.[1]

Winnie and I expect to be with you the evening of Dec. 11. We should like to stay till the morning of the 13th, if it doesn't seem too hard on you.[2]   Yours ever

W. D. Howells.

1. The notice which Howells enclosed has not survived, but Clemens's interest in *Allen Bay, A Story,* by S. O. Stedman (Philadelphia, 1876), is apparent in the burlesque review he wrote of the book, with long quotations illustrating its "divine melancholy," its mixed metaphors, and its consistent failure to deviate into sense (Paine 59, unpublished MS of 38 pp., MTP).

2. Howells was to lecture twice in Hartford: on the evening of Wednesday, 12 December, in the Seminary Hall course, on Gibbon; and next morning, on Venice, before an extra meeting of the Saturday Morning Club, the organization of young women sponsored by Clemens. Howells told Warner he expected to make a fool of himself before a picked audience (Cambridge, 19 November 1877, Watkinson, AGM TS), but his fears proved to be groundless. The *Courant* reported (13 December, p. 2) that the largest audience of the series maintained a "breathless silence" throughout the lecture on Gibbon. The *Courant* praised the "exquisite finish" of the lecture as well as its "subtle analysis of character." Mark Twain introduced the lecturer by saying: "The gentleman who is now to address you is the editor of the Atlantic Monthly. He has a reputation in the literary world which I need not say anything about. I am only here to back up his moral character" (Hartford *Times,* 13 December, p. [2]). Howells wrote his father on 22 December: "My lecture [on Gibbon] was very well received, and I certainly enjoyed giving it" (Cambridge, Houghton). Howells and Winnie stayed several days with the Clemenses. On the evening of 14 December, Twichell and his wife came to dinner, and Twichell noted in his Journal: "W. D. H. is the most pleasing personally of all the literary folk I have met. He seems to be a downright and simple good *man.* There are certain Christian savors about him that one percieves yet can hardly describe" (Yale). The lecture on Gibbon was based on Howells's essay introducing Gibbon's *Memoirs,* to be published by Osgood a month later.

172. HOWELLS TO CLEMENS

[Boston, 18? December 1877]

All right, you poor soul!

W. D. H.

MS. The dating of this note (which is addressed to "S. L. Clemens/ Parker House") rests on the conjecture that it was sent by Howells to Clemens after midnight on the evening of the Whittier Birthday Dinner (see note 1 to letter 174).

GIVE ME YOUR PLAIN ADVICE (1877–1879)

[Cambridge] Dec. 21, 1877.

Dear Clemens:

I send the proof,[1] and beg you to sacrifice the passage on Slip 2, which I'm decidedly afraid of.

I sent you on Tuesday by express the 2 vols. of the Margravine,[2] and 3 of DuBarry.[3] There is a 4th of the latter, but Fairchild[4] has borrowed it, I find. I'll get it of him, and let you have it.

Yours ever

W. D. H.

MS. As the next letter reveals, Mark Twain was much disturbed by the reception of his speech at the Whittier Birthday Dinner given by the *Atlantic Monthly* on 17 December. Howells is no doubt trying to minimize the incident with this business-as-usual letter and the present of books.

1. Probably of "The Loves of Alonzo Fitz Clarence and Rosannah Ethelton" (a story of a courtship conducted over the long-distance telephone between Maine and California), which was published in the *Atlantic* for March 1878 (DE, XIX, 419–446).

2. *Autobiography. Memoirs of Frederica Sophia Wilhelmina, Princess Royal of Prussia,* one of the series of "Choice Autobiographies" which Howells was then editing for James R. Osgood & Co. Howells had contributed an essay to this work and may well have made the translation. Henry W. Fisher, the newspaper man whom Mark Twain knew much later in Europe, says Mark Twain told him Howells translated this book while he was United States consul in Venice during the Civil War. Mark Twain thought that the Princess, sister of Frederick the Great, was "a corker." He especially admired her humor (*Abroad with Mark Twain and Eugene Field,* New York, 1922, p. 74). He acquired for himself a copy of a new translation of the memoirs published in London in 1887 (*Mark Twain Library Auction Catalogue,* Los Angeles, 1951, Item 8a), and he began a historical novel about her, of which one chapter and some notes — 38 pp. of MS — remain in MTP (Paine 212).

3. *Memoirs* of Marie Jeanne Bécu, Comtesse du Barry; a four-volume translation was published in London in 1830 and 1831.

4. Charles W. Fairchild, a friend of Howells and later his Belmont neighbor, whom Mark Twain had met.

174. CLEMENS TO HOWELLS

[Hartford] Sunday Night [23 December 1877].

My Dear Howells:

My sense of disgrace does not abate.[1] It grows. I see that it is going to add itself to my list of permanencies — a list of humiliations that extends back to when I was seven years old, & which keep on persecuting me regardless of my repentancies.

I feel that my misfortune has injured me all over the country; therefore it will be best that I retire from before the public at present. It will hurt the Atlantic for me to appear in its pages, now. So it is my opinion & my wife's, that the telephone story had better be suppressed.

Will you return those proofs or revises[2] to me, so that I can use the same on some future occasion.

It seems as if I must have been insane when I wrote that speech & saw no harm in it, no disrespect toward those men whom I reverenced so much. And what shame I brought upon *you,* after what you said in introducing me! It burns me like fire to think of it.

The whole matter is a dreadful subject — let me drop it here — at least on paper.[3]   Penitently yrs

Mark.

1. Mark Twain refers to the speech he had made at the Whittier Birthday Dinner in Boston on 17 December, in which he described the antics of three tramps who represented themselves to a California miner as Longfellow, Emerson, and Holmes and quoted (or misquoted) these authors frequently in their conversation. Howells had revealed some uneasiness in his introduction of Mark Twain as "a humorist who never makes you blush to have enjoyed his joke; whose generous wit has no meanness in it, whose fun is never at the cost of anything honestly high or good." The two friends had persuaded one another that the speech was grossly insulting to the venerable poets, all of whom had been present, and Mark Twain had been suffering an agony of self-accusation for six days (Henry N. Smith, " 'That Hideous Mistake of Poor Clemens's,' " *Harvard Library Bulletin,* IX, 145–180, Spring 1955).

2. Of "The Loves of Alonzo Fitz Clarence and Rosannah Ethelton."

3. On 25 December, Howells wrote to Warner: "This morning I got a letter from poor Clemens that almost breaks my heart. I hope I shall be able to answer it in just the right way" (Cambridge, Watkinson, AGM TS).

175. HOWELLS TO CLEMENS

[Cambridge] Dec. 25, 1877.

My dear Clemens:

I was just about to ask you to let me postpone your story a month, because I found the Feb'y number overfull, and your paper had come last to hand. But I have no idea of dropping you out of the Atlantic, and Mr. Houghton [1] has still less, if possible. You are going to help and not hurt us many a year yet, if you will. Every one with whom I have talked about your speech regards it as a fatality — one of those sorrows into which a man walks with his eyes wide open, no one knows why. I believe that Emerson, Longfellow and Holmes themselves can easily conceive of it in that light, and while I think your regret does you honor and does you good, I don't want you to dwell too morbidly on the matter. Mr. Norton [2] left a note on my table the other day, expressing just the right feeling towards you about it. One of the most fastidious men here,[3] who *read* the speech, saw no offense in it. But I don't pretend not to agree with you about it. All I want you to do is not to exaggerate the damage. You are not going to be floored by it; there is more justice than that even in *this* world. And especially as regards *me,* just call the sore spot well. I could say more and with better heart in praise of your good-feeling (which was what I always liked in you) since this thing happened than I could before.

— A man isn't hurt by any honest effort at reparation. Why shouldn't you write to each of those men and say frankly that at such and such an hour on the 17th of December you did so and so? They would take it in the right spirit, I'm sure. If they didn't the right would be yours.

Mrs. Howells joins me in cordial regards to Mrs. Clemens and yourself.   Ever yours

W. D. Howells.

1. Henry O. Houghton, publisher of the *Atlantic*.

2. Charles Eliot Norton, of Harvard. Howells had written to him on 19 December saying that Clemens was "completely crushed" by his "hideous mistake" at the Whittier dinner; "for he *has* a good and reverent nature for good things, and his performance was like an effect of demoniacal possession" (Cambridge, LinL, I, 243).

3. Probably Francis J. Child, of whom Howells wrote later: "The morning after the dreadful dinner there came a glowing note from Professor Child, who had read the newspaper report of it, praising Clemens's burlesque as the richest piece of humor in the world, and betraying no sense of incongruity in its perpetration in the presence of its victims" (MMT, p. 62).

176. CLEMENS TO HOWELLS

Hartford, Friday [28? December 1877].

My Dear Howells:

Your letter was a godsend; & perhaps the welcomest part of it was your consent that I write to those gentlemen; for you discouraged my hints in that direction that morning in Boston — rightly, too, for my offense was yet too new, then. Warner has tried to hold up our hands like the good fellow he is, but poor Twichell couldn't say a word, & confessed that he would rather take nearly any punishment than face Livy & me. He hasn't been here since!

It is curious, but I pitched early upon Mr. Norton as the very man who would think some generous thing about that matter, whether he said it or not. It is splendid to be a man like that — but it is given to few to be.

I wrote a letter yesterday, & sent a copy to each of the three.[1] I wanted to send a copy to Mr. Whittier also, since the offense was done also against him, being committed in his presence & he the guest of the occasion, besides holding the well nigh sacred place he does in this people's estimation; but I didn't know whether to venture or not, & so ended by doing nothing. It seemed an intrusion to approach him, & even Livy seemed to have her doubts as to the ⟨right⟩ best & properest way to do in the case. I do not reverence Mr. Emerson less, but somehow I could approach him easier.

Send me those proofs, if you have got them handy; I want to submit them to Wylie;[2] he won't show them to anybody.

Had a very pleasant & considerate letter from Mr. Houghton, to-day, & was very glad to receive it.

You can't imagine how brilliant & beautiful that new brass fender is,[3] & how perfectly naturally it takes its place under the carved oak. How they did scour it up before they sent it! I lied a good deal about it when I came home — so for *once* I kept a secret & surprised Livy on a Christmas morning!

I haven't done a stroke of work since the Atlantic dinner; have only moped around. But I'm going to try tomorrow. How could I ever have —

Ah, well, I am a great & sublime fool. But then I am God's fool, & all His works must be contemplated with respect.

Livy & I join in the warmest regards to you & yours.

Yrs Ever

Mark

1. The letter of apology and replies from Longfellow, Holmes, and Emerson's daughter have survived. The supposed victims assured him they felt no offense, and Emerson was described as really not having heard or understood very clearly what Clemens had said. It seems probable, in fact, that Howells and Clemens had believed the offense to be greater than it actually was.

2. Not now identifiable.

3. Part of some bric-a-brac which Mark Twain had bought the morning after the Whittier dinner (MMT, p. 61).

[Hartford] Jan. 4 [1878].

My Dear Howells:

The play [1] is enchanting. I laughed & cried all the way through it. The dialogue is intolerably brilliant; one hadn't time to see where one lightning-burst struck before another followed. I cannot remember when I have spent so delightful an evening in a theatre. Ah, if I only had my old fool of a detective [2] mooning & meddling along through a play like that, once, his fame & fortune would be made. My wife, & Lily Warner enjoyed the piece as heartily & unreservedly as I did.

Love to you all.   Ys Ever

S. L. C.

Dear me, Winnie didn't put her name in our Visitor's Register! Ask her to send it to me on a slip of paper, so that I can paste it in.

1. *A Counterfeit Presentment,* which had reached Hartford in its tour of New England.

2. Simon Wheeler, the principal character in the play he had written in 1877 (see letters 156, 158, and 159).

[Cambridge] Jan. 6, 1877 [1]

My dear Clemens:

Your letter about the play gave me great joy, and so did Warner's most kindly criticism in the Courant.[2] I am very happy in your liking for it. We shall yet write a play together; but you must not expect any profit out of it if we do. I am the champion prosperity-extinguisher. To tell you the truth, I'm awfully discouraged at the failure of the comedy to draw houses in New England. I don't suppose it paid expenses in either Worcester,

Providence, Springfield or Hartford, and I shall not blame Barrett if he withdraws it.[3] I wonder if you had any talk with him about it?

— I was with Mr. Longfellow the morning he got your letter. He spoke of it as "most pathetic," and said everyone seemed to care more for that affair than he did.[4] I know you had the right sort of answer from him. — I couldn't help reading to Mr. Norton, the other day, what you had said of him,[5] and it gave him the greatest pleasure.

Winny will send her name. She now sends her love to your tribe with all of us.   Yours ever

W. D. Howells.

1. An error for 1878.

2. In his unsigned review Warner said that the performance of *A Counterfeit Presentment* at the Hartford Opera House (2 January 1878) had removed his doubts about whether the play contained enough incident to sustain interest, and whether the actors could manage roles requiring subtle rather than pronounced characterization. Howells, he asserted, had successfully undertaken in New England what Goldoni undertook in Venice — "pure comedy of unexaggerated, real life." The reviewer found the play distinguished for "pure humor and keen analysis of character." The added third act he reported as often amusing, but slow (Hartford *Courant*, 3 January 1878, p. 1). Howells thanked Warner for the notice, and agreed with him that the third act was "over-literal" (Cambridge, 12 January, Watkinson, AGM TS).

3. Despite poor houses in parts of New England, Lawrence Barrett brought the play to the Boston Museum for a successful week early in April. Fourteen months later, Howells confessed to Lowell: "My comedy was played some thirty times but is now in abeyance — not to use a harsher expression. They played it charmingly at the Museum, to packed houses, and I in my simple soul thought it beautiful. There is no delight like seeing one's play acted" (Cambridge, 22 June 1879, Houghton). *A Counterfeit Presentment* never achieved lasting popularity. Barrett finally dropped it, and neither Joseph Jefferson nor William Gillette could be persuaded to revive it (Meserve).

4. Longfellow replied to Clemens's letter of apology with a very reassuring note (Cambridge, 6 January 1878; texts of both letters are in *Harvard Library Bulletin*, IX, 164, 167, Spring 1955).

5. In letter 176.

179. HOWELLS TO CLEMENS

[Cambridge] February 24, 1878.

My dear Clemens:

I never was in Berlin and don't know any family hotel there. I shd be glad I didn't, if it would keep you from going.[1] You deserve to put up at the Sign of the Savage in Vienna.[2] Really, it's a great blow to me to hear of that protracted sojourn. It's a shame. I must see you somehow, before you go. I'm in dreadfully low spirits about it.   Yours ever

W. D. H.

I was afraid your silence meant something wicked.

1. A letter of Clemens containing the first intimation to Howells that he intended taking his family to Europe seems to be missing.

2. "At the Sign of the Savage" is the title of a story by Howells which had appeared in the *Atlantic* for July 1877. It concerns a hostelry in Vienna — agreeable enough, apparently — called the "Gasthof zum Wilden Manne."

180. CLEMENS TO HOWELLS

[Hartford] Tuesday [26? February? 1878].

My Dear Howells —

Imagined my silence meant something wicked? — Lord bless me, I never thought of such a thing!

Yes, & I must see *you* before I go; we must all see each other. Now if you folks can by any possibility snatch a few days & run down here before March 25, — *any* time — one date as good as another for us — we shall be ever so grateful. It seems mean to ask this concession of you when we stand so largely in your debt on visiting account, but you know this is a pretty big concern to tear up, disband & put in order for a year or two's absence, so I doubt if the month before us is any more time than necessary for the madam to accomplish it in. My own affairs require a little attention from day to day, too, since I must leave them as straight as I can.

Here you will find no atmosphere of work whatever, because I've laid aside the pen till I reach Europe, so if you can come here we shall have an utter respite from the "shop" & all its belongings, & you may even be able to forget, for the time, that you are an editor & fettered with obligations. Send me a card to say how the chances are.

Our plan is to leave here for Elmira March 25. We have taken 2 staterooms in the Holsatia, which sails for Hamburg April 11. Miss Clara Spaulding [1] (who is here) goes with us — also Rosa & the children. We shall leave nobody here but Patrick & the horses.   Ys Ever

Mark.

over.[2]

P.S. Have written Frank Pixley [3] that I would speak to you when I see you, & if you were willing to simultane with the Argonaut, I would write him so; if you were unwilling I would indicate it by not writing. I didn't tell him you *wouldn't,* because I'm not authorized to speak for you — but told him to write you himself if he preferred. He is a good fellow, but Dam the Argonaut.

Mark.

1. A girlhood friend of Livy's, from Elmira.
2. The postscript is written on the back of the last sheet.
3. Frank M. Pixley, whom Clemens had known in 1864 in Nevada, had founded the *Argonaut* in San Francisco in March 1877. On 17 February 1878 he wrote to ask Clemens for a contribution to the magazine. "We have worked over your old diggins somewhat," he said, "filching anything of yours that we can find: but would prefer to be honest and deal with you direct." Pixley wondered whether Clemens could allow the *Argonaut* to publish a MS simultaneously with some Eastern journal, since "we are 3000 miles away from the Eastern market, and territorial jurisdiction is distinct." Besides, the circulation of the *Argonaut* was only "6000 copies for distribution mostly upon this coast" (San Francisco, MTP). The *Argonaut*'s prospecting seems already to have extended beyond Mark Twain's "old diggins" of articles published long before in Nevada and California: the

issue of the *Argonaut* dated 23 February 1878 (II, No. 7) contained his sketch, "The Loves of Alonzo Fitz Clarence and Rosannah Ethelton," which appeared in the *Atlantic* for March 1878. (Copies of the *Atlantic* reached subscribers about the middle of the month preceding the printed date of publication; and the *Argonaut* may have been a few days behind its weekly schedule.)

181. CLEMENS TO ELINOR M. HOWELLS

[Hartford, 26? February? 1878]

P.S.

Dear Mrs. Howells:

Mrs. Clemens wrote you a letter, & handed it to me half an hour ago, while I was folding mine to Mr. Howells. I laid that letter on this table before me while I added the paragraph about Pixley's application. Since then I have been hunting & swearing, & swearing [and] hunting, but I can't find a sign of that letter. It is the most astonishing disappearance I ever heard of. Mrs. Clemens has gone off driving — so I will have to try & give you an idea of her communication from memory. Mainly it consisted of an urgent desire that you come & see us next week if you can possibly manage it, for that will be a reposeful time, the tur-moil of breaking up beginning the week after. She wants you to tell her about Italy, & advise her in that connection, if you will. Then she spoke of her plans — *hers,* mind you, for I never have anything quite so definite as a plan. She proposes to stop a fort-night in (confound the place, I've forgotten what it was,) — then go on & *live* in Dresden till some time in the summer; then retire to Switzerland for the hottest season, then stay a while in Venice & put in the winter in Munich — this program subject to modification according to circumstances. She said something about some little by-trips here & there, but they didn't stick in my memory because the idea doesn't charm me.

(They have just telephoned me from the Courant office

that Bayard Taylor & family have taken rooms in our ship, the Holsatia, for the 11th of April.) [1]

Do come, if you possibly can! — & remember & don't forget to avoid letting Mrs. Clemens find out I lost her letter. Just answer her the same as if you had got it.   Sincerely Yours

S. L. Clemens

MS. This letter was probably enclosed with Clemens's letter to Howells of 26? February?

1. Taylor had been appointed United States minister to Germany. On 2 March he wrote Clemens confirming his intention to cross on the *Holsatia* "if the Gov't. will allow me that much time at home," and added: "I saw your name in the book, which is another inducement. But I dare n't positively engage passage until after the Senate has acted" (New York, MTP).

182. HOWELLS TO CLEMENS (POSTCARD)

[Cambridge, 2 March 1878?]

How would Saturday of next week [1] do for that projected visit? I could come down on the 9 (?) o'clock train, and stay till Monday morning.

W. D. H.

1. If this note is properly dated it proposes a visit of Howells alone to Hartford on 9–11 March.

183. HOWELLS TO CLEMENS

[Cambridge] March 3, 1878.

My dear Clemens:

Mrs. Howells starts to New York on Wednesday, and I propose to go with her as far as Hartford, where if convenient for you we will both stop off till one o'clock the next day.[1] We shall leave Boston on the 3 p.m. train. In spite of the kind reassurances of

Mrs. Clemens we feel the visit at this time to be an infliction, but it's a pleasure which we can't deny ourselves. My wife wants to talk over the proposed travel with Mrs. Clemens.

— All this to hold good in case Wednesday *is not furiously tempestuous.* In that event Mrs. H. feels that it would not be safe to slip off — I don't know why.   Yours ever

W. D. Howells.

Don't bother to meet us at the station. We know the way.

I don't believe our people would simultane.[2] You see it isn't like simultaning with a foreign country.

1. This note revises the proposal of the day before concerning a date for visiting Hartford, and includes both the Howellses in the plan. Wednesday would have been 6 March. Elinor Howells was going to New York to visit her relatives the Augustus D. Shepards in New Jersey.

2. A reply to Clemens's question in letter 180 about the San Francisco *Argonaut.*

184. CLEMENS TO HOWELLS

[Hartford, 4? or 5? March? 1878?]

P.S. Later. My facts are astray. We return home *Wednesday.* So, what-ever day you come, we shall be here & expecting you.

S. L. C.

MS. The body of the letter to which this postscript belongs has been lost.

185. CLEMENS TO HOWELLS

[Hartford] Mch 15 [1878].

My Dear Howells:

If you print this [1] will you see that simultane-sheets go to the Canadian Monthly & to Chatto & Windus 74 Piccadilly, London.[2] That is, if I'm out of the country by that time.

I'm going to be away out in Elmira, 300 miles from N. Y when the Taylor banquet [3] comes off, so I shall have to decline, I suppose.

I was *determined* to have one more look at you, in Boston, before we go, but I've just been 2 days in New York [4] & Livy had no sleep while I was gone. I dasn't rob her of another nights rest, for she has to be on her feet & hard at work from now till we leave, 26th. The drawing- & pink rooms have a melancholy look, to-day — uncarpeted & wholly stripped & empty. This work of desolation is to go right on, day after day.

I am called — Good-bye, for today!   Yrs Ever

Mark.

1. Probably "About Magnanimous-Incident Literature," published in the *Atlantic* for May 1878 (DE, XIX, 326–334).

2. Clemens wishes to send advance proofs of the article to the *Canadian Monthly*, Toronto, in order to forestall piracy by *Belford's Monthly* (letter 164). But the article was not published in either of these Canadian magazines, perhaps because Clemens soon changed his mind about "simultaning" in Canada (letter 188). The proofs sent to Chatto & Windus were for publication in their magazine *Belgravia*, where the article appeared in the issue for May 1878, under the title "Fables and Their Sequels."

3. The farewell banquet for Taylor took place on 4 April, at Delmonico's in New York. Mark Twain was able to attend after all, and made a short speech, the text of which is not extant (MTB, p. 617).

4. The brief trip to New York was on business, the nature of which remains obscure. A notebook entry for 1878 reads: "Mch. 13 (I think it was, that Lester & I talked at Rossmore [Hotel, in New York] & he made promises" (#12, TS, p. 2, MTP). The business involved Charles J. Langdon, Livy's brother, and J. D. F. Slee, of the Langdon family coal business in Elmira, who hoped that Clemens could help them; and Senator John P. Jones of Nevada, whose associate was the Lester mentioned in the notebook entry (Slee to SLC, Elmira, 23 March 1878, MTP). Whatever the business may have been, it left Clemens intensely annoyed with Jones, who figures prominently in notebook entries of this period as a man "whose proper place is shyster in a Tombs court."

186. HOWELLS TO CLEMENS

[Cambridge] March 16, 1878.

Dear Clemens:

The new thing you send me [1] is perfectly delicious. It went right home every time. What a fancy you *have* got! And what sense!

It was such a clear case that Mrs. Howells and I had the best time in the world at your house last week that it seemed useless to say so and a sort of folly to thank you for it. — I know how you must feel about those desolated rooms. "I'm a mother, myself, Mr. Copperfield."

As to being at the Taylor banquet on the 4th, I don't know. Whitelaw Reid [2] has asked me to a dinner he will give T. the night before he sails and I'd much rather go to that — only 25 commensals instead of 200. Perhaps I shall go to both. My missus is coming home to-day and will decide for me. At any rate I shall see you either on the 4th or the 10th.   Yours ever

W. D. Howells.

It's sickening to have you going away.

1. "About Magnanimous-Incident Literature."
2. Editor of the New York *Tribune* and a friend of Howells since the winter of 1860–61 (YMY, pp. 213–214). Howells stayed at his house for three days on the occasion of his ten-day visit to New York early in April; and he did, after all, attend the public Taylor banquet on 4 April (LinL, I, 253).

187. ELINOR M. HOWELLS TO OLIVIA L. CLEMENS

Cambridge March 21st [1878]

Dear Mrs Clemens:

Only a word — just to say good bye again and to tell how much both Mr Howells & I enjoyed our visit at your house. You seemed so calm & unruffled; and not a look or movement showed that you were about to go "through the floods" of break-ing-up — which are about as bad as the ocean. We hoped Mr

Clemens would run over here for a night — but he seems to think he cant. But Mr Howells will see you — both I hope — in New York at the time of the Taylor dinner & of your sailing.

One thing I said in Hartford (*several* would bear it) I wish to correct: that Dickens spoke of the Fieldses' Mutton as "*raw.*"[1] Of course it wasn't so. I suppose it rare I meant — but he may have expressed himself in quite another way. I never remember stories as I hear them. You see I am rivalling your husband in truthfulness? But I thought afterwards "what must Mrs Day[2] have thought of my statement"! We are being nipped by an east wind. You are going out to meet the lovely Spring abroad. With feelings of regret — and envy — I see you depart. With this note goes one to Miss Mary Wells[3] saying we cannot come there this Spring. How forlorn Hartford will be without you! The Warners will be there to visit. But you know when I visited you I had never seen them there. Now when I visit them I shall feel the emptiness of your house. Adieu! Adieu!

Elinor M. Howells

1. Elinor Howells, who talked a great deal and very well, is revealed here as repentant over an idle remark concerning the visit of Dickens to Boston ten years earlier. He dined with the James T. Fieldses on 5 March 1868, and Howells was present (LinL, I, 127); but it is not clear that Mrs. Howells was also, and she may have been reporting Dickens's conversation from hearsay.

2. Alice Hooker Day, daughter of Isabella Beecher Hooker and thus niece of Thomas K. Beecher, who had been invited by Livy's father to the pulpit of Park Church in Elmira in 1854. Alice and Livy had been close friends since childhood (NF, p. 250, n. 39).

3. Now unidentifiable.

188. CLEMENS TO HOWELLS

[Hartford] 23^d [March 1878]

My Dear Howells —

No, we won't simultane with Canada unless Houghton can get the Canadian copyright transferred immediately to himself or some personal friend of his in Canada.[1] Won't he try?

O dear! Orion's MS book [2] has come & I've read it all through. There are good places in it, but oh, the manifest apprentice hand!

And that reminds me — ungrateful dog that I am — that I owe as much to your training as the rude country job printer owes to the city boss who takes him in hand & teaches him the right way to handle his art. I was talking to Mrs. Clemens about this the other day & grieving because I had never mentioned it to you, thereby seeming to ignore it or be unaware of it. Nothing that has passed under your eye needs any revision before going into a volume, while all my other stuff does require so *much*.[3]

I'm glad you like this last sketch — I begin to like it myself, now.

The trunks are being packed — the furniture is boxed — we depart out of this home next Wednesday. But for the madam's sleepless nights when I am away, I should certainly ring your door bell this evening at 7. Mrs. C. is full of pleasure over Mrs. Howells's letter.   Yrs Ever

                                                              Mark.

1. It will be recalled that on 15 March Clemens had asked Howells to see that proof sheets of "About Magnanimous-Incident Literature" were sent to the *Canadian Monthly*. He now acknowledges a difficulty, perhaps brought to his attention in a letter from Howells now lost. The *Canadian Monthly* was to be taken over by Clemens's hated enemies the Belfords with the issue for July 1878, and some rumor of this impending change had apparently reached Boston. Clemens would have suffered agonies if he had helped the Belfords get Canadian copyright to any of his work by sending it himself to a magazine they were about to acquire.

2. A work of fiction describing an imaginary expedition through "Symmes's Hole," supposedly an opening at the North Pole, to the interior of the earth. When he began writing it, Orion had never heard of Jules Verne's *Journey to the Centre of the Earth* (first published 1864; English translations, Boston, 1874, etc.), but at Clemens's suggestion he had subsequently tried to make his book into a burlesque of Verne (Orion to SLC, Keokuk, 5, 26 February 1878, MTP).

3. Mark Twain's hearty and explicit acknowledgment of the value of Howells's criticism for him is impressive. Although he once made a comparable (but less enthusiastic) record of his indebtedness to Bret Harte

(SLC to TBA, Buffalo, 28 January 1871, MTL, I, 182–183), he spoke of no critic save Livy with the warmth of approval he shows here for Howells.

189. CLEMENS TO HOWELLS

May 4 [1878]. Frankfort on the Main

My Dear Howells —

I only propose to write a single line to say we are still ⟨alive⟩ around. Ah, I have such a deep, grateful, unutterable sense of being "out of it all." I think I foretaste some of the advantage of being dead. Some of the joy of it. I don't read any newspapers or care for them. When people tell me England has declared war,[1] I drop the subject, feeling that it is none of my business; when they tell me Mrs. Tilton has confessed & Mr. B. denied,[2] I say both of them have done that before, therefore let the worn stub of the Plymouth white-wash brush be brought out once more,[3] & let the faithful spit on their hands & get to work again regardless of me — for I am out of it all.

We had 2 almost devilish weeks at sea (& I tell you Bayard Taylor is a really lovable man — which you already knew); then we staid a week in the beautiful, the *very* beautiful city of Hamburg; & since then we have been fooling along, 4 hours per day by rail, with a courier, spending the other 20 in hotels whose enormous bedchambers & private parlors are an overpowering marvel to me. Day before yesterday, in Cassel, we had a love of a bedroom 31 feet long, & a parlor with 2 sofas, 12 chairs, a writing desk & 4 tables scattered around here & there in it. Made of red silk, too, by George.

The times & times I wish you were along! *You* could throw some fun into the journey; whereas I go on, day by day, in a smileless state of solemn admiration.

What a paradise this land is! What clean clothes, what good faces, what tranquil contentment, what prosperity, what genuine freedom, what superb government! And I am so happy, for I am responsible for none of it. I am only here to enjoy.

How charmed I am when I overhear a German word which I understand!

With love from us 2 to you 2.

Mark.

P.S. — We are not taking six days to go from Hamburg to Heidelberg because we prefer it. Quite the contrary. Mrs. Clemens picked up a dreadful cold & sore throat on board ship & still keeps them in stock — so she could only travel 4 hours a day. She wanted to dive straight through, but I had different notions about the wisdom of it. I found that 4 hours a day was the best she could do. Before I forget it, our permanent address is Care Messrs. Koester & Co., Bankers, Heidelberg. We go there to-morrow.

Poor Susie! From the day we reached German soil, we have required Rosa to speak German to the children — which they hate with all their souls. The other morning in Hanover, Susie came to me (from Rosa, in the nursery,) & said, in halting syllables, "Papa, wie viel Uhr ist es?" — then turned, with pathos in her big eyes, & said, "Mamma, I wish Rosa was made in English."

1. Diplomatic tension between England and Russia growing out of the Russo-Turkish War of 1877–78 fostered such rumors, but the difficulties were resolved by a secret pact between the two countries on 30 May.

2. In 1874 Theodore Tilton, editor of a widely read religious weekly, *The Independent,* had brought suit for alienation of his wife's affections against Henry Ward Beecher. The case had been a front-page sensation throughout the country for six months in 1875. Clemens had been interested enough at the time to go down to Brooklyn with Twichell and spend a whole day (14 April 1875) observing the trial.

3. Although Beecher was almost certainly guilty of adultery with Mrs. Tilton, Tilton's suit ended in a hung jury, and Beecher was declared innocent in various hearings and investigations conducted by his congregation in the Plymouth Church, Brooklyn (Shaplen, *Free Love and Heavenly Sinners,* pp. 215, 253, 266–267). In MMT Howells says (in a transparent allusion that avoids mentioning names): "He [Clemens] believed the accused guilty, but when we met some months after it was over, and I tempted him to speak his mind upon it, he would only say, The man had suffered enough; as if the man had expiated his wrong, and he was not going to do anything to renew his penalty. I found that very curious, very delicate" (p. 68).

190. CLEMENS TO HOWELLS

Schloss-Hotel Heidelberg, May 26 [1878].
Sunday A.M.

My Dear Howells:

[. . .]¹ divinely located. From this airy perch among the shining groves we look down upon Heidelberg Castle, & upon the swift Neckar, & the town, & out over the wide green level of the Rhine valley — a marvelous prospect. We are in a cul de sac formed of hill-ranges & river: we are on the side of a steep mountain; the river at our feet is walled, on its other side, (yes, on both sides,) by a steep & wooded mountain-range which rises abruptly aloft from the water's edge; portions of these mountains are densely wooded; the plain of the Rhine, seen through ⟨the mouth of the opening of⟩ the mouth of this pocket, has many & peculiar charms for the eye.

Our ⟨big⟩ bed-room has two great glass bird-cages (enclosed balconies) one looking toward the Rhine Valley & sunset, the other looking up the Neckar-cul de sac, & naturally we spend nearly all our time in these — when one is sunny the other is shady. We have tables & chairs in them; we do our reading, writing, studying, smoking & suppering in them.

The view from these bird-cages is my despair. The picture changes from one enchanting aspect to another in ceaseless procession, never keeping one form half an hour, & never taking on an unlovely one. To look out upon the Rhine Valley when a thunderstorm is sweeping across it is a [. . .]² day there is a [. . .] the way of a sun [. . .] that the sunrise [. . .] the moonlight dr [. . .] town, bridges & [. . .] soothing & satisfying to the outlooker. And then Heidelberg on a dark night! It is massed, away down there, almost right under us, you know, and stretches off toward the valley. Its curved & interlacing streets are a cobweb, beaded thick with lights — a wonderful thing to see; then the rows of lights on the arched bridges, & their glinting reflections in the water; & away at the ⟨other⟩ far end, the Eisenbahnhof, with its twenty solid acres of glittering gas-jets, a huge garden, as one may say, whose every plant is a flame.

These balconies are the darlingest things. I have spent all this morning in this north one. Counting big & little, it has 256 panes of glass in it; so one is in effect right out in the free sunshine, & yet sheltered from wind & rain — & likewise doored & curtained from whatever may be going on in the bedroom. It must have been a noble genius who devised this hotel. Lord, how blessed is the repose, the tranquillity of this place! Only two sounds: the happy clamor of the birds in the groves, & the muffled music of the Neckar, tumbling over the opposing dikes. It is no hardship to lie awake awhile, nights, for this subdued roar has exactly the sound of a steady rain beating upon a roof. It is so healing to the spirit; & it bears up the thread of one's imaginings as the accompaniment bears up a song.[3]

While Livy & Miss Spaulding have been writing at this table, I have sat tilted back, near by, with a pipe & the last Atlantic, & read Charley Warner's article [4] with prodigious enjoyment. I think it is exquisite. I think it must be the roundest & broadest & completest short essay he has ever written. It is clear, & compact, & charmingly done.

The hotel grounds join & communicate with the Castle grounds; so we & the children loaf in the winding paths of those leafy vastnesses a great deal, & drink beer & listen to excellent music.

When we first came to this hotel, a couple of weeks ago, I pointed to a house across the river, by the water's edge, & said I meant to rent the centre room on the 3ᵈ floor for a work-room. Jokingly we got to speaking of it as my office; & amused ourselves with watching "my people" daily in their small grounds & trying to make out what we could of their dress, &c., without a glass. Well, I loafed along there one day & found on that house the only sign of the kind on that side of the river: "Moblirte Wohnung zu Vermiethen!" I went in & rented that very room which I had long ago selected. There was only one other room in the whole double-house unrented.

(It occurs to me that I made a great mistake in not thinking to deliver a very bad German speech (every other sentence pieced out with English,) at the Bayard Taylor banquet in New York;[5] I think I could have made it one of the features of the occasion.)

We left Hartford before the end of ⟨April⟩ March, & I have been idle ever since. I have waited for a "call" to go to work — I knew it would come. Well, it began to come a week ago; my note-book comes out more & more frequently every day since; 3 days ago I concluded to move my manuscripts over to my den. *Now* the call is loud & decided, at last. So, tomorrow I shall begin regular, steady work, & stick to it till middle of July or 1st August, when I look for Twichell;[6] we will then walk about Germany 2 or 3 weeks & then I'll go to work again — (perhaps in Munich.)

We both send a power of love to the Howellses, & we do wish you were here. Are you in the new house? Tell us about it.

Yrs Ever

Mark.

1. The upper left corner of the first sheet of the letter has been cut off.

2. The mutilation affects p. 3 also.

3. The Neckar Valley, the castle, the hotel, the glass-enclosed balconies, the view of the city at night, etc., are described also in Chapter II of *A Tramp Abroad,* with a number of verbal echoes of this letter.

4. One of the installments in a series entitled "The Adirondacks Verified," which ran January–June 1878; perhaps the article in the May number, "A Character Study," devoted to a philosophic guide named Orson Phelps.

5. Mark Twain used this plan for his speech at a Fourth of July celebration sponsored by the Anglo-American Club of Heidelberg. He describes it in one of the passages omitted from *A Tramp Abroad:*

"I had written a little seven-minute speech, chiefly in execrable German, three days before, & had put in a great deal of hard but successful work in getting it by heart. The difficulty had not been to memorize the words, but the pauses, the pretended embarrassments, the hesitations, the taking compulsory refuge in English occasionally, — in a word, the various & sundry tricks of manner & utterance which give to a set speech the struggling, diffident, & confused look of a lame impromptu performance.

"I had expected to have a charming good time out of my oration, but the absurdity of it soon began to try me severely, & before I got to the middle I laughed. It was a strange accident, for when one is talking nonsense to an audience he usually feels serious almost to sadness, & has no impulse toward the opposite direction.

"I sat down, of course. It would have been useless to try to keep up the pretense of being in deep & sincere trouble after having laughed" (DV 4, pp. 368–372, MTP).

6. Twichell was to come to Europe as Mark Twain's guest for the "pedestrian tour" described in *A Tramp Abroad*. In this narrative Twichell figures as "Harris."

191. HOWELLS TO CLEMENS

[Boston] [1] June 2, 1878.

My dear Clemens:

Ich habe Ihren herzerfreuenden Brief erhalten — or do you prefer English by this time? There is at least one American family whom your absence from the country truly bereaves, and I need not tell you your letter was truly welcome, and duly read aloud at the breakfast table the morning it came. We are still in Cambridge, and we no longer put our faith in joiners. The Belmont house [2] is promised us in a month — and was so a month ago. But the weather remains charmingly cool in Cambridge, and as nobody wants to buy or to hire this house, it costs us nothing to stay in it. Just now we are excited about a horse and phaeton which we are to buy, and I suppose that by the end of a fortnight I shall be the worst sold ass in Massachusetts. But to a literary man all these things are gain: they turn into material, as we all know.[3] The only thing that doesn't is a displeasure with an actor: that's a thing that one likes to keep to one's self. — I am working away steadily at my new story,[4] which promises to be a long one, and I am venturing on some untried paths in it. Think of so domestic a man as I wrecking his hero on a coral island — an uninhabited *atoll* — in the South Pacific! There's courage for you! [5] Till I get this done, I try not even to think of a play, though to tell you the truth I would ten times rather write plays than anything else, and I shall tackle the Steam Generator [6] at the earliest opportunity. I have had a very pleasant letter from your cub-dramatist in Hartford,[7] renouncing — or rather disclaiming — all right and title to Clews.[8]

— Osgood goes abroad this month, with Waring. Aldrich spends the summer at Swampscott. John Hay is, I suppose, in Europe by this time: from a short note he sent me before sailing, I'm afraid his health is delicate. Him and O. you would like to see, and will, I dare say. Harte, you know, has got a consular appointment somewhere in Germany.[9] So you see you are likely to be joined by the whole fraternity during the summer. I alone shall stay at home. In fact, I find that I have outlived all longing for Europe: you are now the principal attraction of that elderly enchantress, as far as I'm concerned. — I hope you'll find all the hoped-for leisure there, and that you'll not be able to keep from writing for The Atlantic. Otherwise I must begin printing your private letters to satisfy the popular demand. People are constantly asking when you're going to begin. (That's a pleasant thorn to plant in a friend's side.) — When I parted from you, that dismal day in New York, I saw that the weather was capable of anything, and I'm not surprised to hear how it used you; but I hope that by this time Mrs. Clemens is all well of her cold, and that poor Susie is more reconciled to Rosa's composition. Really, however, I could imagine the German going harder with you, for you always seemed to me a man who liked to be understood with the least possible personal inconvenience. The worst thing about any foreign country is its language, which the natives never can speak with our accent. — What a stupid letter. But give me another chance, by answering. You know that at my dullest, my heart is in the right place. Mrs. Howells joins me in love to both of you.   Affectionately,

W. D. Howells.

Tell me about Capt. Wakeman in Heaven, and all your other enterprises.

1. The editorial offices of the *Atlantic* had been moved from Cambridge to Winthrop Square, Boston, about 1 April.

2. Designed by Elinor's brother, William Rutherford Mead of the firm of McKim, Mead, & White, in the then very modern Queen Anne style. The house was named Red-Top from the long sloping red roof. It com-

manded a magnificent view over Cambridge and Boston. In back were "lovely hill-tops, and gardened slopes" with a road fraying off into "the most delightful country lane to be found anywhere within a hundred miles of Boston" (Cady, *Road to Realism*, p. 199; LinL, I, 270). The house held the finest of Howells's studies, with a broad fireplace, ample bookshelves, and the Shakespearian inscription "From Venice as far as Belmont," the hint for which may well have come from the Emersonian dictum "written in perennial brass" over the fireplace in Clemens's Hartford library, "The ornament of a house is the friends who frequent it" (MMT, p. 37). The Howells family moved during the week of 8 July, and on the fourteenth Howells wrote Warner: "We have had a perfect 'hell of a time' . . . with the carpenters and painters, since we moved in; but they're all out now, *about*; and we're ready for friends" (Belmont, Watkinson).

3. Howells's "Buying a Horse" was published in the *Atlantic* for June 1879.

4. *A Woman's Reason,* not completed and published until 1883.

5. Even with the help of Thomas S. Collier, a young naval officer who knew the Pacific and the China coast, and of Edmund Gosse, who could tell him of Hong Kong, Howells could not make probable the long separation of his hero from his heroine by shipwreck and sojourn on an atoll in the South Pacific. *A Woman's Reason* is one of Howells's few ventures into melodramatic action, the "moving accidents" and dire catastrophes which he would soon insist were not the stock in trade of "the new school" of realists in fiction (George W. Arms, "A Novel and Two Letters," *Journal of the Rutgers University Library,* VIII, 9–13, December 1944).

6. "The Steam Generator" is probably the project for a collaborative play that Clemens had proposed to Howells. Another early title for the play was "Orme's Motor"; it was eventually called *Colonel Sellers as a Scientist.*

7. The cub dramatist cannot be identified unless he is William Gillette, young brother of Lilly Warner, who was struggling to make his way in the theatre as actor and dramatist. Clemens had helped him get a small part in *Colonel Sellers* and had lent him $3000 to finance his apprenticeship. But there is no evidence to connect Gillette with Clemens's efforts at writing plays.

8. An alternative title for "Cap'n Simon Wheeler, The Amateur Detective."

9. Despite Clemens's violent opposition to a consular appointment for Harte, Howells had quietly helped secure the Crefeld consular post for him because he had become convinced that Harte was "really making an effort to reform" (LinL, I, 251–252).

192. CLEMENS TO HOWELLS

Schloss Hotel [Heidelberg], June 27 [1878].

My Dear Howells:

What do the newspapers say about Harte's appointment? Billiardly-speaking, the President ⟨(through persuasion of Evarts,[1] I judge)⟩ scored 400 points on each, when he appointed Lowell & Taylor[2] — but when he appointed Harte he simply pocketed his own ball. — Now just take a realizing sense of what this fellow is, when one names things by their plain dictionary names — to wit: Harte is a liar, a thief, a swindler, a snob, a sot, a sponge, a coward, a Jeremy Diddler, he is brim full of treachery, & he conceals his Jewish birth as carefully as if he considered it a disgrace. How do I know? By the best of all evidence, personal observation. With one exception: I don't know him, myself, to be a thief, but John Carmany, publisher of the Overland Monthly, charges him with stealing money delivered to him to be paid to contributors, & the defrauded contributors back Mr. Carmany. I think Charley Stoddard said Harte had never ventured to deny this in print, though W. A. Kendall, who published the charge in the San Francisco Chronicle, not only invited him to deny it, but dared him to do it.[3] O, the loveliness of putting Harte into the public service, after removing Geo. H. Butler[4] from it for lack of character! If he had only been made a home official, I think I could stand it; but to send this nasty creature to puke upon the American name in a foreign land is too much.

I don't deny that I feel personally snubbed; for it seems only fair that after the letter I wrote last summer the President should not have silently ignored my testimony, but should have given me a chance to prove what I had said against Harte. I think I could have piled up facts enough to show that Harte was fitted for the highest office in the gift of the city of New York.

Now there's one thing that *shan't* happen. Harte shan't swindle the Germans if I can help it. Tell me what German

235

town he is to filthify with his presence; then I will write the authorities there that he is a persistent borrower who never pays. They need not believe it unless they choose — that is their affair, not mine.

Have you heard any literary men express an opinion about the appointment? Who were they — & what said they?

Ah, don't I wish I could venture to write for the Atlantic! The only thing in the way is Canada. If Mr. Houghton can copyright my stuff in Canada & hold it *himself*, & will prosecute & stop any infringement, I shall be glad enough to write; but I can't trust any more Canadians after my late experience.[5] I suppose they are all born pirates. I do not know that I have any printable stuff just now — separatable stuff, that is, — but I shall have, by & by. It is very gratifying to hear that it is wanted by anybody. I stand always prepared to hear the reverse, & am constantly surprised that it is delayed so long. Consequently it is not going to astonish me when it comes.

Mrs. Clemens, who even reads note-books in her hunger for culture, was rather startled to run across this paragraph in mine, last night:

"Have all sorts of heavens — have a gate for each sort. Wakeman visits these various heavens. One gate where they receive a barkeeper with artillery salutes, swarms of angels in the sky, & a noble torchlight procession. *He* thinks he is *the* lion of Heaven. Procession over, he drops at once into solid obscurity. But the roughest part of it is, that he has to do 30 weeks' penance — day & night he must carry a torch & shout himself hoarse to do honor to some poor scrub whom he wishes had gone to hell." [6]

I wish I was writing that Wakeman book, but I suppose I shan't get at it again before next year.[7]

Privately, I have some good news to tell you. That is, I believe it will gratify you — in fact I am sure it will — though I am not acquainted with a great many people whom it would please. It is this: *we've quit feeling poor!* Isn't that splendid? You know that for two years we have been coming to want, every little while, & have straightway gone to economising. ⟨Well, the annual report from the coal firm [8] came yesterday, & with that as a basis) Yesterday we fell to figuring & discovered that we have more than income enough, from investments, to live in Hartford on a generous scale. Well, now that we are fixed at last, of course the communists & the asinine government will go to work & smash it all. No matter, we have resolved to quit feeling poor for a little while, any way. This thing was so gratifying to me that my first impulse was to run to you with it.

Drat this German tongue, I never shall be able to learn it. I think I could learn a little conversational stuff, maybe, if I could attend to it, but I found I couldn't spare the time. I took lessons two weeks & got so I could understand the talk going on around me, & even answer back, after a fashion. But I neither talk nor listen, now, so I can't even understand the language any more. Mrs. Clemens is getting along fast, & Miss Spaulding & our little Susie talk the devilish tongue without difficulty. But the Bay scorns the language. The nurse & the governess blandish around her in vain. She maintains the calm & persistent attitude of not caring a damn for German. There is a good deal of character in the Bay — such as it is.

Look here, Howells, when I choose to gratify my passions by writing great long letters to you, you are not to consider anything but the briefest answers necessary — & not even those when you have got things to do. Don't forget that. A lengthy letter from you is a great prize & a welcome, but it gives me a reproach, because I seem to have robbed a busy man of time which he ought not to have spared.

Well, good bye & good luck attend you. We both send love to you & yours.   As Ever

Mark.

over.

All day to-day I have been having an experience — & it results in this maxim:

To man all things are possible but one — he cannot have a hole in the seat of his breeches & keep his fingers out of it.

A man does seem to feel more distress & more persistent & distracting solicitude about such a thing than he could about a sick child that was threatening to grow worse every time he took his attention away from it. (Mrs. Clemens said you wouldn't understand the maxim unless I explained it!)

1. William M. Evarts, Secretary of State in Hayes's Cabinet.

2. Hayes had appointed James Russell Lowell minister to Spain and Bayard Taylor minister to Germany.

3. These charges refer to the late 1860's, before Harte came East from San Francisco.

4. In letter 199 Clemens indicates that Butler had been appointed to a diplomatic post but was dismissed "before he got there" because he got drunk. The editors have not been able to document the incident.

5. On 4 January 1878 Eustace Conway, eldest son of Moncure D. Conway, wrote to Clemens from London that a Canadian publisher had brought out au unauthorized edition of his "Old Times on the Mississippi" papers in the *Atlantic,* and that there was danger of an unauthorized edition in England (MTP). Howells had also suffered from the Canadians: Belford Bros. had pirated *Their Wedding Journey* and *A Chance Acquaintance (Belford's Monthly,* I, 133, December 1876). They were to continue their depredations. In 1879 Howells complained that the Belford edition of *A Counterfeit Presentment,* selling for $1, was made to resemble the authorized $2 edition, and copies were being sold not only in Canada but in the United States (to WCH, 11 May, LinL, I, 268). Belford Bros. published at least five editions of *The Lady of the Aroostook* (letter 201).

6. The notebook entry which Mark Twain transcribes (with some rearrangement of sentences) occurs under the date 20 March 1878 (#12, TS, p. 4, MTP); the original has "3 weeks" instead of "30 weeks." The torchlight procession greeting the barkeep is described in "Extract from Captain Stormfield's Visit to Heaven" (*Harper's,* January 1908), but the narrative breaks off at that point and there is no indication that Mark Twain ever continued it (Dixon Wecter, ed., *Report from Paradise,* New York, 1952).

7. On 23 March 1878 Clemens wrote his brother Orion that he had mapped out "A Journey to Heaven" in 1869, had written a first draft in 1870, had rewritten it in 1873, and had discussed the piece frequently with Howells, who had repeatedly advised redoing it. At last, in March 1878, Howells had approved Mark Twain's plan and urged him to develop the story into a book for publication first in England with an endorsement by Arthur Stanley, Dean of Westminster, to "draw *some* of the teeth of the religious press." Mark Twain added: "Neither Howells nor I believe in hell or the divinity of the Savior, but no matter, the Savior is none the less a sacred Personage & a man should have no desire or disposition to refer to him lightly, profanely, or otherwise than with the profoundest reverence" (Hartford, MTP).

8. Livy Clemens had inherited a substantial interest in her father's coal

company upon his death in 1870. The business was probably recovering from the effects of the Panic of 1873.

193. CLEMENS TO HOWELLS

Venice, Sept. 27 [1878].

My Dear Howells:

Have I offended you in some way? The Lord knows it is my disposition, my infirmity, to do such things; but if I have done it in your case, I can truthfully say that if I had known it at the time, I would not have done it, & if it were to do again I would not do it — & in any case I am sorry.

I started to write a thing today which has been in my mind, but these thoughts came into my head instead.

I wish you were Consul here,[1] for we want to stay a year, & would do so in that case — but as it is, I suppose we shall stay only 3 or 4 weeks.   Yrs Sincerely

S. L. Clemens

Our address (for want of a better) is still Heidelberg, Care of Consul E. M. Smith, Lang's Hotel. — Drop us a postal-card when you get this.

1. Howells had been United States consul in Venice 1861–1865.

194. CLEMENS TO HOWELLS

No. 1ᵃ· Karlstrasse, 2ᵉ Stock.
Munich, Nov. 17 [1878].
Care Fraülein Dahlweiner.

My Dear Howells —

We arrived here night before last, pretty well fagged: an 8-hour pull from Rome to Florence; a rest there of a day & two nights; then 5 1/2 hours to Bologna; one night's rest; then from

239

noon to 10.30 pm carried us to Trent, in the Austrian Tyrol, where the confounded hotel had not received our message, & so at that miserable hour, in that snowy region, the tribe had to shiver together in fireless rooms while beds were prepared & warmed; then up at 6 in the morning & a noble view of snow-peaks glittering in the rich light of a full moon while the hotel-devils lazily deranged a breakfast for us in the dreary gloom of blinking candles; then a solid 12-hour pull through the loveliest snow-ranges & snow-draped forests — & at 7 pm we hauled up, in drizzle & fog at the domicil which had been engaged for us ten months before. Munich did seem the horriblest place, the most desolate place, the most unendurable place! — & the rooms were *so* small, the conveniences so meagre, & the porcelain stoves so grim, ghastly, dismal, intolerable! So Livy & Clara sat down forlorn, & cried, & I retired to a private place to pray. By & by we all retired to our narrow German beds; & when Livy & I finished talking across the room, it was all decided that we would rest 24 hours, then pay whatever damages were required, & straightway fly to the south of France.

But you see, that was simply fatigue. Next morning the tribe fell in love with the rooms, with the weather, with Munich, & head over heels in love with Fraülein Dahlweiner. We got a larger parlor — an ample one — threw two communicating bedrooms into one, for the children, & now we are entirely comfortable. The only apprehension, now, is that the climate may not be just right for the children — in which case we shall *have* to go to France, but it will be with the sincerest regret.

Now *I* brought the tribe through from Rome, myself. We never had so little trouble before. The next time anybody has a courier to put out to nurse, I shall not be in the market.

Last night the forlornities had all disappeared; so we gathered around the lamp, after supper, with our beer & my pipe, & in a condition of grateful snugness tackled the new magazines. I read your new story [1] aloud, amid thunders of applause, & we all agreed that Captain Jenness & the old man with the accordion hat are lovely people and most skilfully drawn — & that cabin-boy, too, we like. Of course we are all glad the girl is gone to Venice — for there is no place like Venice. Now I easily understand that the old man couldn't go, because you have a purpose in sending Lyddy by herself; but you could send the old man over in another ship, & we particularly want him along. Suppose you *don't* need him there? What of that? Can't you let him feed the doves? Can't you let him fall in the Canal occasionally? Can't you let his good-natured purse be a daily prey to guides and beggar-boys? Can't you let the cheerful gondoliers canvas his hat? Can't you let him find peace & rest & fellowship under père Jacopo's [2] kindly wing? (However you are writing the book, not I, — still, I am one of the people you are writing it *for,* you understand.) I only want to insist, in a friendly way, that the old man shall shed his sweet influence frequently upon the page — that is all.

The first time we called at the convent, père Jacopo was absent; the next (just at this moment Miss Spaulding spoke up & said something about père Jacopo — there is more in this acting of one mind upon another than people think) time, he was there, & gave us preserved rose-leaves to eat, & talked about you, & Mrs. Howells, & Winnie, & brought out his photographs, & showed us a picture of "the library of your new house," but not so — it was the study in your Cambridge house. He was very sweet & good. He called on us next day; & the day after that we left Venice, after a pleasant sojourn of 3 or 4 weeks. He expects to spend this winter in Munich & will see us often, he said.

Pretty soon, I'm going to write something, & when I finish it I shall know whether to put it to itself or in the "Contributor's Club." That "Contributor's Club" was a most happy idea. The idiot does not more unfailingly turn first to the "Drawer" [3] than does the wise man to the "C.C." By the way, *I* think that the man who wrote the paragraph beginning at the bottom of page 643 [4] has said a mighty sound and sensible thing. I wish his suggestion could be adopted.

It is lovely of you to keep that old pipe [5] in such a place of honor.

While it occurs to me, I must tell you Susie's last. She is sorely badgered with dreams; & her stock dream is that she is being eaten up by bears. She is a grave & thoughtful child, as you will remember. Last night she had the usual dream. This morning she stood apart (after telling it,) for some time, looking vacantly at the floor, & absorbed in meditation. At last she looked up, & with the pathos of one who feels he has not been dealt by with even-handed fairness, said, "But mamma, the trouble is, that I am never the *bear,* but always the PERSON." It would not have occurred to me that there might be an advantage, even in a dream, in occasionally being the eater, instead of always the party eaten, but I easily perceived that her point was well taken.

I'm sending to Heidelberg for your letter & Winnie's, & I do hope they haven't been lost. My wife & I send love to you all.   Yrs Ever

Mark.

Notes — *April, 1909.*[6]

1. Thirty-six hours of railroading! It makes me shudder to think of it. I seem to have gotten a measure of enjoyment out of it, but it probably wasn't a very large measure. From childhood up to the "Innocents Abroad" excursion I was a natural human being, with a natural human being's desires; one of them being a hungry desire to travel — but the Excursion, with its five or six months of ceaseless & exhausting gadding around, surfeited me, surfeited me thoroughly, & for good & all. That was 42 years ago, & I have never gone a journey since, either short or long, that could honorably be avoided.

Meantime I have made more than 40 sea voyages & numberless land-trips, & have gone clear around the globe once. This seems a hard fate. No, not seems — it *was* a hard fate. I made all those journeys because I could not help myself — made them with rebellion in my heart, & bitterness. Human life is maliciously planned with one principal object in view: to make you do all the different kinds of things you particularly don't want to do.

You notice that our little family arrived at Fräulein Dahlweiner's on time — where the rooms had been engaged for us ten months before. That was not all of it: we arrived *exactly* on time — on the very day & by the very train as planned out by Mrs. Clemens ten months before. Fräulein Dahlweiner was at the door with a lantern in her hand, waiting for us. Mrs. Clemens was an extraordinary planner. We left home to be gone 14 months; to abide a given number of days in one place, weeks in another & months in another, then reach our home in America again on a certain date. Date by date it all came out just as she had planned it.

We acquired a great affection for Fräulein Dahlweiner; acquired it at once, & it outlasted the winter we spent in her house. While it was not difficult to get fond of her, it was less easy to take Gretchen to our hearts. Gretchen was the maid — the maid of all work. She was 15 years old, & earnest & gentle & quiet & grave enough to be a hundred & fifty. She made the fires in the monument at dawn; she scrubbed the naked parlor floor at intervals, at other intervals swept it; at all intervals neglected the naked halls; she washed the dishes, she waited on the table; she was hard at work all day long & well into the night — my, how permanently tired that child must have been! She was a pathetic little figure, with her patient old-young face, which made our hearts ache to look at. We pitied her from the start, but it took us ten days to learn to love her. This was because her sole & only frock was *so* soiled & timeworn & shabby; & because her towhead was *so* frowsy & unkempt; & because her garters were *so* inefficient, & her discouraged stockings so given to drowsing in folds about her ancles; & because her hands & her face were *so* caked with petrified real estate. She was baptised when she was a little baby, & it was her last wash. For a time she blighted our appetites when she passed the plates & dishes — it was just the *look* of her hands, those stove-polishy hands! — & it seemed as if we *couldn't* endure her.

But that was just a superstition. Her heart was right, & she was a dear good child — so she had the essentials, she held the winning cards, & she walked into our affections with a sure & steady stride. *Then* we could have had her washed, but we didn't want to. She wouldn't be *our* Gretchen any more. We shouldn't know her, she would be a stranger, her charm a memory & no more. We couldn't bear to see her so. We wanted her just as she was. As she was, she was *our* Gretchen, all ours: *our* love, *our* friend, *our* dear, *our* personal property, *our* real estate, & we wouldn't allow a single ⟨stratum of it to be pried⟩ layer of it to be planed off. And so, all the pleasant winter we left it just as it was — stratified. How long it is since I have thought of that gentle little spirit — thirty-one years! She is 46, now, & has fossils.

2. "*I* brought the tribe through from Rome." Probably a lie.

3. Apparently somebody "said a mighty sensible thing." Very well, then, why didn't I quote it? If it was worth mentioning, it was worth quoting. I am reading Lowell's Letters, & in them he commits that irritating crime all the time, & the compiler of the Letters makes himself an accessory after the fact by not inserting the thing mentioned.[7] However, I am reflecting upon myself. And I want to change the subject anyway.

1. *The Lady of the Aroostook,* which began running serially in the *Atlantic* for November 1878. Clemens was reading the January 1879 installment.

2. Padre Giacomo Issaverdenz of the Armenian Monastery at San Lazzaro was one of Howells's old Venetian friends to whom he directed Americans he especially liked when they visited Venice. Padre Giacomo was the prototype of Padre Girolamo in *A Foregone Conclusion* (James L. Woodress, *Howells and Italy,* Durham, 1952, p. 161).

3. The "Editor's Drawer," a regular department edited by William A. Seaver in *Harper's,* which had probably suggested the idea of the "Contributors' Club" to Howells.

4. Discussing the unsigned article by J. B. Harrison in the October issue, entitled "Certain Dangerous Tendencies in American Life." The writer objects to Harrison's conclusion that such tendencies may be remedied by education. He maintains instead that all men not born in the United States and all Negroes should be disfranchised, that immigration should be stopped, that nine out of ten newspapers should be suppressed, and that the public-school system should be replaced by dame schools teaching the three R's. Clemens, on second thought, would not have subscribed to all these views (he was certainly not hostile toward Negroes, and in letter 199 he opposes shutting off immigration of Chinese). But in these years he was concerned about the danger of the ballot in the hands of "the ignorant and non-tax-

paying classes," "the bottom layer of society," as he had indicated in "The Curious Republic of Gondour" (*Atlantic,* October 1875).

5. The references to the pipe and to "père Jacopo" indicate that one or more letters from Howells to Clemens have been lost. The Howellses had made a candleholder of an old pipe Clemens had left at their house (see letter 199).

6. Added when Clemens was looking over letters Albert B. Paine had borrowed from Howells for use in writing the biography (MTP).

7. The editors find in this passage an indication that Clemens would have approved the intention (if not necessarily the result) of their labors at annotation of his correspondence.

195. CLEMENS TO HOWELLS

Munich, Jan. 21 [1879].

My Dear Howells —

It's no use, — your letter miscarried in some way & is lost. The consul has made a thorough search & says he has not been able to trace it. It is unaccountable, for all the letters I did *not* want arrived without a single grateful failure. Well, I have read-up, now, as far [as] you have got, — that is, to where there's a storm at sea approaching, — & we three think you are clear out-Howellsing Howells. If your literature has not struck perfection now we are not able to see what is lacking. — It is all such truth — truth to the life; everywhere your pen falls it leaves a photograph. I *did* imagine that everything had been said about life at sea that could be said, — but no matter, it was all a failure & lies, nothing but lies with a thin varnish of fact, — only *you* have stated it as it absolutely *is.*[1] And only you see people & their ways & their insides & outsides as they *are,* & make them talk as they *do* talk. I think you are the very greatest artist in these tremendous mysteries that ever lived. There doesn't seem to be anything that can be concealed from your awful all-seeing eye. It must be a cheerful thing for one to live with you & be aware that you are going up & down in him like another conscience all the time. Possibly you will not be a fully accepted

245

classic until you have been dead a hundred years, — it is the fate of the Shakspeares & of all genuine prophets, — but *then* your books will be as common as Bibles, I believe. You ain't a weed, but an oak; you ain't a summer-house, but a cathedral. In that day *I* shall still be in the Cyclopedias, too, — thus: "Mark Twain; history & occupation unknown — but he was personally acquainted with Howells." There — I could sing your praises all day, & feel & believe every bit of it.

My book [2] is half finished; I wish to heaven it was done. I have given up writing a detective novel — can't write a novel, for I lack the faculty; but when the detectives were nosing around after Stewart's loud remains, I threw a chapter into my present book in which I have very extravagantly burlesqued the detective business [3] — if it *is* possible to burlesque that business extravagantly. You know I was going to send you that Detective play,[4] so that you could re-write it. Well I didn't do it because I couldn't find a single idea in it that could be useful to you. It was dreadfully witless & flat. I knew it would sadden you & unfit you for work.

I have always been sorry we threw up that play embodying Orion which you began.[5] It was a mistake to do that. Do keep that MS & tackle it again. It will work out all right, you will see. I don't believe that that character exists in literature in so well developed a condition as it exists in Orion's person. Now won't you put Orion in a *story*? Then he will go handsomely into a play afterwards. How deliciously you could paint him — it would make fascinating reading, — the sort that makes a reader laugh & cry at the same time, for Orion is as good & ridiculous a soul as ever was.

We thought we were going to lose our little Clara yesterday, but the danger is gone, to-day, apparently.

Ah, to think of Bayard Taylor! [6] It is too sad to talk about. I was so glad there was not a single sting & so many good praiseful words in the Atlantic's criticism of Deukalion.[7]

Love to you all   Yrs Ever

               Mark.

We remain here till middle of March.

GIVE ME YOUR PLAIN ADVICE (1877–1879)

1. *The Lady of the Aroostook,* then running serially in the *Atlantic,* was "the first story that I ever began to print before I had finished it; so that I may claim now to be a regular-built novelist," Howells wrote Warner (Boston, 19 February 1879, Watkinson, AGM TS). Although Howells had already published his first true novel, *A Foregone Conclusion* (1875), *The Lady of the Aroostook* reverts to the travel formula of *Their Wedding Journey* (1872) and *A Chance Acquaintance* (1873). It takes an American girl much like Daisy Miller on a voyage to Italy. She is the only female on board the ship. Howells wrote to his father that he knew of a young lady's going to Malta "under such circumstances," and added: "a friend of Elinor's went so to Cuba; and Mark Twain told me of a girl coming alone with him to San Francisco from Honolulu" (Boston, 3 November 1878, Houghton). The dramatic presentation of Lydia Blood especially impressed Clemens, and his spontaneous tribute to the novel shows his complete acceptance of Howells's emphasis on "truth to the life" as a prime virtue of literature.

2. *A Tramp Abroad.*

3. "The Stolen White Elephant," which was eventually omitted from *A Tramp Abroad* and became instead the title piece in a volume of sketches published in 1882 (DE, XIX, 215–241). The body of Alexander T. Stewart, one of the wealthiest merchants of New York, which had been buried on 13 April 1878, was stolen from a vault in Weehawken Cemetery early on the morning of 7 November. For two weeks or more the newspapers — especially the New York *Herald* — were filled with sensational details concerning the efforts of police and numerous private detectives to recover the body. There was another flurry of interest in the case in January 1879, when representatives of the Stewart family issued a statement that a ransom of $50,000 had been paid and the body returned. This statement, however, was a falsehood designed to get the case out of the newspapers. In July 1880, the body was finally returned and a ransom paid of undisclosed amount. The criminals were apparently never apprehended. Many details borrowed from newspaper accounts of this case are turned to purposes of burlesque in "The Stolen White Elephant."

4. "Cap'n Simon Wheeler, The Amateur Detective."

5. The project mentioned in Howells's letter of 2 June 1878 which eventually developed into *Colonel Sellers as a Scientist.*

6. Taylor had died in Berlin on 19 December, less than a year after his arrival as American minister.

7. Taylor's play *Prince Deukalion* was reviewed in the January number.

196. CLEMENS TO HOWELLS

1ª Karlsstrasse, 2ᵉ Stock,
Munich, Jan. 30 [1879].

My Dear Howells —

It took a great burden off my heart this morning when your letter arrived ⟨& said⟩ & I found my 2 articles [1] had not been lost *in transitu.* I was going to write today & ask about them. Ordinarily I should trouble myself but little about the loss of 2 articles, for the loss could not rob me of the chief thing, i.e., the pleasure the writing them had afforded me, — but when a body is yoked down to the grinding out of a 600-page 8-vo. book, to lose a chapter is like losing a child. I was not at all sure that I should use both of those chapters in my book, but to *have them around,* in case of need, would give that added comfort which comes of having a life-preserver handy in a ship which *might* go down though nobody is expecting such a thing. But you speak so kindly of them that I shall probably venture to use them both. I have destroyed such lots of MS written for this book! And I suppose there are such lots left which ought to be destroyed. If it should be, it *shall* be, — that is certain. I have rung in that fragrant account of the Limberger cheese & the coffin-box full of guns. [2] Had I better leave that out? Give me your plain, square advice, for I propose to follow it. The back of my big job is broken, now, for the book is rather more than half done; so from this out I can tear up MS without a pang.

You sent me 2 copies of the *first* slip of Pitcairn, but no copy of the remaining half of the article. However, I have mailed one first-slip to Chatto & Windus & asked them to send me one of their second-slips, in exchange.

I wish I *could* give those sharp satires on European life which you mention, but of course a man can't write successful satire except he be in a calm judicial good-humor — whereas I *hate* travel, & I *hate* hotels, & I *hate* the opera, & I *hate* the Old Masters — in truth I don't ever seem to be in a good enough humor with ANYthing to *satirize* it; no, I want to stand up before it & *curse* it, & foam at the mouth, — or take a ⟨club & beat it⟩ club & pound it to rags & pulp. I have got in two or three chapters about Wagner's Operas, & managed to do it without showing temper — but the strain of another such effort would burst me. — (Mind, whatever I say about the book is a *secret*; — my publisher shall know little or nothing about the book till he gets the MS, for I can't trust his tongue — I am trusting *nobody* but you & Twichell. I like mighty well to tell my plans & swap opinions about them, but I don't like them to get around.) I have exposed the German language in two or three chapters, & I have shown what I consider to be the needed improvements in it. I mean to describe a German newspaper, but not satirically — simply in a plain matter of fact way. I wrote the chapter satirically, but found that a plain statement was rather the better satire. In my book I allow it to appear, — casually & without stress, — that I am over here to make the tour of Europe *on foot*. I am in pedestrian costume, as a general thing, & *start* on pedestrian tours, but mount the first convey-ance that offers, making but slight explanation or excuse, & endeavoring to seem unconscious that this is not legitimate pedestrianizing. My second object here is to become a German scholar; my third, to study Art, & learn to paint. I have a notion to put a few hideous pen & ink sketches of my own in my book, & explain their merits & defects in the technical language of art. But I shall not put many in — better artists shall do nineteen-twentieths of the illustrating. I have made a pedestrian trip up the Neckar to Heilbronn, with muslin-wound hat, leathern leg-gings, sun-umbrella, alpenstock, &c — *by rail,* — with my agent, — I employ an agent on a salary, & he does the real work when any is to be done, though I appropriate his emotions to myself & do his marvelling for him — & in yesterday's chapter we have started back to Heidelberg on a raft, & are having a good time. The raft is mine, since I have chartered it, & I shall pick up useful passengers here & there to tell me the legends of the ruined castles, & other things — perhaps the Captain who brought the news of the Pitcairn revolution. I have invented quite a nice little legend for Dilsberg Castle, & maybe that is the only one I *shall* invent — don't know.

I want to make a book which people will *read,* — & I shall make it profitable reading in spots — in spots merely *because* there's not much material for a larger amount. And as soon as it is off my hands I shall take up Wakeman & Heaven at once.

Confound that February number, I wish it would fetch along the Lady of the Aroostook, for we are pretty impatient to see her again. — All right, tell me about the Pacific coast trip [3] — I wish we were going with you.

So Aldrich is gone — but he won't go to Egypt if this plague continues to spread. I sent him a paragraph from a German paper the other day: Scientist discovered a Roman vessel near Regensburg of a sort which has long been supposed to have been used to burn fragrant herbs in during cremation of corpses, but there was no proof. He set this one on the stove one day, & presently it began to send out a sweet perfume — resumed its office after a vacation of 1500 years. Thought Aldrich could do a sonnet on it.

Write me here, to above address — for even if the plague drives us away, we shall see to it that our letters follow us all right this time.

With our loves to you & yours —   Yrs Ever

Mark.

We missed Mead [4] in Florence — he arrived from Paris right after we left F.

over

P.S. Are you in the new house?

Père Jacomo is here & has called twice, but I was out both times. Mrs. C was out once & lying down in undress uniform the other time & had to excuse herself. He has never come near us since. I have written to Venice to ask for his address (he didn't leave us any) & am hoping to get it.

Bay Clemens came within an ace of dying, last week — a mighty close shave. She is about well, now.

1. "The Great Revolution in Pitcairn," to be published in the March 1879 *Atlantic* (DE, XIX, 343–359), and probably "The Recent Great French Duel," which was to appear in the *Atlantic* for February 1879, before its inclusion in *A Tramp Abroad* (DE, IX, 49–62).

2. Eventually (doubtless on Howells's recommendation) left out of *A Tramp Abroad,* and published for the first time in *The Stolen White Elephant* (1882) as an insertion just before the end of "Some Rambling Notes of an Idle Excursion," with the following note: "Left out of these 'Rambling Notes,' when originally published in the *Atlantic Monthly,* because it was feared that the story was not true, and at that time there was no way of proving that it was not. — M. T." (pp. 94–95). The piece was again detached from "Some Rambling Notes" for publication in the Definitive Edition as "The Invalid's Story" (XXII, 187–196).

3. Presumably mentioned in a letter from Howells now lost. President Hayes had invited the Howellses to accompany his party on a trip to California originally planned for the early summer of 1879. A special session of Congress, however, forced him to change his plans. On 16 March, Howells wrote to Hayes: "Even before your letter came, we had read the fate of the California trip in the certainty of an extra session, and were prepared for the worst. At least it was a splendid prospect, while it lasted, and I think you would have liked my book about it — if I had written it" (Boston, quoted by Lyon N. Richardson, NEQ, XV, 124, March 1942). Hayes finally set out in September 1880, on a tour that lasted two months and took him to California and Seattle and back by way of Tucson, Santa Fe, and Denver (Charles R. Williams, *Life of Rutherford B. Hayes,* 2 vols., Boston, 1914, II, 288, 293–297), but the Howellses did not go with him.

4. Larkin G. Mead, Elinor Howells's brother, a sculptor who had married the Venetian girl Marietta di Benvenuti.

197. CLEMENS TO HOWELLS

Munich, Feb. 2 [1879].

Dear Howells —

I thought I would call your attention to the following incident, while the dinner table is getting ready for the soup.

There are several families & several little children in this pension. One of these little children, Marie Haüff,[1] has an ailment which requires a peculiar treatment — therefore she is the envy & admiration of the rest of the little tribe.

Scene, Our ⟨Nursery⟩ *Parlor* — *Time, This Afternoon.* —
Enter a male friend from up town & introduces his little daughter, aged 6 or 7. I introduce the little maid into our nursery &
tell our children who she is. My friend & I close the nursery
door, but leave a crack to peep through. Little Miss Minnie
stands bolt upright in the centre of the nursery, in her white
silk head-gear, her hands still in her little muff, & stares at
Susie & Bay, who stand before her and stare back. Presently —

Minnie — *I've* got a cat at home — a *live* one.

Our children can't "call this hand," so they are silent. After
a pause, —

Minnie — And I've got a dog, too, — a live dog.

Our children can't size *this* pile either. Silence, & a pause.
Then —

Minnie — I've seen the *Queen!* — I've seen her *ever* so many
times!

Bay (with triumph) — But you've never seen Marie Haüff.
I have. And I *know* her, too. — She has an injection every day!
So there, now!

That let Miss *Minnie* out, you see.

And now the soup has arrived.   Yrs

Mark.

---

1. Clemens is making progress in his melodramatic struggle with the
German language — his notebooks for this period contain many German words
and sentences, along with such awestruck observations as "26 columns of
über in the dictionary" (#13, TS, p. 39, MTP) — but he still often places the
umlaut over the wrong vowel in diphthongs, as here.

198. CLEMENS TO HOWELLS

Munich, Feb. 9 [1879].

My Dear Howells —

I have just received this letter from Orion [1] — take care of
it, for it is worth preserving. I got as far as 9 pages in my answer
to it, when Mrs. Clemens shut down on it, & said it was cruel, &

made me send the money & simply wish his lectures success. I said I couldn't lose my 9 pages — so she said send them to you. But I will acknowledge that I thought I was writing a very kind letter.

Now just look at this letter of Orion's. Did you ever see the grotesquely absurd & the heart-breakingly pathetic more closely joined together? Mrs. Clemens said "Raise his monthly pension." So I wrote to Perkins [2] to raise it, a trifle.

Now only think of it! He still has 100 pages to write on his lectures, yet in one inking of his pen he has already swooped around the United States & invested the result!

You *must* put him in a book or a play right away. You are the only man capable of doing it. You might die at any moment, & your very greatest work would be lost to the world. *I* could write Orion's simple biography, & make it effective, too, by merely stating the bald facts — & this I will do if he dies before I do; but *you* must put him into romance. This was the understanding you & I had the day I sailed.

Observe Orion's career — that is, a *little* of it:

He has belonged to as many as five different religious denominations; last March he withdrew from deaconship in a Congregational Church & the superintendency of its Sunday School, in a speech in which he said that for many months (it runs in my mind that he said 13 years,) he had been a confirmed *infidel,* & so felt it to be his duty to retire from ⟨his⟩ the flock.

2. After being a republican for years, he wanted me to buy him a democratic newspaper [3] merely because his prophetic mind told him Tilden would be President — in which case he would be able to get an office for his services.

A few days before the Presidential election, he came out in a speech & publicly went over to the democrats; but at the last moment, while voting for Tilden & 6 State democrats, he prudently "hedged" by voting for 6 State republicans, also. He said it might make him safe, no matter who won.

The new convert was made one of the secretaries of a democratic meeting, & placed in the list of speakers. He wrote me jubilantly of what a ten-strike he was going to make with that speech. All right — but think of his innocent & pathetic candor in writing me something like this, a week later: "I was more diffident than I had expected to be, & this was increased by the silence with which I was received when I came forward; so I seemed unable to get the fire into my speech which I had calculated upon, & presently they began to get up & go out; & in a few minutes they all rose up & went away."

How *could* a man uncover such a sore as that & show it to another? Not a word of complaint, you see — only a patient, sad surprise.

3. His next project was to write a burlesque upon Paradise Lost.

4. Then, learning that the Times was paying Harte $100 a column for stories, he concluded to write some for the same price. I read his first one & persuaded him not to write any more.

4. Then he read proof in the N.Y. Eve. Post at $10 a week, & meekly observed that the foreman swore at him & ordered him around "like a steamboat mate."

5. Being discharged from that post, he wanted to try agriculture — was sure he could make a fortune out of a chicken farm. I gave him $900 & he went to a ten-house village 2 miles above Keokuk on the river bank — this place was a railway station. He soon asked for money to buy a horse & light wagon, — because the trains did not run at church time on Sunday, & his wife found it rather far to walk.

For a long time I answered demands for "loans," & by next mail always received his check for the interest due me to date. In the most guileless way he let it leak out that he did not underestimate the value of his custom to me, since it was not likely that any other customer of mine paid his interest *quarterly*, & thus enabled me to use my capital twice in 6 months instead of only once. But alas, when the debt at last reached $1500 or $2500 (I have forgotten which,) the interest ate too formidably into his borrowings, & so he quietly ceased to pay it or speak of it. At the end of two years I found that the chicken farm had long ago been abandoned, & he had moved into Keokuk. Later, in one of his casual moments, he casually observed that his books had shown that there was no money in fattening a chicken on 65 cents worth of corn & then selling it for 50.

6. Finally, if I would lend him $500 a year for 2 years (this was 4 or 5 years ago,) he *knew* he could make a success as a lawyer, & would prove it. — This is the pension which we have just increased to $600. The first year his legal business brought him $5. It also brought him an unremunerative case where some villains were trying to chouse some negro orphans out of $700. He still has this case. He has waggled it around through various courts & made some booming speeches on it. The negro children have grown up & married off, now, I believe, & their litigated town-lot has been dug up & carted off by somebody — but Orion still infests the courts with his documents & makes the welkin ring with his venerable case. The second year, he didn't make anything. The third, he made $6, & I made Bliss put a case in his hands — about half an hour's work.[4] Orion charged $50 for it — Bliss paid him $15. Thus four or five years of lawing has brought him $26, but this will doubtless be increased when he gets done lecturing & buys that "law library." Meantime his office rent has been $60 a year, & he has stuck to that lair day by day as patiently as a spider.

7. Then he by & by conceived the idea of lecturing around America as "Mark Twain's Brother" — that to be on the bills. Subject of proposed lecture, "On the Formation of Character."

8. I protested, & he got on his war-paint, couched his lance, & ran a bold tilt against Total Abstinence & the Red Ribbon fanatics.[5] It raised a fine stink among the virtuous Keokukians.

9. I wrote to encourage him in his good work, but I had let a mail intervene; so by the time my letter reached him he was already winning laurels as a Red Ribbon Howler.

10. Afterward he took a rabid part in a prayer meeting epidemic; dropped that to travesty Jules Verne;[6] dropped that, in the middle of the last chapter, last March, to digest the matter of an infidel book which he proposed to write; & now he comes to the surface to rescue our "noble & beautiful religion" from the sacrilegious talons of Bob Ingersoll.[7]

Now come! Don't fool away this treasure which Providence has laid at your feet, but take it up & use it. — One can let his imagination run riot in portraying Orion, for there is nothing so extravagant as to be out of character with him.[8]

And then his wife is the only woman who could have so rounded & perfected Orion's character. She was a bald-headed old maid. She was poor & taboo; she wanted position & clothes, oh, so badly; she had the snaffle on this ass before he knew what he was about — for he was editor of a daily paper & a good catch. She is saturated to the marrow with the most malignant form of Presbyterianism, — that sort which considers the saving one's own paltry soul the first & supreme end & object of life. So you see she has harried him into the church several times, & then made religion so intolerable to him with her prayings & Bible readings & her other & eternal pious clack-clack that it has had the effect of harrying him out of it again. He is a printer, but she won't allow him to work at his trade because she can't abide the thought of being a mechanic's wife. She prefers to keep boarding-house & make him let on to be a lawyer. He wrote piteously once, how the governor or somebody gave a blow out, with a broad general invitation to lawyers & their wives to be present, & she made him go, & take her, — & it was the year that he didn't have a case or make a cent, & those people all knew it. Moreover, he hadn't any decent clothes, for she gobbles all the money & buys clothes & new wigs for herself with it. The only way we can keep him from being ragged is to send him money distinctly for *himself* occasionally. Then he treats himself to something "for Sunday & weddings" & a pair of "bi-focal spectacles" — that is, if bi-focal spectacles happen to be the newest & freshest astonisher in the spectacle market. For he wouldn't give a curse for a pair that hadn't anything surprising about them. She won't let him work at a trade, but in the privacy of the boarding-house she makes him get up in the cold gray dawns of winter & go from one lodger's room to another (young fellows not half his age, — & they pity him & protest, too,) & build the fires, & go down on his knees & bow his gray head & blow them, to save the parlor bellows from wear & tear.[9]

Orion is in his 54th year. He & she are two curses which are dove-tailed together with marvelous exactness. She is such a vain, proud fool; he is so utterly devoid of pride. He is a curse to her, & she is a curse to him. And these two curses have been yoked fast together for five & twenty years! If Orion ever goes to hell, he will be likely to say,

"I don't think *this* place is much of an invention." And if she ever goes to heaven, she will be likely to say, "I am disappointed; I did not think so many would be saved."

Well, — good-bye, & a short life & a merry one be yours. Poor old Methuselah, how did he manage to stand it so long?

Yrs Ever

Mark.

Munich, Feb. 9.

My Dear Bro —

Yours has just arrived. I enclose a draft on Hartford for $25. You will have abandoned the project you wanted it for, by the time it arrives, — but no matter, apply it to your newer & present project, whatever it is. You see I have an ineradicable faith in your unsteadfastness, — but mind you, *I* didn't invent that faith, you conferred it on me yourself. But fire away, fire away! — I don't see why a changeable man shouldn't get as much enjoyment out of his changes, & transformations & transfigurations as a steadfast man gets out of standing still & pegging at the same old monotonous thing all the time. That is to say, I don't see why a Kaleidoscope shouldn't enjoy itself as much as a telescope, nor a grindstone have as good a time as a whetstone, nor a barometer as good a time as a yard stick. I don't feel like girding at you any more about fickleness of purpose, because I recognize & realize at last that it is incurable; but before I learned to accept this truth, each new weekly project of yours possessed the power of throwing me into the most exhausting & helpless convulsions of profanity. But fire away, now! Your magic has lost its might. I am able to view your inspirations dispassionately & judicially, now, & say "This one or that one or the other one is not up to your average flight, or is above it, or below it."

257

And so, without passion, or prejudice, or bias of any kind, I sit in judgment upon your lecture project & say it was up to your average, it was indeed above it, for it had possibilities in it, & ⟨not only that⟩ even *practical* ones. While I am not sorry you abandoned it, I should not be sorry if you had stuck to it & given it a trial. But on the whole you did the wise thing to lay it aside, I think, because a lecture is a most easy thing to fail in; & at your time of life, & in your own town, such a failure would make a deep & cruel wound in your heart & in your pride. It was decidedly unwise in you to think for a moment of coming before a community who knew you, with such a course of lectures; because Keokuk is not unaware that you have been a Swedenborgian, a Presbyterian, a Congregationalist, & a Methodist (on probation,) & that just a year ago you were an infidel. If Keokuk had gone to your lecture-course, it would have gone to be amused, not instructed, — for when a man is known to have no settled convictions of his own he can't convict other people. They would have gone to be amused, & that would have been a deep humiliation to you. It could have been safe for you to appear only where you were unknown — then many of your hearers would think you were in earnest. And they would be right. You *are* in earnest while your convictions are new. But, taking it by & large, you probably did best to discard that project altogether. But I leave you to judge of that, for you are the worst judge I know of.

1. The letter has been lost, although many of the events Clemens summarizes are mentioned in earlier letters from Orion in MTP.

2. Charles E. Perkins of Hartford, Clemens's lawyer and business manager.

3. The Keokuk *Constitution* (Orion Clemens to SLC, Keokuk, 26 June 1876, MTP).

4. Orion was to warn a Keokuk bookseller against selling copies of the pirated Belford edition of *Tom Sawyer* (Orion Clemens to Elisha Bliss, Keokuk, 1 February 1877, MTP).

5. The Red Ribbon Reform Clubs were an outgrowth of the Bangor (Me.) Reform Club, founded in 1874 by Dr. Henry A. Reynolds. Membership was limited to drinkers who had taken the pledge of total abstinence from intoxicating liquors. In 1877 the movement had been carried into

the Mississippi Valley by John B. Finch, who was said to have secured a hundred thousand signatures to the pledge in Nebraska alone (August F. Fehlandt, *A Century of Drink Reform in the United States,* Cincinnati & New York, 1904, p. 232).

6. See note 2 to letter 188.

7. According to Howells, Clemens "greatly admired Robert Ingersoll, whom he called an angelic orator, and regarded as an evangel of a new gospel — the gospel of free thought" (MMT, p. 31).

8. This opinion led to such improbabilities in *Colonel Sellers as a Scientist* as to make the play unusable in the theatre.

9. Here, as elsewhere, the helpless pity for Orion that underlies Mark Twain's exasperation with him shows through.

199. CLEMENS TO HOWELLS

Hotel Normandy
7 rue de l'Echelle
Paris, Apl. 15 [1879].

Dear Howells —   7. P.M.

Have just got Livy L. Clemens & Miss Spaulding off to the Opera in charge of an old friend — (for I cannot stand anything that is in the nature of an Opera) — & here I find a letter from Susie Warner to Mrs. Clemens — I open it & my goodness, how she raves over the exquisiteness of Belmont; & the wonderful view; & Mrs. Howells's brilliancy, & her deadly accuracy in the matter of detecting & driving the bulls-eye of a sham; & the attractiveness of the children; & your own "sweetness" (Why, do they call *you* that? — that is what they generally call *me*); & the indescribably good time which she & Charley had; & my old pipe dressed up in ribbons & holding a candle, & making an unique & graceful ornament of itself — & I thank you for paying these kindly honors to the old pipe, — if the dull plebeian thing half appreciated them it would have turned to gold-mounted malachite by this time.

So the reading of that letter has set me going, when it was my purpose to turn in, immediately, & read & smoke. However,

I'll cut myself short, for once. Mr. Mead called yesterday (not Larkin G.,) [1] just as I was starting off to the neighborhood of the Triumphal Arch on business, so he walked with me to the rue de Rivoli & up the Champs Elysèe half way to the Arch — which gave us a chance to talk a good deal about you & your disappointment in the matter of the Pacific Excursion, (what a real pity that was,) & other matters. He is going to call again, & come in the evening, when we are business-free.

⟨Well, I had a very curious experience, Sunday, day before yesterday. Since I was⟩ [2]

(Pages 5, 6, 7 and 8 torn up.)

It was splendid in the President to appoint Mr. White. [3] The more I think of the matter the more I am satisfied that the President never appointed Bret Harte. Evarts simply *crowded* that shameless scoundrel in. You have seen by the papers that Harte has deliberately swindled two German publishing houses, by selling each the *sole* right to print one of his books. Poor Boyesen [4] is here in this expensive city, & has got to *stay* here till his wife is confined in July, & every cent of silver is worth its weight in gold to him; well, two German publishers were going to buy some of his literature, but all of a sudden comes a letter from a famous German author a week or so ago, freighted with disappointment — the publishers have reconsidered the matter, & say in plain terms that they must decline to buy anything of an American author, now, *unless he will give bond to indemnify them in case he has sold the sole right to some other German publisher*! It comes hard on Boyesen. We like Boyesen & his wife, heartily. Poor fellow, there are *12* Orions in his family. That's enough to make anybody warm to him. —

Do you know, I wanted to take that German author's letter & send it to the President & say "When your Excellency found that George Butler was drunk, on his way to his new post, you dismissed him before he got there; here is a new appointee who is also a drunkard, & is a thief besides: is it not a case for dismissal?" — But I couldn't seem to word a formal state paper just right in my mind, & I wouldn't send one that wasn't in every way a proper thing for the head of our country to read — so

I've dropped it for the present. I told Bret Harte, just before the Presidential election, that the New York Custom house was the right place for him, & that I thought him an unfit person for our foreign service. I would think so yet, only the Custom house has latterly become too clean a place for such a dirty bird as he is.

Good night, my boy —   Yrs Ever

Mark

Continued.

Chatto sent me Harte's new book of Sketches,[5] the other day, ("An Heiress of Red Dog," etc). I have read it twice — the first time through tears of rage over the fellow's inborn hypocrisy & snobbishness, his apprentice-art, his artificialities, his mannerisms, his pet phrases, (such as the frequent "I regret to say,") — his laboriously acquired ignorance, & his jejune anxiety to display it. O, my God! He rings in *Strasse* when street would answer every purpose, and *Bahnhof* when it carries no sharper significance to the reader ⟨than depot⟩ than "station" would; he peppers in his seven little French words (you can find them in all his sketches, for he learned them in California 14 years ago,), — he begins his German substantives with "lower case" generally, & sometimes mis-spells them — all this with a dictionary at his very elbow — what an illustration of his slovenly laziness it is! And Jack Hamlin [6] talks like a Bowery gutter-snipe on one page, & like a courtier of Louis XV's time on the very next one. And he has a "nigger" who talks a "dialect" which is utterly original. The struggle after the pathetic is more pathetic than the pathos itself; if he were to write about an Orphan Princess who lost a Peanut he would feel obliged to try to make somebody snuffle over it.

The second time I read the book I saw a most decided brightness on every page of it — & here & there evidences of genius. I saw enough to make me think, "Well, if this slovenly shoemaker-work is able to command the applause of three or four nations, what *mightn't* this ass accomplish if he would do his work honestly & with pains?" If I ever get my tedious book finished, I mean to weed out some of my prejudices & write an article on "Bret Harte as an Artist" — & print it if it ⟨would⟩ will not be unfair to print it without signature.

Tauchnitz called the other day — a mighty nice old gentleman. He paid me 425 francs for the Innocents — I think he paid me about 6 or 700 fr. for Tom Sawyer (it being new); he is going to print Roughing It by & by, & has engaged advanced sheets of my new book. Don't know what he will pay for the two latter — I leave that to him — one can't have the heart to dicker with a publisher who won't steal.[7]

Can't you get up a plot for a "skeleton novelette" & find two or three fellows to join us in writing the stories? Five of us would do. I can't seem to give up that idea.

I knew the President would veto that infamous Chinese bill.[8] I wish I knew whether Belmont was a P.O. or a country seat.

Yrs Ever

Mark.

P.S. If I should think of anything more to say about Harte, I will telegraph.

1. Probably William Rutherford Mead, another brother of Elinor Mead Howells.

2. Four pages are missing at this point.

3. Andrew D. White (1832–1918), founder of Cornell University (1867) and its first president, whom Hayes had just appointed to succeed Bayard Taylor as minister to Germany. After only two years in this post, he returned to Cornell and served again as president until ill health forced him to retire in 1885.

4. Hjalmar H. Boyesen (1848–1895), an immigrant to the United States from Norway, whose work as novelist and critic Howells had published in the *Atlantic*. Boyesen, who was professor of German at Cornell, may well have told Clemens of White's appointment.

5. *An Heiress of Red Dog, and Other Tales,* published by Chatto & Windus in 1879.

6. A handsome gambler who figures in several of Harte's stories of California.

7. The sums paid by the publisher Bernhard Tauchnitz, of Leipzig, for the right to bring out Mark Twain's works in English for sale on the Continent seem surprisingly small, even negligible, as lump-sum payments rather than royalties; but doubtless, as Mark Twain says, even small payments seemed better than nothing when there were no legal means of compelling any payment at all.

8. An act designed initially to prohibit Chinese immigration into the United States. It forbade any shipmaster from bringing to this country more than fifteen Chinese at any one time, and directed the President to announce the abrogation of certain articles of the Burlingame Treaty of 1868 — a procedure in violation of international law (Williams, *Hayes,* II, 213–215). Four years later, in the administration of Chester A. Arthur, a Chinese Exclusion Act which was equally unilateral became a law.

V

A MILLION THINGS
I WANTED TO SAY

(1 8 7 9 – 1 8 8 0)

V

(1 8 7 9 – 1 8 8 0)

"I have thought of upwards of a million things I wanted to say to you — but that is always the way. Probably there is an eternity" (SLC to WDH, Hartford, 19 April 1880, Houghton)

After the return of the Clemens family from Europe in the autumn of 1879 their life in Hartford, and that of the Howellses in Belmont, went on much as it had all through the 1870's. In November 1879 Clemens attended the Grand Reunion of the Army of the Tennessee in Chicago, delivered a highly successful humorous tribute to Grant, and returned home enraptured with the Bloody Shirt oratory of Robert Ingersoll and other Republican Stalwarts. He had at last finished *A Tramp Abroad*, which Howells reviewed with his usual discerning praise in the *Atlantic* in May 1880. Howells's *The Undiscovered Country* was being serialized in the *Atlantic* and Lawrence Barrett was still occasionally playing his adaptation of *Un Drama Nuevo* by Tamayo y Baus. In October 1880, Clemens delivered the official speech welcoming Grant to Hartford and a few days later addressed a Republican mass meeting on the iniquities of Democratic proposals for a lower tariff. Both friends were, of course, gratified by the election of Garfield. At Howells's insistence Clemens appeared on the program of the *Atlantic* breakfast honoring Oliver Wendell Holmes on 3 December 1879 with a graceful tribute that made amends for the supposed offense of his speech at the Whittier dinner three years before. But Howells's connection with the *Atlantic* was nearing an end. The dissolution of the publishing firm of Houghton, Osgood & Co. resulted in his resignation from the editorship early in January 1881.

200. CLEMENS TO HOWELLS

[Elmira] Sept 8 1879

My Dear Howells:

Are you *dead* — or only sleepeth? [1]
We are all well, & send love to you & yours by the hand of
Yrs Ever
Mark.

1. The Clemenses had landed in New York on 3 September.

201. HOWELLS TO CLEMENS

[Boston] September 9, 1879.

My dear Clemens:

Sleepeth is the matter — the sleep of a torpid conscience. I will feign that I didn't know where to write you; but I love you and all yours, and I am tremendously glad that you are at home again. When and where shall we meet? I want to see you and talk with you. Have you come home with your pockets full of Atlanticable papers? How about the two books? How about all the family in the flesh and the MS.?

Thanks to your generous interest in the matter, Tauchnitz is putting some of my books into his library.[1] He has already put F. Conclusion in, and the L. of the Aroostook goes next. He has sent me $70 for the first — and the Canadian villains,[2] who have got out *five* editions of the Aroostook, never a cent.

Mrs. Howells unconsciously joins me in love to you all. We go to Toronto the first week in October to see my father. Till then we are at home, and we shall be at home about the 20th of October on our return. When do you get back to Hartford?
Yours ever
W. D. Howells.

1. A letter from Bernhard Tauchnitz to Clemens written from Leipzig on 19 February 1879 (in MTP) says in part: "I have also to thank you heartily for what you say about your friend Mr. Howell and I shall be happy to receive his books and to pay every attention to their republication."

2. Belford Bros., of Toronto.

202. CLEMENS TO HOWELLS

Elmira, Sep. 15 [1879].

My Dear Howells:

When & where? Here on the farm would be an elegant place to meet, but of course you cannot come so far. So we will say Hartford or Belmont, about the beginning of November. The date of our return to Hartford is uncertain, but will be three or four weeks hence, I judge. I hope to finish my book [1] here before migrating.

I think maybe I've got some Atlanticable stuff in my head, but there's none in MS I believe.

Say — a friend of mine wants to write a play with me, I to furnish the broad-comedy cuss.[2] — I don't know anything about his ability, but his letter serves to remind me of *our* old projects. If you haven't used Orion or Old Wakeman (Amateur Detective),[3] don't you think you & I can get together & grind out a play with one of those fellows in it? Orion is a field which grows richer & richer the more he manures it with each new top-dressing of religion or other guano. — Drop me an immediate line about this, won't you? I imagine I see Orion on the stage, always gentle, always melancholy, always changing his politics & religion, & trying to reform the world, always inventing something, & losing a limb by a new kind of explosion at the end of each of the four acts. Poor old chap, he is good material. I can imagine his wife or his sweetheart reluctantly adopting each of his new religions in turn, just in time to see him waltz into the next one & leave her isolated once more. — (*Mem.* Orion's wife *has* followed him into the outer darkness, after 30 years' rabid membership in the Presbyterian church.)

Well, with the sincerest & most abounding love to you & yours, from all this family, I am   Yrs Ever

Mark.

What *is* your P.O. address?

1. *A Tramp Abroad.*
2. The friend cannot now be identified.
3. This interesting association of Captain Wakeman and Simon Wheeler persisted in Mark Twain's mind. Even after Captain Wakeman was re-named Captain Stormfield, and "Stormfield's Visit to Heaven" existed in MS (Clemens refers to it in October 1893, Notebook #27, TS, p. 33, MTP), he mentions "Si Wheeler's arrival in Heaven" (Notebook #27, TS, p. 35).

203. HOWELLS TO CLEMENS

[Boston] (Belmont is my P.O.) Sept. 17, 1879.

My dear Clemens:

We have projected a journey northward and westward, which we expect to set out on, either the first of October, or the first of November. But the date will be decided soon, and then I will make appointments for meeting, accordingly.

— More than once I've taken out the skeleton of that comedy of ours, and viewed it with tears. You know I hate to say or do anything definitive; but I really have a compunction or two about helping to put your brother into drama. You can say that he is your brother, to do what you like with him; but the alien hand might inflict an incurable hurt to his tender heart. That's the way I have felt since your enclosure of his letter to me. I might think differently, — and probably should, as soon as the chance of cooperating with you was gone. I would prefer to talk with you about the matter. As usual my old complaint troubles me — want of time. I am just finishing a longer story [1] than I've written before, and I'm tempted to jump into another, as soon as that is done, by the fact that the editor of Cornhill is ready to simultane. — By the way, why don't your publishers put an injunction on the sale of the Canadian ed. of *Piloting on the M'ppi?* I have seen it for sale at the Albany depot here? Harpers stopped a reprint of a book of theirs by suing every man that sold it. — I have just seen Waring, who had met you since your return. That bro't us very near.

Yours ever

W. D. Howells

1. *The Undiscovered Country,* to be serialized in the *Atlantic* January–July 1880.

204. CLEMENS TO HOWELLS

[Hartford, late September–early October 1879]

My Dear Howells:

If you should find you do not need this for the Contributors' Club, will you please return it to me, as they want it for the Christian Union? [1]   Yrs Ever

Mark.

1. A religious weekly edited by Henry Ward Beecher and Lyman Abbott, of very large circulation. Clemens is repeating one of his cherished jokes in pretending to offer an unpublishable MS to Howells for the *Atlantic* before he sends it to the *Christian Union.* As Howells's reply (letter 205) makes clear, in addition to a "paragraph" designed to shock readers with conventional religious beliefs, Clemens had also sent the MS of his ribald *1601. Conversation, as It Was by the Social Fireside, in the Time of the Tudors.* Howells and his wife, then in Toronto, were to visit the John Hays in Cleveland on their way home, and Howells may well have been responsible for Clemens's sending the MS to Hay a few months later. On 16 July 1880 Hay wrote Clemens to express his gratitude for "that most exquisite bit of English morality, 1601. . . . I don't wonder Howells declined it. It would have set so high a standard in the *Atlantic* that subsequent numbers would have shown a ruinous decline" (Washington, MTP). On 16 August, Hay wrote, enclosing the MS together with proof sheets of a printed version: "Here is the Meisterstück. It got into such appreciative hands among the Vampire Club [in Cleveland] that it was read into rags . . . and then the noble-minded Vampires, being pricked in the conscience, did have it copied, as you see. . . . Do not think it has been vulgarized — only a half-dozen

proofs were pulled and the type was faithfully distributed. It remains **RRR**" (Washington, MTP). This letter corrects Merle Johnson's conjecture that only four copies of the "Cleveland Edition" were printed (*Bibliography of the Works of Mark Twain*, rev. ed., New York, 1935, p. 35). There is no record of a comment by Howells on *1601*. He was probably at once amused and distressed by it. After Mark Twain's death he wrote: "Throughout my long acquaintance with him his graphic touch was always allowing itself a freedom which I cannot bring my fainter pencil to illustrate. He had the Southwestern, the Lincolnian, the Elizabethan breadth of parlance, which I suppose one ought not to call coarse without calling one's self prudish; and I was often hiding away in discreet holes and corners the letters in which he had loosed his bold fancy to stoop on rank suggestion; I could not bear to burn them, and I could not, after the first reading, quite bear to look at them" (MMT, pp. 3–4).

205. HOWELLS TO CLEMENS

[Toronto] Oct. 6, 1879.

My dear Clemens:

They've sent me your note here, but kept the enclosure,[1] which I shall see in Boston. But I will never give up that other paragraph [2] to the Christian Union, and I am going to publish it in MS. by showing it to everybody. It's delicious; and like so many of your good things it has a bottom of the awfulest kind of wisdom. How much better the human justice is than the theological-divine justice!

— We have been having a very nice trip, to Montreal, Ottawa and Toronto. Next week we are going on for a day at John Hay's. Hay is deep in politics, and will probably go to Congress next year.

I wish we could stop at Elmira, but we must go home the other way. We left the chicks at Belmont, and we're in a hurry to get back to 'em.

Elinor joins me in love to you both.

Yours ever

W. D. Howells.

1. *1601.*

2. Clemens's letter of 9 October implies that the impropriety of this paragraph involved a quotation from the Bible.

206. CLEMENS TO HOWELLS

Elmira, Oct. 9/79.

My Dear Howells:

Your letter brought me vast relief. It had been my intention to mark that religious squib "Private," but I forgot it, & so was tortured with the fear that it might fall into the hands of the family. One cannot be too careful how he quotes from the Bible, for he may bring a blush where he would be far from wishing to cause such a thing.

Since my return, the mail facilities have enabled Orion to keep me informed as to his intentions. Twenty-eight days ago it was his purpose to complete a work aimed at religion, the preface to which he had already written. Afterward he began to sell off his furniture, with the idea of hurrying to Leadville & tackling silver-mining [1] — threw up his law den & took in his sign. Then he wrote to Chicago & St. Louis newspapers asking for a situation as "paragrapher" — enclosing a taste of his quality in the shape of two stanzas of "humorous rhymes," so labored, so witless, so dreary (I have a copy) as to compel the compassion of the unkindest reader.[2] But only a brute could smile at this eruption of fetid hilarity. By a later mail on the same day he applied to New York & Hartford insurance companies for copying to do.

However, it would take too long to detail all his projects. They comprise a removal to south-west Missouri; application for a reporter's berth on a Keokuk paper; application for a compositor's berth on a St Louis paper; a re-hanging of his attorney's sign, "though it only creaks, & catches no flies;" but last night's letter informs me that he has re-tackled the religious question, hired a distant den to write in, applied to my mother for $50

273

to re-buy his furniture, which has advanced in value since the sale — purposes buying $25 worth of books necessary to his labors, which he had previously been borrowing, & his first chapter is already on its way to me for my decision as to whether it has enough ungodliness in it or not. Poor Orion! [3]

Your letter struck me while I was meditating a project to beguile you, & John Hay & Joe Twichell into a descent upon Chicago which I dream of making, to witness the re-union of the great Commanders of the Western army Corps on the 9th of next month.[4] My sluggish soul needs a fierce upstirring, & if it would not get it when Grant enters the meeting-place I must doubtless "lay" for the final resurrection. Can you & Hay go? At the same time, consound it, I doubt if I can go myself, for this book [5] isn't done yet. But I would give a heap to be there. I do hope Hay will be elected; [6] in any case he will deserve his country's gratitude for trying. Gratitude is the right term — I thought it out before saying it. When such men come forward, it has a good influence, for it emboldens other men of like stamp to do likewise. I mean to heave some holiness into the Hartford primaries when I go back; & if there was a solitary office in the land which majestic ignorance & incapacity, coupled with purity of heart, could fill, I would run for it. This naturally reminds me of Bret Harte — but let him pass.

We propose to leave here for New York Oct. 21, reaching Hartford 24th or 25th. If, upon reflection, you Howellses find you *can* stop over here on your way, I wish you would do it, & telegraph me. — Getting pretty hungry to see you. I had an idea that this was your shortest way home, but like as not my geography is crippled again — it usually is. The Madam & I join in love to you both. Mrs. Clemens wants to add a special word of invitation to Mrs. Howells, but I tell her that as she is abed Mrs. Howells will receive it from me & harbor no hard feelings.

Ys Ever

Mark.

1. On 17 September, Orion had sent Mark Twain the preface of an unwritten book which was "to show that morality and religion are developed independently of each other, and without Divine interference." The same

letter mentions the idea of prospecting for silver in Colorado (Keokuk, MTP).

2. The specimen of what Orion calls his "doggerel" was sent on 3 October (Keokuk, MTP).

3. Clemens was by turns touched, amused, and exasperated by his feckless but indomitably innocent brother. On this occasion his pity got the better of his judgment. Even though he had seen only the preface of Orion's book on religion (the MS had been sent to Hartford instead of Elmira), he allowed him to believe that the book might earn a substantial income. On 6 October (in a letter misdated 6 September) Orion wrote: "I am very thankful to you for your kind letter of Octo. 2, received to-day. I had all things ready for a trip to St. Louis in search of work to-morrow morning; but immediately changed the programme. I had squared off my rent account, and taken down my attorneys' sign. It is well enough. It was only creaking and catching no flies. I shall write at home, and use the rent money to pay instalments on some books I wish to buy — I guess I can get them for $25. They are books I have been borrowing and quoting from." Orion wrote to Jane Clemens on the same day: "Don't send me or Mollie any money. I have heard from Sam. He encourages me to go on with my book, and says it is probably a duty for me to do so. . . . I am going to work very hard, and think I will get done by spring. If it succeeds, it will probably [be] a source of income for 28 years. . . . I find from a letter received from Sam to-day, that his views of religion are precisely the same as my own. . . . I feel that in my book I am pursuing the average line of thought of the time in and out of church" (Keokuk, MTP). Clemens continued to think well of the book after he had read some of it (see letter 208).

4. Although Clemens was thinking this early about attending the Chicago meeting of the Society of the Army of the Tennessee, his formal invitation to respond to a toast at the banquet on the evening of 13 November was dated 25 October (R. S. Tuthill to SLC, Chicago, MTP).

5. *A Tramp Abroad.*

6. Hay was very active as a political speaker in 1879, and was being discussed as a possible Republican candidate for Congress, but he was not nominated. In November, Evarts appointed him Assistant Secretary of State (William R. Thayer, *The Life and Letters of John Hay*, 2 vols., Boston, 1915, I, 431–438).

207. HOWELLS TO CLEMENS

[Boston] Oct. 24, 1879.

My dear Clemens:

We got home last Saturday, and though we had a glorious time in Cleveland and elsewhere, we were *glad* to get home.[1] John Hay lives in superb style, and a lovely house, and the only thing in which I had the better of him was your letter which came there. "Why don't somebody write *me* such letters?" he sang out. "Why don't Clemens do it?" He's no end of a nice fellow, and he has a good wife and charming children. I suspect he is going to Congress next year.

Now Clemens, they are going to give Dr. Holmes a big breakfast on the 3d of December, — the Atlantic folks — and I want, and Mrs. Howells wants, you to come on and be our guest as long before and after that date as you can. Will you? Your invitation to the breakfast, (which isn't *out,* yet,) will reach you in due time.[2]

Yours with our joint love to all your tribe,

W. D. Howells.

1. Howells and his wife had taken a three-weeks trip to Canada to see his father, returning by way of Cleveland to visit the Hays. In these months Howells was advising President Hayes concerning ministerial and consular appointments, for Lowell and Harte successfully and for J. W. De Forest and C. W. Stoddard unsuccessfully (Cady, *Road to Realism,* p. 179).

2. Howells saw in this occasion an opportunity for Clemens to rehabilitate himself in the eyes of literary Boston after what Howells and Clemens both considered the fiasco of Clemens's speech at the Whittier dinner in 1877.

208. CLEMENS TO HOWELLS

Hartford Oct. 27/79

My Dear Howells —

Will I come? O *hell*-yes! — as the energetic Arkansaw student said to Rev. Joe Twichell in the Black Forest when Joe asked

him if he was home-sick. O *hell*yes! I'll come a day or two before the 3d (if Mrs. Clemens will permit), & stay a day or
two after it *any*way.

Hang it, I wish John Hay & his wife would give *us* a call,
next time they look in on you. David Gray is coming, by & by,
& you must see him & get better acquainted with that rare
spirit. By the way, in my letter to you,[1] speaking of Hay, I said
"The presence of such a man in politics is like a vase of attar of
roses in a glue-factory — it can't extinguish the stink, but it
modifies it." Mrs. Clemens said, "That will apply to Gen.
Hawley, too — take it out of your letter & put it in your speech
when you introduce Hawley to his audience — your speech *needs*
a snapper on the end of it, for it flats out, as it is at present — &
just say *stench,* that is strong enough." It was pretty good advice, & I followed it.[2]

Orion is really writing quite a readable book. He uses an
assumed name — fearing to injure me with pious people if he
used his own — & he goes for religion in a very capable & dignified way.

Mrs. Clemens usually helps me beat ingenious autograph-
hunters like the enclosed, but her hands are frightfully full,
just now. Will you ask Winnie or John to write on the postal
cards & ship them. Let both be dated ⟨Boston⟩ Hartford, &
signed "S L Clemens — Per J. L. McWilliams."[3] I have written
form of reply across the end of one of the cards & at the bottom
of the note-sheet. It is wonderful how that little "per" does take
the stuffing out of an autograph.

We-all send a power of love to you-all.   Yrs Ever

Mark.

Warner says your new book[4] is your best yet, according to Mrs.
Howells's judgment. You can imagine how that gratified us.

---

1. Of 9 October 1879.

2. The substitution of "stench" for "stink" is representative of Livy's
celebrated censorship of her husband's writing. Here, as often, the distinction seems to concern levels of elegance in diction rather than substan-
tive meaning. And it is significant that, with the revision in language, Livy
wanted the passage used emphatically in a public address in Elmira, the

home of many of her relatives and friends, where Clemens was to introduce Joseph R. Hawley.

3. "McWilliams" will be recalled as the name of the family described in Mark Twain's "The Experience of the McWilliamses with the Membranous Croup" (*Sketches, New and Old,* 1875; DE, VII, 85–94), "Mrs. McWilliams and the Lightning" (*Atlantic,* September 1880; DE, XV, 330–340), and "The McWilliamses and the Burglar Alarm" (*Harper's Christmas,* 1882; DE, XXVII, 315–324).

4. *The Undiscovered Country,* completed but still in MS.

209. HOWELLS TO CLEMENS

[Boston] Nov. 14, 1879.

My dear Clemens:

Do you suppose you could be got to lecture on anything before the Young Ladies' Saturday Morning Club of Boston, the mother of your Hartford Y.L.C.,[1] on the 20th of December?

Yours ever,

W. D. Howells.

1. The Saturday Morning Club, before which Howells had lectured in 1877 (see note 2 to letter 171).

210. CLEMENS TO HOWELLS

Hartford, Nov. 17/79.

My Dear Howells —

Just got home from Chicago at 2.30 this morning, after a solid week of unpareleled dissipation.[1] I was up all night Monday, Tuesday, Wednesday and Thursday nights, & was in bed only four & five hours a day during three of those days — the first (Monday,) I was up at 6 AM & did not go to bed till 7 the next morning. Still, I have not at any time felt tired, and hardly even drowsy. But of course the fatigue is in me somewhere, & will begin to come to the surface now.

I wish you had gone out there — you would have been glad all your life. I doubt if America has ever seen anything quite equal to it; I am well satisfied I shall not live to see its equal again. — How pale those speeches are in print — but how radiant, how full of color, how blinding they were in the delivery! Bob Ingersoll's speech [2] was sadly crippled by the proof-readers, but its music will sing through my memory always as the divinest that ever enchanted my ears. And I shall always see him as he stood that night on a dinner table, under the flash of lights & banners, in the midst of seven hundred frantic shouters, the most beautiful human creature that ever lived. "They fought that a mother might own her child" [3] — the words look like any other print, but Lord bless me, he borrowed the very accent of the angel of Mercy to say them in, & you should have seen that vast house rise to its feet, & you should have heard the hurricane that followed. That's the *only* test! — people may shout, clap their hands, stamp, wave their napkins, but none but the master can make them *get up on their feet.*

I heard four speeches which carried away all my wits & made me drunk with enthusiasm.[4] When I look at them in print they don't seem the same — their still sentences seem rather the prone dead forms of a host whom I had lately seen moving to the assault in the fire & smoke & tumult of battle, with flags flying & drums beating & the clarion voice of command ringing out above the thunder of the guns. Lord, there's nothing like the human organ to make words live & throb, & lift the hearer to the full altitudes of their meaning.

But — what I set out to say was, I can't talk before those ladies because I'm not going to have the time. If I had the time, & *could* talk about the wonders I saw in Chicago, & those ladies cared for anything so uninstructive, I'd do that; but I couldn't, for I choke up with the mere memory of it — to talk of it would simply be impossible. Imagine what it was like, to see a bullet-shredded old battle-flag reverently unfolded to the gaze of a thousand middle-aged soldiers most of whom hadn't seen it since they saw it advancing over victorious fields when they were in their prime. And imagine what it was like when Grant, their first commander, stepped into view while they were still going mad over the flag — & then right in the midst of it all, somebody struck up "When we were Marching through Georgia." Well, you should have heard the thousand voices lift that chorus & seen the tears stream down. If I live a hundred years I shan't ever forget these things — nor be able to talk about them. I shan't ever forget that I saw Phil Sheridan, with martial cloak & plumed chapeau, riding his big black horse in the midst of his own cannon — by all odds the superbest figure of a soldier *I* ever looked upon.

Grand times, my boy, grand times. Gen. Grant sat at the banquet like a statue of iron & listened without the faintest suggestion of emotion to fourteen speeches which tore other people all to shreds, but when I lit in with the fifteenth & last, his time was come![5] I shook him up like dynamite & he sat there fifteen minutes & laughed & cried like the mortalest of mortals. But bless you I had measured this unconquerable conqueror, & went at my work with the confidence of conviction, for I knew I could lick him. He told me he had shaken hands with 15,000 people that day & come out of it without an ache or pain, but that my truths had racked all the bones of his body apart. General Sherman said — well, no matter what he said, but it was mighty hearty & flattering, & most admirably worded — for he knows how to handle English.

But this postscript is extending itself too much. Its object is — now that I seem to have got down to it — to wail over the fact that my proof-sheets have begun to pile in on me at last, & *that* means, the dozen closing chapters of my book[6] have got to be ⟨written now⟩ tackled now & stuck to without interruption till they are all written & completed — & this bars me out of the Holmes breakfast & my visit with you; & I just can't bear to think of it. I've been imagining that visit, & the lovely talks in the lovely new house, & the delightful times we should have — & now it is all "up." But you've got to extend the time, & allow me to come as soon as my confinement with this book is over & I'm able to be around again.   Yrs Ever

                                                                            Mark.

1. Clemens had gone to Chicago to attend the "Citizen's Reception and Grand Re-Union of the Army of the Tennessee." For a fuller account of this celebration, see Appendix.

2. A printed copy of Robert G. Ingersoll's speech at the Grant banquet, in response to the twelfth toast: "The Volunteer Soldiers of the Union, whose valor and patriotism saved the world 'a government of the people, by the people, and for the people,'" is in MTP with Clemens's endorsement: "Ingersoll's great speech. Sent to me by him."

3. In the printed version, the passage reads as follows: "Grander than the Greek, nobler than the Roman, the soldiers of the Republic, with patriotism as shoreless as the air, battled for the rights of others, for the nobility of labor, fought that mothers might own their babes, that arrogant idleness might not scar the back of patient toil, and that our country should not be a many-headed monster made of warring states, but a nation, sovereign, great, and free."

4. Paine says that the four speeches were, in additon to Ingersoll's, that of Emery A. Storrs (responding to the thirteenth toast, "The Patriotic People of the United States, who fed, clothed and encouraged our Armies, and stood by us in Defeat as well as in Victory"), Colonel W. F. Vilas (responding to the fourth toast, "Our First Commander, General U. S. Grant"), and General John A. Logan (responding to the second toast, "The President and Congress of the United States") (MTB, p. 655). George Warner wrote to Lilly Warner from Des Moines on 19 November: "the Western papers all say Marks speech was No. 3. Ingersoll 1 Vilas 2" (MTP).

5. Mark Twain's speech (DE, XXVIII, 135–137) was in response to a toast of his own devising: "The Babies — As they comfort us in our sorrows, let us not forget them in our festivities" (MTB, p. 653).

6. Still *A Tramp Abroad*.

211. CLEMENS TO HOWELLS

[Hartford] Sunday [23 November 1879].

My Dear Howells:

My book is really finished at last[1] — every care is off my mind, everything is out of my way — so I have accepted the invitation to be at the Holmes breakfast.[2]

I'll bet a million my bed in your house has meantime been turned over to another; but if (on your honor) it hasn't, & I

won't be incommoding you in the least, may I still come to you
— say Dec. 2? Yrs Ever

Mark.

1. *A Tramp Abroad* was to be published by the American Publishing
Co. on 13 March 1880.

2. In spite of his great success with his speech recently in Chicago, it
will be noted that Clemens had written five days earlier to Howells that
he could not come to the Holmes breakfast. Warner seems to have helped
Clemens overcome his qualms, for he wrote to Howells this same day:
"Coming home yesterday, I found Mark in a mood to decline. I have urged
him to go, which he can now do — having finished his book — as well as
not. I have told him he will make a great mistake to stay away. He should
act just as if nothing has happened. . . . It seems to me very clear for his
own sake that he should go. If you agree with me, I wish you would tell
him so, for I know he values your judgment more than any others. He said
he had written to you and got no reply" (Hartford, 23 November 1879,
Houghton).

212. HOWELLS TO CLEMENS (POSTCARD)

[Belmont, 25 November 1879]

Your sober second thought received. — Awfully glad you are
coming. I wrote you yesterday.[1]

W. D. Howells.

1. The missing letter of Howells written on 24 November must have
urged Clemens to attend and speak at the Holmes breakfast, and may have
spoken of Johnny Howells's "conclusion to become an outlaw," to which
Clemens refers in his reply of 28 November.

213. CLEMENS TO HOWELLS (POSTCARD)

[Hartford, 27 November 1879]

Warner & I go up Tuesday, 2d, reaching Boston about 6
P.M. He goes to friends in the Highlands. He thinks I leave

for Belmont from the Fitchburg-Old Colony-Boston-&-Albany Station; but I do not think he knows anything about it — he talks like a man who is simply trying to let on to know everything. But if *you* say that is the station to leave from, I will believe you, for you have no motive to deceive. Speak up.

Ys

Mark

214. CLEMENS TO HOWELLS

Hartford, Nov. 28 [1879]

My Dear Howells —

If anybody talks, there, I shall claim the right to say a word myself, & be heard among the very *earliest* — else it would be confoundedly awkward for me — & for the rest, too.[1] But you may read what I say, beforehand, & strike out whatever you choose.[2]

Of course I thought it wisest not to be there at all; but Warner took the opposite view, & most strenuously.

Speaking of Johnny's conclusion to become an outlaw, reminds me of Susie's newest & very earnest longing — to have crooked teeth & glasses — "like mamma."

I would like to look into a child's head, once, & see what its processes are.

Yr Ever

S. L. Clemens

1. Clemens remembers the Whittier Birthday Dinner in December 1877. The Holmes breakfast presented an opportunity for him to make amends for his earlier blunder before a similarly imposing audience of Boston intellectuals.

2. The speech which Mark Twain delivered at the Holmes breakfast ("Unconscious Plagiarism," DE, XXVIII, 77–79) asserts that the dedication of *The Innocents Abroad* ("To my most patient reader and most charitable critic, my aged Mother . . . ") was inadvertently based upon Holmes's dedication in his *Songs in Many Keys*, which Mark Twain had "read and re-read" during an illness in the Sandwich Islands. When a friend brought the parallel to his attention and he wrote Holmes in apology, the genial

283

doctor had "said in the kindest way that it was all right and no harm done; and added that he believed we all unconsciously worked over ideas gathered in reading and hearing, imagining they were original with ourselves." It was a re-enactment in miniature of the pattern of unintentional offense and generous forgiveness which Mark Twain wanted to believe had characterized the incident of the Whittier dinner, and it had the desired effect. He appeared with credit on a program that also included a long list of New England celebrities, from Mrs. Julia Ward Howe to President Charles S. Eliot (Gilman, "Atlantic Dinners," *Atlantic,* C, 653–655). Despite the cordial reception of his speech, however, Mark Twain later recalled further offenses he thought he had committed. In his notebook for 1897–1899 (#32b II, TS, p. 50, MTP), along with reminiscences of the Whittier dinner, appears the following cryptic statement: "Breakfast to Holmes, when I made 3 blunders — the last with a man I worshiped — Francis Parkman."

215. CLEMENS TO HOWELLS

Hartford, Dec. 9 [1879].

My Dear Howells:

Am very much obliged for the trouble you have taken in the telegraphic matter.[1] It is all right, now. — I think the employment of "Young ladies" to do a servant's work in a waiting-room is a mistake — Young ladies who flaunt that obsolete title are bound to be conspicuous for the lack of the good manners which belong with it.

But what do you send back the proofs [2] for? They were for you, not me. The idea is to send them in batches, so you can read them when you have nothing pressing on hand, & be able finally to write a notice without being obliged to skim through the whole vast mass at one sitting. (I have struck out that little yarn, as you suggested.) [3]

In this morning's Courant I make an effort to blast the Post Master General's private secretary [4] from *his* lucrative position. I think I've rather got him.   Yrs Ever

Mark.

Had an awful good time at Belmont,[5] but it was intolerably short.

1. "Once in a telegraph office at a railway station," Howells remembered, "he [Clemens] was treated with such insolent neglect by the young lady in charge, who was preoccupied in a flirtation with a 'gentleman friend,' that . . . he told her he should report her to her superiors, and . . . did so. He went back to Hartford, and in due time the poor girl came to me in terror and in tears; for I had abetted Clemens in his action, and had joined my name to his in his appeal to the authorities. She was threatened with dismissal unless she made full apology to him and brought back assurance of its acceptance. I felt able to give this, and, of course, he eagerly approved. . . " (MMT, p. 42).

2. Of *A Tramp Abroad,* which Mark Twain was sending to Howells as the type was set.

3. The little yarn was not omitted, because the page had already been stereotyped, but the ending was changed "so as to make it inoffensive" (letter 217). Unfortunately, the passage cannot be identified.

4. The blast at Thomas B. Kirby, private secretary of Postmaster General David M. Key, appeared in the Hartford *Courant* under the title "The Postal Order Business." The affair had begun a couple of weeks earlier when Mark Twain had written a letter to the *Courant* in protest against new postal regulations requiring addresses to be written out in full. As he interpreted the rules, he would no longer be allowed to write on an envelope simply "Editor, 'Atlantic Monthly,' Boston," but would be obliged to write, "Editor, 'Atlantic Monthly,' care Messrs. Houghton, Osgood & Co., Winthrop Square, Boston, Mass." — a waste, by his count, of nine words. Computing how much time and ink would be wasted in the country as a whole, he arrived at an astronomical figure. He had received a rather saucy half-humorous note from Kirby dated 30 November, and proceeded to send it to the *Courant* together with a reply constituting a specimen of the verbal mayhem of which he was capable when his temper was inflamed (Frank C. Willson, "Twain Spanks a Government Employee for Unofficial Impertinence," *Twainian,* January 1945, pp. 2–4; "Twain 'Ciphers' Loss from Postal Decree," *ibid.,* March–April 1947, pp. 3–4).

5. When he came to Boston for the Holmes breakfast, and stayed with the Howellses.

216. CLEMENS TO HOWELLS

[Hartford] Dec. 10. '79.

Dear Howells —

Will you place this cuss's name & address alongside Chatto's,

& order "simultane" sheets to be sent to him & Chatto at the same time — when there are any? [1]

I hoped he wouldn't bother any more about these things, but as I promised him I suppose I must keep my word — not as creating a precedent, but for the novelty of it.   Yrs Ever

Mark.

1. The "cuss" was possibly H. Mortimer Franklyn, editor of the *Victorian Review* (Melbourne), who wrote Clemens on 21 January 1881 thanking him for an offer apparently made at an earlier date to send advance sheets of articles scheduled for publication in the *Atlantic* and *Belgravia* (MTP). The *Victorian Review,* given over entirely to nonfiction of a very solemn cast, was an unlikely medium of publication for Mark Twain, but Franklyn expected to begin publishing a weekly that would presumably be less forbidding in tone. Mark Twain's forthcoming piece in the *Atlantic* was his speech at the Holmes breakfast, to appear in the supplement to the February 1880 issue under the title "Mark Twain's Explanation."

217. CLEMENS TO HOWELLS

Htfd. Jan. 8./80

My Dear Howells:

Am waiting for Patrick to come with the carriage — Mrs. Clemens & I are starting (without the children!) to stay indefinitely in Elmira. — The wear & tear of settling the house broke her down, & she has been growing weaker & weaker for a fortnight. All that time — in fact ever since I saw you — I have been fighting a life-&-death battle with this infernal book [1] & *hoping* to get done some day. I required 300 pages of MS, & I have written near 600 since I saw you — & tore it all up except 288. This I was about to tear up yesterday & begin again, when Mrs. Perkins [2] came up to the billiard room & said, "You will never get any woman to do the thing necessary to save her life by mere *persuasion*; you see you have wasted your words for 3 weeks; it is time to use *force*; she *must* have a change; take her home & leave the children here." —

I said, "If there is one death that is painfuller than another, may I get it if I don't do that thing."

So I took the 288 pages to Bliss & told him that was the very last line I should ever write on this book. (A book which required 2600 pages, of MS, & I have written nearer four thousand, first & last.

I am as soary (& flighty) as a rocket, to-day, with the unutterable joy of getting that Old Man of the Sea off my back, where he has been roosting more than a year & a half. Next time I make a contract before writing the book, may I suffer the righteous penalty & be burnt, like the injudicious believer.

I am mighty glad you are done [with] your book [3] (this is from a man who, above all others, feels how much that sentence means) & am also mighty glad you have begun the next [4] (this is also from a man who knows the felicity of *that*, & means straightway to enjoy it.) The Undiscovered starts off delightfully — I have read it aloud to Mrs. C. & we vastly enjoyed it.

Yes, I'll return you those proofs. [5] I struck out that anecdote, as you recommended; but when I found the page had been stereotyped, in due order, I reinstated it & changed the ending so as to make it inoffensive. [6]

Well, time's about up — must drop a line to Aldrich.

Ys Ever

Mark.

1. *A Tramp Abroad*, which Mark Twain had said was "really finished at last" on 23 November 1879.

2. Mrs. Mary Beecher Perkins, wife of Thomas C. Perkins, a neighbor and intimate friend of the Clemenses.

3. *The Undiscovered Country*, of which the first installment appeared in the *Atlantic* for January 1880.

4. Presumably the *nouvelle, A Fearful Responsibility,* which would appear in *Scribner's Monthly* for June and July 1881.

5. Of *A Tramp Abroad*, which Mark Twain had been sending along in batches for some weeks so that Howells might have more time to read the book in preparation for reviewing it. Howells had returned some of the proofs with a suggestion for revision.

6. See letter 215.

218. CLEMENS TO HOWELLS

Elmira, Jan. 24/80.

Say — are you dead again? And did you go to the Tile Club dinner in New York?[1] I should have gone, sure, if my wife had had two husbands, so one could stay here & give the medicine. I've read the Feb. Undiscovered,[2] & it is perfectly wrote — as Susy says. — What a master hand you are to ⟨hand⟩ jabber the nauseating professional slang of spiritism — it flows from you like your native language. I see that that poor old man & that poor girl[3] are going to pain me more & more, to the end.

Supper? Well, then, I must cut short & go.

I didn't dare to sign the enclosed article[4] — the histories are too thinly disguised.

We reach Hartford next Saturday — leave here Tuesday & take 2 days to go to New York, & stay there a day or two.

Ys Ever

Mark.

You perceive the madam mends apace.

1. The Tile Club was an informal group of artists who met in one another's studios in New York on Wednesday evenings from 1877 to 1884. W. Mackay Laffan, artist and drama critic of the New York *Sun,* had written to Clemens in Hartford on 13 January (with a second letter on 15 January addressed to Elmira; New York, MTP) inviting him to dine with the Club at the studio of William M. Chase on West 10th St. on 24 January. Laffan said that James R. Osgood was coming down from Boston for the occasion.

2. The second installment of Howells's *The Undiscovered Country,* in the *Atlantic* for February 1880.

3. "Doctor" Boynton, a self-deluded dabbler in spiritualism, and his daughter Egeria, whom he considers to be gifted as a medium. Howells had first encountered spiritualism as a boy when his family moved to the Western Reserve, "lately . . . swept by the fires of spiritualism, which left behind a great deal of smoke and ashes where the inherited New England orthodoxy had been" (YMY, p. 88). At the Dante readings in Longfellow's home in 1866, he had heard Holmes argue spiritualism with Thomas

Appleton, and very probably had heard Holmes's description of a showman and his daughter of thirteen who pretended to summon up the spirits of the dead and make them talk and sing (T. F. Currier, *Bibliography of Oliver Wendell Holmes,* New York, 1953, p. 488). With Hawthorne's *The Blithedale Romance* as a guide, in *The Undiscovered Country* Howells tried to deal seriously with the delusion of spiritualism as a substitute for failing religious faith.

4. It concerned among other matters a poor girl who married a Senator, and an idiot (as Howells indicates in his reply, letter 219); the article is not extant.

219. HOWELLS TO CLEMENS

[Boston] Feb. 3, 1880.

My dear Clemens:

I am glad to hear of Mrs. Clemens's improved health. I am just going to follow your main-force example, and take *my* wife away. She has been in the house and the greater part of the time, and in bed ever since you were here; and last week her long sickness culminated in a carbuncle. So we are going to wander round for change of air.

— This sketch — or part of it — has the making of something uncommonly fine in it: as good as your True Story.[1] I mean that part relating to the poor girl who married the Senator. The touch about the idiot brought a lump into my throat.[2] Do that story in full, Clemens, and let me have it with your name. This sketch as it stands, is not good enough to go without your name, and your name is too good for it. The cataloguing, in it, fails of its purpose, I think. — You know what a beast I feel like, to be saying this, especially as you like what I'm doing now. I hope you and Mrs. Clemens will have a kindness for Boynton, to the end. — That Tile Club Dinner, I'm told, was great affair: darkies in fezes and yataghans waiting on the guests, and narghiles ad libitum. Yours ever

W. D. Howells.

1. "A True Story, Repeated Word for Word as I Heard It," Mark Twain's first contribution to the *Atlantic* (November 1874).

2. In part, perhaps, because Howells's younger brother Henry had been rendered feeble-minded for life by a head injury in early childhood.

2 2 0. CLEMENS TO HOWELLS

Hartford, Mch 5/80

Dear Howells —

I reckon you are dead again,[1] but no matter, I will heave a line at the corpse. I have really nothing to say, though, except that Mrs. C. & I are going to spend a week secretly in a Boston hotel, by & by, & hope you & Mrs. Howells will not be sorry to hear it — for, upon the honor of a man & a scribe, we shall not be incensed if you do nothing more than drop in & say howdy-do, for we know what it is to be busy & have a wife whose health requires peace, & rest from ⟨intrusion.⟩ social taxing.

That most infernally troublesome book[2] is at last hidden from my sight & mind in the jaws of three steam presses. Orders received for 25,000 copies — not a very satisfactory start, but the diligent Canadian[3] has warned everybody that he will glut the market at half-a-dollar within ten days after we issue; proclaims that he has bought advance-sheets right along from pressmen & understrappers in the three printing-offices, attending to the matter in person here under an assumed name. Such is Belford! However, these things discomfort me not in the slightest degree. My joy in getting the book out of my hands fills me up & leaves no room for trivial griefs.

I have reached (MS) page 326 on my historical tale of "The Little Prince & the Little Pauper" & if I knew it would never sell a copy my jubilant delight in writing it would not suffer any diminution. Love to you all.   Yrs Ever

Mark.

1. Howells had been submerged in work. Late in January he had pleaded this excuse in declining an invitation to visit President Hayes in the

White House (WDH to Rutherford B. Hayes, Boston, 23 January, NEQ, XV, 123, March 1942).

2. Still *A Tramp Abroad.*

3. Alexander Belford, of Belford Bros., Toronto. Moncure D. Conway wrote to Clemens from London on 20 December 1880 that "the Canadian appropriators" had sold twenty thousand copies of *A Tramp Abroad* (MTP). The legitimate sale in the United States at that time had reached eighty thousand.

221. CLEMENS TO HOWELLS

[Hartford] Mch. 11/80

My Dear Howells —

Many thanks — I have telephoned & district-messengered Bliss to start the book [1] to you immediately. It will be on its way per the noon train today.

I take so much pleasure in my story [2] that I am loth to hurry, not wanting to get it done. Did I ever till you the plot of it? It begins at 9 a.m., Jan. 27, 1547, seventeen & a half hours before Henry VIII[s] death, by the swapping of clothes *and places,* between the prince of Wales & a pauper boy of the same age & countenance (& half as much learning & still more genius & imagination) and & after that, the rightful small king has a rough time among tramps & ruffians in the country parts of Kent, whilst the small bogus king has a gilded & worshiped & dreary & restrained & cussed time of it on the throne — & this all goes on for three weeks — till the midst of the coronation grandeurs in Westminster Abbey Feb. 20, when the ragged true king forces his way in but cannot prove his genuineness — but the bogus king, by a remembered incident of the first day is able to prove it *for* him — whereupon clothes are changed & the coronation proceeds under the new & rightful conditions.

My idea is to afford a realizing sense of the exceeding severity of the laws of that day [3] by inflicting some of their penalties upon the king himself & allowing him a chance to see the rest of them applied to others — all of which is to account for certain mildnesses which distinguished Edward VI⁸ reign from those that preceded & followed it.

Imagine *this* fact — I have even fascinated Mrs. Clemens with this yarn for youth. My stuff generally gets considerable damning with faint praise out of her, but this time it is all the other way. She is become the horse-leech's daughter & my mill doesn't grind fast enough to suit her. This is no mean triumph, my dear sir.

Last night, for the first time in ages, we went to the theatre — to see Yorick's Love.⁴ The magnificence of it is beyond praise. The language is so beautiful, the passion so fine, the plot so ingenious, the whole thing so stirring, so charming, so pathetic! But I will clip from the Courant — it says it right.⁵ And what a good company it is, & how like *live* people they all acted! The "thee's" & the "thou's" had a pleasant sound, since it is the language of the Prince & the Pauper. You've done the country a service in that admirable work.

Say — couldn't you Howellses run down here & give us a visit? Come, now, say you will? Do — we'll have a quiet & comfortable good time. Mrs. Clemens distinctly & cordially invites Mrs. Howells, & would write it herself, only I tell her these rigid ceremonies *can't* be necessary between these two families of friends. Say — will you do it?

You see, I judge we don't go to Boston before the middle or end of April — thank you very much for those offers, & the same are hereby enthusiastically accepted.   Yrs Ever

Mark.

1. *A Tramp Abroad.*
2. *The Prince and the Pauper.*
3. This looks forward to *A Connecticut Yankee in King Arthur's Court.*
4. The tragedy adapted by Howells from *Un Drama Nuevo* by Manuel Tamayo y Baus. Concerning the play, see Appendix.
5. The *Courant* reviewer called *Yorick's Love* "one of the most powerful of modern plays . . . a really great tragedy." Barrett's performance, he said, "deserves the highest praise" (11 March 1880, p. 2).

222. HOWELLS TO CLEMENS

[Boston] March 22, 1880.

My dear Clemens:

I have been feebly trying to give the Atlantic readers some notion of the charm and the solid delightfulness of your book;[1] and now I must tell you privately what a joy it has been to Mrs. Howells and me. Since I have read it, I feel sorry for I shall not be able to read it again for a week, and in what else shall I lose myself so wholly? Mrs. Howells declares it the wittiest book she ever read, and I say there is *sense* enough in it for ten books. That is the idea which my review will try to fracture the average numbscull with.[2] — Well, you are a blessing. You ought to believe in God's goodness, since he has bestowed upon the world such a delightful genius as yours to lighten its troubles.

Love from both of us to Mrs. Clemens. We wish we could come to see you, but we are many promises deep to the Warners, and our first visit must be to them. We shall hope for you here by mid-April.　　　　　Yours ever

W. D. Howells

MS. At the top of p. 1 of the letter Clemens wrote, "Remail this to me, Joe. *Mark*," and a note from Twichell to Clemens on 25 March acknowledges receipt of Howells's letter (Hartford, MTP).

1. Howells's review of *A Tramp Abroad* was to appear in the *Atlantic* for May 1880 (p. 686) and is reprinted in MMT (pp. 129–133).

2. The review emphasizes "the serious undercurrent of the book" and concludes that the reader will find in it "much to enlighten as well as amuse him, much to comfort and stay him in such Americanism as is worth having, and nothing to flatter him in a mistaken national vanity or a stupid national prejudice."

[Hartford] March 24/80.

My Dear Howells —

Your & Mrs. Howells's praises have been the greatest up-lifting I ever had. When a body is not even remotely expecting such things, how the surprise takes the breath away! We had been interpreting your stillness to melancholy & depression caused by that book. This is honest. Why *everything* looks brighter, now. A check for untold cash could not have made our hearts sing as your letter has done.

I long ago forbade any copies to go to anybody connected with the press except you & David Gray — couldn't send to Warner without sending to the others here.[1] You were the three men whom I could trust to say the good thing if it could be honestly said; or be & remain charitably silent. I am justified in being afraid of the general press, because it killed the "Gilded Age" before you had a chance to point out that there were merits in that book.[2] The sale ceased almost *utterly* until the adverse criticisms were forgotten — then began again, & has kept smoothly on. During the past 12 months (to Jan. 1) it has sold a trifle over 1500 copies — not greatly behind Innocents & Tom Sawyer, each of which sold a fraction under 2200 copies — & hardly *any* behind Roughing It, which sold 1800.

Tauchnitz proposes to use casts of our pictures & issue an illustrated edition of the new book in addition to putting it in the "Series." So I judge the advance sheets have favorably impressed him.

When Mrs. Clemens read about your being so "many promises deep," she made that noise which one creates by suddenly detaching the tongue from the roof of the mouth, & which eloquently expresses aggravation. That did not deceive the Recording Angel a bit; I knew the entry that was being set down in the great book opposite the name Livy L. Clemens, to-wit:

"March 24, 1880 — at breakfast — unarticulated remark reflecting the thought, *'Damn those Warners.'* " —

To get this woman to give up the baneful habit of underhanded swearing, is one of those things which I have long ago been obliged to give up, as being among the reforms which cannot be accomplished. But the poor children don't suspect, I thank God for that.

What she said afterward, (shot full of silent oaths & curses & general blasphemy which made my flesh crawl & my hair stand,) was this:

"That is an old debt, & I suppose one must allow that it is just to pay it — though it does seem unfair, somehow — but why have the Warners allowed it to run so long? — here we have been away a year & a half; they have had abundance of time to collect — it does seem to me rightdown hard; I believe such indebtednesses should come under some sort of law of limitation, like moneyed ones."

There was reason in that. The first time Susie Warner is sick again, I'll telegraph you & you come down & visit them, along with Mrs. Howells. They cant receive when they are sick, of course, & that will set things all straight.   Yrs Ever

Mark.

P.S. Madam says you've visited the Warners since you visited us. Now doesn't that knock those promises?

I have just written Congress asking for a law making the selling of ⟨Cana⟩ pirated books a penal offense, punishable by fine & imprisonment, like dealing in any other kind of stolen goods.[3] Wish we could have had something of the sort recommended in the President's message.[4] This thing is Bliss's idea, & I do not see why it is not sound & sensible.

---

1. Clemens means he could not send a copy of *A Tramp Abroad* for Warner to review in the Hartford *Courant* without sending copies to the other Hartford papers, and he was reluctant to do this.

2. Clemens exaggerates the hostility of the newspapers toward *The Gilded Age*. It is true that the Chicago *Tribune* denounced the book on the score that it lacked the delicacy of Warner's earlier work and the "quaint and fertile humor" of Mark Twain, and quoted a charge made by the St. Louis

Democrat that the book was a hoax, having been written by "several obscure . . . local reporters." Elsewhere, however, critical opinion was at least divided. Although the construction of the plot was generally condemned, the characterization was praised by the Boston *Transcript* and by *Old and New*, and the satiric power of the book was praised by *Appleton's* (Arthur L. Vogelback, "The Literary Reputation of Mark Twain in America, 1869–1885," pp. 79, 80, 85, 101).

3. There is no evidence that the petition was actually submitted to Congress.

4. President Hayes had sent a special message to Congress (concerning the plan for a canal connecting the Atlantic and the Pacific) on 8 March.

[*See Additional Letter 223A, p. 880.*]

224. CLEMENS TO HOWELLS

[Hartford] Thursday, Apl. 1/80.

My Dear Howells:

That [1] is perfectly lovely, & it came with its reviving breath just at the right moment — for I had just laid down a long letter from Orion & was feeling haggard, — a letter which actually contains these following propositions & statements:

Having reached 20th chapter of his work whose purpose is to destroy Christianity, sent eleven pages of it (under assumed name,) to the publishers of "The Bible for Learners," & inquired if they desired the rest? MS. returned without comment. Whereupon, he abandoned the work, & — on the same day — began "The Autobiography of an Ass," & encloses Chapter 1 to me for revision, opinion, & suggestion; will send me one chapter *every day*, & wishes it sent immediately back, for the work is to be driven night & day to completion. Afterthought — sent the 11 pages to the Investigator, Boston, (assumed name again) with application for editorial position — if none open, Editor please let him know of any vacancy on any republican or independent paper. If favorably answered will go to Boston at once — has begun preparations to that end. Been down town to newspaper office, & brought home armfull of exchanges — has written to a Worcester, Mass., paper, a Colorado paper, & to one in West Virginia & one in Alabama, asking editorial position. Also has subscribed 6 months to a New York advertising journal, & means to watch it for notices of "editors wanted." In Colorado exchanges, he is fired by some rich silver strikes, & proposes that I send him out there, with enough money to buy furniture & fit up a house; he will prospect, & give me half he finds, though thinks it quicker & richer work if I furnish a moderate sum monthly & he watch the market warily, & speculate — always being careful to "buy on a rising market & sell on a falling one" — sees, now, that the reason he did not succeed in Nevada was because he followed the opposite course. Will give me any share of the profits "(if any)" that I require. Please answer "immediately," & he will be off the same day. Will make preparations at once. Has just written to an old printer-friend in St Louis for "subbing" — if favorable answer returned, will telegraph me his St Louis address. Has written to three country papers, inquiring upon what terms he can buy in — in case of favorable answer, what amount can I let him have, "at 8 per cent — the property to be bought in your name & held by you, so as to secure you utterly from loss." Proposes to set up a correspondence-bureau in New York, & mail 12 copies of the same letter daily to 12 widely-scattered papers "at $1 each — or less, if they will not pay that." "This could be made to grow into something enormous, by careful work & strict & unwavering attention to the business." Will need a little capital till the thing "gets to running smoothly."

Well, let the rest go. I thought I could give the whole list, but I see I have got only halfway down. Three of his daily batches of Autobiography of an Ass have arrived in a bunch — but it will stop there — he is at another "work" before this.

Your most generous review has saved me; if I could have a new book & a new review every time Orion assaults me, I could defy him & tell him to do his worst. Last year — aged 54 — he proposed to learn German, go to Germany, & get rich teaching English.

Mrs. Clemens says we leave for Boston "Monday after next, or the Monday after that." I never knew her mind to be thus shackly before; never knew her to stick the adverb *or* in, before — heretofore she has always known her dates with a grisly & awful exactness.

With a world of sincere thanks,   Yrs Ever
(over) [2]   Mark.

1. Howells's review of *A Tramp Abroad,* which was to appear in the May *Atlantic.*

2. The note from Livy to Howells which appears on the verso of the sheet is printed as the next item in the correspondence.

225. OLIVIA L. CLEMENS TO HOWELLS

[Hartford, 1 April 1880]

Dear Mr. Howells

We do thank you most heartily for your notice of Mr Clemens book — I have wondered so many times why some one did not take note of certain things in Mr Clemens which seemed to me his strong points, and now you have spoken of them so of course I am peculiarly pleased [1] —

We do want to see you and Mrs Howells here — your last visit here was to the Warners we must take possession of you next time

With love to Mrs Howells I am
with sincere regards   Yours

Olivia L. Clemens

MS. The note is written on the verso of the last sheet of Clemens's letter of this date.

1. The point which gratifies Livy is beyond question Howells's assertion that Mark Twain's humor "springs from a certain intensity of common sense, a passionate love of justice, and a generous scorn of what is petty and mean. . . . Its wildest extravagance is the break and fling from a deep feeling, a wrath with some folly which disquiets him worse than other men, a personal hatred for some humbug or pretension that embitters him beyond anything but laughter" (MMT, p. 130).

226. CLEMENS TO HOWELLS

[Hartford, 12? April 1880]

If you've got that letter, yet, wherein I told you about the sable hero John Lewis & his miraculous feat the time Ida Langdon's horse ran away,[1] here's an addition for it, being an autograph letter from Lewis.[2]   Yrs

Mark.

MS. An endorsement on a letter to Clemens from John T. Lewis, Elmira, 11 April 1880 (Houghton).

1. Clemens's letter of 25 [–27] August 1877 contains a full account of the incident.

2. The Negro farmer on the Cranes' Quarry Farm near Elmira. He thanks Clemens for a copy of *A Tramp Abroad*.

227. CLEMENS TO HOWELLS

Hartford, Apl. 19[–20]/80.

My Dear Howells:

I have just "wrotened" this stuff [1] to-day — as Bay says — maybe you may need it to fill up with.

We had a most elegant good time in Boston, & Mrs. Clemens has two imperishable topics, now, the museum of andirons which she collected, & your dinner. It is hard to tell which she admires the most. Sometimes she leans one way, & sometimes the other; but I lean pretty steadily toward the dinner, because I can appreciate that, whereas I am no prophet in andirons. There has been a procession of Adams Express wagons filing before the door all day, delivering andirons.

Well what a good time we had at old Mr. Fields's.[2] And what lovable people the Bulls [3] are — both of them. Did you notice her dress? — what a piece of perfection that was. — And what a master-hand she is with a piano. And if Ole Bull had been born without arms, what a rank he would have taken among the poets — because it is in him, & if he couldn't violin it out, he would talk it out, since of course it would have to *come* out. It would be lovely if they would come & visit us.

I have thought of upwards of a million things I wanted to say to you — but that is always the way. Probably there *is* an eternity.

Mrs. C. seems settled in her mind that Mrs. Howells is a perfectly wonderful woman — in fact this poor girl has come home dazed. Boston has been too many for her. Her opinion of herself was low enough, before — it has gone down out of soundings, now. I don't ever have any of that sort of sweats.

We couldn't go to the Fairchilds's [4] & the tile factory & Chelsea both; so we gave up the latter & attempted the former. It was a failure, & we were very sorry to miss them. Fairchild was out, & Mrs. F at home; the porter was at the speaking tube a good while & then brought an excuse; I saw he still had our cards, so I wasn't at all sure he had sent up our names at all, but doubtless he did. I'm always suspecting people when they pretend to talk through a tube. I always imagine there isn't anybody at the other end.

Mrs. Clemens finds this house pretty dull, now, & housekeeping a new trouble, but I reckon she will quiet down presently. With love to all,   Ys Ever

                                        Mark.

Apl. 20. — P.S. ⟨I have ch⟩ Mrs. Clemens has changed her mind. She says it is an atrocious article (in *motif*) & she will not publish it.

Joe Twichell was here last night, wild with delight over your notice of the "Tramp." Said it was such an able notice, such literature, etc — & added absently & to himself, resting his hands on knees & head bent down, "And to think that old *Howells* has said that — old Howells — well, it's a form of immortality in itself!"

Upon second thought I interlined Joe's *attitude,* it is so common to him & he is so handsome in it, & so unbearably aggravating to Mrs. Clemens when her voice ceases from an animated narrative, & Joe responds "Well, Livy, how are they all at Elmira?" (not having heard a word of her yarn.)

1. Apparently suppressed; in the postscript, Mark Twain says it did not earn Livy's approval.

2. James T. Fields, who had retired from editorship of the *Atlantic* in 1871 and had sold it to H. O. Houghton & Co. in 1873.

3. Ole Bull, the celebrated Norwegian violinist, and his American wife. According to a letter from Howells to his father (Boston, 17 April 1880, LinL, I, 283), the Fieldses gave a luncheon for the Bulls on 16 April which Howells attended with his daughter Winifred; presumably this was the occasion on which the Clemenses also met the Bulls. "We had a sit-down lunch," wrote Howells, "and uproarious story-telling gayety, and after lunch Ole Bull made his fiddle sing to us. It was wonderful: the fiddle did everything but walk round the room. Ole Bull is very white haired, and it was fine to see him as well as hear him playing. His wife was with him — an American, half his age — who accompanied him on the piano: a very gentle and charming person."

4. Charles Fairchild was the wealthy friend of the Howellses who had induced them to build on his acreage in Belmont.

228. CLEMENS TO HOWELLS

[Hartford] Thursday [22 April 1880].

My Dear Howells:

I have scribbled this [1] to-day — maybe it may do for the Club, I dunno.

When you can, I want you to give me the exact date of your hegira or exodus into Hartford, (if that is the right phrase,) because I want to fetch up the Rightful Earl [2] & have that interview. He has invented a swimming apparatus, & wants me to lend him $200 to shove it with, but I don't calculate to do that.   Ys Ever

                                                    Mark.

1. Probably the piece which Howells calls "obituary eloquence" in his letter of 25 April. Although Howells then said that the piece would go into

the Contributors' Club of the July *Atlantic,* it was not published until November 1881. The sketch is an amusing dissection of the mixed metaphors and inflated rhetoric in the obituary notice of a man who had lived "out toward the rear of a Western state."

2. Jesse M. Leathers. Concerning him, see Appendix.

229. CLEMENS TO HOWELLS

[Hartford] Apl. 23/80.

Dear Howells —

If you want this,[1] won't you either have some of your office-folks copy it — or put it in type — at once, so I can have it in the course of 4 or 5 days? I wrote it to read at a private house next week (among other stuff) for the benefit of a charity. If you will send me 2 proofs, I'll send one to Chatto myself, & write him a soft-spoken letter & mollify him a little, — though it is through his own carelessness that he is out behind us with the new book & therefore has doubtless lost his English copyright.[2]

Ys Ever

Mark.

P.S. It may be that this subject has been treated by somebody while we were gone over the water; in which case we will suppress this [.]

1. "A Telephonic Conversation," which appeared as a separate piece over Mark Twain's signature in the *Atlantic* for June 1880 (DE, XXIV, 204–208). It is a charming satire on women's conversation in the form of a "verbatim" record of one side of a dialogue over the telephone.

2. Chatto & Windus were not mollified; they insisted that the American Publishing Co. had brought out the American edition of *A Tramp Abroad* "without giving us sufficient notice" (Chatto & Windus to SLC, London, 9 May 1880, MTP), and Clemens's friend and literary agent Moncure D. Conway wrote that "Bliss did not do his duty . . . the proof of the text of the book was not in Chatto's hands until the work was out in America" (Turnham Green, England, 4 May 1880, MTP). A work could be copyrighted in England only if it were published there before publication in any other country. Fortunately, Chatto's edition was not forestalled by a pirated edition in England.

[Boston] April 25, 1880.

My dear Clemens:

I sent the Conversation by Telephone to the printers at once, with orders to set it and send you proofs instantly. It is one of the best things you have done, and we both think it shows great skill in the treatment of female character. It's delicious. And we've been laughing over the way Twichell takes Mrs. Clemens's conversation — that's cruel good. — The obituary eloquence will go into the next month's Club — July's.

Mrs. Howells has written to Mrs. Clemens and I hope has told her how much we all enjoyed the visit you made us.[1] It was a noble time, but as you found, it left something over for eternity. The incompleteness — the unfinishable incompleteness — of everything in life, ought to point to something, as Dr. Boynton[2] would have said. Well, we can hitch on again at Hartford, either next week or week after — a Maypole dancing-party of the children has to decide for us. But we will let you know in good time for the rightful earl. — I think you've only to ask Ole Bull, if you want him to visit you. What a beautiful old man he is! I suppose neither of us will ever look so, though we might together. We can do anything together.   Yours ever

W. D. Howells

1. Howells wrote to his father on 17 April that the Clemenses spent "a day and night with us," apparently 15–16 April (Boston, LinL, I, 283).
2. The muddled spiritualist of *The Undiscovered Country.*

[Hartford] Apl. 29/80.

My Dear Howells:

I return the simultaning copy[1] to you enveloped & stamped for transmission *at the proper time.* I don't know which No.

of the Atlantic it is to appear in — that's why I don't transmit it myself — afraid it might get back here in the English mag.[2] before it had appeared in the Atlantic. And then, again, if it is to be in your June No, I would not ship it to Chatto at all. I'm not particular about simultaning now-a-days, though I used to was — that is, I'm not at all particular if it must cost us any delay or inconvenience. A squib like this is so likely to be thought of & done by somebody else, you see, while we fool around waiting on an English mag.

Just see how lucky a body is, sometimes! During four weeks Hartford hasn't dared to quench its thirst with a drop of water, for the pipes deliver only a fearfully-stinking fluid which is thick with rotten fish — one has to hold his ⟨nose⟩ breath whilst he washes his face. I am not overstating it. Well, a fortnight ago we added a strip of 25 feet of ground to our south line, by purchase, & the very next day, just within the bounds of that strip, we struck a spring of cold, sweet, limpid & abundant water worth many millions of dollars! There's enough of it for the cooking & drinking of a dozen families. Our other spring (just below the conservatory) was long ago destroyed by the plumbers in repairing a neighbor's drain. May this one abide! (Unberufen!) [3]   Yrs Ever

                                                             Mark.

1. Of "A Telephonic Conversation."

2. Chatto's *Belgravia*. But the piece was not published there.

3. This expression — which became a household word in the Clemens family — is explained by an entry in Mark Twain's notebook made in April 1878, on board the *Holsatia*: "Unberufen! & *knock under* the table or other wood 3 times — the superstition being that [if] the evil spirits hear you say 'What fine weather it is!' they will immediately change it unless you ward it off [by] the invocation 'Unberufen!' " (#12, TS, p. 14, MTP).

[Boston] April 30, 1880.

My dear Clemens:

I want to put the Conversation into the next number, and so I suppose you *can't* simultane. I return the letter, and a proof of a Club ¶.[1]

I dont think I told you how very good I found that letter of your black hero's.[2] Isn't the incident old enough to let you let me Club it? I want to. And this letter of his — it's beautiful.

— Your finding the spring *was* luck! — That is, it wasn't merit, I suppose, or we should have a geyser, here.

Yours ever

W. D. Howells

1. Conceivably the piece on obituary eloquence which Howells held for some months and which his successor, Aldrich, published in November 1881. Howells called items for the Contributors' Club "paragraphs" even when they ran to a page or more.
2. John T. Lewis.

[Hartford] Thursday, 6th. [-7 May]/80.

My Dear Howells:

There you stick, at Belmont, & now I'm going to Washington for a few days; & of course, between you & Providence that visit is going to get mixed, & you'll have been here & gone again just about the time I get back. Bother it all, I wanted to astonish you with a chapter or two from Orion's *latest* book — not the seventeen which he has begun in the last four months, but the one which he began last week.

Last night, when I went to bed, Mrs. Clemens said, "George

didn't take the cat down to the cellar — Rosa says he has left it shut up in the conservatory." So I went down to attend to Abner (the cat.) About 3 in the morning Mrs. C. woke me & said, "I do believe I hear that cat in the drawing-room — what did you do with him?" I answered up with the ⟨satisfaction⟩ confidence of a man who has managed to do the right thing for once, & said, "I opened the conservatory doors, took the library off the alarm, & spread everything open, so that there wasn't any obstruction between him & the cellar." Language wasn't capable of conveying this woman's disgust. But the sense of what she said, was, "He couldn't have done any harm in the conservatory — so you must go & make the entire house free to him & the burglars, imagining that he will prefer the coal-bins to the drawing-room. If you had had Mr. Howells to help you, I should have admired but not been astonished, because I should know that *together* you would be equal to it; but how you managed to contrive such a stately blunder all by yourself, is what I cannot understand." [1]

So, you see, even *she* knows how to appreciate our gifts.

Brisk times here. — Saturday, these things happened: Our neighbor Chas. Smith was stricken with heart disease, & came near joining the majority; my publisher, Bliss, ditto ditto; a neighbor's child died; neighbor Whitmore's sixth child added to his five other cases of measles; neighbor Niles sent for, & responded; Susie Warner down, abed; Mrs. George Warner threatened with death during several hours; her son Frank, whilst imitating the marvels in Barnum's circus bills, thrown from his aged horse & brought home insensible; Warner's friend Max Yortzburgh, shot in the back by a locomotive & broken into 32 distinct pieces & his life threatened; [2] & Mrs. Clemens, after writing all these cheerful things to Clara Spaulding, taken at midnight, & if the doctor had not been pretty prompt the contemplated Clemens would have called before his apartments were ready.

However, everybody is all right, now, except Yortzburg, & he is mending — that is, he is *being* mended. I knocked off, during these stirring times, & don't intend to go to work again till we go away for the summer, 5 or 6 weeks hence. So I am writing to you; not because I have anything to say, but because you don't have to answer, & I need something to do, this afternoon.

The rightful earl has

Friday, 7th.

Well, never mind about the rightful earl [3] — he merely wanted to borrow money — I never knew an American earl that didn't.

But Warner has just telephoned me about you.[4] It is a great disappointment, but Mrs. Clemens says — & I repeat — that you are doing the right thing; when one is short for time, he should be free to alter arrangements with friends, without prejudice or cussedness (I wish in my heart she would drop that word) — & that it is hard enough that one can't have the same righteous privilege with more distantly-related folk.

Well, we hope you will have a good time, & I wish I was going; but I have given it up. I have a letter from a Congressman [5] this morning, & he says Congress *couldn't* be persuaded to bother about Canadian pirates at a time like this when *all* legislation must have a political & Presidential bearing, else Congress won't look at it. So I have changed my mind & my course; I go north, to kill a pirate. I must procure repose *some* way, else I cannot get down to work again.

Pray offer my most sincere & respectful approval to the President — is approval the proper word? I find it is the one I most value here in the household, & seldomest get.

With our affection to you both,   Ys Ever

Mark.

1. This incident became the basis for Mark Twain's extravaganza "The McWilliamses and the Burglar Alarm" (*Harper's Christmas,* 1882; DE, XXVII, 315–324).

2. Of the neighbors mentioned in Clemens's casualty list, Elisha Bliss and the Warners are familiar to the reader, and the only other person of consequence in Clemens's life is Frank G. Whitmore, a member of the Friday Evening Club, later Mark Twain's local business agent. "Max Yortzburgh" is probably an invention.

3. Leathers had written again from New York on 6 May repeating his request for a loan of $200 to develop his "swimmer invention" and add-

3 0 7

ing a request for $100 to enable him to go to Louisville, get his three small motherless daughters, and take them to Binghamton, N.Y., where he had found a foster mother for them (MTP).

4. To say that the Howellses were not coming to Hartford because they were leaving for Washington to spend six days with President and Mrs. Hayes in the White House.

5. Probably Rollin M. Daggett, whom Clemens had known in Nevada in the 1860's. On 3 May, Daggett wrote to Clemens offering to introduce any amendment to the copyright law that Clemens wished "and the country will stand," and remarking, "Blaine is too busy to attend to anything but his fences" (Washington, 3 May 1880, MTP).

234. CLEMENS TO HOWELLS

Hartford, May 18/80.

My Dear Howells —

I know you hate Clubs — at least they are an unpleasant suggestion to you, & doubtless they are borous to you — still I have been urged to ask you to consent to join a Club — the easiest way to disburden myself of the matter is to unload it onto you, & leave you to consent or refuse, as shall seem best. I wish to hold myself purely neutral & say nothing to influence you, one way or the other. The Club would be proud to have your name; that goes without saying; the membership is consonant with yourself, for it is refined, cultured, more than ordinarily talented, & of exceptionally high character. These facts are in its favor; but I think I ought not to conceal a fact of another sort — one which I must ask you to treat as confidential: the intent of the Club is, by superior weight, character & influence, to impair & eventually destroy the influence of ⟨[illegible]⟩ [1] — not from any base feeling, but from a belief that this is a thing required in the interest of the public good. The name of the new organization is peculiar — The Modest Club — & the first & main qualification for membership is modesty. At present, I am the only member; & as the modesty required must be of a quite aggravated type, the enterprize did seem for a time doomed to stop dead still with myself, for lack of further material; but upon reflection I have come to the conclusion that you are eligible. — Therefore I have held a meeting & voted to offer you the distinction of membership. I do not know that we can find any others, though I have had some thought of Hay, Warner, Twichell, Aldrich, Osgood, Fields, Higginson, & a few more — together with Mrs. Howells, Mrs. Clemens, & certain others of the sex.

But I will append the "Laws," & you just drop me a line & say whether you & Mrs. Howells would care to belong — & John Hay. I have long felt that there ought to be an organized gang *of our kind.*   Yrs Ever

Mark.

LAWS.

The organization shall sue & be sued, persecute & be persecuted, & eat, drink, & be merry, under the name & style, of THE MODEST CLUB of the United States of America.
OVER.

The object of the Club shall be, to eat & talk.[2]
over again.

Qualification for membership shall be, aggravated modesty, unobtrusiveness, native humility; learning, talent, intelligence; and unassailable character.

Both sexes admitted.

Two adverse votes shall destroy the applicant.

Any member may call a meeting, when & where he or she may choose.

Two members shall constitute a quorum; & a meeting thus inaugurated shall be competent to eat & talk.

There shall be no fees or dues. There shall be no regular place of meeting.

There Shall be no ⟨permanent⟩ officers, except a President; & any member who has anything to eat & talk about, may constitute himself President for the time being, & call in any member or members he pleases, to help him devour & expatiate.

At all Club gatherings the membership shall wear the official symbol of the order, a single violet.

Any brother or sister of the order finding a brother or sister in imminent deadly peril, shall forsake his own concerns, no matter at what cost, & call the police.

Any member knowing anything scandalous about himself, shall immediately inform the Club, so that they may call a meeting & have the first chance to talk about it.

Any member who shall

1. Almost certainly Bret Harte. The cancellation here is of a type used by Howells rather than by Clemens.
2. Insert written on verso of p. 1.

235. HOWELLS TO CLEMENS

[Boston] May 23, 1880.

My dear Clemens:

The only reason I have for not joining the Modest Club is that I am too modest: that is, I am afraid that I am not modest enough. If I could ever get over this difficulty, I should like to join, for I approve highly of the Club and its objects: it is calculated to do a great deal of good, and it ought to be given an annual dinner at the public expense. If *you* think I am not too modest, you may put my name down, and I will try to think the same of you. Mrs. Howells applauded the notion of the Club from the very first. She said she knew *one* thing: that *she* was modest enough, *any* way. Her manner of saying it implied that the other persons you had named were not, and created a painful impression in my mind. — I have sent your letter and the rules to Hay.[1] But I doubt his modesty; he will think he has a *right* to belong as much as you or I; whereas other people ought only to be admitted on sufferance. — We had a magnificent time in Washington, and were six days at the White House. I wish you could have come on, as you intended, but as your friend advised, I suppose it would have been useless as far as copyright is concerned. I spoke about international copyright treaty to the President, one day, and he said that the administration would be willing to act if the authors and publishers would agree among themselves on some basis. Now, could they not agree on this basis: Englishmen to have copyright if they have an American publisher, and Americans, vice versa. Our publishers would never agree to anything else, and this would secure us our rights. If some such house as Harpers would send this proposition to all the authors and decent publishers for signature, I believe that it would be universally signed, and that if presented as a memorial to the State Department, it would before this administration goes out, become a treaty.[2] I am going to write to the Harpers about it.

    With regards to all from all   Yours ever,

W. D. Howells.

1. John Hay replied to Howells on 24 May from Washington (where he was serving as Assistant Secretary of State) that Clemens's idea was as judicious as it was daring, and that "a club which would hold him and you and me, and then reach out for H. [igginson?] etc., — and still keep modest, — staggers and fatigues the faculty of wonder" (Thayer, *Life of John Hay*, I, 439). He proposed that Howells and Clemens should come down to hold the first meeting at his house.

2. In 1878, Harper & Bros. had submitted to Secretary of State Evarts a draft of a proposed treaty concerning copyright between Great Britain and the United States.

236. CLEMENS TO HOWELLS

[Hartford] June 9/80

Well, old practical joker, the corpse of Mr. B.[1] has been here, & I have bedded it & fed it, & put down my work during 24 hours & tried my level best to make it do something, or say something, or appreciate something — or even stink — but no, it was *worse* than Lazarus. A kind-hearted, well-meaning corpse was this Boston young man, but lawsy bless me, horribly dull company. Now old man, unless you have great confidence in Mr.

B.s judgment, you ought to make him submit his article to you before he prints it.[2] For only think how true I was to you: Every hour that he was here I was saying, gloatingly, "O G — d you, when you are in bed & your light out, I will fix you" (meaning to kill him) — but then the thought would follow — "No, Howells sent him — he shall be spared, he shall be respected — he shall travel hellwards by his own route." [3]

Breakfast is frozen by this time, & Mrs. Clemens correspondingly hot. Goodbye   Yrs Ever

Mark.

1. Sylvester Baxter, a young newspaper man from Boston who had come to Hartford with a note of introduction from Howells in order to interview Clemens and Warner. Howells assured Warner that Baxter would respect his "mental infirmities and moral obliquities" (Boston, 2 June 1880, Watkinson, AGM TS).

2. Howells responded to Clemens's request by writing to Baxter: "Can you let me see what you have written about Warner and Clemens before it goes into print? They are particularly sensitive, and as you went from me to them, I am anxious to know what report you give" (Boston, 10 June 1880, Barrett, AGM TS).

3. Baxter and Clemens later became good friends and corresponded cordially about their shared political enthusiasms (SLC to Baxter, Hartford, 20 November 1889, Berg; Baxter to SLC, Boston, 22, 30 November, 9 December 1889, MTP).

237. CLEMENS TO HOWELLS

[Hartford] June 9/80.

My Dear Howells:

Some time ago, I told Orion to sit down & write his autobiography — & do it in a plain, simple, truthful way, suppressing none of the disagreeables — & said that in order to be able to really accomplish this, he must use genuine names & genuine dates & localities — & that when the thing was finished he could then lay his history in some other State, change the real dates & names to fictitious ones, use a feigned name for himself, & nobody would ever know who wrote it.

He started in — & I think the result is killingly entertaining; in parts absolutely delicious. I'm going to mail you 100 pages or so of the MS.[1] Read it; keep his secret; & tell me, if, after surplusage has been weeded out, & I ring into the MS here & there a characteristic letter of his, you'll buy the stuff for the Atlantic at the ordinary rates for anonymous matter from unknown writers.   Ys Ever

Mark.

1. Orion's autobiography occupied him at intervals for many years. Albert B. Paine had access to portions of the MS when he was writing his biography of Mark Twain. "A quantity of Orion's manuscript has been lost and destroyed," he said, "but enough fragments of it remain to show its fidelity to the original plan. It is just one long record of fleeting hope, futile effort, and humiliation. It is the story of a life of disappointment; of a man who has been defeated and beaten down and crushed by the world until he has nothing but confession left to surrender." In a footnote Paine adds that "the earliest of these chapters were preserved, and, as the reader may remember, furnished much of the childhood details for this biography" (MTB, pp. 676–677). The references to Orion's MS and quotations from it in Paine's biography are all in the first hundred pages. Paine may have paraphrased some material from the MS which he did not specifically acknowledge, but the inference is inescapable that he used nothing except childhood recollections. Only seven pages of the MS are now in MTP: two alternative openings of a first chapter written apparently in 1883; one page numbered 341; and one numbered 1027½. These fragments contain nothing of special interest.

238. CLEMENS TO HOWELLS

[Hartford, 10? June 1880]

I think that when this batch is culled & reduced 50 per cent, it will be worth printing, Howells — & that is a pretty fair result for a lunatic like the author of it, poor fellow. Lord what a hard time of it he has had.   Yrs

Mark.

Read it at your leisure — then mail it to me at Elmira, N.Y., (whither we journey for the summer next week, June 15.)

MS. This covering note for the portion of Orion's autobiography promised in Clemens's letter of 9 June may have been sent the same day, but more probably the next. The MS had arrived in Boston when Howells replied on 12 June.

239. HOWELLS TO CLEMENS

[Boston] June 12, 1880.

You poor old fellow:

I didn't expect that you would ask that man to *live* with you. What I was afraid of was that you would turn him out of doors, on sight, and so I tried to put in a good word for him. After this, when I want you to board people, I'll ask you. — I'm sorry for your suffering. I suppose I have mostly lost my smell for bores; but yours is preternaturally keen. I shall begin to be afraid that *I* bore you. (How does that make you feel?)

B. has really written a most blameless and pretty account of you,[1] with appreciation which he got out of my review.[2]

Your brother's life has come, and I'm eager to get at it.

That sketch of yours (about the two cousins)[3] is *wunderbar.* — Winny's school master now recommends A Tramp Abroad to all his young ladies. Yours ever

W. D. Howells.

How will Garfield do?[4] You Grant men ought to have muzzled Conkling.[5]

1. Sylvester Baxter's interview, which was printed in the Boston Sunday *Herald* of 20 June 1880 (p. 10), chiefly concerns Clemens's house and his views on copyright.

2. Of *A Tramp Abroad,* in the May *Atlantic.*

3. "Edward Mills and George Benton: A Tale," a sardonic fable using Mark Twain's cherished theme of the good boy and the bad boy to attack the sentimental cult of reformed drunkards and convicts. It was published in the *Atlantic* for August 1880 (DE, XXIV, 209–217).

4. James A. Garfield, the Republican nominee, had been William Cooper Howells's protégé and was a lifelong friend of the Howells family.

5. Roscoe Conkling, boss of the Republican machine, had been bitterly

opposed to the reformist tendencies of the Hayes administration, and had led the Stalwart faction urging the nomination of Grant for a third term. Howells apparently felt that Conkling's speech of 5 June nominating Grant had damaged Grant's prospects, brought on the deadlock in the convention, and thus led to the choice of Garfield, a dark horse, on the thirty-fifth ballot.

240. HOWELLS TO CLEMENS

[Boston] June 14, 1880.

My dear Clemens:

I have read the autobiography with close and painful interest. It wrung my heart, and I felt haggard after I had finished it. There is no doubt about its interest to *me*; but I got to questioning whether this interest was not mostly from my knowledge of you and your brother — whether the reader would not need some sort of "inside track" for its appreciation. The best touches in it are those which make us acquainted with *you*; and they will be valuable material hereafter. But the writer's soul is laid *too* bare: it is shocking. I can't risk the paper in the Atlantic; and if you print it anywhere, I hope you wont let your love of the naked truth prevent you from striking out some of the most intimate pages. Don't let any one else even see those passages about the autopsy.[1] The light on your father's character is most pathetic.   Yours ever

W. D. Howells.

1. On the basis of this reference, together with a notebook entry by Clemens in 1903, Dixon Wecter argues convincingly in *Sam Clemens of Hannibal* (Boston, 1952, pp. 116–117) that the twelve-year-old Sam Clemens had the traumatic experience of witnessing, perhaps through a keyhole, a post-mortem performed on his father by the family doctor, "later unburdening his secret, no doubt, to his elder brother." Howells's neurotic breakdown at nineteen, manifested in a fear of hydrophobia and of insanity and death, left in him an unusually strong tendency to shrink from violence or even the description of it. The course of the illness of his daughter, Winnie, which led to her death in 1889, and the idiocy of his youngest brother,

315

Henry, must have served to keep his fears alive, though Howells had long been in control of them.

241. CLEMENS TO HOWELLS

[Hartford] June 15/80.

My Dear Howells:

The family are assembling at the front door for immediate flight to Elmira. Your letter just received. Well, I'm mighty glad the grave Baxter didn't "give me away." I breathe freer, now.

Patrick will express to you, to-day or tomorrow four little roots, & says all you've got to do is to plant them close up to the wall & trust in God; they will take care of themselves, & give you no trouble; they'll soon spread over & cover the wall.

Garfield suits me thoroughly & exactly. I prefer him to Grant ('s friends.) The presidency can't add anything to Grant — he will shine on, without it. It is ephemeral, he is eternal.

I think Winnie's teacher has excellent judgement [1] — but I shouldn't have thought it before your review converted me from my ill opinion of the book.

I'm called — Good bye & love to you & yours.

Yrs Ever

Mark.

1. Winnie's teacher, it will be recalled, had urged his pupils to read *A Tramp Abroad,* as Howells reported in his letter of 12 June.

242. HOWELLS TO CLEMENS

Belmont, June 20, 1880.

Dear Clemens:

I guess those plants are going to be one of our successes: they haven't come to hand yet, but I'm prophetically grateful.

I met an old friend of yours the other day — Capt. Morland of the Cunard service.[1] Very entertaining, and thinks you're mad at him. Going to quit the water and take to milk — cow farm in Colorado.

This sketch [2] of yours is uncommon good.

Yours ever

W. D. H.

Sent my book [3] to you at Hartford.

1. Master of the Cunard liner *Batavia* when the Clemens family crossed to England in her in 1873. During the voyage Livy wrote to her mother that the Captain was "just about perfection, he has done every thing that he possibly could to make us comfortable . . . he and Clara take long walks on the deck together — I do not know hardly what we should do if it was not for his chart room, the baby [Susy] goes there early in the forenoon & stays until her bed time. It crowds Capt. Morland very much but he insists that it does not . . ." (May 1873, Jervis Langdon, TS in MTP).

2. "Mrs. McWilliams and the Lightning," which was published in the *Atlantic* for September 1880 (DE, XV, 330–340).

3. Probably *The Undiscovered Country,* issued in book form on 24 June.

243. HOWELLS TO CLEMENS

[Boston] July 18, 1880.

My dear Clemens:

It is all very well to send things to the Atlantic, but why begrudge my private ear a word? We are none of us quite well without your letters, and Mrs. Howells, who has to do her own violence when you don't write, is almost worn out. She says McWilliams is only a palliative, not a cure.

— Are you going to visit Mr. Norton at Ashfield,[1] in August? Better do so. Warner is going, and so are Winny and I; and Curtis will be there. We shall have a famous time, and you will enjoy yourself, and make every body else happy.

I hope Mrs. Clemens is well — I *know* you are.

Mrs. Howells joins me in love to you all.

Yours ever

W. D. Howells.

1. Charles Eliot Norton's summer home was at Ashfield, in the Berkshire Hills of northwestern Massachusetts, where George W. Curtis also maintained a summer place. Concerning the occasion to which Howells refers, see letter 275.

244. CLEMENS TO HOWELLS

Elmira, July 26/80.

My Dear Howells:

I have been up all night helping to receive Miss Clemens,[1] who arrived perfectly sound but with no more baggage than I had when I was on the river. I will go to bed, now — merely adding that ⟨it is a girl again &⟩ mother & child are doing quite well & the latter weighs about 7 pounds. That is a pretty big one — for us.

I sincerely wish I could go, with you & Warner & Aldrich,[2] but the journey is too prodigious; moreover, as Mrs. Clemens gets only harassed cat-naps instead of honest sleep when I am away, I shan't venture to leave her for a month or two yet.

Ys Ever

Mark.

1. The baby was named Jane Lampton, but was always called Jean.
2. To the Ashfield Academy Dinner.

245. CLEMENS TO HOWELLS

Elmira, Aug. 1/80.

Say — Howells, dear, would it be too much trouble for you to drop in at Estes & Lauriat's, 301 Washington street, next time you are in town & look at a book there for me? — an Audubon; I think the price is $150. It can't be in very good condition, I suppose, at that figure; but if it is, & is complete, & of Audubon's own issue (however, I believe no one has ever issued an edition *but* Audubon,) won't you please ask them to ship it to *Hartford,* & send bill to *Elmira?* [1] If the figure wasn't $150 in their catalogue, I know it wasn't any *more.* And if it is off your route, will you have the thing done by somebody who *does* travel Washington street? It'll be a great favor to me.

The new baby is thoroughly satisfactory, as far as it goes; but we did hope it was going to be twins. We were alarmed about Mrs. Clemens during 2 or 3 days, but she seems to be coming along all right, now.   Yrs Ever

Mark.

1. Howells must have secured the copy of Audubon's *Birds of America;* for in the spring of 1884 Clemens and Cable "took down a volume of Audubon to identify a bird they had noticed through the window" of the Hartford house (Arlin Turner, *George W. Cable,* Durham, 1956, p. 151) and many years later Clemens referred familiarly to the book as being worth a thousand dollars "in the market" ("James Hammond Trumbull, The Tribute of a Neighbor," *Century,* LV, 154, November 1897).

246. CLEMENS TO HOWELLS

Elmira, Aug. 9 [1880].

My Dear Howells:

The box came yesterday, & I enclose check — at least I *mean* to, though one of the hardest things in this life to remember is to enclose a thing — even a dog — in the letter one is writing. It most always goes in another envelop, half an hour later, tottering under a load of profanity which runs it aground at the postoffice for insufficient postage. The hair restorer (is that what it is?) is very welcome, indeed, & Mrs. Clemens is greatly obliged. It is in good time, for Mrs. Clemens is abed yet & can't go to restoring till she is up; the baby was born well fixed on top; & the thing *I* need is something that will make the hair come out. Mrs. Clemens told me some days ago to tell Mrs. Howells she is keeping her hair unparted, all through this episode, for her wise advice's sake.

I have been thinking things over, & have changed my mind

to this complexion: I would rather the N.Y. Times & all the other journals *would* copy my stuff — it keeps a body more alive & known to the broad & general public, for the Atlantic ⟨only⟩ ⟨only⟩ goes to only (dam that "Boston Girl")[1] the select high few. Yes, I would rather write for the modester wage of one whose articles increase not the subscription list, & then be copied in the general press; for I should find my vast reward in the augmented sales of my books. However, maybe they *do* copy — hope they do — for I have this moment opened a letter from Michigan which speaks of reading "Benton & Mills"[2] in the Yonkers Gazette; but all the other letters which have come to me shouting the praises of that little moral tale (lord, how inscrutably constructed we are! — I never really expected you to print that article; so when I came to, after you accepted it, I said to myself, "All right, if he wants all the pious people after his scalp, let him go ahead — it will be a spectacle not without interest") have spoken of seeing it in the Atlantic. By-the-way, these praiseful letters have usually come from strong church-members — think of that! — & they take *me* to be one — think also of that! Blame it, they are the very people I expected to make skip around & cuss. I will enclose this last one to let you see — you can read it, then throw it away.

We all vote that the baby is the prettiest & perfectest little creature we have turned out yet. Susie & Bay could not worship it more if it were a cat — & the same formula will fit my case. Livy is doing finely.

Whilst not working — for one can't work during a lying-in season — I have written 60 pages of the most ridiculous stuff[3] — burlesque foreign travel, steeped in complacency & placid ignorance — & I mean to go along & see how it comes out.

Yrs Ever

Mark.

Bliss's check has come for first 1/4 of Tramp Abroad — nearly $19,000 — very good.

1. Mark Twain had made a letter written to him by "A Boston Girl" (commenting on his placing of adverbs in sentences and his "tautology")

the occasion of one of his longest and best contributions to the Contributors' Club, in the June *Atlantic*. Admitting freely that "I am dead to adverbs; they cannot excite me," he went on to say that "though this young lady's grammar be as the drifted snow for purity, she will never, never, never learn to punctuate while she lives; this is her demon, the adverb is mine." He added, "Tautology cannot scare me." In anticipation of his note at the beginning of *Huckleberry Finn*, he argued that dialect writing "is exceedingly difficult; it has rarely been done well," and that Harte could "reproduce" California scenery but wrote impossible dialect. This is recognizably the writer of whom Howells once said to Garland, "Mark uses words as if they had never been used by other writers" (quoted in Alma B. Martin, *A Vocabulary Study of "The Gilded Age,"* Webster Groves, Mo., 1930, p. 3).

2. The sketch by Mark Twain published in the August number of the *Atlantic*. It prefigures the futile attempt of the pious townspeople of St. Petersburg to reform Pap Finn, and the rivalry of the "twins" in *Pudd'nhead Wilson*.

3. Not now identifiable.

247. ELINOR M. HOWELLS TO OLIVIA L. CLEMENS

Belmont Aug. 13th [1880]

My dear Mrs Clemens:

The check (3.50) has arrived to pay for the hairtonic, which I at last induced Fleming to send you. As she has probably sent both brown & white tonic, with exactly the same label on each bottle I write to explain a little: the brown is to be rubbed into the parting and is to make the hair *grow* — (the head being washed first with juniper-tar soap) and the white tonic keeps the head delightfully clean. The smell of the brown is rather disagreeable to me, so I only use the white. Having despatched business let me have the pleasure of congratulating you on your new daughter. What is her name, who is she most like, and why didn't you *tell* me! I am always in the wrong as to your intentions it seems. I would like to say that when you get back to Hartford I would run on to see all your children. You know I missed them in Boston! [1] — but my poor spine still troubles me so that I dread car riding. Please tell me about

— or rather if, you were at Dr Taylor's establishment in New York, and whether it did you good. Or do you know any doctor who makes the spine a specialty? Excuse this mixed up letter which I write not feeling well,

Most Affectionately yours
Elinor M. Howells.

1. Presumably when Mark Twain and Livy were in Boston in April (see letter 227). There is, however, no other indication that the Clemens children were taken along on that trip.

248. ELINOR M. HOWELLS TO OLIVIA L. CLEMENS

[Belmont] Aug. 16 [1880]

My dear Mrs. Clemens:

Your husband wrote that you were not yet in a condition to use the tonic — so I have yet time to add one exceedingly important item: — that the brown tonic must be well shaken and then a little poured into a saucer and applied with a sponge. The white tonic has a cork with a fixture in it which can be unscrewed so you can sprinkle the liquid on through it — after which it must be screwed down again very tightly. Mr Howells & Winnie started for Ashfield this morning. This is royal weather for you to get well in. Mrs. Fairchild carried some wine whey to an Irish woman the other day when her baby was three days old — or perhaps five — and found her up doing her washing.

Affectionately
Elinor M. Howells

249. CLEMENS TO ELINOR M. HOWELLS

Elmira, N.Y. Quarry Farm, Aug 17/80.

Dear Mrs. Howells —

O hang my grandmother, did I make that check $3.50! [1] I meant to make it right — (i.e. $4.50) — & the stub in my check-book says I *did*. Figures won't lie, of course, but stubs may; therefore won't you please look into this matter & (in case I have made the mistake) let me know? There were 6 bottles — all white.

REPLIES. 1. Jane Lampton Clemens, (after my mother.) She (the child,) is addressed as Jean, & also as Jessie, in non-official intercourse — her official name doesn't seem to be over-popular with the hill tribe.

2. ⟨She is "most like" — well, say an orange that is a little mildewed in spots.⟩ No — I discover you don't mean complexion, but *who* is she most like? That is easily answered: Mrs. Crane says, Livy; Livy says, my mother; Bay Clemens says, me; Susie Clemens says, Bay; *I* think she looks most like a successful attempt to resemble nobody. Take your choice.

Expunged, by order.

3. ⟨Didn't "tell you," because we weren't certain; thought it was flesh; supposed it would wear off. But we changed, as time rolled on; toward the last we estimated it at twins, at the very outside.⟩

4. No — O, no, I don't think she had any really definite "intentions" at that time. ("Intentions" is mighty good!)

O dear, I never imagined you were drifting into invalidity as a settled thing. I think we both always looked upon you as a sort of Leyden jar, or Rumkoff coil, or Voltaic battery, or whatever that thing is which holds lightning & mighty forces captive in a vessel which is apparently much too frail for its office, & yet after all isn't. But the spine! — come, this is a surprise, & anything but a pleasant one.

There are two Taylors in the business — Dr. *George H.* Taylor is the only right one — bear that in mind. — Livy had a high opinion of him & his methods & his establishment; he did her great good. But this was 12 or 15 years ago; so her testimony is rather stale; she has had the impression, latterly, that his place has become a resort for fashionables — a mere swell boarding-house — & that its efficiency had rather fallen off. Therefore we have applied for later information to Livy's physician, Mrs. Zippie Brooks[2] — & she is an able one & her testimony can be trusted. She was down there [3] lately, & says it is a mistake; & that Dr. Taylor is as full of enthusiasm as ever, & as attentive to his patients; & that he gives his *personal* attention to the patients, & has fine success with spinal diseases — curvatures & all sorts. Therefore go to him. He is located out toward the Park — 50th street, or thereabouts.

It is too bad that you cannot travel by rail, for now you will go by boat — otherwise we might hope you would break your journey with us in Hartford. Maybe you can do that on your return. Let us hope so.

We have at last got Livy, greatly against her will, to let the wet nurse do *all* the nursing. Both child & mother are already the gainers by it. Both are prospering tolerably fairly. Livy has been lifted into a rocking chair & hauled out on to the porch, to-day, for the first time, & had the matchless air & the lovely prospect from our high perch. She has had good luck all these 3 weeks of confinement — only one hot day in the lot — open fire in the room a good part of the time.

Love to Winny, & John, & Howells. And speaking of Howells, he ought to use the stylographic pen,[4] the best fountain-pen yet invented — he *ought* to, but of course he *won't* — a blamed old sodden-headed conservative — but you see, yourself, what nice clean uniform MS it makes. John Hay sent me his speech [5] — a rattling good one.

Most Truly Yours
Mark.

Livy not able to write, yet — so begs you to let me represent her this time — & she sends her love to you & the house.

— & she also sends her very best thanks for the trouble you have so kindly taken about the hair tonic.

1. Clemens is answering Mrs. Howells's letter to Livy of 13 August.
2. Of Elmira.
3. New York.
4. The only letter for which Howells seems to have used a stylographic pen (an early effort at a practicable fountain pen) is that of 13 December 1880. The improvement in the legibility of his all but indecipher-

able handwriting is enormous, but the pen was apparently unsatisfactory for mechanical reasons. Clemens himself soon abandoned it.

5. On 11 August 1880 Hay had written Clemens, "I sent you my speech the other day" (Washington, MTP). It was presumably in support of Garfield, in whose behalf Hay was very active during the Presidential campaign.

250. CLEMENS TO HOWELLS

Quarry Farm [Elmira], Sep. 3 [1880].

My Dear Howells:

Like enough, you are having too good a time. Well, then, I will interfere. I have got to lose my day's work, on account of good old Frank Soulés letter,[1] because it has taken me clear away from my book;[2] but I mean to get even by taking the tuck out of one of your junketing days[3] — I am going to shove this matter over onto you. —

This looks highhanded, but there are fair & honorable reasons for it. Frank Soulé *was* one of the sweetest and whitest & loveliest spirits that ever wandered into this world by mistake; I seem somehow to have got the impression that he has of late years become sour & querulous; cannot tell — it has been 13 years since I worked at his side in the Morning Call office; in San Francisco;[4] but no matter, he has believed for 36 years, that he would next year, & then next year, & still next year, be recognized as a poet — & all these slow years have come & gone, & each in its turn has lied to him. Soured? — why anybody would be, that had been served so. Therefore, don't you mind whether he is sour or sweet; you just go to the Alta[5] office & call on him — it is the right courtesy from a young successful man to an old unsuccessful one — an old unsuccessful one who has seen the day when a young fellow right up stairs over his head (Harte), & another one at his elbow (me), looked upon a compliment from Frank Soulé as praise from Sir Hubert. And he was not stingy of his applause; whoever earned it, got it. Frank Soulé had that sort of a face which is so rare — I mean a face that is *always*

325

welcome, that makes you happy all through, just to see it. And Lordy, to think that this fine & sensitive & beautiful & proud spirit had to grind, & grind, like a pitiful slave, on that degraded "Morning Call," whose mission from hell & politics was to lick the boots of the Irish & throw bold brave mud at the Chinamen. And he is a slave yet!

Now I am not done yet. You see he asks very little: only that his book shall be published, that is all; royalties & copyrights are not in the question. You ask him to put a selection of his poems into your hands, to be read at your hotel or on the road; & tell him you will tell Osgood or some publisher just what you think of them, leaving the publisher to decide whether to take the book or decline it. O, dear, it was always a painful thing to me to see the Emperor (Norton I., of San Francisco) [6] begging; for although nobody else believed he was an Emperor, *he* believed it. And Frank Soulé believes himself a poet (& many others believe it, too) & it is sad enough to see him on the street begging for the charity of mere notice.

What an odd thing it is, that neither Frank Soulé, nor Charley Warren Stoddard, nor I, nor Bret Harte the Immortal Bilk, nor any other professionally literary person of S.F., has ever "written up" the Emperor Norton. Nobody has ever written him up who was able to see any but his ⟨ludicrous or his⟩ grotesque side; but I think that with all his dirt & unsavoriness there was a pathetic side to him. Anybody who said so in print would be laughed at in S.F., doubtless, but no matter, I have seen the Emperor when his dignity was wounded; and when he was both hurt & indignant at the dishonoring of an imperial draft; & when he was full of trouble & bodings on account of the presence of the Russian fleet, he connecting it with his refusal to ally himself with the Romanoffs by marriage, & believing these ships were come to take advantage of his entanglements with Peru & Bolivia; I have seen him in *all* his various moods & tenses, & there was always more room for pity than laughter. He believed he was a natural son of one of the English Georges — but I wander from my subject.

I shall write Soulé that I am not a judge of poetry, but

that if you find merit in his book I shall then know it is ⟨mere-tricious⟩ meritorious, & will cheerfully hunt down a publisher for him, if it be possible, either in conjunction with you or alone. As for the correspondence, I am up a stump, there — I don't seem to know any editors at all, personally, except one or two upon whose lives I have designs. Besides, I never have heard of a newspaper that *wanted* a San Francisco correspondence; bless us, it wouldn't have the least interest for anybody. Well, I'll tell him that.

And I shall tell him that if circumstances give you a chance, you will look in on him.

There's some more things to go in this letter — I'll add them in a P.S. this evening.   Yrs Ever

                                      Mark.

Now you attend to this thing, do you hear? You will be old yourself some day. Yes, & neglected, too, if *I*'m any judge of literature.

Frank Soulé has written some mighty good poetry — I have heard Harte & honester men say so.

Never mind the other things, I'll add them another time — but mind, you just let up on some of your debauching, & run in & see old Soulé. O, you don't get away from *me*, simply by in-serting a few thousand miles between us. I offer my affections to Mrs. Howells, & my respects to the President.

1. To Clemens (San Francisco, 22 August 1880, MTP). Soulé en-closed "my last Fourth of July Poem" (clipped from a newspaper) and asked whether Clemens could find a publisher for his poems — "Say, a volume of 200 pages. I'll give him the manuscript if he will take the chances." Soulé added: "I must publish soon or never, for time and I are to have a settlement soon and the accounts must be squared."

2. *The Prince and the Pauper*.

3. President Hayes had invited Howells to join his party on a transcontinental tour and at one time Howells had apparently thought of doing so. But he refused invitations twice in August because, as he wrote to Hayes, "though fat I am not strong" (Duxbury, 7 August; Belmont, 28 August, Hayes Memorial Library, AGM TS). Clemens's project to have Howells call on Soulé thus came to nothing (Frank Soulé to SLC, San Fran-

cisco, 22 August 1880, MTP). Unaware that Howells had not gone, Clemens wrote to Aldrich on 15 September: "I hope Howells is enjoying his journey to the Pacific. He wrote me that you and Osgood were going, also, but I doubted it, believing he was in liquor when he wrote it. [This letter from Howells to Clemens has been lost.] In my opinion, this universal applause over his book is going to land that man in a Retreat inside of two months" (Elmira, MTL, p. 386).

4. Mark Twain had a job as a reporter on the San Francisco *Call* for about four months, June through October 1864.

5. The *Alta California* was a San Francisco newspaper for which Mark Twain had written most of the dispatches collected in *The Innocents Abroad*.

6. Joshua A. Norton, a harmless lunatic, widely known in San Francisco in the 1860's, who imagined himself to be Emperor of the United States of America and Protector of Mexico. His belief that he was the natural son of one of the English Georges enrolls him in the list of American claimants who fascinated Mark Twain.

251. HOWELLS TO CLEMENS

[Boston] Oct. 1, 1880.

My dear Clemens:

I was immensely glad to see your hand again, and to get the piece you sent for the Club.[1] Ever since your letter to Mrs. Howells came, I have been wanting to tell you how wonderfully good that comparison of her to a Leyden-jar was. She never *does* quite go to pieces, but it always looks like a thing that might happen. I hope that you are all going back to Hartford in glorious health and spirits. It seems as if we might now hope sometime to see you again, and at Elmira you were fearfully far away. I am sorry you could not have come to Ashfield in August, upon Norton's invitation. We had a good time, and much talk about you. Curtis was there, and we also talked politics, in which he was more hopeful then than I suppose I should find him now. What a *great* speech that was of Grant's at Warren![2] I should think all speakers hereafter would feel that nothing had been left for them to say. I had a little note from Hay, the other day. He says that on the 4th of March he goes out of office forever;

but he shall always take a hand in every campaign. He thinks the outlook for us is rather blue. — I congratulate you on the great sale of A Tramp Abroad. I am running a slow race after you with The Undis. Coun. which has sold about 11,000. I have translated another play for Barrett. He has paid up in full the $2500 promised me for Yorick.

All join me in love to you all.　　　Yours ever

W. D. Howells.

1. Apparently a paragraph on the admirable behavior of the German publisher, Bernhard Tauchnitz, in making payments to American authors whose books he reprinted even though he was under no legal obligation to do so. Howells published this paragraph in the *Atlantic* for January 1881.

2. Grant had spoken at Warren, Ohio, on 28 September. He had emphasized the denial of free speech to Republicans in the fourteen states of the Solid South, the duplicity of the Democrats in advancing contradictory proposals in different sections of the country, and the concern of the Republican party to provide equality of opportunity for everyone (George P. Edgar, comp., *Gems of the Campaign of 1880 by Generals Grant and Garfield*, Jersey City, 1881, pp. 13–17).

252. CLEMENS TO HOWELLS

[Hartford] 13th [October 1880]

My Dear Howells — I expect to reach the Brunswick, in Boston, tomorrow about 6 p.m. (on this Grant reception matter in Hartford.)[1] I go a day ahead of the rest, so as to see you & House.[2] You'll be likely to be in town Thursday — I want to see you.　　　Yrs Ever

Mark.

MS. This note is written on the back of a card containing a printed statement that Mark Twain has "quitted the platform permanently."

1. The reception committee which went to Boston in order to accompany Grant back to Hartford consisted of nine men, including Clemens and Mayor Morgan G. Buckley. The *Transcript* placed Clemens's name at the head of the list (16 October 1880, p. 3).

2. Edward H. House, correspondent for the New York *Tribune,* who was traveling with Grant's party (Boston *Transcript,* 14 October 1880, p. 1). Clemens had known him in New York in 1867, when House was on the staff of the *Tribune* and Clemens was writing for California newspapers, and they both (as Clemens wrote House later) were members of "the Pfaff gang, in that old day when bohemianism was respectable — ah, more than respectable, heroic" (Hartford, 14 January 1884, Barrett). In the interim House had spent almost ten years in Japan and had only recently returned, accompanied by a Japanese girl named Koto whom he presented as his adopted daughter but whom the reporter for the *Transcript* took to be his wife. The acquaintance between House and Clemens had been renewed before 13 September 1880, when House wrote to Clemens from Boston describing a visit in Buffalo with their mutual friend David Gray (MTP).

253. CLEMENS TO HOWELLS (TELEGRAM)

Boston Oct. 15 1880

W D Howells

Belmont Ms

Via Arlington Ms

I will bet you thirty (30) dollars to ten (10) cents that you wont get this telegram before supper which comes of living out in the woods and the money is up in House's hands but we start at eleven fifteen 11.15 any way —[1]

S L Clements

1. Having come to Boston the day before, Clemens now proposes to bring his friend Edward H. House out to see Howells in Belmont. Concerning this visit, Howells told his father: "Warner was out here, one day, and Clemens, the next — both hot Republicans, and full of rejoicing" (Belmont, 17 October 1880, Houghton).

254. HOWELLS TO CLEMENS

[Belmont] Oct. 18, 1880.

Dear Clemens:

Osgood says Gebbie is a hard-headed, close-fisted, reliable, enterprising Scotchman, who will do what he says, and will make the closest bargain he can with you;[1] but I told him you would be a match for him *there*. I hope this will not seem fulsome.

— You were charming, the other day — never better — and endeared yourself to this family anew. I saw House at the Houghton lunch [2] to-day. We had a pleasant time, and I wish you had been there.

How did your speech [3] suit? I heard several express their satisfaction in it, as a "change," and something that would set people thinking — and blushing, I hope.   Yours ever

W. D. Howells.

1. When Clemens and House called on Howells on 15 October, Clemens had evidently asked him to consult James R. Osgood for information about the Philadelphia publisher George Gebbie. Gebbie had proposed that Clemens should compile an anthology of humor to be published by subscription, and had named Osgood as a reference (Gebbie to SLC, Philadelphia, 14, 17 July 1880, MTP).

2. Presumably given for contributors to the *Atlantic*.

3. Clemens made the official speech welcoming Grant to Hartford on 16 October, after having accompanied him on the special train from Boston. Clemens pointed out that Britain had made Wellington a duke and had given him $4,000,000 as a reward for his victory at Waterloo, whereas the United States had done nothing of the sort to recognize the many victories of Grant, each of them equal to Waterloo in importance. He added: ". . . thank God! this vast and rich and mighty republic is imbued to the core with a delicacy which will forever preserve her from so degrading you. . . . Your country stands ready from this day forth to testify her measureless love and pride and gratitude toward you in every conceivable — *inexpensive* way. Welcome to Hartford, great soldier, honored statesman, unselfish citizen" (MTB, pp. 692–693).

255. CLEMENS TO HOWELLS

[Hartford] Oct. 19/80.

My Dear Howells: Read the letter to Mrs. Handy,[1] & then mail it. The idea of that printed biography [2] is a noble good one: saves me time, rage, excuses, declinations, disgust, humiliation; & from frenzies of blasphemy which exhaust me physically as well

331

as morally; & besides, it at the same time furnishes to the in-quiring idiot connected with the literary society exactly what he has ASKED for, & softly & neatly chouses him out of the thing he was really after, viz., a humorous autograph letter which would make him the most important ass connected with the Society for one whole evening. You may use that idea — no charge.

I send you a paper with the speech. Gen. Grant came near laughing his entire head off. Therefore, as I only needed one hearty & unequivocal laugh out of him, I skipped, & left out the clause explaining why there were two welcomers. There was a couple of minutes' laughter over my break-down; (it was on a sentence which would *not* stay in my memory) or rather, over my explaining to Gen. Grant in a sort of confidential way how it happened — at which his "grim smile" became very audible, & of course that set the whole multitude off again. It was one more laugh than was needed, maybe, but no matter. The words "in every conceivable . . . . inexpensive way" invoked the loudest shout, & the longest, & the most full-hearted that was heard in Hartford that day. It started in laughter but ended in a thunder of endorsement.

MS. The letter, written on both sides of two cards, is unsigned and apparently incomplete.

1. Not extant, but its contents are explained by Clemens.

2. Reprinted from *Men of the Time,* 10th ed., revised by Thompson Cooper, and published by G. Routledge & Sons, London, 1879. The account, about five hundred words long, emphasizes Clemens's meager formal schooling and his later efforts "to improve his education." It is otherwise austerely factual. A photostat of the reprint is in MTP.

256. CLEMENS TO HOWELLS

[Hartford] Sunday Oct 24/80

My Dear Howells —

Here's a letter which I wrote you to San Francisco the second time you didn't go there. Soulé has written again (see enclosed) [1] & now I have just admonished him to ship his poems to you & you'll tell Osgood squarely what you think of them & he will accept or decline them as he pleases. I told Soulé he needn't write you, but simply send the MS to you. O dear, dear, it is dreadful to be an unrecognized poet. How wise it was in Ch — W — Stoddard to take in his sign & go for some other calling while still young.[2]

I'm a laying for that Encyclopediacal Scotchman; & he'll need to lock the door behind him, when he comes in; otherwise when he hears my proposed tariff his skin will probably crawl away with him. He is accustomed to seeing the publisher impoverish the author — that spectacle must be getting stale to him — if he contracts with the undersigned he will experience a change in that programme that will make the enamel peel off his teeth for very surprise — & joy. No, that is what Mrs. Clemens thinks — but it ain't so. The proposed work is growing, mightily, in my estimation, day by day; & I'm not going to throw it away for any mere trifle. If I make a contract with the canny Scot, I will then tell him the plan which you & I have devised (that of taking in the humor of *all* countries) — otherwise I'll keep it to myself, I think. Why should we assist our fellow-man for mere love of God?   Yrs Ever

Mark.

Baxter was here yesterday — I liked him quite well.[3]
O, no, you were not "fulsome."

1. Although Soulé returned Clemens's letter addressed to Howells in his care in San Francisco, it has not survived. In his letter to Clemens, Soulé referred again to his difficulty in finding a publisher for his poems. "I do not anticipate making money by publishing," he said, "but yet think I have some thousands of lines worth preserving. The fifth canto of a Poem depicting the settlement of California by the gold seekers, I believe would be read with interest by many" (San Francisco, 11 October 1880, MTP).

2. Stoddard, who had been another poet in the literary group Clemens had known in San Francisco, had eventually become a lecturer at Notre Dame and the Catholic University in Washington.

3. Clemens has revised his opinion of Sylvester Baxter since Baxter visited him in the early summer (letter 236).

257. CLEMENS TO HOWELLS

[Hartford] Oct. 28 [1880].

Dear Howells — Receive a lesson. This is a plan which I have used for many years to get the advantage of a bad memory. I keep the hieroglyphics [1] in my pocket, but don't have to refer to them.

Mark.

1. Mark Twain's hieroglyphics are reproduced on the next page. They were his notes for a speech before a Republican mass meeting in the Hartford Opera House on 26 October 1880. The relation of the hieroglyphics to the speech is explained in the Appendix, p. 871.

258. CLEMENS TO HOWELLS

Hartford, Oct. 30 [1880].

My Dear Howells:

Will the proposed treaty [1] protect us *(& effectually)* against Canadian piracy? Because if it doesn't, there is not a single argument in favor of international copyright which a rational American Senate could entertain for a moment. My notions have mightily changed, lately. Under this recent & brand-new system of piracy in New York, this country is being flooded with the best of English literature at prices which make a package of water closet paper seem an "edition de luxe" in comparison. I can buy Macaulay's History, 3 vols., bound, for $1.25. Chambers's Cyclopedia, 15 vols., cloth, for $7.25. (we paid $60), & other English copyrights in proportion; I can buy a lot of the great copyright classics, in paper, at from 3 cents to 30 cents apiece. These things must find their way into the very kitchens & hovels of the country. A generation of this sort of thing ought to make this the most intelligent & the best-read nation in the world. International copyright must becloud this sun & bring on the former darkness and dime-novel reading.

Morally, this is all wrong — governmentally it is all right;

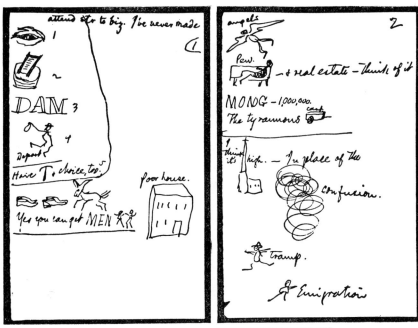

Mark Twain's notes for a political speech.
(See letter 257.)

for it is the *duty* of governments — & families — to be selfish, & look out simply for their own. International copyright would benefit a few English authors, & a lot of American publishers, & be a profound detriment to 20,000,000 Americans; it would benefit a dozen American authors a few dollars a year, & there an end. The *real* advantages all go to English authors & American publishers.

And even if the treaty *will* kill Canadian piracy, & thus save me an average of $5,000 a year, I'm down on it anyway — & I'd like cussed well to write an article opposing the treaty. Dern England! Such is *my* sentiments.   Yrs Ever

Mark.

Gebbie's coming here soon.

   Contrib

   Club.[2]

— Here is one definition of the word "Journalism" which has lately been offered to the dictionary makers — & declined; for what reason, is not stated: "Journalism is the one solitary respectable profession which honors theft (when committed in the ⟨pecuniary⟩ interest of a journal,) & admires the thief." In view of the filching of a President's message by one metropolitan journal,[3] & the stealing of General Grant's article,[4] by another, the definition seems to have more or less force. — However, these same journals combat despicable crimes quite valiantly — when committed in other quarters. For so complacent & boastful a public teacher as a journalist to steal, is not worse than it would be for an archbishop to commit a rape; but perhaps this is all that can be said in praise of it.

1. A draft of a proposed treaty with Great Britain concerning international copyright had been submitted by Harper & Bros. to Secretary of State Evarts in 1878; with minor revisions, it was presented to the British government in 1880 by James Russell Lowell, then American minister in London (George H. Putnam, *The Question of Copyright,* 3rd ed., New York, 1904, p. 44). Clemens's ability to recognize the cultural benefits to the United States from the absence of a copyright agreement with Britain is remarkable in view of the headlong fashion in which he usually supported the causes in which he was interested.

2. Howells did not use this piece for the Contributors' Club of the

Atlantic, if indeed Clemens was serious in submitting his paragraph.

3. The editors have not been able to document this allusion.

4. The Cincinnati *Gazette* (on 4 October) and the New York *Times* (on 6 October, p. 1) had published a part of an interview with Grant which the Reverend Dr. C. H. Fowler (Missionary Secretary of the Methodist Episcopal Church) had written for the issue of the Chicago *Inter-Ocean* due to be published on 6 October. General Grant had been persuaded to attack General Winfield S. Hancock, the Democratic Presidential nominee, with reference both to his character ("He is a weak, vain man . . . the most selfish man I know") and his supposed undue leniency toward the South during Reconstruction (*Nation,* XXXI, 245, 7 October 1880; New York *Herald,* 6 October 1880, p. 5, and 7 October, p. 6).

259. HOWELLS TO CLEMENS

[Boston] Oct. 31, 1880.

My dear Clemens:

I have read your Hartford speech twice; and your memoranda, even, can't put it out of my mind, though they are pretty effective in that way. But I'm going to keep them and try hard to get at the secret of remembering one's good things. We could all say just as good things as you if we could remember them.

Soule's MS. hasn't come yet; but you have touched me in regard to him, and I will deal gently with his poetry. This printed piece is *not* poetry,[1] and I return it lest it should prejudice me against the rest. Poor old fellow! I can imagine him, and how hard he must have to struggle not to be hard or sour. I wish now I *had* gone with the President, if only to see him.

I await with curiosity your result with the Scotchman. If he does not behave honorably, the question for us to consider will be how we can honorably steal his idea. But if we try to be good, we shall be helped.   Yours ever

W. D. Howells.

Your speech was wonderfully good. I should like to have heard it, and seen the effect.

1. The clipping of a Fourth of July poem by Frank Soulé which Howells

returns shows that one of his faults as a poet was logorrhea: it runs to twenty stanzas, of which the first two are as follows:

> When toasts are uttered "to the dead!"
> With brows unclad we silent drain
> The pledge; but in the heart and head
> They live again.

> In presence of the dead who died
> For hearth, and home, and native land,
> By faith inspired, by battle tried,
> We seem to stand.

260. HOWELLS TO CLEMENS

Belmont, Dec. 13, 1880.

My dear Clemens:

I have read the Two Ps,[1] and I like it immensely. It begins well, and it ends well, but there are things in the middle that are not so good. The whipping-boy's story[2] seemed poor fun; and the accounts of the court ceremonials are too long, unless you *droll* them more than you have done. I think you might have let in a little more of your humor the whole way through, and satirized things more. This would not have hurt the story for the children, and would have helped it for the grownies. As it is, the book is marvellously good. It realizes most vividly the time. All the *picaresque* part — the tramps, outlaws, etc., — all the infernal clumsiness and cruelties of the law — are incomparable. The whole intention, the allegory, is splendid, and powerfully enforced. The subordinate stories, like that of Hendon, are well assimilated and thoroughly interesting.

I think the book will be a great success unless some marauding ass, who does not snuff his wonted pasturage there should prevail on all the other asses to turn up their noses in pure ignorance. It is such a book as *I* would expect from you, knowing what a bottom of fury there is to your fun; but the public at large ought to be *led* to expect it, and must be.

No white man ought to use a stylographic pen,[3] any how. You will be surprised, perhaps, that I have written you at all about the book, but Osgood sent it to me, and it took five good hours out of me on Saturday, and I think I have a right to say something. And I say it is *good* — and only long-winded in places. You ought to look out for those. The interest of the story mounts continually; there are passages that are tremendously moving; and it is full of good things.　　　Yours ever

　　　　　　　　　　　　　　　　　　W. D. Howells.

Hendon's mock — and growingly real — subordination to the prince is delightful — one of a hundred fine traits of the story.

1. *The Prince and the Pauper.*
2. See Appendix.
3. Howells abandons the stylographic pen at this point.

261. CLEMENS TO HOWELLS

　　　　　　　　　　　[Hartford] Xmas Eve, 1880.

My Dear Howells:

I was prodigiously delighted with what you said about the book — so, on the whole I've concluded to publish intrepidly, instead of concealing the authorship. I shall leave out that bull story.[1]

I wish you had gone to New York. The company was small, & we had a first-rate time. Smith's an enjoyable fellow.[2] I liked Barrett, too. And the oysters were as good as the rest of the company. It was worth going there to learn how to cook them.

Next day I attended to business — which was, to introduce Twichell to Gen. Grant & procure a private talk in the interest of the Chinese Educational Mission here in the U.S.[3] Well, it was very funny. Joe had been sitting up nights building facts & arguments together into a mighty & unassailable array, & had studied them out & got them by heart — all with the trembling half-hearted hope of getting Grant to add his signature to a sort of petition to the Viceroy of China; but Grant took in the whole situation in a jiffy, & before Joe had more than fairly got started, the old man said: *"I'll write the Viceroy a letter* — a separate letter — & bring strong reasons to bear upon him; I know him well, & what I say will have weight with him; I will attend to it right away. No, no thanks — I shall be *glad* to do it — it will be a labor of love."

So all Joe's laborious hours were for naught! It was as if he had come to borrow a dollar, & been offered a thousand before he could unfold his case. When we came away, he said that if he could have ventured upon the familiarity, he would have appealed to the General's generosity & said, "But General, consider! I have been a week getting up this case & perfecting it, & I *know* it is admirable — & now this most pleasant, but at the same time most destructive haste of yours, has made it useless & thrown it on my hands a valueless property. If you would only retract your approval, & sit down & give me a chance, it would be a grateful favor to me. I know I could convince you all over again, sure."

But it's getting dark. Merry Christmas to all of you.

Yrs Ever

Mark.

1. See Appendix.

2. It will be recalled that Clemens had been invited to a meeting of the Tile Club in January 1880 (letter 218), but had not been able to go. The present letter shows that he had at last attended a meeting of the Club in the studio of F. Hopkinson Smith in New York, on 20 December. Smith's letter of invitation (New York [13] December 1880, MTP) has some of the self-consciousness that characterized the Club: "In the top of my house is my studio, and in the studio is an open wood fire place, and on the night of Dec 20, immediately after Barretts performance at the Park Theatre in Howells play, we do propose to cook upon that fire a variety of oyster hitherto unknown in a way peculiar to the First familie's of Virginia from whom I am descended. There will be a man named [W. Mackay] Laffan descended from an Irish King who will brew a punch, the smell of which will ascend to Heaven *first* and *descend* later to a better place. May I ask you to join us?"

3. Established by order of Viceroy Li Hung Chang in 1872 with headquarters in Hartford, under the direction of Yung Wing. According to Yung's

original plan, some thirty Chinese boys were to be sent to the United States each year to receive a Western education. They were to remain fifteen years living at first with American families and receiving instruction in both Chinese and English, then, when they were adequately prepared, entering college. About one hundred in all were sent, but in 1881 personal rivalries within the Chinese bureaucracy and a resurgence of conservative anti-Western feeling led to the abolition of the Mission. Twichell's efforts were fruitless, as was a formal protest addressed to the Chinese Foreign Office by Noah Porter, Anthony Seelye, F. T. Frelinghuysen, John Russell Young, and Mark Twain. All the students were recalled to China (Yung Wing, *My Life in China and America,* New York, 1909, esp. pp. 210–215). Grant enclosed his letter to the Viceroy in a letter to Clemens from New York on 24 December (MTP).

VI

AN INDIGNANT SENSE OF RIGHT AND WRONG

(1 8 8 1 – 1 8 8 2)

VI

(1 8 8 1 – 1 8 8 2)

". . . I warn the reader that if he leaves out of the account an indignant sense of right and wrong, a scorn of all affectation and pretense, an ardent hate of meanness and injustice, he will come indefinitely short of knowing Mark Twain" (WDH in the Century, *September 1882*)

When the firm of Houghton, Osgood & Company was dissolved, Howells decided upon Osgood as his publisher, in return for a guaranteed monthly income. Clemens, who had lost confidence in the American Publishing Company upon the death of the president, Elisha H. Bliss, entered into a rather different contract which made Osgood his publishing agent with capital provided by Clemens. The two friends revived the project of a collaborative *Library of Humor,* and Clemens proposed they should take up the comedy about Colonel Sellers which they had often discussed. Winifred Howells, then a girl of seventeen with precocious literary gifts, suffered a nervous breakdown which a "rest cure" did little to help. Perhaps through sorrow over his daughter's illness, perhaps through overwork in his effort to make a living without a regular editorial post, Howells himself became seriously ill in the autumn of 1881 and was incapacitated for more than two months. But as he was able, he continued to serve as editor and critic for Clemens, supervising the choice of materials for *The Stolen White Elephant, Etc.,* reading the proofs of *The Prince and the Pauper,* and reviewing this book in the usually hostile New York *Tribune* under the terms of a benign conspiracy with John Hay. Howells's *A Modern Instance,* one of his best novels, was serialized in the *Century* (December 1881–October 1882), to Clemens's rapturous applause. In the spring of 1882 Clemens returned to the Mississippi to make notes for expanding his "Old Times" sketches into a book. The Howellses sailed for Europe in July, hoping that travel might benefit both Winifred and her father. In the September issue of the *Century* Howells published a full-length appraisal of Clemens's work, the first serious effort by a critic to take account of

345

his career as a whole. As 1882 ended Clemens was engaged in a prolonged effort to complete *Life on the Mississippi* and the Howellses, after resting several weeks in Switzerland, had established themselves in Florence for the winter.

262. CLEMENS TO HOWELLS

[Hartford] Jan 14/81.

My Dear Howells —

Here is Gebbie's letter,[1] received last night. Now if you are still in the mind to tackle this Cyclopedia with me, drop me a line *right away* — for I have put Gebbie off two or three days on purpose to give myself time to hear from you. I still like the idea of going into this thing, as much as ever; & I hope you do, also.

———————————

On *3 different days,* last week, Bay, & the baby, & the house, came within the *half* of a hair's breadth of being *burned up!*[2] Stirring adventures enough for *one* small week, ain't it?

Ys Ever

Mark.

1. In his letter to Clemens (Philadelphia, 12 January 1881, MTP) George Gebbie proposed to call on Clemens in Hartford "on the business which we have already mooted." Gebbie did come, several weeks later, but the interview seems to have been unfortunate and the discussions led to nothing (letter 266).

2. The fires were caused by an alcohol lamp under a croup kettle which set fire to the canopy of Clara's crib, a spark from the fireplace which fell on the lace covering of baby Jean's crib, and sparks from another fireplace which ignited the woodwork supporting the mantel in the schoolroom adjoining the nursery (MTB, pp. 699–700).

263. HOWELLS TO CLEMENS

[Boston] Jan. 17, 1881.

My dear Clemens:

Yes, I shall be very glad to co-operate with you in making Gebbie's Cyclopaedia. You spoke of giving me $3000 or $5000 for my work. Make such terms with him that you can give me the latter sum, which is somehow more attractive to the imagination, and for one year replaces a certain salary. I believe we can make a very good book together, and whenever you are ready to begin, I will be ready to plan it with you. Consider me heartily in for it.

Two cases of measles — very bad — one low fever, and one habitual debility indefinitely intensified, as well as an attack of two publishers,[1] against your conflagrations!

Yours ever

W. D. Howells.

1. Henry O. Houghton and James R. Osgood. When Houghton bought out Osgood, and the firm of Houghton, Osgood & Co. was dissolved, in 1880, they had made an agreement concerning which man should take each of the authors published by the firm. Houghton kept the *Atlantic Monthly* but Howells wished to place his books with Osgood. Houghton and Osgood disagreed over the meaning of their arrangement as it applied to Howells. On 10 January 1881 he wrote both men saying, "I cannot suffer myself to be made your battle-ground in fighting out your different interpretations." By 2 February he had resigned as editor of the *Atlantic* (LinL, I, 293–294).

264. CLEMENS TO HOWELLS

Hartford Feb. 4/81.

My Dear Howells —

Don't you remember the Southern author who invented a fire-kindler & kept the article for sale? I *want* some patent fire-kindlings very badly. Can you tell me where to send my order?

Sir Gebbie was to be here to-day, but has telegraphed & postponed till *next* Friday. If ever I make a contract with this dallying Scot, it will be drawn almighty tight, as sure as he is born.   Yrs Ever

Mark.

P.S. Oh, yes, if I can't make a contract with him that will enable me to pay you $5,000, you can rest most assured that there won't be any contract made.

S L C

265. HOWELLS TO CLEMENS

[Boston] Feb. 13, 1881.

My dear Clemens:

That wretched man was merely trying to introduce light-wood knots; but he found no market for them, and he went into the Census business and no doubt helped to get up that super-abundant population in the South. (This sounds dreadful.)

Osgood has told me of closing his contract with you, and no doubt he has told you of closing one with me.[1] I know that I owe you the advantage of mine,[2] and some day when I get you alone I will thank you for it. In the meantime you understand that you are at the mercy of my gratitude.

Winny and Mrs. Howells are at a hotel in Boston for a week, and John and Pil and I are keeping house in Belmont. You know perhaps that Winny is quite broken down. She has not been in school for five months, and for a while she could not cross the room alone. She is now much better than that, and her mother takes her in town to give her what amusement she can, at the theatres, etc.

If Sir Gebbie doesn't come to time, can you honorably steal his scheme, and get it realized elsewhere?

Yours ever

W. D. Howells.

1. After resigning as editor of the *Atlantic* and thus severing all connection with Houghton, Howells had proposed to Osgood that Osgood should become his publisher, and this letter announces the conclusion of the arrangement. In return for a fixed weekly salary amounting to about $7500 a year for a novel a year plus shorter pieces, Osgood got the right to sell 10,000 copies of each of Howells's books before he began paying royalty on them. Back royalties and other incidental sources of revenue probably brought Howells's income to $10,000 a year — enough to enable him to give up editing and devote his time more exclusively to writing novels (Cady, *Road to Realism,* p. 200).

2. Clemens was able to exert influence on Osgood because he himself was in the market for a publisher. Elisha H. Bliss, president of the American Publishing Co. of Hartford, who had been Clemens's publisher since *The Innocents Abroad* in 1869, had died on 28 September 1880 (Frank E. Bliss to SLC, Hartford, 28 September 1880, MTP). On 24 October, Clemens had written to Orion, " . . . I shall probably go to a new publisher 6 or 8 months hence, for I am afraid Frank [Bliss, son of Elisha], with his poor health, will lack push and drive" (Hartford, MTL, p. 389). And on 27 November he wrote Orion that he had already made a contract for publication of *The Prince and the Pauper* with a new publisher — that is, Osgood (Hartford, MTBM, pp. 147–148). Actually, the contract made Osgood an employee of Clemens rather than an independent publisher; for the author was to provide all the capital for manufacture of the books and was to take all the profits except a royalty of 7½ per cent which Osgood received for selling them (SLC to Pamela Clemens Moffett, Hartford, 16 March 1881, MTBM, pp. 150–151; MTB, p. 707).

266. CLEMENS TO HOWELLS

Hartford Feb. 15/81.

My Dear Howells:

I'm not going to have any further personal intercourse with Sir Gebbie. If he writes me again, I shall tell him that he may contract with me through Osgood if he can, but that I will not see him myself.[1]

If *I* did not tell Osgood about Gebbie's plan I don't know but that it would be legitimate for me to entertain the same plan coming to me from Osgood, (in case we arrive at no conclusion with Gebbie); but if Osgood heard of Gebbie's plan *through me,* I judge that that would shut me out from entertaining that plan when coming from Osgood. It would be like betraying a confidence. It would be like Gebbie's revealing to me the locality of a Captain Kidd deposit, & my sailing in with another fellow to dig it up.

The news about Winny is too bad, too bad. But you have done the wise thing, I think. We must canvass this thing when I come to Boston the 23d.   Yrs Ever

Mark.

Mighty glad you are out of that cussed mill, that gilded slavery.²

1. Clemens's irritation with Gebbie is explained in his letter to James R. Osgood on 12 February from Hartford: "Now as to Gebbie. He failed of his appointment yesterday (as usual). He can make no more appointments with me. . . . If he will treat with me *through you,* (if you are willing,) all right — but there ain't any other way" (Harvard Theatre Collection, TS in MTP).

2. The editorship of the *Atlantic.* " . . . I have grown terribly, miserably tired of editing," Howells had written Horace Scudder a week earlier. "I think my nerves have given way under the fifteen years' fret and substantial unsuccess. At any rate the MSS., the proofs, the books, the letters became insupportable. Many a time in the past four years I have been minded to jump out and take the consequences — to throw myself upon the market as you did, *braver Mann!* — rather than continue the work which I was conscious of wishing to slight. . . . The chance came to *light soft,* and I jumped out" (Boston, 8 February 1881, LinL, I, 294–295). Howells's resignation from the *Atlantic* seems to have revived the idea of a diplomatic appointment for him. On 19 February, Clemens wrote to Edward H. House that the newspapers said Howells was "going to Switzerland as our Minister." Clemens added, "I hope it is true. Winny's health is getting mighty bad & that country would build her up" (Hartford, Barrett).

267. CLEMENS TO HOWELLS

Private & Confidential.

Hartford Feb. 21, 1881.

My Dear Howells —

Well, here is our romance.

It happened in this way. One morning, a month ago — no,

three weeks — Livy, & Clara Spaulding & I were at breakfast, at 10 A.M., & I was in an irritable mood, for the barber was up stairs waiting & his hot water getting cold, when the colored George returned from answering the bell & said —

"There's a lady in the drawing room wants to see you."

"A book agent!" says I, with heat. "I won't see her; I will die in my tracks, first."

Then I got up with a soul full of rage, & went in there & bent scowling over that person, & began a succession of rude & raspy questions — & without even offering to sit down.

Not even the defendant's youth & beauty & ⟨apparent⟩ (seeming) timidity were able to modify my savagery, for a time — & meantime question & answer were going on. She had risen to her feet with the first question; & there she stood, with her pretty face bent floorward whilst I inquired, but always with her honest eyes looking me in the face when it came her turn to answer.

And this was her tale, & her plea — diffidently stated, but straightforwardly; & bravely, & most winningly simply & earnestly: I put it in my own fashion, for I do not remember her words:

Mr. Karl Gerhardt, who works in Pratt & Whitney's machine shops, has made a statue in clay, & would I be so kind as to come & look at it, & tell him if there is any promise in it? He has none to go to, & he would be so glad.

"O, dear me," I said, "I don't know anything about art — there's nothing *I* could tell him."

But she went on, just as earnestly & as simply as before, with her plea — & so she did after repeated rebuffs; & dull as I am, even *I* began by & by, to admire this brave & gentle persistence, & to perceive how her heart of hearts was in this thing, & how she *couldn't* give it up, but *must* carry her point. So at last I wavered, & promised in general terms that I would come down the first day that fell idle — & as I conducted her to the door, I tamed more & more, & said I would come during the very next week — "We shall be so glad — but — but, would you please come early in the week? — the statue is just finished, & we are

351

so anxious — & — & — we did hope you could come this week
— and" — well, I came down another peg, & said I would come
Monday, as sure as death; & before I got to the dining room remorse was doing its work & I was saying to myself, "Damnation,
how can a man be such a hound? — why didn't I go with her
now?" Yes, & how mean I should have felt if I had known that
out of her poverty she had hired a hack & brought it along to convey me. But luckily for what was left of my peace of mind, I didn't
know that.

Well, it appears that from here she went to Charley Warner's. There was a better light, there, & the eloquence of her
face had a better chance to do its office. Warner fought, as I
had done; & he was in the midst of an article & very busy; but
no matter, she won him completely. He laid aside his MS &
said, "Come, let us go & see your father's statue. That is — is he
your father?" "No, he is my husband." So this child was married, you see.

This was a Saturday. Next day Warner came to dinner, &
said, "*Go!* — go tomorrow — don't fail." He was in love with the
girl, & with her husband, too. And he said he believed there
was merit in the statue. Pretty crude work, maybe, but merit in it.

Patrick & I hunted up the place, next day; the girl saw us
driving up, & flew down stairs & received me. Her quarters
were the second story of a little wooden house — another family
on the ground floor. The husband was at the machine-shop,
the wife kept no servant; she was there alone. She had a little
parlor, with a chair or two & a sofa; & the artist-husband's hand
was visible in a couple of plaster busts, one of the wife, the other
of a neighbor's child; visible also, in a couple of water colors,
of flowers & birds; an ambitious unfinished portrait of the wife
in oils; some paint-decorations of the pine mantel; & an excellent human ear, done in some plastic material at 16.

Then we went into the neat kitchen, & the girl flew around,
with enthusiasm, & snatched rag after rag from a tall something in the corner, & presently there stood the clay statue, life
size — a graceful girlish creature, ⟨life size⟩ nude to the waist,
& holding up a single garment with one hand — the expression

attempted being a modified scare — she was interrupted when about to enter the bath.

Then this young wife posed herself along side the image & so remained — a thing I didn't understand. But presently I did — then I said —

"O, it's *you!*"

"Yes," she said, "I was the model. He has no model but me. I have stood for this, many & many an hour — & you can't think how it does tire one! But I don't mind it. He works all day at the shop; & then, nights & Sundays he works on his statue as long as I can keep up."

She got a big chisel, to use as a lever, & between us we managed to twist the pedestal round & round, so as to afford a view of the statue from all points. Well, sir, it was perfectly charming, this girl's innocence & purity — exhibiting her naked self, as it were, to a stranger & alone, & never once dreaming that there was the slightest indelicacy about the matter. And so there wasn't; but it will be many a long day before I run across another woman who can do the like & show no trace of self-consciousness.

Well, then we sat down, & I took a smoke, & she told me all about her people in Massachusetts — her father is a physician & it is an old & respectable family — (I am able to believe anything she says.) And she told me how "Karl" is 26 years old; & how he has had passionate longings all his life, toward art, but has always been poor & obliged to struggle for his daily bread; & how he felt sure that if he could only have *one* or *two* lessons in —

"Lessons? Hasn't he had any lessons?"

No. He had never had a lesson.

And presently it was dinner time, & "Karl" arrived — a slender young fellow with a marvelous head & a noble eye — & he was as simple, & natural, & as beautiful in spirit as his wife was. But *she* had to do the talking — mainly — there was too much thought behind his cavernous eyes for glib speech.

I went home enchanted. Told Livy & Clara [1] all about the paradise down yonder where those two enthusiasts are happy with a yearly expense of $350. Livy & Clara went there next day & came away enchanted. A few nights later the Gerhardts kept their promise & came here for the evening. It was billiard night & I had company & so was not down; but Livy & Clara became more charmed with these children than ever.

Warner & I planned to get somebody to criticise the statue whose judgment would be worth something. So I laid for Champney,[2] & after two failures I captured him & took him around; & he said "this statue is full of faults — but it has merits enough in it to make up for them" — whereat the young wife danced around as delighted as a child. When we came away, Champney said, "I did not want to say too much there, but the truth is, it seems to me an extraordinary performance for an untrained hand. You ask if there is promise enough there, to justify the Hartford folk in going to the expense of training this young man. *I* should say, *yes,* decidedly; but still, to make everything safe, you had better get the judgment of a sculptor."

Warner was in New York. I wrote him, & he said he would fetch up Ward [3] — which he did. Yesterday they went to the Gerhardts & spent 2 hours, & Ward came away bewitched with those people & marveling at the winning innocence of the young wife, who dropped naturally into her model-attitude beside the statue (which is stark naked from head to heel, now — G. had removed the drapery, fearing Ward would think he was afraid to try legs & hips) just as she has always done before.

Livy & I had two long talks with Ward yesterday evening. He spoke strongly. He said, "if any stranger had told me that this apprentice did not model that thing from plaster casts, I would not have believed it — I *couldn't* have believed it." He said "it is full of crudities, but it is full of genius, too. It is such a statue as the man of average talent would achieve after two years' training in the schools. And the *boldness* of the fellow, in going straight at *nature*! He is an apprentice — his work shows that, all over; but the stuff is in him, sure. Hartford must send him to Paris — two years; then if the promise holds good, keep him there 3 more — & warn him to study, study, work, work, &

keep his name out of the papers, & neither ask for orders nor accept them when offered."

Well, you see, that's all *we* wanted. After Ward was gone Livy came out with the thing that was in my mind. She said, "Go privately & start the Gerhardts off to Paris, & say nothing about it to anyone else."

So I tramped down this morning in the snow-storm — & there was a stirring time. They will sail a week or ten days from now.

* * * * *

As I was starting out at the front door, with Gerhardt beside me & the young wife dancing & jubilating behind, this latter cried out impulsively, "Tell Mrs. Clemens I want to hug her — I want to hug you *both*!"

I gave them my old French book, & they are going to tackle the language, straight off.

Now this letter is a secret — keep it quiet — I don't think Livy would mind my telling you these things, but then she might, you know, for she is a queer girl.　　　Ys Ever

Mark.

1. Clara Spaulding.

2. James W. Champney, painter and illustrator, of New York; Clemens and Warner persuaded him to make a special trip to Hartford to see Gerhardt's work (MTB, p. 703).

3. John Quincy Adams Ward, sculptor, president of the National Academy of Design, whom Howells had talked to, walked with, and watched modeling a statue of Simon Kenton, the Indian fighter, in Columbus in 1861 (YMY, pp. 214–215).

268. CLEMENS TO HOWELLS

Hartford Feb. 27 [1881].

My Dear Howells —

I go to West Point with Twichell tomorrow, but shall be back Tuesday or Wednesday; [1] & then just as soon thereafter as you

& Mrs. Howells & Winny can come you will find us ready & most glad to see you — & the longer you can stay the gladder we shall be. I am not going to have a thing to do, but you shall work if you want to. On the evening of March 10th, I am going to read to the colored folk in the African church here, (no whites admitted except such as I bring with me,) & a choir of colored folk will sing Jubilee songs. I count on a good time, & shall hope to have you folks there, & Livy. I read in Twichell's chapel Friday night, & had a most rattling high time — but the thing that went best of all was Uncle Remus's Tar Baby [2] — I mean to try that on my dusky audience. They've all heard that tale from childhood — at least the older members have.

I arrived home in time to make a most noble blunder — invited Charley Warner here (in Livy's name,) to dinner with the Gerhardts', & told him Livy had invited his wife *by letter* & by word of mouth also. I don't know where I got these inspirations, but I came home feeling as one does ⟨who came mighty near⟩ who realizes that he has done a neat thing for *once* & left no flaws or loop-holes — & it seemed to me, for a while, that Livy would certainly take the roof off the house. She said she had never told me to invite Charley & she hadn't dreamed of inviting Susie, & moreover there wasn't any dinner but just one lean duck. But Susy Warner's intuitions were correct — so she choked off Charley, & staid home herself — we waited dinner an hour, & you ought to have seen that duck when he was done drying up in the oven. (The G.'s tea here tonight & leave for New York & Europe tomorrow.)

Mark.

P.S. Livy's going to write Mrs. Howells.

1. Clemens went to West Point with Twichell, presumably at Twichell's solicitation, to read before the literary society of the U.S. Military Academy, of which Twichell's parishioner, Cadet "Andy" Hammond, was president. In his Journal Twichell noted that on 28 February Clemens "read to them, in the course of the evening, as much as an hour and a half, and produced extreme delight" (Yale, TS in MTP). Twichell and Clemens returned to Hartford on Wednesday, 2 March.

2. Joel Chandler Harris's "Brer Rabbit, Brer Fox, and the Tar Baby"

had been published first in the Atlanta *Constitution* on 10 November 1879, but Mark Twain had probably encountered it in *Uncle Remus: His Songs and Sayings,* published by Appleton in November 1880.

269. OLIVIA L. CLEMENS TO ELINOR M. HOWELLS

[Hartford] Monday [28 February 1881] [1]

My dear Mrs Howells

I am so delighted that you & Mr Howells & Winnie are coming to us as soon as you can make it convenient. We shall be so glad to see you this week or next or any time now when you can come — but let it be as soon as it is convenient for you.

Mr & Mrs Gerhardt start for New York today & for Paris on Saturday — every time we see them we are more in love with them, they seem like story book people — he is mature & fine. She is young & charming & with quick intuitions — They are just the people to have experiences —

I do hope that Winnie is better than when Mr Clemens was in Boston. Hoping to see you very soon I am affectionately

Livy L Clemens.

1. The date is inferred from the Gerhardts' sailing for France on Saturday, 5 March.

270. CLEMENS TO HOWELLS

[Hartford] Mch. 3 [1881].

Dear Howells —

Did you get my letter telling of the blunder I made about dinner & the Warners — & asking you & Mrs. Howells & Winny to come as soon as you can & stay as long as you can spare time for? I ask because Mrs. Clemens says she kept it back from the mail to have a lot of slanders upon her knocked out of it,[1] & she thinks it was then mislaid & lost.   Ys Ever

Mark.

357

1. This note documents once again the household routine according to which Livy frequently read outgoing mail.

271. CLEMENS TO HOWELLS

Hartford, Mch. 4/81.

My Dear Howells —

1. Read the enclosed,¹ ⟨then send it to⟩ 2 then see Osgood & show it to him — *3* then mail *my* letter to *Leathers*;² 4, have Osgood send Leathers a check for $10 (not ⟨by⟩ the same ⟨day⟩ mail, but *next* mail, say; 5, preserve Leathers's letter & the envelop (addresses his ragship as "Col.," & leaves off the "Mr." from his friend's name). Of course I am responsible for the $25 ³ — I stand behind Osgood.

Now, here is my little game: I won't have this tramp under my roof, nor on my hands; yet at the same time he is a perfectly stunning literary bonanza, & *must* be dug up & put on the market. You must get his entire biography out of him, & have it ready for Osgood's new magazine.⁴ Even if it isn't worth printing you must have it, anyway, & use it one of these days in one of your stories or in a play. Yes, & you must SEE him & talk with him, too — not at your house, but at Osgood's store (or in the Earl's quarters in N.Y. — which is better still, if it could be managed.) You would point out to him places in his MS. where from self-love he had left out interesting stuff — hadn't entered into detail sufficiently, etc.

YOU are protected — you can act under cold business orders from Osgood, & keep the thing on a cold business basis from first to last; but my case is different, the bond being blood-kinship & sentiment.

I've an idea that this bummer (judging by that envelop & other things) will write an inflated lot of rot that will make delicious reading. I *know* it — for I read one of his political articles written when he was "working" for the Dem. party at $28 for 4 months.

Come, hurry along down here just the earliest minute you *can.* Yrs Ever

Mark.

If you won't see him, Osgood must.

1. A letter to Clemens from Jesse M. Leathers (not extant). Concerning the "rightful earl," see Appendix.
2. This letter is also lost.
3. Clemens seems to have forgotten he had just mentioned the sum of $10.
4. The projected new magazine was never established.

272. HOWELLS TO CLEMENS

March 5, 1881. 28 Brimmer St. [Boston]

My dear Clemens:

I should think the American earl's autobiography would be delightful; but I dread to have him put in possession of my name as that of one having anything to do with his MS. While he lived, I don't see how I could use his history; and that kind of man survives everybody. Really, it seems to me that I can't do anything about it; and if I can't, I suppose you want your letters back.[1]

— Mrs. Fairchild was speaking, last night, about a suggestion she made to you that you should write a burlesque book of etiquette. The idea struck me as enormously good. Don't give it up. Such a book — 150 or 200 pp. 18mo — put into the trade would go like wildfire. Think what a chance to satirize the greed, solemn selfishness and cruel dullness of society! It's a wonderful opportunity, and you were made for it.[2]

We *did* get that letter; and it made me happy for twenty-four hours. I argued that if you had not been fresh from me[3] you could not have achieved that enormity. Some time when we have got a whole Saturday, I want to tell you how I forgot that Mrs. Howells was to go to a tea-party with me, went alone, excused her according to custom, and involved myself in domestic and social consequences without end. The worst of these things is that you never can keep them secret.

At present Mrs. Howells is grappling with a tooth, which binds her to an inspired dentist here with hooks of steel, and she has written to Mrs. Clemens asking her to Boston. As soon as the tooth lets up we shall turn our faces towards Hartford.

— The earl's letter is delicious.   Yours ever

W. D. Howells.

1. The letters from Leathers which Howells seems to have sent back to Clemens have not survived.

2. On 7 March, Clemens wrote to Osgood: " . . . *yes,* send me a collection of etiquette books; Mrs. Fairchild's idea is a mighty good one, I think" (Hartford, Harvard Theatre Collection, TS in MTP). Clemens began writing the burlesque book of etiquette, although at what date is not certain. More than 70 pp. of MS survive, on such topics as "At a Funeral" and "At a Fire" (DV 68, MTP). The discussion of "Visiting Cards" is especially amusing, since it develops into an extravaganza on how playing cards might be used to convey delicate sentiments in a courtship. Albert B. Paine publishes a page of the burlesque etiquette MS (MTB, pp. 705–706).

3. This remark, and Livy's remark in letter 269, imply that Clemens carried out his intention (announced in letter 266) of going to Boston on 23 February. The visit is otherwise unrecorded.

273. HOWELLS TO CLEMENS

Boston, April 17, 1881.

My Dear Clemens:

I have written to Osgood to-day about the Library of Humor, and have asked him to read my letter to you; but Mrs. Howells, who has charge of my sense of decency — I wish she didn't brag so about her superior management of it — suggests that *you* ought to hear from me first. Osgood tells me that you and he are about to strike a bargain,[1] and he wants to know if I'm ready to go to work. He also tells me that you would like to push the job through before you go to Elmira. I suppose he doesn't perhaps quite understand; but I could not agree to work at it except in the most leisurely way; you spoke of an hour a day; and I don't see how I could give more time. You see that I have to get ready a novel [2] for Scribner by November 1st, so as to let them have the opening chapters for January; and I wish to finish it by Dec. 31, and cut for Europe.[3] I don't know exactly how hard this work will be; but it wont be very light; and I don't know how big a book you wish to make. With the rashness of youth, I agreed to do anything, when I was at your house; but I now wish you to let me suspend my decision till I see Osgood, and get your latest ideas from him. I think also I should prefer to return to your first idea of paying me a stipulated sum — $5000 — and leave the rich possibilities of the venture to you. I believe that I could help you to that extent; but I could not afford to lose my labor if the work failed. I hope this wont seem fickle or unreasonable. The questions with me are: I How many volumes and how large? II Whether I can decently spring the notion of a stipulated sum on you instead of a royalty? III Whether I could undertake the work experimentally, and back out if I found it too hard?

Mrs. Howells is feeling badly at not having written to Mrs. Clemens and thanked her for the good time she made us have at your house.[4] She has been in bed the greater part of the past fortnight; but she is up now, and will start the universe on the right basis again in a few days. She joins me in love to all of you.

Please write me at Belmont: we go back on Thursday.

Yours ever

W. D. Howells.

P.S. My difficulty in finishing ⟨up⟩ the two-number story that I've just ended [5] has given me a scare about loading up with more work till I see my way through the novel. If I were not able to go to Europe in December, then I should have a clear three months before I began another story, and should be glad and humbly thankful to help you on the L. of H. Or if you and Osgood can agree on terms, and leave the time blank, I can still be your man. What I dread is to enter on work that I can't decently back out from. Why don't you go on with the Etiquette Book, and let the L. of H. rest awhile? I *don't* want to give it up; but I don't want to begin it till the way is clearer to me.

1. JRO to WDH, Boston, 15 April 1881, Houghton.

2. *A Modern Instance,* which was serialized from December 1881 through October 1882 in the *Century Magazine,* successor to *Scribner's Monthly.* The characters and plot of this book, Howells's first long novel, had been turning over in his mind ever since April 1875, when he had been greatly moved by Fanny Janauschek's re-creation of the jealous passion of Medea in a Boston performance of Euripides' play. He had begun writing by September of the following year, but only now, in the spring of 1881, had he found the time for a major effort such as he intended. To Osgood, his agent in placing serial rights, he described his subject for "The New Medea," in a letter of 18 February (Belmont, AGM TS), as "one of the few which are both great and simple," and claimed a *"great* motive" that was strong without being tendentious. "I propose to take a couple who are up to a certain point about equally to blame for their misery," he said, whose "love marriage falls into ruin through the undisciplined character of both," though the deserted wife would necessarily receive more sympathy in the end. His setting would include "Equity," Me.; Boston; and an Indiana divorce court. His treatment of the separation and divorce would be tragic. Through the summer and fall, before his serious illness in December, Howells read aloud portions of his MS to Clemens when they met, as letter 310 indicates. (The genesis of the novel is described more fully in William M. Gibson, "Introduction," *A Modern Instance,* Boston, 1957, pp. v–ix.)

3. Howells wanted to go to Europe for the sake of Winifred's precarious health.

4. The Howellses' visit to Hartford in the latter part of March, promised in Howells's letter of 5 March, is not otherwise recorded.

5. "A Fearful Responsibility," which would appear in *Scribner's Monthly* for June and July.

274. CLEMENS TO HOWELLS

'Artford, Hapril 19/81.

My Dear 'Owells —

Good idea! That is exactly what we will do: *"leave the time blank."* That is sensible; I wonder you ever thought of it. If you were not married, I should believe you *did* think of it. Anyway, it is sound, it is wisdom.

I appreciate all you say, & sympathize with your dreads of manacles & fetters, & of speculative uncertainties. Therefore we will retrograde to the original proposition, & make it a distinct sum, $5,000, to be paid by me, whether the book succeeds or fails.

⟨Now if I *do* reach an agreement with the Osgood,⟩ This would leave you where you could back out, or die, without obloquy attaching to the act.

If God takes an interest in this Library of Humor (a thing which would make me feel a good deal set up, if I could really believe it & realize it, I can tell you,) *he* knows how big a book & how many volumes it will be, but it would be nonsense for the rest of us to try to guess, so early as this. I know this, however: if the work were to consist of 15 octavo volumes, the labor would amount to nothing — anything that was pretty good could go right in — there would be a sufficiency of room; but to have to sift & select for a mere pitiful one or two big volumes, *that* is WORK — & don't you forget it. This latter is the very job that is before us.

Well, now, as follows is my idea: If I do succeed in agreeing with the Osgood, I will hire a capable man, at a good salary, to tackle libraries, catalogues, dictionaries of authors, &c., & make out an exhaustive list of American books & authors for us. If I can get the man I want (Charley Clark), this will take him several months, for his main time will belong to the Courant. — When Osgood shall have raked together the books in said list, Clark & I will sail in & read & select. By the time you are back

363

from Europe, we shall be ready, no doubt, for you to go through our said stack of selections, & knock out, approve — & add to, too, if you want to. In this way you will be relieved of the realest drudgery of the thing.[1] In a heaven of a hurry,

Yrs Ever

Mark

1. "We can do anything together," the conclusion of Howells's letter to Clemens of 25 April 1880, becomes almost a refrain in their correspondence, although it seems ironic now because none of their joint projects really thrived. The *Library of Humor* of this letter is a typical example. Clemens did hire Charles Hopkins Clark, managing editor of the Hartford *Courant,* to help Howells choose the selections and prepare copy; but the book was not published until 1888, without Howells's name on the title page, and Clemens made almost no money from it (letters 451, 453, 458, 459; Harold Blodgett, "A Note on *Mark Twain's Library of Humor,*" AL, X, 78–80, March 1938).

The gap of nearly three months here in the correspondence cannot be explained; no doubt letters by both Clemens and Howells have been lost. On 17 July, Clemens wrote to George W. Cable (whom he had met for the first time in June) that Howells "spent a day with me last week" and that he was "still in the mind to go to New Orleans with me in November for the Mississippi trip . . . " (Hartford, TS in MTP).

275. CLEMENS TO HOWELLS

Elmira, Aug. 12/81.

My Dear Howells —

Say — I am going to Ashfield, Mass. Aug 25th.[1] Tell me — what does a body have to do there? Talk? And if so, who are the audience? 1. Is it a school? 2. If so, is it male, or female, or both? 3. Boys & girls? or bigger bucks & fillies? [2]

Are you going?

In a hurry,

Yrs Ever

Mark.

1. In 1879 Charles Eliot Norton had begun sponsoring an annual midsummer Academy Dinner at Ashfield, in the hills of northwestern

Massachusetts, where he had long maintained his summer home. Each year Norton invited some celebrated friend or acquaintance to speak; tickets were sold at one dollar each, and the proceeds were donated to Ashfield Academy, in which Norton and George W. Curtis, who also had a summer place at Ashfield, had interested themselves. "With Norton to preside at those 'dinners'; with Curtis, whose persuasive eloquence in the fearless exposure of corruption can never be forgotten by anyone who heard him speak; with Lowell, Howells, Choate, Moorfield Storey, Booker Washington, and many others, guests in Ashfield and speakers at that mid-summer feast, it was not surprising that the occasion became, as the years went on, well known. It was regarded from outside as an event of national interest, since the speakers addressed an audience that listened from be-yond the encircling hills of Ashfield. Their words might be denounced as 'Mugwump oratory'; they might themselves be regarded as 'renegade to party'; but this did not deter these lovers of America, these leaders in such causes as those of Civil Service Reform, Tariff Reform, Negro educa-tion, Anti-Imperialism, from coming to Ashfield to speak on subjects about which free speech was expected there" (Sarah Norton and M. A. De Wolfe Howe, eds., *Letters of Charles Eliot Norton with Biographical Comment,* 2 vols., Boston, 1913, II, 89–90). The dinners continued to be held until 1903.

2. It is interesting that Clemens had accepted the invitation to speak when he knew so little about the occasion. His notion that the audience might consist of boys and girls was doubtless suggested by the phrase "Ashfield Academy Dinners." It will be recalled that Howells, with his daughter and Charles Dudley Warner, had visited Norton at Ashfield in August 1880 (letter 243), and had presumably delivered a lecture.

276. HOWELLS TO CLEMENS

Belmont, Aug. 16, 1881.

Dear Clemens:

Your Ashfield audience will be the farmer-folks of the re-gion, quiet and dull on top, but full of grit and fun; they're fond of speaking, and rather cultivated, but not spoiled. They know *you,* like a book, and you can trust all your points to them. Their life is one of deadly solitude and suffocating frugality; but they are smart. They will stand lots of human nature from you. You speak at a cold public dinner in the

Town Hall. — I can't go: we are a hospital: our dear girl has to lie *abed* now all the time — rest cure. I wrote you at Montewese [1] on Friday. How I wish you could give us a day whilst you're on this side of the mountain.   Yours ever

W. D. H.

1. The Clemenses went to the Montowese House, Branford, Conn., on 4 June and remained there until they moved on to Elmira on 4 August (MTBM, pp. 158–162; SLC to [Benjamin?] Ticknor, Branford, Conn., 1 August 1881, Yale, TS in MTP).

277. CLEMENS TO HOWELLS

Elmira, Aug. 18./81.

Dear Howells —

Your news about Winny is too distressing; & is altogether a surprise, too, for the idea that she has been really an invalid all these months never took a realizing grip upon my mind. Of course you have our deepest sympathy, it is not necessary to say that; & we do hope a better day will come soon. What *can* have brought her to this state, I wonder?

If the President remains in this critical state; or if we lose him — which latter is a bitter thing to contemplate, but yet is the disaster in store for us, I seem almost to know [1] — I cannot go to Ashfield, for I should not enjoy a festival of any sort, at such a time, nor be able to help anybody else enjoy it.[2]

I have to see Osgood, however, & shall see him either in N.Y. or Boston. If the latter, you must run into town for a day, if you possibly can; but if you just *can't,* I'll run out there. With love & best hopes to Winny, & the same to the rest,

Yrs Ever

Mark.

I wrote Clark.[3]

1. Garfield was shot by Charles J. Guiteau in a railway station at Washington on 2 July 1881; he died 19 September. His death was especially

disheartening for men of Clemens's political views because Chester A. Arthur, the Vice-President, whom Hayes had removed from his post as collector of customs for the Port of New York, had been nominated as a concession to the Stalwart faction of the Republican party dominated by Roscoe Conkling (H. J. Eckenrode, *Rutherford B. Hayes, Statesman of Reunion,* New York, 1930, pp. 267–278; Williams, *Hayes,* II, 238–239).

2. On 23 August, Clemens wrote to Charles Eliot Norton from Elmira that he had "finished loading myself up with my speech" and had "ordered a sleeping-section for Albany in to-night's train." But bad news concerning Garfield's condition made it impossible for him to deliver the speech he had planned at Ashfield. "The idea of making a light & nonsensical speech to possibly appear in print in the midst of columns of heart-break walled in from top to bottom with the black bars of mourning for the head of the nation, was appalling." He would have had "no heart to talk nonsense, nor the people to listen to it," and a speech in unison with the sorrowful circumstances would merely have added another pang (TS in MTP). But as he told Norton he would be compelled to do, he made his business trip to Hartford and Boston anyway.

3. Charles Hopkins Clark, who was to assist in compiling the *Library of Humor.*

278. ELINOR M. HOWELLS TO OLIVIA L. CLEMENS

Redtop [Belmont],
August 26th [1881]

My dear Mrs. Clemens:

It always seems like an "opportunity" to write you when Mr. Clemens is here, — though I know there is nothing to prevent me at other times. You will smile when I tell you that I *was* just going to write, and that I have hardly been myself enough to write before since I left Hartford — owing first to my having been sick, and then to my great anxiety about Winnie.

Now, although she has not left her bed a moment for more than a month and will be in bed some months longer, I feel light-hearted, for I am sure we are at last acting in the right direction and that she is really gaining in flesh and strength. We changed from the old treatment — of keeping her lively and stirred up — to one of perfect rest, some like Weir Mitchell's [1]

— under the direction of Dr. Putnam,[2] a nervous specialist. She actually takes eight meals or lunches a day — so that we have named her the Lunch Fiend.

Of course she has a nurse — so that I am not at all worn out; but it has been a very wearisome Summer. I hardly think we will get off to Europe before next Summer, and in that case shall go in to Boston for the Winter. Winnie will be quite well by that time, and you will make us that visit you did not make last Spring. You will soon be looking forward to getting settled in your own house after all those repairs.[3] Mr Clemens speaks enthusiastically of the improvements — but it never occured to me that the outside *could* be improved. Branford seems to have agreed with Mr Clemens. I hope you are all in as good condition as he. Mr Howells is going down to Manchester next week to pay his respects to Mrs Fields, whom we have not seen since her husband's death. She could not see people at first. Today Osgood has a lunch — *without* ladies. I think it will hardly be as jolly as usual on account of the state of the President.

Much love to Susy & Ba   Affectionately

Elinor M. Howells

1. Dr. S. Weir Mitchell of Philadelphia, known in literary history for his novels, was the originator of the "rest cure" for neurasthenia, which he had described in *Fat and Blood* (1877) and *Lectures on Diseases of the Nervous System* (1881). See David M. Rein, *S. Weir Mitchell as a Psychiatric Novelist,* New York, 1952, pp. 46–47.

2. Dr. James Jackson Putnam of the Harvard Medical School, a pioneer neurologist, later a close friend of Sigmund Freud.

3. The repairs and alterations to the Clemens house in Hartford — costing $10,000 (MTBM, p. 246) — had been begun in March 1881, when Clemens paid $1200 to a neighbor named Chamberlain for "100 feet of land adjoining our east line" to stop him from building a house there (MTBM, pp. 150–151). Clemens described the work to Mrs. Fairbanks as follows: "We have rebuilt our kitchen & doubled its size; we have torn out the reception room & made the main hall larger by that much; we have carried the driveway off to the right, past the greenhouse, & it now enters the avenue a hundred feet east of where it did before; & we have lowered that ground & brought the house up into view" (Elmira, 18 September 1881, MTMF, pp. 245–246).

Elmira, Sept. 3, 1881.

Private

My Dear Howells —

What I call my mind, has been in a state of fierce ⟨uncontrollable⟩ irruption during three successive days. The consequence is, I am on my back, burnt out, devastated, & merely smouldering. At your house (I think it was) an old idea came again into my head which I had missed from that treasury during seven or eight years or more: that of adding a character to ⟨Shakspeare's⟩ Hamlet. I did the thing once — nine years ago; the addition was a country cousin of Hamlet's. But it did not suit me, & I burnt it. A cousin wouldn't answer; the family could not consistently ignore him; one couldn't rationally explain a *cousin's* standing around the stage during 5 acts & never being spoken to: yet of course the added character must *not* be spoken to; for the sacrilegious scribbler who ventured to put words into Shakspeare's mouth would probably be hanged.[1] But I've got a character, now, who is all right. He goes & comes as he pleases; yet he does not need to be spoken to.[2] I've done the first & second Acts; but this was too much work for three days; so I am in bed. But I am in bed really as a precaution, only; it is to guard against wandering up to the study; I should go to work, sure — & I have had some rough lessons in the matter of over-work.

I say *"private"* up there, because I would not like my secret to go out of the family till my work is done — & you know I generally drop my work in the middle & then take it up again next year. I am doing this thing for the enjoyment I get out of it; therefore there is no hurry. Shall return to "Etiquette" presently.

Your experience in the matter of "Dr. Breen" & the authoress of its Doppelganger,[3] adds a rattling strong instance to my list of cases of "mental telegraphing." I guess that by the time that that magazine article is finished, it will make curious & interesting reading.[4] Seems to me there were other cases mentioned when yours was spoken of. Why the nation did I let them slip out of my mind?

Take it all around, it was a pretty fat visit that I made to Boston & Belmont.[5] Among other things, that visit cast in my way an idea toward perfecting an invention of mine; it gave me the right character for my Hamlet; the incident for my "mental telegraphy;" chapter on international etiquette; mighty nice dog; a staving good time at your house & Fairchild's — yes, & the great day of mourning, in Boston, that memorable Friday, when one could almost feel the heart of the nation beat.[6]

But I might as well be at *work* as writing 600 words & calling it recreation — wherefore, good bye, & mind you keep Winnie right where she is — it is the sure remedy. I am her fellow-rest-curist, today.   Ys Ever

Mark.

1. A reader of the present day may not be able to grasp Mark Twain's distinction between the sacrilege of putting words into Shakespeare's mouth, and what he considered the acceptable plan of adding a character to the play. In Mark Twain's defense it should be pointed out that dramatic burlesque had an extraordinary development in France, England, and the United States in the nineteenth century. There were many burlesques of Shakespeare, including several of *Hamlet,* of which W. S. Gilbert's *Rosenkrans and Guildenstern* (1891) is an example. The notion of a character who is present on the stage but ignored by all the other characters may have been suggested to Mark Twain by the character of the Lone Fisherman in the burlesque *Evangeline* of E. E. Rice and Cheever Goodwin (1877), "always present, but never speaking," who was for years "one of the commanding comic figures of burlesque" on the American stage (Odell, *Annals,* X, 193). An unfinished MS version of Act I and part of Act II of Mark Twain's burlesque *Hamlet* is in MTP.

2. The added character is a subscription book agent named Basil Stockmar, "the farmer's humble baby who was foster-brother to Hamlet, & milked the same plebeian breast along with him at a time when he wasn't as particular about the style of his company as he is now, perhaps" (DV 320, p. 3, MTP). Although Basil is farcically frightened by the ghost, he tries to get the ghost and other characters to subscribe for the book he is selling. He calls Claudius "Boss." A note for future development of the burlesque reads: "Appears with umbrella, in royal procession." Concern-

ing the other characters, Basil announces to the audience in a soliloquy: "They're on the high horse all the time . . . they swell around, & talk the grandest kind of book-talk, & look just as if they were on exhibition. It's the most unnatural stuff! Why, it ain't *human* talk; nobody that ever lived, ever talked the way they do. Even the flunkies can't say the simplest thing the way a human being would say it" (pp. 28–29). (And he gives an eighteen-line illustration of how a Shakespearian butler would order the carriage for his master.) In short, despite occasional efforts to make him speak like a stage Cockney, Basil Stockmar is an easily recognizable literary ancestor of the Connecticut Yankee.

3. When *Dr. Breen's Practice* was written and partly in type, Elizabeth Stuart Phelps submitted to the *Atlantic* her novel *Doctor Zay*, which in some of its outlines resembled Howells's story. With a note by Howells explaining the coincidence, dated Belmont, 28 October 1881, *Doctor Zay* began to appear in the *Atlantic* in April of 1882. At almost the same time that Miss Phelps told Howells the plot of her novel, he received a third story dealing with a "lady doctress" from a younger and less well-known writer. To prevent "all suspicion among our friends that I stole your plot," as he said, he took the proofs to the suburban house where the young woman lived and offered to show them to her; but she "courteously refused" to look at them, and destroyed her own MS (LinL, I, 299; J. Henry Harper, *I Remember,* New York, 1934, pp. 154–155).

4. Clemens's collection of examples of "thought transference" reached print as "Mental Telegraphy" in *Harper's Monthly* for December 1891 (DE, XXII, 111–137). An author's note stated that most of the article was written in 1878 for inclusion in *A Tramp Abroad* but omitted because he "feared that the public would treat the thing as a joke and throw it aside, whereas I was in earnest."

5. Clemens was in Boston and Belmont on 25–26 August 1881, and possibly a day or two longer (SLC to OLC, Boston, 25 August 1881, Doheny, TS in MTP; the Friday mentioned below was 26 August).

6. Howells wrote Warner that when Clemens was in Belmont, Garfield was at his lowest ebb, and the group all but shed tears (Belmont, 3 September 1881, Watkinson, AGM TS). The Howellses had close personal ties with Garfield. William Cooper Howells had advised and supported Garfield as a boy and helped groom him for Congress. Garfield in turn had secured from Grant in 1874 the appointment of W. C. Howells as consul at Quebec, and had arranged through Hayes the elder Howells's promotion to Toronto (Cady, *Road to Realism,* pp. 45, 179–180). Howells recalled staying overnight with his father at Garfield's home in Hiram, Ohio, in the early 1870's. Garfield, to whom the young editor was talking of Holmes and Longfellow and Lowell and Whittier, called his neighbors over to the veranda to listen to Howells's talk about the famous poets, "and I went on," he said, "while the whippoorwills whirred and whistled round, and the hours drew

toward midnight" (YMY, pp. 204–207). At Garfield's death, Howells wrote an obituary tribute for the November *Atlantic*, speaking of his typically American origin and character and characterizing him as "from the people, of the people, for the people."

280. CLEMENS TO HOWELLS

Elmira, Sept. 5/81.

My Dear Howells —

Osgood says something about your projecting a play. Now I think that the play for you to write would be one entitled "Col. Mulberry Sellers in Age" (75) — with that fool of a Lafayette Hawkins (aged 50) still sticking to him & believing in him, & calling him "my lord" (S. being American earl of Durham) — & has cherished his delusion until he & his chuckle-headed household believe he *is* the rightful earl & that he is being shamefully treated by the house of Lords. He is a "special-ist" & a "scientist" in various ways; makes collections of pebbles & brickbats & discourses garrulously & ignorantly over them & projects original geological "theories" &c. ⟨A selfish old hog & hypocrite, surrounded by sap-headed worshipers.⟩ Has a lot of impossible inventions, which cost somebody a good deal & then blow up & cripple disinterested parties, or poison them. Let the patent for his earldom actually arrive from England just as he is dying.[1]

Your ⟨delicate⟩ refined people & purity of speech would make the best possible back ground for this coarse old ass. And when you were done, I could take your MS & re-write the Colonel's speeches & make him properly vulgar & extravagant. For this service I would require only 3/4 of the pecuniary result. (How liberal, how lavish I seem to grow, these days!) And I would ⟨give⟩ let the play to Raymond,[2] & bind him up with a contract that would give him the belly-ache every time he read it. (I made $70,000 out of that devil with the other play.)

372

Shall we think this over? — or drop it, as being nonsense. Madam says we shall go home about two weeks hence.

Ys Ever

Mark.

1. Howells consented to collaborate with Clemens in writing the play suggested in this letter. Under various titles ("Orme's Motor," "The Steam Generator," *Colonel Sellers as a Scientist,* and finally *The American Claimant*) the project is mentioned often in this correspondence during the 1880's.

2. John T. Raymond, who had played Colonel Sellers with such success.

281. HOWELLS TO CLEMENS

Belmont, Sept. 11, 1881.

My dear Clemens:

That is a famous idea about the Hamlet, and I should like ever so much to see your play when it's done. Of course you'll put it on the stage, and I prophesy a great triumph for it. — You know I had *two* rivals in the celebration of a doctress; now comes a pretty young doctress who had written out her own adventures! How is that for mental telegraphy?

Osgood told me of your very generous willingness to pay me for my Library of humor work in advance. I know you let him know this because you supposed I needed money; but I assure you that I do not. I am as deeply touched, though, and as grateful as if I could let you do such a thing. I can wait perfectly well till the work is ready to be done. — I have written to Hay, and he has commissioned me [to] write a review of The P. and the P. for The Tribune.[1] I'm now merely waiting for the sheets.

Winny is still trying the rest cure; but we are going to get her up as soon as the doctor comes home. If she could have been allowed to read, I think the experiment might have succeeded; but I think the privation has thrown her thoughts back upon her, and made her morbid and hypochondriacal.

373

You know how fond we are of you; and I needn't tell you that we were very happy in your fruitful visit here. The only trouble is that we don't meet often enough.

— How fortunate Garfield's removal was![2] He might have been well by this time if they'd moved him a month ago. — Yesterday I wrote 30 pages on my story.[3]

Yours ever

W. D. Howells.

When do you return to Hartford?

1. This arrangement was a friendly conspiracy suggested by the absence of Whitelaw Reid, editor of the *Tribune,* on a honeymoon tour of Europe. Hay had been on the staff of the paper from 1870 to 1875. When he retired from the State Department with the advent of Garfield's administration, he returned to serve as editor from April to October 1881 (Thayer, *Hay,* I, 335, 351–352, 405, 450, 455). Clemens was eager to take advantage of this circumstance, for he believed that Reid was hostile to him and that the criticism of the powerful *Tribune* had hampered the sale of his books (letter 292). Some years later Clemens said that Edward H. House had offered to review *The Gilded Age* in the *Tribune* in 1873 "before some other journal should get a chance to give it a start which might not be to its advantage." But, according to Clemens, House reported that when he approached Reid, Reid "abused him and charged him with bringing a dishonorable proposal from Warner and me. That seemed strange; indeed unaccountable, for there was nothing improper about the proposition, and would not have been if it really had come from Warner and me. Eight or ten years later I made a like proposition to Col. John Hay when he was temporarily editing the Tribune, and when [he] accepted it I inquired into the former case. He said that the explanation of that case was, that Reid did not like House, and would not have entertained a proposition of any kind from him. However, I had taken House's report at its face value . . . I withdrew my smile from Reid, and did not speak to him again for twelve or thirteen years . . . " ("Concerning the Scoundrel Edward H. House. . . ," DV 305, TS, pp. 4–5, MTP). As a result of the arrangement whereby Howells's review was to be published before Reid's return, it appeared on 25 October 1881, despite the fact that the book was not published in the United States until the middle of December (Johnson, *Bibliography,* pp. 40–41). The title page bore the date 1882.

2. On 6 September, Garfield, who had been nursed in the White House, was moved by train to the seaside resort at Elberon, N.J. where his family was staying.

3. *A Modern Instance.* The first installment was to appear in the

Century Magazine for December. One day's composition of thirty pages (containing about one hundred words each) indicates how hard Howells was driving himself to complete a long novel.

282. HOWELLS TO CLEMENS

Belmont, Oct. 12, 1881.

My dear Clemens:

I send some pages with words queried.[1] These and other things I have found in the book seem rather strong milk for babes — more like milk-punch in fact. If you give me leave I will correct them in the plates for you;[2] but such a thing as that on p. 154,[3] I can't cope with. I don't think such words as devil, and hick (for person) and basting (for beating,) ought to be suffered in your own narration. I have found about 20 such.

Winny is at last beginning to get up. She had got into a very low condition. Yours ever

W. D. Howells.

I'm reading your book for review.

1. Howells was editing page proof of *The Prince and the Pauper* — the "sheets" mentioned in his letter of 11 September — and, as he says in his postscript, was at the same time reading the book for review.

2. Since Clemens gives his enthusiastic permission in his letter of 15 October, Howells presumably made the proposed changes in the stereotype plates.

3. A ballad supposed to be sung in snatches by Miles Hendon. Clemens revised it to remove the language Howells objected to. The printed text of the first edition shows by a slight difference of type and inking that the three words enclosed in brackets below have been changed in the plate (p. 154):

There was a woman in our town,
   In our town did dwell —
She loved her husband dearilee,
But another man [he loved she, —]

The last line quoted must originally have read,

But another man twice as well.

For further discussion of the ballad and Mark Twain's use of it, see Appendix.

283. HOWELLS TO CLEMENS

[Belmont, 13 October 1881]

My dear Clemens:

I send some passages marked, which I don't think are fit to go into a book for boys: [1] your picture doesn't gain strength from [them] and [they] would justly tell against it. I venture to bring them to your notice in your own interest; and I hope you wont think I'm meddling.   Yours ever

W. D. H.

1. Howells is continuing his careful scrutiny of page proofs of *The Prince and the Pauper*. The passages he objected to cannot now be identified. Clemens endorsed this letter on the envelope: "1881 Howells corrects Boys Story" (MTP).

284. CLEMENS TO HOWELLS

Hartford, Oct. 15/81.

My Dear Howells —

Slash away, with entire freedom; & the more you slash, the better I shall like it & the more I shall be cordially obliged to you. Alter any and everything you choose — don't hesitate.

The news from Winny is most acceptable & welcome. I do hope she will go straight on, now, to sound health, without an interruption.

I am hard at work on Capt. Ned Wakeman's adventures in heaven [1] — merely for the love of it; for laws bless you, it can't ever be published. At least not unless I trim it like everything & then father it on some good man — say Osgood. This is my purpose at present.

Twichell & I walked out to the Tower [2] & back, yesterday. He mentioned that a Yale scientist believes we shall contrive a way to communicate with the people in other planets by & by

— (by my system of Mental Telegraphy, maybe.) No other way will be possible, because only *thoughts* could be transmitted — not language, since neither of us could understand the other. As for myself, I have no difficulty in believing that our newspapers will by & by contain news, not 24 hours old, from Jupiter *et al* — mainly astronomical corrections & weather indications; with now & then ⟨an irritating⟩ a sarcastic fling at the only true religion. Ys Ever

Mark

1. Eventually published in part as "Captain Stormfield's Visit to Heaven" in *Harper's Magazine* (December 1907 and January 1908), and as a small book in 1909 under the title *Extract from Captain Stormfield's Visit to Heaven*. All the surviving text (which is, however, unfinished) was published by Dixon Wecter in *Report from Paradise*.

2. Mark Twain and Twichell often walked together to Talcott's Tower, "a wooden structure about five miles from Hartford" (MTB, p. 527).

285. CLEMENS TO HOWELLS

Hartford Oct 26/81.

My Dear Howells —

I am delighted with your review,[1] & so is Mrs. Clemens. What you have said, there, will convince anybody that reads it; a body cannot help it. That is the kind of a review to have; the doubtful man, even the prejudiced man, is persuaded, & succumbs. Henry Robinson[2] met me on the street, yesterday, & shouted in his vigorous way: "Seen that review in the Tribune? it's a good one, *mighty* good one, Clemens — done by a master, Clemens, done by a master — hope the book's half as good as the review; yes, & I hope it's half as good as the reviewer thinks it is & *believes* it is."

That document takes care of the opinions of the general press pretty effectually. That was my main solicitude; I can drop it out of my mind, now.

What a queer blunder that was, about the baronet.[3] I can't quite see how I ever made it. There was an opulent abundance of things I *didn't* know; & consequently no need to trench upon the vest-pocketful of things I *did* know, to get material for a blunder.

Charley Warren Stoddard has gone to the Sandwich Islands permanently.[4] Lucky devil. It is the only supremely delightful place on earth. It does seem that the more advantages a body doesn't earn here, the more of them God throws at his head. This fellow's postal card has set the vision of those gracious islands before my mind, again, with not a leaf withered, nor a rainbow vanished, nor a sun-flash missing from the waves, & now it will be months, I reckon, before I can drive it away again. It is beautiful company, but it makes one restless & dissatisfied.[5]

With love & thanks,   Yrs Ever

                                        Mark.

1. Of *The Prince and the Pauper,* in the New York *Tribune,* 25 October 1881, p. 6; unsigned. "I have written it solely in the interest of that unappreciated serious side of Clemens's curious genius," Howells wrote Hay. "The book has a thousand blemishes and triumphs over them" (Belmont, 16 October 1881, LinL, I, 303). In his review he emphasized Mark Twain's descriptive and narrative power as contrasted with his gifts as a humorist, which were more often praised: "Like all other romances, [the book] asks that the reader shall take its possibility for granted, but this once granted its events follow each other not only with probability but with realistic force. The fascination of the narrative and the strength of the implied moral are felt at once, and increase together to the end in a degree which will surprise those who have found nothing but drollery in Mark Twain's books, and have not perceived the artistic sense and the strain of deep earnestness underlying his humor." In its satire on monarchy, Howells declared, the book "is a manual of republicanism which might fitly be introduced in the schools."

2. A lawyer, former mayor of Hartford, and member of the Monday Evening Club.

3. It consisted in making Miles Hendon's father a baronet at a date before the rank and title existed in England. For a discussion of the problem, see Appendix.

4. Stoddard's plan had to be postponed. He wrote Mark Twain from Honolulu on 15 December 1881 that he expected to continue another year

as an editorial writer for "one of the local weeklies" in San Francisco (MTP).

5. In January 1884, not long after he finished writing *Huckleberry Finn*, Mark Twain began a novel laid in the Hawaiian Islands, which are described as a dreamy "haven of refuge for a worn and weary spirit" (DV 111, MTP; letter 344).

286. CLEMENS TO ELINOR M. HOWELLS

Hartford Nov. 25/81.

Dear Mrs. Howells —

How you startle me! Can a man so near by, fall sick, & linger along, & approach death, & a body never hear of it?[1] This is the most surprising thing that has come under my notice lately — for I am in correspondence with Boston all the time, these days.[2] I supposed Howells went to Toronto the 20th, & that he would fetch around & join Osgood & me in Montreal three or four days from now. I was counting on this programme with the entirest confidence.

I reach Boston tonight, & leave for Montreal by the earliest train in the morning. Doubtless visitors would be an incumbrance, now; nevertheless if I had got your letter an hour sooner I could have caught the noon train, & so would have looked in on you a moment this evening, ⟨if⟩ (after inquiring of the Fairchilds as to the propriety of it.)

It seems to me that Winny's long illness filled up your share of trouble; but then these things never trickle, they pour. Well, that the danger is over, is a good deal to be thankful for, anyway. Mrs. Clemens sends her love & sympathy.

Sincerely Yours

S. L. Clemens

1. In a letter now lost, Elinor Howells had evidently informed Clemens of her husband's illness. Howells said in his letter to Clemens of 19 December that he had been confined to his bed for five weeks. He told his father on 15 November 1881 that he was "down with some sort of fever . . . the result of long worry and sleeplessness from overwork . . . " (LinL, I,

303). Although he added reassuringly that it was "nothing at all serious," and that he was already recovering, the illness was evidently grave: Elinor Howells had considered him near death, and on 20 January 1882 Howells told Clemens he was five years older than he had been two months before. The "long worry" may well have been over Winifred Howells's prolonged bad health.

2. That is, with Osgood, about the publication of *The Prince and the Pauper* and the proposed trip to Canada.

287. CLEMENS TO HOWELLS

Hartford, Dec. 16/81.

My Dear Howells —

It was a sharp disappointment — your inability to connect, on the Canadian raid.[1] What a gaudy good time we should have had! Osgood & I *had* a good time, true, in the tranquil & restful practice of the vices; but we needed *you* — needed the foil & spice of a virtuous presence. The cause of your absence made the absence all the harder to bear, too.[2] Disappointed, again, when I got back to Boston; for I was promising myself half an hour's look at you, in Belmont; but your note to Osgood showed that that could not be allowed yet.

The Atlantic arrived an hour ago, & your faultless & delicious Police Report[3] brought that blamed Joe Twichell powerfully before me. *There's* a man who can tell such things himself (by word of mouth,) & has as sure an eye for detecting a thing that is before his eyes, as any man in the world, perhaps — then why in the nation can't he report himself with a pen? But he can't. One of those drenching days last week, he slopped down town with his cubs, & visited a poor little beggarly shed where were a dwarf, a fat woman, & a giant of honest eight feet, on exhibition behind tawdry show-canvases, but with nobody to exhibit to. The giant had a broom, & was cleaning up & fixing around, diligently. Joe conceived the idea of getting some talk out of him. Now that *never* would have occurred to me. So he dropped in under the man's elbow, dogged him patiently around, prodding him with questions & getting irritated snarls in return which would have finished me early — but at last one of Joe's random shafts drove the centre of that giant's sympathies somehow, & fetched him. The fountains of his great deep were broken up, & he rained a flood of personal history that was unspeakably entertaining.

Among other things it turned out that he had been a Turkish (native) Colonel, & had fought all through the Crimean war — & so, for the first time Joe got a picture of the Charge of the Six Hundred that made him *see* the living spectacle, the flash of flag & tongue-flame, the rolling smoke, & hear the booming of the guns; & for the first time also, he heard the *reasons* for that wild charge delivered ⟨from by⟩ from the mouth of a master, & realized that nobody had "blundered," but that a cold, logical, military brain had perceived this one & sole way to win an already lost battle, & so gave the command & *did* achieve the victory. And mind you Joe was able to come up here, days afterwards, & reproduce that giant's picturesque & admirable history. But dern him, he can't *write* it — which is all wrong, & not as it should be.

And he has gone & raked up the MS autobiography (written in 1848,) of Mrs. Phebe Brown,[4] (author of "I love to Steal a while Away,") who educated Yung Wing in her family when he was a little boy; & by George I came near not getting to bed at all, last night, on account of the lurid fascinations of it. Why in the nation it has never got into print, I can't understand.

But by jings the postman will be here in a minute; so, congratulations upon your mending health, & gratitude that it *is* mending; — & love to you all.   Yrs Ever

                                                                              Mark.

Don't answer — I spare the sick.

1. Clemens left for Montreal 26 November (MTBM, p. 178) in order to establish "residence" in Canada as a basis for a Canadian copyright on *The Prince and the Pauper.* He was there as late as 8 December (SLC to JRO, Montreal, 8 December 1881, AAA-Anderson Galleries catalogue, Sale No. 4217, 8–9 January 1936, Item 63). He was back in Hartford by

12 December (SLC to Joel Chandler Harris, Hartford, 12 December 1881, TS in MTP).

2. Howells was still convalescent from his long and critical illness when Clemens reached Boston on his way home (letter 288).

3. Howells's "Police Report," in the *Atlantic* for January 1882, is essentially reportage, possibly influenced by his interest in Zola, which would soon lead him to read "everything . . . I can lay my hands on" of that writer (LinL, I, 311). A decade before, Howells had sketched the recovery of a drowned prostitute's body from the Charles River in "Scene," one of the *Suburban Sketches,* but the piece was impressionistic, self-conscious, and too clearly derived from Hawthorne's *Blithedale Romance.* Here the rendering of the speech, and the appearance of the petty thieves and chronic drunkards and quarreling wives and husbands, is hard and clear. At the end of his sketch, Howells pointed up the weary patience of the magistrate and the sameness of the trials with a kind of despairing irony.

4. Phoebe Hinsdale Brown (1783–1861) was the mother of the Reverend S. R. Brown (Yale 1832), a missionary to China who served as director of the Morrison Education Society School at Macao from 1839 to 1842 and at Hongkong from 1842 to 1846, when he came back to the United States. He brought three Chinese youths to be educated here, using funds he had solicited from British and American patrons in China. The three youths boarded with Mrs. Brown near Monson, Mass., while they attended Monson Academy for a year. One of these Chinese students, Yung Wing, was able to take his A.B. from Yale and later was the first director of the Chinese Educational Mission at Hartford. In his autobiography, Yung characterizes Mrs. Brown as "a woman of surpassing strength of moral and religious character" (*My Life in China and America,* pp. 13–18, 25–30, *et seq.*).

288. HOWELLS TO CLEMENS

6, Garden St., Cambridge, Dec. 19, 1881.

Dear Clemens:

I write this from my bed, where I have now been five weeks. Most of the time I have been *recovering*; so you see how bad I must have been, to begin with. But now I am out of any first-class pain; I have a good appetite, and I am as abusive and peremptory as Guiteau.[1] These are said to be good signs.

You cannot do a greater charity than drop me a line now and

then. Notice the address: I came down here to be near the doctor.

Regards to Mrs. Clemens.　　　　Yours ever

W. D. Howells.

1. The assassin of Garfield.

289.　WINIFRED HOWELLS TO CLEMENS

Boston, Jan. 18th, 1882.

Dear Mr. Clemens

Thank you very much for that beautiful book you sent me.[1] The binding is so exquisite that I hardly dare handle it, and I have to keep looking back to the first page, on which you have written, to assure myself that it is really mine and "from the Author." It seems almost too good to believe.

I have not finished it yet, but I think the loveliest place I have read is where the Prince finds the calf in the barn and is so glad to cuddle up to something warm and alive. After his horror at first feeling something beside him it was such a relief to find what it really was that I was almost angry with the picture for letting me know a little too soon.

I was very sorry to be obliged to leave the Prince and Miles Hendon in prison today when I finished reading for, though I know it is all coming out right, I cannot bear to have such a splendid fellow as Miles suffering such indignities.

I never knew or realized before how in old times the Laws hindered instead of helping justice; and now they seem to me much worse than if there had been none.

But most of all the book makes me glad to think that I live in these times.

Please let me thank you again for remembering me in such a lovely way.　　　　Very Sincerely Yours,

Winifred Howells.

383

1. A copy of the Franklin Press edition of *The Prince and the Pauper,* printed on special paper, and bound in white cloth stamped in gold. There were apparently only fourteen copies in this edition (Johnson, *Bibliography,* p. 40); it was intended for private circulation as gifts to Susy, Clara, Edward H. House's adopted Japanese daughter Koto, and other special friends (SLC to Edward H. House [Hartford], 27 December 1881, Barrett).

290. CLEMENS TO HOWELLS

Hartford, Jan. 18, '82.

My Dear Howells —

I haven't written, partly because there wasn't anything to write about, particularly, & partly because I have been expecting to get a chance to run up to Boston for a day. However, I haven't made out to get that chance, yet, & it still hangs out in the dim remotenesses & doesn't approach worth a —— We have had a most pleasant visit from House & Koto; but they talk of leaving us tomorrow for Boston. Koto has been ill during several days, but is up & around again, now.

Charley Warner writes to Twichell (whether it was confidential or not I do not remember,) that Mrs. Dan Fisk died in the belief that she had left to her husband her splendid new palace & all its rich & painstakingly-gathered belongings (the whole worth a million) but it turns out that by an oversight which is probably embittering her heaven to-day, these things were not referred to in her will at all. Consequently they come under the head of "residue," unprovided-for, & therefore go in a solid block to the library of Cornell University. How poor, how impotent, does profanity seem when it is confronted with a *real* occasion.

Enclosed is a note from that girl of nineteen — one of our Gerhardt's.[1] You see how happily it reports progress. Return me the letter, will you. If I had that child's artless way of saying the moving thing, I would quit humor & write on the higher plane. No matter how brief a note she writes, or how scrawly or ill-spelled it may be, she is always sure to get in a sentence

or two that makes me think the Creator intended her for a
writer.   Yrs Ever

                                                          Mark.

I hear you are strong, & your old self again — Is it so?

1. Hattie Gerhardt's letter to Mrs. Clemens (Paris, 1 January 1882,
MTP) thanks the Clemenses for their generosity, mentions a visit from the
Warners, and expresses the hope that the Clemenses will come to Europe
the following summer. Karl's teacher, she adds, has said that "as a compliment to his talent & progress next week his figure should be cast in
plaster at the expense of the school. . . . It does not seem like Karl and I at all;
[semicolon supplied by Clemens] I have to pinch myself to believe it is
so — does n't it seem like a beautiful dream?"

291. HOWELLS TO CLEMENS

                  16 Louisburg Square, Boston, Jan. 20, 1882.
My dear Clemens:

    Thank you for a sight of La Gerhardt's letter. The ideal
perfection of some things in life persuades me more and more
never to meddle with the ideal in fiction: it is impossible to com-
pete with the facts. How we should all be down upon the fellow
who cheaply invented the things that these fairy-paupers are
daily living!

    There isn't anything I should like so much as the sight of
you. Do come, if you can! I can't offer you a bed, because I
haven't a house, (only a boarding-house,) but here is a room
to smoke in, and I can place three meals a day at your disposal.

    I'm *not* myself, by any means. I'm five years older than I
was ⟨six⟩ two months ago.[1] I may young up again, but that is
the present fact. The worst of it is that I work feebly and in-
effectually.[2] But I'm glad to be here on any terms: not because
this is a *very* good place, but because it's the only place I'm
sure of, and it *is* very fairish. (I mean this world; not 16
Louisburg Sq.)

    I told Osgood, the other day that I should write you about
— or against — your dynamitic life of Reid;[3] but I concluded

not to do so, partly because I did not know how you would take unprovoked good intentions from me, and partly because I believe you will be sick of the thing long before you reach the printing point.

What a beautiful book that Prince and Pauper on India paper which you gave Winny is. (There's a High Dutch sentence for you. It made me wish to spoil my small market by having my books printed no otherwise evermore.

Yours ever

W. D. Howells.

John has read the P. & P. through twice, and Pill I don't know how many times.

1. Because of his illness in November and December.
2. On *A Modern Instance*.
3. Described in Clemens's reply (letter 292).

292. CLEMENS TO HOWELLS

Hartford Jan. 28/82.

My Dear Howells:

Nobody knows, better than I, that there are times when swearing cannot meet the emergency. How sharply I feel that, at this moment. Not a single profane word has issued from my lips this morning — I have not even had the *impulse* to swear, so wholly ineffectual would swearing have manifestly been, in the circumstances. But I will tell you about it:

About three weeks ago, a sensitive friend,[1] approaching his revelation cautiously, intimated that the N.Y. Tribune was engaged in a kind of crusade against me. This seemed a higher compliment than I deserved; but no matter, it made me very angry. I asked many questions, & gathered, in substance, this: Since Reid's return from Europe, the Tribune had been flinging sneers & brutalities at me with such persistent frequency "as to attract general remark." I was an angered — which is just as good an expression, I take it, as an hungered. Next, I learned that Osgood, among the rest of the "general," was worrying over these constant & pitiless attacks. Next came the testimony of another friend, that the attacks were not merely "frequent," but "almost *daily*." Reflect upon that: "Almost *daily*" insults, for two months on a stretch. What would you have done?

As for me, I did the thing which was the natural thing for me to do; that is, I set about contriving a plan to accomplish one or the other of two things: 1. Force a peace; or, 2, Get revenge. When I got my plan finished, it pleased me marvelously. It was in six or seven sections, each section to be used in its turn & by itself; the assault to be begun at once with No. 1, & the rest to follow, one after the other, to keep the communications open while I wrote my biography of Reid.[2] I meant to wind up with this latter great work, & then dismiss the subject for good.

Well, ever since then I have worked day & night making notes & collecting & classifying material. I've got collectors at work in England. I went to New York & sat three hours taking evidence while a stenographer set it down. As my labors grew, so also grew my fascination. Malice & malignity faded out of me — or maybe I *drove* them out of me, knowing that a malignant book would hurt nobody but the fool who wrote it. I got thoroughly in love with this work; for I saw that I was going to write a book which the very devils & angels themselves would delight to read, & which would draw disapproval from nobody but the hero of it, (*and* Mrs. Clemens, who is bitter against the whole thing.) One part of my plan was so delicious that I *had* to try my hand on it right away, just for the luxury of it. I set about it, & sure enough it panned out to admiration. I wrote that chapter most carefully, & I couldn't find a fault with it. (*It* was not for the biography — no, it belonged to an immediate & deadlier project.)

Well, five days ago, this thought came into my mind — (from Mrs. Clemens's): "Wouldn't it be well to make *sure* that the attacks have been 'almost daily?' — & to also make sure that their number & character will justify me in doing what I am proposing to do?"

I at once set a man [3] to work in New York to seek out &
copy every unpleasant reference which had been made to me
in the Tribune from Nov. 1 to date. On my own part I began
to watch the current numbers, for I had subscribed for the
paper.

The result arrived from my New York man this morning. O,
what a pitiable wreck of high hopes! The "almost daily" assaults,
for two months, consist of — 1. Adverse criticism of P. & P.
from an enraged idiot in the London Atheneum; 2, Paragraph
from some indignant Englishman in the Pall Mall Gazette who
pays me the vast compliment of gravely rebuking some imaginary ass who has set me up in the neighborhood of Rabelais;
3, A remark of the Tribune's about the Montreal dinner,
touched with an almost invisible satire; & 4, A remark of the
Tribune's about refusal of Canadian copyright, not complimentary, but not necessarily malicious — & of course adverse criticism
which is not malicious is a thing which none but fools irritate
themselves about.

There — that is the prodigious bugaboo, in its entirety! Can
you conceive of a man's getting himself into a sweat over so
diminutive a provocation? I am sure I can't. What the devil
can those friends of mine have been thinking about, to spread
these 3 or 4 harmless things out into two months of daily sneers
& affronts? The whole offense boiled down, amounts to just
this: *one* uncourteous remark of the Tribune about my *book*
— not me — between Nov. 1 & Dec. 20; & a couple of foreign
criticisms (of my *writings,* not me,) between Nov. 1 & Jan. 26!
If I can't stand that amount of friction, I certainly need reconstruction. Further boiled down, this vast outpouring of malice
amounts to simply this: *one* jest from the Tribune (one can
make nothing more serious than that out of it.) One jest — &
that is all; for the foreign criticisms do not count, they being
matters of news, & proper for publication in anybody's newspaper.

And to offset that one jest, the Tribune paid me one compliment, Dec. 23, by publishing my note declining the New
York New England dinner, while merely (in the same breath,)

mentioning that similar letters were read from General Sherman & other men whom we all know to be persons of *real* consequence.

Well, my mountain has brought forth its mouse; & a sufficiently small mouse it is, God knows. And my three weeks' hard work have got to go into the ignominious pigeon-hole. Confound it, I could have earned ten thousand dollars with infinitely less trouble. However, I shouldn't have done it; for I am too lazy, now, in my sere & yellow leaf, to be willing to work for anything but love.

Being now idle once more, I could go to Boston for a day, but House & Koto are coming Monday. They leave again Tuesday. Don't you think you & Mrs. Howells could leave the children for a day or two & run down here next Tuesday or Wednesday or Thursday? Don't you think that stepping out of the rut for a moment might be both pleasant & wholesome? Mrs. Clemens & I hope you will feel that way about it & say yes to the proposition. Louis Frèchette [4] is coming to visit us Thursday Feb. 2. If you *can* come, come then, or before, or after — any date will suit us that will suit you.

I kind of envy you people who are permitted for your righteousness' sake, to dwell in a boarding house; not that I should want to *always* live in one, but I should like the change occasionally from this housekeeping slavery to that wild independence. A life of don't-care-a-damn in a boarding house is what I have asked for in many a secret prayer. I shall come by & by & require of you what you have offered me there.

I won't fret you & worry you by insisting & insisting that you & Mrs. Howells come down here, for nothing is quite so utterly hellish as one of these bowelless & implacable insisters — but I shall *yearn* for you just the same.

I wish the godly Osgood would drop in on us a little oftener. All our rooms are finished & habitable, now — & there's rugs enough, you bet! for Mrs. Clemens has been to New York.

Yours Ever

Mark

1. Warner (MMT, p. 69).

2. Clemens's Notebooks #15 and #16 contain many entries concerning the proposed biography, beginning early in December 1881 and continuing into January 1882. This incident is the prime illustration of the extraordinary violence of his anger when it was fully aroused. In a fragmentary and often cryptic list of charges, insults, and ideas for more elaborate forms of abuse which he meant to launch at Reid, the following are representative: "direct ownership of Reid by Jay Gould"; "Grant calls him Outlaw Reid"; "was Chase's dog"; "Reid the Esthete"; "chased after all the rich girls in California" (#15, TS, pp. 43–44); "In prosperity turned his back upon the man who housed & sheltered him when he came poor to N.Y. Get his name. H. L. Stewart" (#16, TS, p. 2); "There are men who require in the future wife two qualities, only — money & sex" (TS, p. 3); "Steel portraits of him as a sort of idiot, from infancy up — a dozen scattered through book — all should resemble him" (TS, p. 4); "Tribune wanted Grant to have a Brutus & be assassinated" (TS, p. 6). And — perhaps most significantly: "Preface. (Here follow slurs & sneers from Tribune, dating back to '73, & all signed WR . . .)" (TS, p. 4).

3. Clemens's nephew, Charles L. Webster, to whom Clemens wrote on 21 January 1882: "Suppose you put in an hour or two of your time for me at one of the big advertising agencies where they keep full files of the daily papers. Just quietly copy off & send to me every remark which the Tribune has made about me *since the end of October,* up to present date" (Hartford, MTBM, p. 183). On 25 January, John Russell Young (of the New York *Herald*) wrote to Clemens: "I will have *The Tribune* files looked over to see if Mr. Webster's report is confirmed. It would be a pity to make this experiment without provocation. All the effort would be lost" (New York, MTP).

4. The Montreal writer, husband of Annie Howells, who had been very gracious to Clemens during his visit there a couple of months earlier.

293. HOWELLS TO CLEMENS

16 Louisburg Square, Boston, Jan. 31, 1882.

My dear Clemens:

Your letter was an immense relief to me, for although I had an abiding faith that you would get sick of your enterprise, I wasn't easy till I knew that you had given it up. It only remains now that you should see Reid some day, and have it out with him — in perfect friendliness, as I know you can — about the original grief between you.[1] I never believed that he was a man capable of persecuting you, or systematically nagging you.

Mrs. Howells and I would like to come to your house; but for the present it isn't possible. I long to see you here, however; a thousand things are rotting in my breast for want of saying. For example, I should like to reconsider with you that play we once blocked out together.[2] Every once in a while that seems to me a great play. What did you ever do with your amended Hamlet? That was a famous idea. — I am working away all the time at the story now running in The Century.[3] I had written 1466 MS. pages before I fell sick, and I have had to revise nearly all that since I got up; and I have still 300 or 400 pages to write before the story is finished. I find that every mental effort costs about twice as much as it used, and the result seems to lack texture. I ought to have had a clean rest of three months when I began to get well.[4]

My brother Joe has a boy four years old,[5] whose favorite work is Tom Sawyer — "the fightingest and excitingest parts." This fact gave me an idea of fame. If you were John Bunyan could you expect more? I wonder how long you will last, confound you? Sometimes I think we others shall be remembered merely as your friends and correspondents.

Mrs. Howells joins me in love to both of you.

Yours ever

W. D. Howells.

1. Possibly the incident of 1873, described in note 1 to letter 281, which caused Clemens to refuse to speak to Reid for "twelve or thirteen years." Edward H. House was involved in this early affair and may possibly have been "another friend" who, in addition to Warner, told Clemens he was being persecuted by the *Tribune*.

2. About Colonel Sellers (see letter 280).

3. *A Modern Instance* (serialized in the *Century* December 1881– October 1882).

4. Howells's protracted and serious illness, as he realized, was to have its effect upon the novel he considered his "strongest." He unconsciously allowed the focus of interest to be blurred by a pair of secondary figures before he arrived at the planned conclusion of Bartley Hubbard's suit for divorce against his wife Marcia. The divorce goes through by default after

Marcia's father suffers a stroke while defending her in court against her perjured husband (Cady, *Road to Realism,* pp. 210–211; Gibson, "Introduction," *A Modern Instance,* pp. xiv–xv).

5. Joseph A. Howells, Jr.

294. HOWELLS TO CLEMENS

Boston, March 2, 1882.

My dear Clemens:

Osgood has sent me your telegram saying, "wont let howells Back out." I suppose that this means come; and I expect to be down on you by the train leaving here at 4 Saturday afternoon.[1]

Yours ever

W. D. Howells.

1. The previous correspondence concerning this proposed visit is lost. In a letter to George W. Cable dated 7 March, Howells says he had been "at Mark Twain's" the day before, "and we read aloud from the Grandissimes . . . Clemens and I went about talking Creole all day . . . " (Boston, Tilton, AGM TS). On 18 March he wrote to John Hay: "I have lately been at Hartford, and have seen a great deal of Mark Twain. We confessed to each other that the years had tamed us, and we no longer had any literary ambition: before we went to bed we had planned a play, a lecturing tour, a book of travel and a library of humor. In fact, he has life enough in him for ten generations, but his moods are now all colossal, and they seem to be mostly in the direction of co-operative literature" (Boston, LinL, I, 311–312).

295. CLEMENS TO HOWELLS

Hartford Conn. March 14th. 1882.

My Dear Howells:

That hotel bill has arrived, and in it I find this sentence, "Mr. Howells account $6.85." You need not bother to send me the money; just hand it to Osgood sometime or other, and he will credit me with it, on his books. I got finely satirized for coming home empty of information, as regards the intentions of my mother, and sister; but I said you were waiting at the door, and I could not very well stop to ask a lot of irrelevant questions. Then I was asked how long I was there, and as I had to confess to three quarters of an hour, the thing was botched again, so I dropped the subject. If I do not hear from the General within the stipulated week, I will stir him up according to the agreement.   Yours as ever,

Mark.

MS. This letter is the first of eight (295, 299, 301, 308, 317, 318, 321, 323) that are typed on a machine using sans-serif capitals with no lower-case letters. Since shorthand notes for one of them (317) are in the notebook kept by Clemens's secretary Roswell Phelps during the Mississippi River trip in the spring of 1882 (p. 16-B, MTP), the inference is that all eight letters were typed by Phelps from Clemens's dictation. A shorthand note dictated by Clemens to Phelps for an earlier letter ("Sign letter Clemens," p. 14-B) accounts for the fact that even the signatures are typed in the eight letters to Howells. Clemens does not seem to have read the letters after they were typed. They show a few corrections in a hand other than his, and contain mis-spellings and oddities of hyphenation and punctuation quite uncharacteristic of his style.

This rather cryptic letter refers to a trip which Howells and Clemens made to New York for the purpose of asking Grant — "the General" — to intercede with President Arthur in behalf of Howells's father, then U.S. consul at Toronto. With the death of Garfield, the elder Howells feared he might be discharged to make room for a new appointee. Clemens saw Grant on 10 March, and Grant promised to write the President at once (WDH to WCH, New York, 10 March 1882, LinL, I, 308–309). Howells and Clemens stayed at the Hotel Brunswick, and Howells's expenses were entered on Clemens's bill. Clemens's mother Jane and his sister Pamela were in New York visiting Charles L. Webster and his wife Annie, Pamela's daughter (Pamela Clemens Moffett to Samuel E. Moffett, Hartford, 14 March 1882, MTP). Since Jane and Pamela intended soon to come for a visit in Hartford, Livy was naturally eager to know just when they expected to arrive. Clemens had called on them, probably at Webster's house on West 57th St., in company with Howells but had neglected to establish this important date. Jane Clemens and Pamela arrived in Hartford on 13 March and stayed until 8 April (Pamela Clemens Moffett to Samuel E. Moffett, New York, 6 April 1882, MTP).

393

296. CLEMENS TO HOWELLS (SECOND LETTER)

Hartford, Mch. 14/82

My Dear Howells —

The mail has just brought me an envelop addressed to me in General Grant's handwriting, & enclosing an autograph note from the Secretary of State, worded as follows:

"Department of State,

Washington, Mch. 11/82.

My Dear General —

You may inform Mr. Clemens that it is not our purpose to make a change in the Consulate at Toronto.

"Yours Very Truly,

"Fredᵏ T. Frelinghuysen

"Genˡ. U. S. Grant." [1]

This settles the matter — at least for some time to come — & permanently, I imagine. You see the General is a pretty prompt man. Yrs ever

Mark

1. The letter from Frelinghuysen is in MTP. Howells forwarded Clemens's letter to his father with an endorsement which reads in part: "I've just got this from Clemens. It seems to me as distinct a promise for your continuance as could be given, and it leaves you to stay at Toronto if you like. Grant told Clemens at their interview that Arthur was most reluctant to make changes and that there was no probability of your removal; but in order to make matters sure he would write. Which he did, with this result" (Boston, 15 March, Houghton).

297. HOWELLS TO CLEMENS

Boston, March 15, 1882.

My dear Clemens:

Thanks and thanks for all your kindness in my father's affair. I have a letter from him in which he wishes me to express his gratitude to you, and I have just enclosed him yours in which you copy the Sec'y's letter to Grant. Now what can I do to show my sense of Grant's kindness. Would it be too hard on him if I sent him two of my books — Venetian Life and Italian Journeys? (I *can't* suppose he'd care for the novel-books.) — What a bare-faced pretence is that bill of $6.85! You have got on such a string of misrepresentations in regard to your mother's visit that you can't tell the truth about *anything*. Why, the breakfast-bacon that I ate was alone worth $6.85. But I'll settle with you! — I had such a good time that I can hardly believe our mission was not an utter failure. If I hadn't been so thoroughly broken up about my work, by going away twice, I *couldn't* believe it. But that partly persuades me. You can't think what a sneaking desire I had to get into the carriage, that day, and drive home with you and Mrs. Clemens.[1]

Yours ever,
W. D. Howells.

1. Howells and Clemens returned from New York on the same train, and Livy met Clemens with the Clemenses' carriage at the Hartford station.

298. HOWELLS TO CLEMENS

Boston, March 22, 1882.

My dear Clemens:

I hate to seem to be punching you up about the Library of Humor;[1] but I should be very glad if you could let me know whether you're likely to be able to do any work on it this summer. It's plain that you'll have no time before you go South with Osgood;[2] but do you suppose you can do your share of the reading at Elmira while you are writing at the Mississippi book? If you could, and would pass the material along to me as fast as you got it done, I would wait till October before going to Europe. I'm anxious to have the copy ready before I start, because it would give somebody a chance to cut in if we waited very long before publishing, and because life is uncertain. But if there is no hope of your working at it this summer, I had better go abroad as soon as possible, and get back the quicker.

Please give the matter consideration, and let me hear from you soon.   Yours ever

W. D. Howells.

1. Concerning the *Library of Humor,* see letter 274, note 1.

2. The trip was planned as a return to the Mississippi to gather material for chapters to be added to the "Old Times on the Mississippi" sketches that had been published in the *Atlantic* in 1875, the whole to be brought out as a subscription book.

299. CLEMENS TO HOWELLS

Hartford Conn. March 23d. 1882.

My Dear Howells: —

What would you do about the counter copy-right convention, submitted by the present British minister?. I cannot see that it differs from the one which we propose,[1] except that the foriegn author may with-hold publications of his book, during several months, and still hold his copy-right; whereas in ours, he must publish in both countries simultaneously, in order to make his copy-right good. If I have read the thing aright, this is an improvement. I am at work upon Bret Harte,[2] but am not enjoying it. He is the worst literary shoe-maker, I know. He is as blind as a bat. He never sees anything correctly, except Californian scenery. He is as slovenly as Thackeray, and as dull as Charles Lamb. The things which you and Clark have marked, are plenty good enough in their way, but to my jaundiced eye, they do seem to be lamentably barren of humor. Still I think we want some funereal rot in the book as a foil.

Ever yours,

Mark.

MS. This is one of the letters presumably typed by Roswell Phelps. See MS note to letter 295.

1. A memorial on the need for a treaty with Great Britain concerning international copyright had been drafted by Harper & Bros. in 1878 and, after widespread discussion, submitted to the State Department in 1880 over the signatures of sixty-two writers (including Clemens and Howells) and forty-four publishers. James Russell Lowell, then American minister in London, conveyed the proposals to the British government without substantial change. The basic provision of the proposed treaty was that a citizen of either country might secure copyright in the other if his book was manufactured there, published "simultaneously with its original publication in the country of the author or proprietor," and deposited for copyright within three months. The British counterproposal, submitted 22 November 1881, accepted the main outlines of the American memorial, but made the period of grace six months (*Confidential. International Copyright. Suggestions of American Authors and Publishers for an International Copyright Convention, Submitted in August, 1880, and Counter-Project Submitted by The British Minister, The Honorable L. S. Sackville West, November 22, 1881,* Department of State, Washington, February 1882 [printed, unbound], MTP).

2. Clemens was reading Harte to choose passages for inclusion in the proposed *Library of Humor.*

300. CLEMENS TO JAMES R. OSGOOD

[Hartford, late March 1882]

Dear Osgood —

Submit this to Howells, first.

S L C.[1]

P.S. It was written when the search was being made for A. T. Stewart's carcass.[2]

This from Clemens is wonderfully good

W. D. H.[3]

1. This note accompanied the MS of "The Stolen White Elephant," and the date must be shortly before 27 March 1882, when Clemens thanks Howells for reading it. Osgood was planning to bring out a volume of Clemens's stories and sketches. On 4 March, Clemens had written (using a dialect suggested by his enthusiasm for the Uncle Remus stories of Joel Chandler Harris): "I's gwyne to sen' you de stuff jis' as she stan', now; an' you an' Misto Howls kin weed out enuff o' dem 93,000 words fer to

crowd de book down to *one* book; or you kin shove in enuff er dat ole Contrib-Club truck fer to swell her up en bust her in two an' make *two* books outen her" (Hartford, Berg, TS in MTP). Osgood wrote on 15 March that he had "Explored the '*Atlantic*' files for your short articles" and listed thirteen, ranging in date from 1874 to 1880. He reported that Howells had mentioned material published elsewhere, and suggested that "perhaps you have something in MS." He continued, "There is matter enough for a book of 250 to 300 pp. 16 mo. or 12 mo. to sell for $1.00, $1.25 or $1.50" (Boston, MTP).

2. See letter 195, note 3.

3. Howells's endorsement, on the verso of the sheet.

301. CLEMENS TO HOWELLS

Hartford Conn. March 27th. 1882.

My Dear Howells: —

I can imagine the shock at Mr. Longfellows door.[1] The news of his death had a peculiar affect upon me; for it brought back that infernal breakfast[2] and made me feel like an unforgiven criminal. I think there is no reasonable doubt that I can read all summer[3] without any inconvenience. I can read all the Saturdays and Sundays and also an hour each evening prehaps. This added up makes about a month of pretty steady reading and ought to accomplish the business. I am very much obliged to you for reading "The White Elephant"[4] and also for having such a good opinion of it.   Yours as ever,

S. L. Clemens.

MS. This is one of the letters presumably typed by Roswell Phelps. See MS note to letter 295.

1. Longfellow died of peritonitis on 24 March at the age of seventy-five. The letter from Howells describing the "shock at Mr. Longfellows door" is missing from the correspondence.

2. The Whittier Birthday Dinner of 17 December 1877, discussed in letter 174, note 1. Clemens has confused this dinner with the breakfast honoring Holmes, 3 December 1879, at which he spoke with great success.

3. For the *Library of Humor*. The exact procedure was worked out on 1 April and is set forth in a memorandum submitted that day to Clemens by Osgood, with the approval of Howells and Charles H. Clark (in MTP):

   I. Mr. Clark to read first and send to Mr. Howells.

  II. Mr. Howells to read and select from Mr. Clark's Readings.

 III. Mr. Howells to cut out all matter selected by Mr. Clark and then to separate from it the material he prefers.

  IV. Mr. Howells to submit to Mr. Clemens in separate form both the material he accepts and the material he rejects from Mr. Clark's readings.

   V. After Mr. Clemens has looked at these separate groups of material, Mr. Howells to make up the book.

  VI. Mr. Howells objects to any elaborate system of classification by mutual marks but prefers the plan adopted in Hartford, viz. to mark the best 1A and the second best 1B these being intended for Volume 1 and to mark material for a possible second volume 2A & 2B.

 VII. Mr. Clark marks his selections with red and blue pencil in order of his preference, but as Mr. Howells reads *all* Mr. Clark's selections and discriminates between them Mr. Clemens is to disregard Mr. Clark's marks altogether, except so far as he prefers to go over the material which Mr. Howells rejects.

   4. "The Stolen White Elephant" was to become the title piece of the miscellany of Mark Twain's stories, essays, and speeches that Osgood was preparing to publish.

302. HOWELLS TO CLEMENS

Boston, April 7, 1882.

My dear Clemens:

We shall be glad to feed you at the appointed hour next Friday, and we shall all three [1] be at Osgoods by one o'clock waiting for you.

Mrs. Howells and I are both extremely sorry we could not come down for Sunday, but she has been away the whole week. Please remember me cordially to Miss Spaulding and give our love to Mrs. Clemens.

I've been over your material for the new book, and there is stuff for a mighty good one. That new piece about Lying [2] is capital.

Osgood will write you about the book. [3]

Yours ever

W. D. Howells.

399

1. The other two guests at the luncheon were to be Osgood and Aldrich (WDH to TBA, Boston, 11 April 1882, Houghton, AGM TS).

2. "On the Decay of the Art of Lying," which would appear as the ninth item in *The Stolen White Elephant, Etc.* (DE, XIX, 360–368). It should be pointed out that Howells was a very busy man, entirely dependent on his own labor for a livelihood. His generosity in contributing expert editorial services to his wealthier friend is even more remarkable than Clemens's nonchalance in turning over to Osgood and Howells the responsibility for deciding what to include in the book.

3. On 8 April, Osgood wrote to Clemens that Howells had advised omitting ten pieces (which are named), and continued: "This leaves 18 pieces, making in all about 80,000 words. If this is too much he has indicated 8 more which might be omitted, viz Encounter with Interviewer" (Boston, MTP) — the rest of the letter is missing. The book as published contains eighteen pieces amounting to about eighty thousand words, and includes none of the nine items Howells definitely listed for omission. Since "An Encounter with an Interviewer" is the eleventh item in the final table of contents, the inference is inescapable that Howells marked for possible omission the following additional seven pieces which appeared in the volume: "Paris Notes," "Legend of Sagenfeld, in Germany," "Speech on the Babies," "Speech on the Weather," "Concerning the American Language," "Rogers," and "The Loves of Alonzo Fitz Clarence and Rosannah Ethelton" (all in DE, XIX, 384–446).

303. CLEMENS TO HOWELLS

Hartford, Sunday, Apl [16] /82

Dear Howells —

O dear! I came home jubilant, thinking that for once I had gone through a two-day trip & come out without a crime on my soul: but it was all a delusion, nothing but a delusion — as I soon found out as I glided along in my narrative of how Aldrich — but no, I have suffered enough already, through Mrs. Clemens's measureless scorn & almost measureless vituperation. — There has been administered to me punishment enough for ten crimes; & I have punished myself enough for fifty, just in tossing, in impotent regret & humiliation, over one shameful detail after another, pointed out by Mrs. Clemens; & which cause me just as real anguish as if I could see, *myself*, that they were brutalities & stupidities & crimes, & *how* they are & *why* they are; & it makes me wish, in the bottom of my broken heart, that this might be a lesson to me, & so burnt in & *comprehended*, that I could depend on going right back there tomorrow & not only not duplicate the whole performance, but not get up another one, by inspiration, a thundering sight worse. — But oh, hell, there is no hope for a person who is built like me; — because there is no cure, no cure. If I could only *know* when I have committed a crime: then I could conceal it & not go stupidly dribbling it out, circumstance by circumstance, into the ears of a person who will give no sign till the confession is complete; & then the sudden damnation drops on a body like the released pile-driver, & he finds himself in the earth ⟨up⟩ down to his chin. When he merely supposed he was being entertaining.

But thanks be to God, there is one detail of the miserable chapter that I *didn't* tell her — because she dropped on me too soon & didn't give me a chance. And that is why my chin is still above ground. ⟨When the day comes that⟩ When I add *that* detail to her information, it will be because my wounds are not brisk enough for my requirements, & seem to need some turpentine in them.[1]

Good by. Send a line, addressed to "S. L. Samuel, Southern Hotel, St. Louis, Mo.,"[2] to say that you & Mrs. Howells & Winnie can endure a knave but can't stand a fool; & then you will feel as I do about it. And Mrs. Clemens.   Yrs Ever

Mark.

P.S.[3]

Dear Mr Howells

In spite of the apparent flippancy of Mr Clemens note he is in earnest, and last night was so troubled by what he feared (he was not quite certain) was a discourtesy toward you, that he said if he was not starting for the South tomorrow, he would go to Boston and make his apologies to you.

Although he represents me as abusing him so terribly, I think he feels that it was entirely deserved — and that a guilty conscience added to the bitterness of his sufferings.

I was very sorry that you and Mrs Howells could not come down for last Sunday as we wanted so much to have Miss Spaulding see you both. I hope we may have you all here at some not far distant time.

With cordial greeting to Mrs Howells and hoping that you will forgive Mr Clemens I am very sincerely yours

Olivia L. Clemens

1. Albert B. Paine says that the offense Clemens committed during his visit to Boston "is not remembered now" — which means that Clemens himself had forgotten what it was (MTB, p. 735). It was doubtless trivial. Clemens had all his life a tendency toward rather melodramatic self-accusation.

2. Clemens left the next day on his Mississippi journey, with Osgood and a secretary.

3. The postscript is in the handwriting of Livy Clemens.

304. HOWELLS TO CLEMENS

Boston, April 18, 1882.

You dear old fellow —

If you had given me time *I* should have written *you* a letter of humiliation and prayer; for I long ago learned (from Mrs. Howells) that I am to blame for everything; and I went to bed sick at heart, that night, wondering what I had done to spoil our arrangements, and going down among the lees and dregs of despair in self-accusation. But I'm glad you owned up, first; for now I can show your letter to Mrs. Howells and prove that *I'm* all right. But you arrogant and ridiculous boaster — did you think that *you alone* could arrange a thing so complete as that? No, sir; that failure bears the stamp of our *joint effort,* and deserves to be stored away with the Concord Centennial expedition.[1] — If General Grant had not been there to neutralize us, I think we should have had my father turned out of his place and imprisoned for life, when we went on to New York. I used to tremble when I thought of our success in that matter. "Have we lost our cunning?" I asked myself. But I need not have been troubled; this last affair shows that *when there is no outside interference,* we cannot *fail* to fail. — I am sorry that Osgood is with you on this Mississippi trip; I foresee that it will be a contemptible half-success instead of the illustrious and colossal failure *we* could have made it. But we still have our chance in the Library of Humor, (unless Clark ties our hands) and what can we not hope from the Circus? [2]

— *Ah,* how I should like to be with Osgood and you! Give my love to the young willows (not widows) along the Mississippi shore, and good bye and good luck to you both.

Yours ever

W. D. Howells.

Mrs. Howells is off at Lexington. I'll send her your letter.

1. See letter 65, note 3.
2. Howells described the "Circus" thus: "He had a magnificent scheme for touring the country with Aldrich and Mr. G. W. Cable and myself, in a private car, with a cook of our own, and every facility for living on the fat of the land. We should read only four times a week, in an entertainment that should not last more than an hour and a half. He would be the impresario, and would guarantee us others at least seventy-five dollars a day, and pay every expense of the enterprise, which he provisionally called the Circus, himself" (MMT, p. 53).

305. HOWELLS TO CLEMENS

Lexington, May 28, 1882.

My dear Clemens:

I hope you are safely and triumphantly at home again, and that you are bulging at the new book. I have heard from Osgood what a glorious time you had. — I suppose you got my letter at St. Louis.[1] We have been here for a month, and we expect to spend June at Belmont; then we go to see my father at Toronto, and we sail from Quebec July 22d. I do not know that I shall be able to see you, before we go. When are you off for Elmira?

— My brother-in-law Shepard,[2] of the American Bank Note Co., is here, and he wishes me to say to you that if you have made up your mind to buy any of their stock, he can get it for you some dollars cheaper than you can buy it in Harvard [Hartford]. They make a dividend in June. This is well-nigh Greek to me but I suppose you understand it.   Yours ever

W. D. Howells.

I'm going to write your life for The Century.[3] When and why were you born?

1. It is not extant.
2. Augustus D. Shepard, of New York, had married Elinor's sister.
3. Howells's "Mark Twain," prepared for the *Century Magazine* of September (collected in MMT, pp. 134–144), is a milestone in Mark Twain criticism, for no critic before this time had written a full-dress article about Clemens's "burning resentment of all manner of cruelty and wrong," his appeal to the experience of the average American who has "been there" too, the "ethical intelligence which underlies his humor," and the "uncommon power" of his artistry as a storyteller in the tradition of Defoe. The essay was accompanied by Abbot H. Thayer's engraving of a portrait of Clemens in an idealized, almost somber mood. Howells followed it up in the November issue of the *Century* with an equally penetrating discussion of the art of Henry James. Howells's analytic papers had been preceded in the March number by Thomas Sergeant Perry's "William Dean Howells."

306. HOWELLS TO CLEMENS

Lexington, May 30, 1882.

My dear Clemens:

Mrs. Howells knows how busy Mrs. Clemens must be, getting ready for Elmira, but she sets Europe a little higher as an exaction, and she hopes and begs that the visit may be to us.

We are going to spend the month of June at Belmont, where you can have the quietest time possible, with nine o'clock breakfast, and only Mrs. Fairchild[1] to call.

404

Come next Wednesday, and we will drive out from Boston, if the day is fine. I will meet you at the Albany depot.

Yours ever

W. D. Howells.

1. The Charles Fairchilds were close neighbors and friends of the Howellses in Belmont.

307. CLEMENS TO HOWELLS

[Hartford] June 16/82.

My Dear Howells —

I have enveloped it & prepared it to go to the Century, after Mrs. Clemens shall have had a perusal of it. Of *course* it pleases *me* — that goes without saying — & I hope the public will be willing to see me with your eyes. I shouldn't ask anything better than that. Well, I am mighty glad you had time & the disposition to write it.

We leave here the 22d,[1] D.V., — for Mrs. Clemens never alters a schedule: once decided, always decided, with her. Pity we can't see you folks again, but evidently both these families are too busy with journey-preparations to allow of any present visitings.

I don't think I ever knew Mrs. Clemens to take such a strong liking for anybody on a first acquaintance as she took to Col. Fairchild;[2] so you can assure him that if we *could* have got to Boston for his dinner, it would most surely have been done. We both wanted to go, badly enough.   Ever Yrs

Mark.

1. For Elmira.

2. The implication is that the Clemenses had made the visit to Belmont which Howells had urged on them in his letter of 30 May, and that Livy had then first met Howells's friend and neighbor Charles Fairchild. Clemens had known Fairchild for some time. In April 1880, when Clemens and Livy were visiting in Boston, they had called upon the Fairchilds but had "missed them" (letter 227).

308. CLEMENS TO HOWELLS

Hartford Conn. June 20th. 1882.

My Dear Howells:

After infinite labor and fatigue, Mrs. Clemens has got her menagerie ready to move, but now we are brought to a halt by Jean's illness. She has had hoarseness and a pretty sick time of it in one way or another, during the past four or five days, and now a rash has broken out on her which the doctor is not willing to say is not scarlet fever. So we shall stay still and wait a day or two, and then go or stay according to results.

If you would like to have $3000.00. on account,[1] I will send it with pleasure. I mention this because Osgood was here last night and says he thought you wanted to finish paying for your house before you sailed for Europe. If the money will be a convenience to you, all right; it will be no inconvenience to me to pay it.

I not only had a prodigiously good time at your house, but as usual I brought away some material results. I wrote an article for the Tile Club,[2] which would never have been written if I had not gone to Belmont. I always make expenses, and a hundred dollars or so besides out of a visit to you.

Yours as ever,

Mark.

MS. This is one of the letters presumably typed by Roswell Phelps. See MS note to letter 295.

1. Part of the fee ($5000) promised Howells for his editorial work on the *Library of Humor.*

2. "The McWilliamses and the Burglar Alarm," published in *Harper's Christmas, 1882* (pp. 28–29; DE, XXVII, 315–324), a special illustrated supplement to *Harper's Monthly,* edited by members of the Tile Club, in the form of a very large thirty-two page folio. Clemens had described the experience on which the sketch is based in his letter of 6 May 1880; his recent conversation with Howells evidently reminded him of the incident. The coincidental appearance of Howells's "The Sleeping-Car, A Farce" in the supplement (p. 2) points to a genre in which Clemens and Howells

The Clemens family in Hartford, 1884. The children, from left to right, are Clara, Jean, and Susy.

Jesse M. Leathers, American claimant to the earldom of Durham, about 1880. (See letter 228 and Appendix, pp. 869–871.)

Orion Clemens, Mark Twain's elder brother, about 1880.

wrote very much like each other — farce comedy, transmuted and heightened, from their own domestic and social experience. "Experience of the Mc-Williamses with Membranous Croup" (DE, VII, 85–94), "Mrs. McWilliams and the Lightning" (*Atlantic,* September 1880; DE, XV, 330–340), and the "Burglar Alarm" piece are dramatic sketches strongly reminiscent of the vein which Howells worked with Basil and Isabel March in his fiction and with the Robertses and the Campbells in a series of farces and comedies.

309. CLEMENS TO HOWELLS

[Hartford] June 22/82.

My Dear Howells —

I am in a state of wild enthusiasm over this July instalment of your story.[1] It's perfectly dazzling — it's masterly — incomparable. Yet I heard you read it — without losing my balance. Well, the difference between your reading & your writing is — remarkable — I mean, in the effects produced & the impressions left behind. Why, the one is to the other as is as one of Joe Twichell's booming yarns repeated by a somnambulist. Goodness gracious, you read me a chapter, & it is a gentle, pearly dawn, with a sprinkle of faint stars in it; & by & by I strike it in print, & shout to myself, "God bless us, how *has* that pallid former spectacle been turned into these gorgeous sunset splendors!"

Well, *I* don't care how much you read your truck to me, you can't permanently damage it for me that way. It is always perfectly fresh & dazzling when I come on it in the magazine. Of course I recognize the *form* of it as being familiar — but that is all. That is, I remember it as pyrotechnic figures which you set up before me, dead & cold, but ready for the match — & *now* I see them touched off & all ablaze with blinding fires. You *can* read, if you want to, but you *don't* read worth a damn. I know you *can* read because your readings of Cable & your repeatings of the German doctor's remarks prove that.

That's the best drunk scene — because the truest — that I ever read. There are touches in it which I never saw any writer take note of before. And they are set before the reader with

407

amazing accuracy. How very drunk, & how recently drunk, & how altogether admirably drunk you must have been to enable you to contrive that masterpiece! [2]

Why *I* [didn't] notice that that religious interview between Marcia & Mrs. Halleck was so deliciously humorous when you read it to me — but dear me, it's just too lovely for anything. (Wrote Clark to collar it for the "Library.")

Hang it, I know where the mystery is, now: When you are reading, you glide right along, & I don't get a chance to let the things soak home; but when I catch it in the magazine, I give a page 20 or 30 minutes in which to gently & thoroughly filter into me. — Your humor is so very subtle, & elusive — (well, often it's just a vanishing breath of perfume, which a body isn't certain he smelt, till he stops & takes another smell) — whereas you can smell other people's all the time. And your sarcasms on women & people — dern it I always take them for compliments, on the first reading.[3]

Evening. — Everything was going so well — so jubilantly. And now evidently Susie is stricken — & savagely — with this dire scarlet fever.[4]

1. *A Modern Instance,* Chapters XXIII–XXVI, in the *Century.*
2. That Mark Twain was especially impressed by the drunk scene and the threat to Bartley Hubbard of having to spend a night in jail may have been due to an episode in his life which a Harper editor persuaded Howells he should not print (in Section VIII, presumably) in MMT (F. A. Duneka to WDH, New York, 28 April 1910, Am. Antiq. Soc., AGM TS). Paine reported Howells as saying (*Notebook,* pp. 399–400) that once at the family dinner table Mark Twain remarked, "I passed a night in jail once," and when Clara, shocked, asked how he came to be in jail, he replied: "Drunk, I guess." A fellow journalist in San Francisco with whom Mark Twain carried on a violent verbal feud in 1865–66 charged that he was arrested and jailed for drunkenness, but the charge may have been a fabrication intended as humor (*Mark Twain: San Francisco Correspondent,* eds. Henry N. Smith and Frederick Anderson, San Francisco, 1957, pp. 10, 38–40).
3. The bottom half of this page has been cut off here.
4. The top of this page has been cut off.

310. HOWELLS TO CLEMENS

[Boston] June 23, 1882.

My dear Clemens:

I hope all fear of scarlet fever in the case of your little ones is past, and that you will soon be on your hill-top at Elmira.

Thank you for your very kind offer — I shall not forget it — to let me have some money on account. But the exigency is now past. I had hoped to buy my plates of Houghton, but on consideration he will not sell. But I'm just as much obliged to you, all the same.

— A composer [1] who can get the Ideals [2] to produce his opera wants me to write his libretto. [3] Will you kindly let me know just what terms you made with Raymond for production of Col. Sellers? Yours ever

W. D. Howells.

1. George Henschel (1850–1934), singer, conductor, and composer, born and trained in Germany, who had come to the United States in 1880, and who a year later had been made the conductor of the newly founded Boston Symphony Orchestra. He subsequently returned to England, had a long and distinguished career in music there, and was knighted in 1914.

2. The Boston Ideal Opera Company, formed in 1879 by Eugene Tompkins and Noble S. Hill, with S. L. Studly as director of the chorus, to produce *H.M.S. Pinafore* (Eugene Tompkins, *History of the Boston Theatre*, Boston, 1908, pp. 262–265).

3. Howells did write the libretto under the title *A Sea-Change or Love's Stowaway, A Lyricated Farce in Two Acts and an Epilogue,* but the opera was not produced until after his death. See letter 387, note 2.

311. HOWELLS TO CLEMENS (POSTCARD)

[Belmont, late June 1882]

Hurrah for your glorious letter. It has done me good! Did you send the Mark Twain review to the Century? [1] I hope the children continue to improve.[2] We are off to-morrow.[3] Good bye!

W. D. H.

MS. The date is inferred from the reference to Clemens's "glorious letter" (of 22 June) and from the postmark, which reads "Jun" although the day of the month is indecipherable.

1. Howells had submitted his essay to Clemens before it went to the magazine. In his frenzied concern over the illness of Jean and Susy, Clemens neglected to answer the question for some time. An undated postscript to a letter now lost, probably written in July, says that "Jean's well at last!" and that the "biography" has "reached the Century all right" (see the last item among the "Undated Letters and Notes" in the Appendix).

2. Apparently a letter from Clemens with reassurance about the children, written after the alarming announcement of 22 June, has been lost.

3. To visit Howells's father in Toronto before going on to Quebec, where they would embark for Europe on 22 July.

312. HOWELLS TO CLEMENS

[Toronto] July 9, 1882.

My dear Clemens:

I want a line from you before I go [1] to tell me how your little ones are. I hope Mrs. Clemens has borne the trouble of their sickness without too much suffering and that their attack has been a mild one. We shall be here a week yet.

My wife joins me in love to all of you.   Yours ever,

W. D. Howells.

1. To Europe. The Howellses were visiting Howells's father before sailing from Quebec.

313. HOWELLS TO CLEMENS

[Toronto] July 14, 1882.

My dear Clemens:

A letter will go by the same post with this to Norton,[1] who will appreciate all the circumstances, and duly hold you excused. I'm glad that you're over the cause of your trouble safely, and that you're fairly off to Elmira at last. Our best love to Mrs. Clemens, and heartfelt congratulations.

— The Madison Square Theatre Mallorys,[2] having never ceased to drum me up for a play, I told them that you and I had a comedy plotted, of which the main idea w'd be yours, and the literature mostly mine.[3] Whereupon they write proposing that I should let them have it for $4000 (the sum I proposed once to take for a play of my own) and pay you $1000 more for your "idea"! I have just written them that this is a totally different affair, and that they must treat with *you* for our joint comedy. Now, I suppose I could send you home the play completed from [your] notes (which I have) and my own; but it ought to be worth the grand cash to us. I have told them to write to you, and if they want it, I hope you'll make them pay for it; and you had better have them in writing at every step. Let me know the result in London (449 Strand, Gillig's American Exchange,) and tell me whether you wish me to go on and write up the play.   Yours ever,
                                                                    W. D. Howells.

If you write me anything before the 19th, and address me at Quebec, I can still hear from you before sailing.

1. Charles Eliot Norton. Concerning his earlier invitation to Clemens to speak at an Ashfield Academy Dinner, see letters 275 and 277. Norton had evidently sent by Howells — possibly by word of mouth — a second invitation for the summer of 1882, and Clemens had declined, in a letter to Howells now lost, on the score of his children's illness and the pressure of his writing schedule.

2. See letter 314, note 2.

3. The play which eventually became *Colonel Sellers as a Scientist.*

314. CLEMENS TO HOWELLS

                                                   Elmira, N.Y., July 24/82.

My Dear Howells —

Many thanks for your mediation with Mr. Norton, who has excused me most gracefully.[1]

Those godly thieves of the Madison Square [2] have not written me, but no matter about that: you write the play & send it along — there's plenty theatres beside the Madison, & I'll not sell it for nothing, be sure of that. And if the Madison should bid & buy, I will see [to] it that they don't play any of their religious games on us.

Jean is nearly well, at last. She has been having a rough teething time for a fortnight, & is a skeleton with the complexion of a ghost, now.

We all send love to you & yours.   Yrs Ever

Mark

You didn't intend Bartley [3] for me, but he *is* me, just the same, & I enjoy him to the utmost uttermost, & without a pang. Mrs. Clemens indignantly says he doesn't resemble me — which is all she knows about it.

1. Norton had written to Clemens from Ashfield on 18 July (MTP): "Howells has just sent me your note to him, and I write at once to do my best to put you at ease in regard to coming this summer to Ashfield. I am truly disappointed that I am again to lose the pleasure of a visit from you, on which I had been counting as *the* pleasure of the summer." Expressing sympathy for Clemens "in all the trouble you are now happily escaped from," Norton added: "Let us be thankful that the children are well, that you have pleasant days for writing your new book, and that we may count on your coming to us next summer."

2. George S. and Marshall H. Mallory, "godly" because George S. Mallory was a clergyman and the brothers edited *The Churchman* (an Episcopal weekly), and "thieves" because they had signed a contract with Steele MacKaye for his services as actor, manager, and author; had fired him before the end of the 486-performance run of his play, *Hazel Kirke*; and then had never paid him a penny in royalties, though the play continued to earn money for them for many years (Odell, *Annals*, XI, 236–237).

3. Bartley Hubbard, in *A Modern Instance*. It is true that Hubbard's quotation from Emerson, "The chief ornament of a house is the guests who frequent it," was carved on the mantelpiece of Clemens's library, and that Clemens, like Hubbard, had been a struggling journalist, and had drunk hot Scotch at night. But very probably the principal external elements of the characterization were taken by Howells from Bret Harte: ease of manner, edged wit, striking good looks and elegant dress, debts, and excessive drinking. Hubbard's separation from his wife and child and even his in-

difference to the Tilden-Hayes election also suggest Harte. More significantly, however, when Howells reread the novel many years later, he told Brander Matthews that he had drawn Bartley, "the false scoundrel," from himself. The conclusion can only be that Howells and Clemens, exemplary and devoted husbands, as novelists possessed the indispensable gifts of empathy and imagination, and that the occasional harshness in Howells's characterization of Bartley revealed a fear of what he himself might become in less fortunate circumstances (Everett Carter, *Howells and the Age of Realism,* Philadelphia, 1954, p. 108; Gibson, "Introduction," *A Modern Instance,* pp. vi, xvii–xviii).

315. HOWELLS TO CLEMENS

London, Sept. 1, 1882.

My dear Clemens:

You ought to have been yesterday with Osgood, Hutton [1] and me at Oxford. We started with the intention of coming back on a Thames steamer. Of course we failed in that, but what I was thinking was that if you were along, you could have kept us, with my help, from getting to Oxford. We had a beautiful time in that beautifulest of old towns, and almost walked our legs off seeing it. We stopped at the Mitre tavern, where they let you choose your dinner from the joints hanging from the rafter, and have passages that you lose yourself in every time you try to go to your room. But you have been there. — We *did* do a few miles of the Thames, in a sort of big steam launch, and if it had not rained all the way, and Osgood hadn't had the rheumatism, and another fellow the diarrhoea, we should have enjoyed it. We came pretty near it, as it was.

We are in the prettiest and comfortablest kind of lodging in South Kensington (address me care American Exchange, however) where our five rooms with private dining-room and exquisite feed cost us only $50 a week (we paid $75 for *two* rooms in Boston) and here we expect to stay a month longer. We have seen lots of nice people, and have been most pleasantly made of; but I would rather have you smoke in my face, and *talk* for half a day — just for *pleasure* — than go to the best house or club in London. And yet some of these people are delightful — Boughton,[2] for example, and Alma Tadema,[3] above all. *What* a good fellow Tadema is! And I am sending you a card by a wonderful painter, Herkomer,[4] who is going to America next month. — John Hay has been here, and Mrs., and they are coming back in a day or two. Couldn't you and Mrs. Clemens step over for a little while? Warner lunched with us on Tuesday, and is to return from Scotland for a big dinner that Osgood gives next Thursday. — W., Gen. Hawley, John Hay, Boughton, Aldrich, Tadema and W. D. H.[5] How does that strike you as a time? — The children and Mrs. Howells are enjoying themselves immensely, and all three of the chicks are keeping diaries. John's is worth reading. He's developing quite a style, and *sees* with eyes all round his head.

Mrs. Howells sends her love to both of you, and rejoices with me that you are so well out of that terrible scarlet fever peril. We quaked for you when we heard what was the matter with your children.

Did you ever hear from the Madison Theatre Mallorys? — I suppose Clark has the consumption again: I don't get any material from him for the Library of H.   Yours ever
W. D. Howells.

1. Laurence Hutton, a New York drama critic and bibliophile.

2. George Henry Boughton, a painter of English birth, who had lived for many years in New York before taking up his residence in London.

3. Sir Lawrence Alma-Tadema, also a painter. He was a native of Holland but had become a British subject.

4. Sir Hubert von Herkomer, yet another painter. Born in Bavaria, he passed six years of his boyhood at Cleveland, Ohio, but had lived in England since 1857 and would become professor of fine arts at Oxford in 1885.

5. In a letter to Clemens written from Boston on 21 September (MTP) soon after his return to the United States, Osgood said that his dinner (on 7 September) at the Hotel Continental in Regent St. was "a great success — no speeches." Among the guests, in addition to those mentioned by Howells, were Henry James, Edwin Booth, Laurence Hutton, Moncure D. Conway, W. Mackay Laffan, Clarence King, and Bret Harte.

316. HOWELLS TO CLEMENS

Le Clos, Villeneuve,
Vaud, Switzerland,
Oct. 17, 1882.

My dear Clemens:

What you want to do is to pack up your family, and come to Florence for the winter. I shall have my story [1] as good as done when I get there early in December, and shall be ready to go to work with you on the great American comedy of "Orme's Motor" which is to enrich us both "beyond the dreams of avarice." Its fate needn't rest with the Madison Squarers.[2] We can get it played. We could have a lot of fun writing it, and you could go home with some of the good old Etruscan malaria in your bones, instead of the wretched pinch-beck Hartford article that you're suffering from now. I know Mrs. Clemens would like to come; and Osgood could collect that royalty for you in H., on your book.[3] If you come, you need not kill Clarke; you could bring his material with you.

We are having a good, dull, wholesome time in this little pension on the shore of Lake Leman, within gunshot of the Castle of Chillon; but a thousand jokes rot in my breast every day for want of companionship. Think of a country where they are so proud of their manure heaps that they plait the edges of the straw that sticks out. John and I make the most of each other; but he finds me poor company, and the fact is his perpetual questions pall upon me.

We have now been here a month, and we have not spoken to an American soul, and to but one English, and that was a she-soul. Think of the amount of talk that must be bottled up in us! And the capacity for listening that I must have acquired. It is a great opportunity for you. Besides, nobody over there likes you half so well as I do. — We are about three miles from Montreux, a little place full of half-sick, indigent English and predatory Russians, and it is worth the voyage across

415

the Atlantic to see the gloomy splendor with which they stare at and wont speak to one another in the street. Sometimes I'm a little down-hearted, but I always cheer up when I go to Montreux. — In London, Hay and King [4] went to hear Bret Harte read a comedy he has been colaborating with a Belgian lady.[5] He has turned the "Luck" of Roaring Camp into a girl, and brought her to Paris, with all his Californians, where she has adventures.[6]

All the family joins me in love to yours.   Yours ever

W. D. Howells.

1. *A Woman's Reason,* partially written in 1878, which Howells was now determined to finish.

2. See letter 314, note 2.

3. Clemens was convinced the American Publishing Co. had not paid him all that was due him in royalties on *The Prince and the Pauper* and other books. During the summer he had had a man going over the books of the company in the hope of discovering some irregularity. He must have mentioned this matter in a letter to Howells now lost (SLC to CLW, Hartford, 8 July 1882; Elmira, 26 July 1882; MTBM, pp. 188–190, 192).

4. Clarence King, whom Clemens had mentioned familiarly to Howells in his letter of 7 May 1875, was the brilliant geologist ("the best and brightest man of his generation," according to Henry Adams) who had become the first director of the U.S. Geological Survey in 1878, at thirty-six, but had resigned in 1881 in order to engage in mining speculations. Howells had published King's papers on "Mountaineering in the Sierra Nevada" in the *Atlantic* in 1871, and he contributed an essay "Meetings with King" to the *Clarence King Memoirs* (New York, 1904) in which he relates an anecdote concerning the dinner given by Osgood in London on 7 September 1882. When King spoke of "several Fortuny watercolors" he had recently bought in Paris, Howells recalled having exclaimed, "Ah, what a fortunate man, to own Fortunys!" King immediately promised to give him one. "I thought that a good bluff," Howells wrote, "and he let me laugh. But the next morning the Fortuny showed itself at my lodgings . . ." (pp. 144–145).

5. Madame Van de Velde, wife of the chancellor of the Belgian Legation in London, and mother of nine children. She and her husband had made Harte almost a member of their household. A literary critic of some standing, she translated several of Harte's stories into French, but was also happy to serve him as amanuensis.

6. Daniel Frohman planned to produce the dramatization of "The Luck of Roaring Camp" at the Madison Square Theatre in the autumn of 1884, but eventually decided against it, and the play was never produced (George R. Stewart, *Bret Harte Argonaut and Exile,* Boston, 1931, pp. 280–281).

317. CLEMENS TO HOWELLS

Hartford Conn. Oct. 30. 1882.

My dear Howells,

I do not expect to find you, so I shan't spend many words on you to wind up in the perdition of some European dead letter office. I only just want to say that the closing installments of the story [1] are prodigious. All along I was afraid it would be impossible for you to keep up so splendidly to the end; but you were only, I see now, striking eleven. It is in these last chapters that you struck eleven [twelve]. Go on and write, you can write good books yet, but you can never match this one. And speaking of the book, I inclose something which has been happening here lately.[2]

We have only just arrived at home,[3] and I have not seen Clark on our matters.[4] I cannot see him or any one else, until I get my book [5] finished. The weather turned cold, and we had to rush home, while I still lacked thirty thousand words. I had been sick and got delayed. I am going to write all day and two thirds of the night, until the thing is done, or break down at it. The spur and burden of the contract are intolerable to me. I can endure the irritation of it no longer. I went to work at nine o'clock yesterday morning, and went to bed an hour after midnight. Result of the day, (mainly stolen from books, tho' credit given,) [6] 9500 words. So I reduced my burden by one third in one day. It was five days work in one. I have nothing more to borrow or steal; the rest must all be writing. It is ten days work, and unless something breaks, it will be finished in five.

We all send love to you and Mrs. Howells, and all the family.

Yours as ever,

Mark.

MS. This is one of the letters presumably typed by Roswell Phelps. See MS note to letter 295.

1. *A Modern Instance.*

2. Apparently a clipping from a newspaper, now lost.

3. From Elmira.

4. The *Library of Humor.*

5. *Life on the Mississippi.*

6. Chapters XXVII and XXIX quote at length from the books of earlier travelers.

318. CLEMENS TO HOWELLS

Hartford, Nov. 4th. 1882.

My dear Howells: —

Yes, it would be profitable to me to do that, because with your society to help me, I should swiftly finish this now apparently intermidable book.¹ But I cannot come, because I am not boss here, and nothing but dynamite can move Mrs. Clemens away from home in the winter season.

I never had such a fight over a book ² in my life before. And the foolishest part of the whole business is, that I started Osgood to editing it before I had finished writing it. As a consequence, large areas of it are condemned here and there and yonder, and I have the burden of these unfilled gaps harassing me and the thought of the broken continuity of the work, while I am at the same time trying to build build the last quarter of the book. However, at last I have said with sufficient positiveness that I will finish the book at no particular date; that I will not hurry it; that I will not hurry myself; that I will take things easy and comfortably, write when I choose to write, leave it alone when I so prefer. The printers must wait, the artists, canvassers, and all the rest. I have got everything at a dead stand-still, and that is where it ought to be, and that is where it must remain; to follow any other policy would be to make the book worse than it already is. I ought to have finished it before showing it to anybody, and then sent it across the ocean to you to be edited, as usual; for you seem to be a great many shades happier than you deserve to be, and if I had thought of this thing earlier, I would have acted upon it and taken the tuck somewhat out of your joyousness.

In the same mail with your letter, arrived the inclosed from

Orme the Motor Man.[3] You will observe that he has an office. I will explain that this is a law office; and I think it probably does him as much good to have a law office without anything to do in it, as it would another man to have one with an active business attached.

You see he is on the electric light lay now. Going to light the city and allow me to take all the stock if I want to. And he will manage it free of charge. It never would occur to this simple soul how much less costly it would be to me, to hire him on a good salary not to manage it. Do you observe the same old eagerness, the same old hurry, springing from the fear that if he does not move with the utmost swiftness, that colossal opportunity will escape him? Now just fancy this same frantic plunging after vast opportunities, going on week after week with this same man, during fifty entire years, and he has not yet learned, in the slightest degree, that there isn't any occasion to hurry; that his vast opportunity will always wait; and that whether it waits or flies, *he* certainly will never catch it. This immortal hopefulness, fortified by its immortal and unteachable stupidity, is the immortal feature of this character, for a play; and we will write that play. We should be fools else. That staccato post-script reads as if some new and mighty business were imminent, for it is slung on the paper telegraphically, all the small words left out. I am afraid something newer and bigger than the electric light is swinging across his orbit. Save this letter for an inspiration. I have got a hundred more.

Cable has been here, creating worshipers on all hands.[4] He is a marvelous talker on a deep subject. I do not see how even Spencer, could unwind a thought more smoothly or orderly, and do it in cleaner, clearer crisper English. He astounded Twichell with his faculty. You know that when it comes down to moral honesty, limpid innocence, and utterly blemishless piety, the apostles were mere policemen to Cable; so with this in mind you must imagine him at a mid-night dinner in Boston the other night, where we gathered around the board of the Summerset Club; Osgood, full, Boyle Oreily,[5] full, Fairchild responsively loaded, and Aldrich and myself possessing the floor, and properly fortified. Cable told Mrs. Clemens when he returned here, that he seemed to have been entertaining himself with horses, and had a dreamy idea that he must have gone to Boston in a cattle-car. It was a very large time. He called it an orgy. And no doubt it was viewed from his standpoint.

I wish I were in Switzerland, and I wish we could go to Florence; but we have to leave these delights to you; there is no helping it. We all join in love to you and all the family,

Yours as ever,

Mark.

MS. This is one of the letters presumably typed by Roswell Phelps. See MS note to letter 295.

1. Clemens is replying to Howells's invitation to join him in Europe.

2. Still *Life on the Mississippi*.

3. Orion Clemens. The letter from him which Clemens sent to Howells has disappeared.

4. George W. Cable had visited the Clemenses in Hartford late in October; he attended a meeting of the Monday Evening Club on the twenty-third (*List of Members of the Monday Evening Club Together with the Record of Papers Read at Their Meetings 1869–1954*, p. 37; Cable to SLC, New Orleans, 7 November 1882, MTP).

5. John Boyle O'Reilly was a Catholic poet who lived in Boston.

VII

A MIGHTY GOOD BOOK

(1 8 8 3 – 1 8 8 4)

VII

(1 8 8 3 – 1 8 8 4)

"I thought that the bits from Huck Finn told the best — at least I enjoyed them the most. That is a mighty good book, and I should like to hear you read it all" (WDH to SLC, Boston, 14 November 1884, MTP)

Life on the Mississippi was published in the spring of 1883, and during the next few months Clemens finished *Huckleberry Finn* in a continuous outpouring of creative energy. The Howellses, returning from their year in Europe in July, rented a house in Louisburg Square on Beacon Hill where they lived until Howells bought a house on Beacon Street a year later. This was a productive period for him also: between July 1883 and the end of 1884 he completed *A Woman's Reason,* wrote all of *The Minister's Charge,* and almost completed *The Rise of Silas Lapham.* Furthermore, he and Clemens worked on several dramatic projects. They finished their play about Colonel Sellers and engaged in complex but ultimately frustrating negotiations for its production, with the Mallory brothers of the Madison Square Theatre and with the actor-manager John T. Raymond. Howells's opera, *A Sea-Change,* with music by George Henschel, was scheduled for production in Boston, but the plan was dropped because of the accidental death of the manager. Clemens was likewise unsuccessful in his efforts to find producers for his dramatizations of *Tom Sawyer* and *The Prince and the Pauper.* Early in 1884 he decided to end his increasing dissatisfaction with Osgood by establishing his own publishing company in New York under the management of his nephew, Charles L. Webster. *Huckleberry Finn* was the first book published by the new firm (early in 1885). Howells devoted even more attention to the manuscript and proofs of this book than he had to earlier books by Clemens. The friends parted company politically in 1884 when Clemens joined the Mugwumps to support Cleveland for President against Blaine.

319. CLEMENS TO HOWELLS

Hartford Feb. 5/83.

Dear Howells:

I haven't anything to write, except all hands well. But I thought I'd send you this, to show you that we are making progress (this family.) OVER

The children's governess required them to set down the names of such celebrities as they could recal. You have here the result.[1]

Achtungsvoll

Mark

MS. The note is written at the bottom and on the back of a sheet of ruled paper containing lists of "Famous Men" and "Famous Women" which Clemens labeled "Clara's." Clemens enclosed a similar sheet which he labeled "Susie's List." The headings and a few corrections of the spelling are in an adult hand, presumably that of the governess, Miss Bridges.

1. Susy's Famous Men were: "Longfellow, Papa (Mark Twain), Columbus, Teneson, Ferdinad," with "Isibela" canceled. Her Famous Women were, with some help from the teacher, "Boadicea, Bloody Mary, Mrs. Lisy Champtney, Isabella." (Mrs. Elizabeth Williams Champney was the wife of the painter J. Wells Champney.) Clara's Famous Men were: "Columbus, Mr. Clemens, Mr. Millet, Henry Hudson, Mr. Dickens"; her Famous Women, "Queen Isebella, Mrs. Stowe, Miss Bridges." In 1906, when Howells returned Clemens's letters for use in the preparation of Albert B. Paine's biography, Clemens wrote the following comments on them (MTP):

"*Notes.* Susy was 11, Clara 9. Mrs. Harriet Beecher Stowe was our nearest neighbor; that accounts for her appearance among the renowned. I suppose fathers are usually great men to their children; so I may not in fairness charge this couple with lifting me among the elect with designs upon me slanting toward candy. But I am not so sure about Miss Bridges's case. She being the governess, ⟨it is possible that⟩ Clara's promotion of her has a suspicious look about it. It seems to me to smell of flattery.

"The Millet referred to is Frank W., the artist. His promotion was prompted by love, & is above criticism. S L C"

424

A MIGHTY GOOD BOOK (1883–1884)

Florence, Feb. 10, 1883.

My dear Clemens:

I have n't written you because I've been ashamed to do so. Our two months in Florence have been the most ridiculous time that ever even half-witted people passed. We have spent them in chasing round after people for whom we cared nothing, and being chased by them. My story [1] isn't finished yet, and what part of it is done bears the fatal marks of haste and distraction. Of course I haven't put pen to paper yet on the play.[2] I wring my hands and beat my breast when I think of how these weeks have been wasted; and how I have been *forced* to waste them by the infernal social circumstance from which I couldn't escape. It appears that a man cannot go and stay where he likes because his fellow-beings are there, and want him to dine and sup with them. In all Florence there are about a dozen persons whom I wished to see, and — But what's the use? Now we are starting to Siena, by way of Pisa, and expect to return here for the last half of March, and shall not let any one know we're here.

I should like to have some news of you, but I suppose it's asking too much, and I shall not blame you if you don't write any more. However, my address is still Gillig's American Exchange, 449 Strand, London, if you feel merciful. There is some prospect that my new story will be so bad that nobody will care to see me more; otherwise, a howling wilderness is what I'm after for a residence. — John Hay and his wife are here, and that's some satisfaction, and I've met half a dozen men of as many nations whom I was extremely glad to meet. Hay seems to be pretty well, but doesn't believe it. He tells a curious story about Clarence King and young Baron Rothschild,[3] who has taken a prodigious fancy to King and all but sleeps with him; chases him round and wants him to come and spend the rest of his life with him. — How comes on the Library of Humor; or has Clark concluded to let it rest till I get home? We expect to be in Venice a month, and to sail from England in August. — Winny is not so well as when we left home; I think the excitement of travel is bad for her, as it is for every reasonable being. We shall not take her to Rome, even if we go; which now seems uncertain.

This is a poor letter, but it will serve to show that I am still   Yours ever

W. D. Howells.

1. *A Woman's Reason,* which had begun serially in the *Century* for February.

2. Eventually to be called *Colonel Sellers as a Scientist.*

3. Lionel Walter Rothschild, second Baron, of the wealthy banking family, at this time fifteen years old.

321. CLEMENS TO HOWELLS

Hartford, March 1st. 1883.

My dear Howells: —

We got ourselves ground up in that same mill, once, in London, and another time in Paris. It is a kind of fore taste of hell. There is no way to avoid it except by the method which you have now chosen. One must live secretly and cut himself utterly off from the human race, or life in Europe becomes an unbearable burden and work an impossibility. I learned something last night, and maybe it may reconcile me to go to Europe again sometime. I attended one of the astonishingly popular lectures of an idiot by the name of Stoddard,[1] who exhibits interesting stereopticon pictures and then knocks the interest all out of them with his chuckleheaded comments upon them. But all the world go there to look and listen, and are apparently well satisfied. And they ought to be fully satisfied, if the lecturer would only keep still, or die in the first act. But he described how retired tradesmen and farmers in Holland load a lazy scow with the family and the household effects, and then loaf along the water-ways of the Low Countries all the summer long, paying no visits, receiving none, and just lazying a heavenly life out in their own private unpestered society, and doing their literary work, if they have any, wholly uninterrupted.[2] If you had hired such a boat and sent for us we should have a couple of satisfactory books ready for the press now with no marks of interruption, vexatious wearinesses, and other hellishnesses visible upon them anywhere. We shall have to do this another time. We have lost an opportunity for the present. Do you forget that heaven is packed with a multitude of all nations and that these people are all on the most familiar how-the-hell-are-you footing with Talmadge swinging around the circle to all eternity hugging the saints and patriarchs and archangels, and forcing you to do the same unless you choose to make yourself an object of remark if you refrain? Then why do you try to get to heaven? Be warned in time.[3]

We have all read your two opening numbers in the Century,[4] and consider them almost beyond praise. I hear no dissent from this verdict. I did not know there was an untouched personage in American life, but I had forgotten the auctioneer. You have photographed him accurately.

I have been an utterly free person for a month or two; and I do not believe I ever so greatly appreciated and enjoyed and realized the absence of the chains of slavery as I do this time. Usually my first waking thought in the morning is, being read [dead?], I have nothing to do today, I belong to nobody, I have ceased from being a slave. Of course the highest pleasure to be got out of freedom, and the having nothing to do [,] is labor. Therefore I labor. But I take my time about it. I work one hour or four as happens to suit my mind, and quit when I please. And so these days are days of entire enjoyment. I told Clark the other day to jog along comfortably and not get in a sweat. I said I believed you would not be able to enjoy editing that library over there, where you have your own legitimate work to do and be pestered to death by society besides; therefore I thought if he got it ready for you against your return, that that would be best and pleasantest.

You remember Governor Jewell,[5] and the night he told about

Russia down in the library. He was taken down with a cold about three weeks ago, and I stepped over one evening, proposing to beguile an idle hour for him with a yarn or two, but was received at the door with whispers, and the information that he was dying. His case had been dangerous during that day only and he died that night two hours after I left. His taking off was a prodigious surprise, and his death has been most widely and sincerely regretted. Wm. E. Dodge, the father-in-law of one of Jewell's daughters, dropped suddenly dead the day before Jewell died, but Jewell died without knowing that. Jewell's widow went down to New York, to Dodge's house, the day after Jewell's funeral, and was to return here day before yesterday. And she did — in a coffin. She fell dead, of heart disease, while her trunks were being packed for her return home. Florence Strong, one of Jewell's daughters, who lives in Detroit, started east on an urgent telegram, but missed a connection somewhere, and did not arrive here in time to see her father alive. She was his favorite child, and they had always been like lovers together. He always sent her a box of fresh flowers once a week to the day of his death; a custom which he never suspended even when he was in Russia. Mrs. Strong had only just reached her western home again, when she was summoned to Hartford to attend her mother's funeral.

If you should visit Paris, I want you and all the family to be sure and look up our little sculptor, Karl Gerhardt, who seems to be coming along admirably. If he does not kill himself with over work — which he is trying his best to do — he is bound to make a fine success in his art. His address is 11 Rue Boissonade.

This is a deadly winter in this region. Pneumonia is slaughtering people right and left. That was Jewell's disease. The death rate of Hartford for the month of January, was twenty-eight to the thousand. This is thirty or thirty-five per cent bigger than it ought to be. Ninety-nine people died of pneumonia alone in New York last week.

I have had the impulse to write you several times, but was just idiot enough to forget how to get a letter to you. I shall try to remember better henceforth.

With sincerest regards to all of you,   Yours as ever,

                                              Mark.

MS. This is one of the letters presumably typed by Roswell Phelps. See MS note to letter 295.

1. John Lawson Stoddard, an immensely successful practitioner of the travelogue, who pioneered in using the stereopticon. He collected his illustrated talks as *John L. Stoddard's Lectures* in 10 volumes in 1897–98.

2. The effect upon Mark Twain of Stoddard's slides depicting a lazy existence aboard a Dutch scow suggests that he may have taken up the MS of *Huckleberry Finn* again, after driving himself hard to complete *Life on the Mississippi.* "You feel mighty free and easy and comfortable on a raft," Huck says (Chapter XVIII). On 22 August 1883 Mark Twain would write Howells that he had almost finished this book.

3. This passage may mean that Mark Twain was also working again on "Captain Stormfield's Visit to Heaven." The Reverend Thomas DeWitt Talmage, a Brooklyn preacher, had avowed in sermons that the first thing he would do when he got to heaven would be to "fling his arms around Abraham, Isaac and Jacob, and kiss them and weep on them" (*Report from Paradise,* ed. Dixon Wecter, p. 60).

4. The first chapters of *A Woman's Reason* in the February and March issues of the *Century,* in which Howells had sketched a lively, unscrupulous young auctioneer selling the old Harkness house on Beacon Hill (Chapter V).

5. Marshall Jewell, the wealthy editor-owner of the Hartford *Courant.* He had been three times Governor of Connecticut, and had served as Postmaster General under Grant (NF, pp. 50, 100–101).

322. HOWELLS TO CLEMENS

Venice, April 22, 1883.

My dear Clemens:

I enclose a letter just come from the Madison Sq. Theatre people,[1] with a note which you can forward if you like. If you can get the right terms from them, with absolute surety as to pay in the event of success, it would be worth our while to give the month of October to working on that play. There is the making of a good comedy in it without any doubt — something that would run like Scheherazade, for A Thousand and One

429

Nights. But they ought to be made to understand that we could not fool away a month's time for nothing: I for my part should want to be assured a Thousand Dollars, whether they ever put the play on the stage or not. Then if they did produce it, the grand cash should be ours. Please let me know whether you write them, and if you do, what, and with what result.

There was a Prince Edwards Island woman in our pension at Siena, who was of Sienese origin, and had returned to her native city after twenty years' of misery in the British Provinces. She had brought from our hemisphere two books: the Bible and — Roughing It; which she appeared to think equally inspired and binding. When we told her that we knew you, the effect was much as if we had said we knew St. Mathew. I give you the bare bones of a feast, on which I'll enlarge when we meet. She said she often took the book — Roughing It — and showed the pictures to her Italian friends.

You wont expect me to say anything about Venice, merely because I'm here, will you? The idea of being here is benumbing and silencing. I feel like the Wandering Jew, or the ghost of the Cardiff Giant.[2] I used sometimes to dream of having come back, but nothing was ever so strange as this reality, for it isn't strange at all — so far as I'm able to express it.[3]

Winny, who had been drooping in Florence, and getting so that she could not sleep, has recovered in her native air as if by magic; she takes the deadly romantic view of Venice,[4] and doesn't hesitate to tell me that I did the place great injustice in my books. It is quite amusing. She thinks it is *all* beauty and gayety; but for my part, the poor old place is forlorner and shabbier than ever. I don't think I began to see the misery of it when I lived here. The rags and dirt I witnessed in a walk this morning sickened me.

All join in regards to you all.　　　Yours ever

W. D. H.

1. Marshall H. Mallory to Howells, New York, 6 April 1883 (MTP). The letter was part of the Mallory brothers' continuing negotiation for *Colonel Sellers as a Scientist*. Explaining that a letter to Clemens had brought no response, Mallory said: "Frankly, I need, and am anxious to

attach your name to the Madison Square Theatre. I say 'need' because I am trying to keep only American plays on my stage and so need American writers, 'anxious' because not only had your name been partially announced, but I must see my way ahead. There is no doubt I can pay you as much as or more than you ever received for any literary work." The note to Mallory enclosed by Howells is not extant.

2. The Cardiff Giant was a supposedly petrified man of giant size which a farmer pretended to have dug up near Cardiff, N.Y., in 1869. The farmer made a considerable sum of money exhibiting his hoax.

3. Howells would soon transmute his sense of the familiar-and-strange in the city he had known so well twenty years earlier, into the feelings of Colville, his point-of-view hero in the novel *Indian Summer*.

4. Winny Howells's attitude toward Venice may have been influenced by the fact that she was born there. In any event, her young enthusiasm would give color to the portrait of Imogene Graham in the same book.

323. CLEMENS TO HOWELLS

Hartford, May 18th. 1883.

My Dear Howells: —

I have just sent your note to the godly Mallory, and said that we would leave the matter just as it stands, not only until your return but until the play shall be completed. Said I did not wish to bind myself to write a play. Next October you will come here and roost with me, and we will lock ourselves up from all the world and put the great American comedy through. If we ever come to deal with those people, we shall not do it in person, but through the ablest legal talent that New York can furnish; and if they get ahead of us they will have to rise early. [1]

When I was in Montreal three or four days ago, acquiring British copyright whilst my new book [2] was being issued in London, that startling news came of the suicide of John Hay's father-in-law.[3] And among the same telegrams was the news that Hay and his wife sailed from Liverpool just in time to escape hearing of the catastrophe. The suicide lies waiting alongside President Garfield, and these children are still enjoying themselves on the Atlantic, unaware of what is in store for them. How odd and strange and wierd all this is. Apparently nothing pleases the Almighty like the picturesque.

I owe much to you. For during all these months, wherein we have been quarantined during the third of a year with wearisome revisitings of scarlet fever, and wherein Mrs. Clemens has been assaulted by many and rather alarming distempers, and been obliged to keep her bed for weeks, my great and sufficient solace has been that it is you who are writhing in the European hell and not me.[4] I have imagined your sufferings, and reflected that they were not mine, and have enjoyed them to ecstasy. Those of us who are not in Europe, and can so conduct ourselves as not to be obliged to go thither, ought never to forget for a single day to be duly and rightly thankful for the partialities thus shown us by a discriminating Providence over our less fortunate friends. Come home; and let this experience be a lesson to you.

If you should strike Paris, you must look up the Gerhardts, 11 rue Boissonnade. Meantime we join in love to you all, and I humbly try to be sorry for you.   Yours as ever,

Mark.

MS. This is one of the letters presumably typed by Roswell Phelps. See MS note to letter 295.

1. Clemens's consistently sardonic attitude toward the Mallory brothers — Marshall H. and George S. — was soon to receive what he considered complete justification. He had lent $3000 to William Gillette to help Gillette finance the production of his play *The Professor,* and on 13 September 1883 Gillette wrote that he was "having no end of trouble" collecting money which the Mallorys owed him. On 19 September 1883 Clemens addressed to the Mallorys one of his characteristic letters to let off steam, which was apparently not mailed:
"Dear Sirs:

"You have a contract with Mr. Will Gillette; & I am aware that you are trying (as usual with you) to sneak out of the performance of its conditions. I am personally interested in the matter; therefore I suggest to you couple of piety-mouthing, hypocritical thieves & liars that you change your customary policy this time.   Truly Yours,

"S. L. Clemens"

(Hartford, MTP; without identification of addressees in PMT, p. 760.)

2. *Life on the Mississippi,* published in England on 12 May by Chatto & Windus. In March, Howells had congratulated Osgood on the big first printing of the American edition, and expressed his pleasure in "Clemens' having done it again" (Florence, 13 March, Columbia, AGM TS). Since a copy of the American edition was not filed for copyright until 17 May, the book was presumably not published in the United States before that date.

3. Amasa Stone, railroad builder, capitalist, and philanthropist, who had insisted on the experimental construction of a railroad bridge at Ashtabula, Ohio, the town in which first William Cooper Howells and then his son Joseph had been publishing the Ashtabula *Sentinel* since 1852. Stone's health had failed after the bridge collapsed under a trainload of people in 1878 and he was blamed for the disaster.

4. This remark is rather ironic in view of the fact that Clemens was to spend in Europe almost ten of the remaining twenty-seven years of his life.

324. HOWELLS TO CLEMENS

> S.S. Parisian, off the Straits
> of Belle Isle, and about
> 180 miles from Greenland,
> July 10, 1883.

My dear Clemens:

We saw the Gerhards in Paris. I took a fiacre and drove literally hell-wards to the region of the Boulevard d'Enfer, near which they live, and found the little woman preparing asparagus for their dinner in his studio. There was a stove in the middle of the room, a lounge-bed for the nurse and baby at one side, and a curtained corner where I suppose the Gerhards slept. It was as primitive and simple as all Chicopee,[1] and virtuous poverty spoke from every appointment of the place. Gerhard was off at work somewhere, but the next day they both came to see us at our hotel, and Mrs. Howells took a great liking to them. She thought Mrs. G. thoroughly good and honest and very ambitious for her husband, and she thought that he was looking a little worn with overwork. I should think that he had used the time you've given him very conscientiously, and that he had studied hard; it seemed to me also that they were keeping a good conscience about living economically, in a city which seems to me rather more expensive than New York. I don't know how far your beneficence is to extend to them; but if you are still paying their way it wouldn't cost any more to let them run down into Italy for three or four months than it would to keep them in Paris — not as much — and Gerhard needs some sort of outing, and he could learn while he was resting in Italy.[2] He seems to be a man of delicate and refined genius; the little medallion which he exhibited of you in the Salon was full of this, and seized your best points; it was artfully concealed from the public in the catalogue as the portrait of "M. Marc Swain," but it was favorably noticed by the critics. — You are those poor little people's god — I don't know but they'd like me to write you with the large G.

If you answer this letter, you can write me to the care of Osgoods in my own blessed Boston, so nearly are my wanderings over, I hope; for we are now supposed to be within three days of Quebec. When we meet I'll tell about my experiences in England and with the English elsewhere: on paper I might seem to brag. — One night I met Thomas Hardy, the novelist, at dinner; and he said, "Why don't people understand that Mark Twain is not merely a great humorist? He's a very remarkable fellow in a very different way," and then went on to praise your Mississippi in a manner that justified all the admiration I had ever felt for his books.

The family join me in love to both Mrs. Clemens and yourself.   Yours ever

W. D. Howells.

1. This has the air of a proverbial expression, but the editors are unable to explain it.

2. Gerhardt described his and his wife's visit with the Howellses in a letter to Clemens on 7 June. He mentioned Howells's suggestion of a visit to Italy, and in a letter of 17 June canvassed the advantages and disadvantages of the idea, asking Clemens's advice (Paris, MTP). He did not, in the end, go to Italy before his return to the United States in the summer of 1884.

Elmira, July 20/83.

My Dear Howells —

We are desperately glad you & your gang are home again — may you never travel again, till you go aloft or alow. Charley Clark has gone to the other side for a run — will be back in August. He had been sick, & needed the trip very much.

Mrs. Clemens had a long & wasting spell of sickness last spring, & is still proportioned like the tongs, but she is pulling up, now, & by & by will get some cushions on her, I reckon. I hope so, anyway — it's been like sleeping with a bed full of baskets. The children are booming, & my health is ridiculous, it's so robust, notwithstanding the newspaper misreports.

I haven't piled up MS so in years as I have done since we came here to the farm three weeks & a half ago. Why, it's like old times, to step straight into the study, damp from the breakfast table, & sail right in & sail right on, the whole day long, without thought of running short of stuff or words. I wrote 4000 words to-day & I touch 3000 & upwards pretty often, & don't fall below 2600 on any working day. And when I get fagged out, I lie abed a couple of days & read & smoke, & then go it again for 6 or 7 days. I have finished one small book,[1] & am away along in a big one that I half-finished two or three years ago.[2] I expect to complete it in a month or six weeks or two months more. And *I* shall *like* it, whether anybody else does or not.[3] It's a kind of companion to Tom Sawyer. There's a raft episode from it in second or third chapter of Life on the Mississippi.

Day before yesterday I struck a dull place in my head,[4] so I knocked off work & ⟨mapped⟩ measured off the reigns of the English Kings on our roadway, (a foot to the year,) from the Conqueror down, & drove a peg in the ground for each King — 21 feet from the Conqueror to Rufus; 13 to Henry I; 35 to Stephen; 19 to Henry II; 35 to Richard; 10 to John; 17 to Henry III; 56 to Edward I — & so on. You get the idea? — so't

435

you can glance out over the grounds & *see* how short or long a king's reign was, by the distance his peg is from the next one. My notion is, to get up an open-air game which shall put all these names & dates & statistics into the children's heads without the bore of study. I got vastly interested in this nonsense, & after I went to bed last night I worked out a plan for making it an indoor game also — play it with cards & a cribbage board. I'm booming, these days — got health & spirits to *waste* — got an overplus; & if I were at home, we would write a play. But we must do it anyhow by & by.

We stay here till Sept. 10; then maybe a week at Indian Neck[5] for sea air. Then home.

We *are* powerful glad you are all back; & send love according.

Yrs Ever

Mark.

1. Possibly the MS which Howells was to comment upon in letter 328, "1002d Arabian Night."

2. *Adventures of Huckleberry Finn* (despite MTW, p. 57n). Mark Twain had written 400 MS pp. of "Huck Finn's Autobiography" in the summer of 1876, taking it up again (probably) in the winter of 1879–80 (Blair, "When Was *Huckleberry Finn* Written?" AL, XXX, 1–25).

3. This assertion should be kept in mind as an offset to Mark Twain's often-quoted comment in 1876 (to Howells, 9 August) that he liked *Huckleberry Finn* "only tolerably well, as far as I have got, & may possibly pigeon-hole or burn the MS when it is done."

4. By inference from Mark Twain's associative patterns of thinking, the dull place might be the point in the novel where Huck tells Jim about kings, at the end of Chapter XXIII; or a point just before that, on the assumption that the game involving kings' reigns served as the stimulus for taking up the novel again with Huck's historical discourse.

5. On the coast below New Haven, near Branford, Conn.

326. HOWELLS TO CLEMENS

4 Louisburg Square, Boston, Aug. 12, 1883.

My dear Clemens:

What I've done to you is to launch a lord at you. The Earl

of Onslow, now eating breakfasts at Newport, was one of our fellow-passengers on the Parisian, and I gave him a letter to you, because I liked him and he liked you.[1] He seemed a simple, quiet, gentlemanly man, with a good taste in literature which he evinced by going about with my books in his pockets and talking of yours. That is the whole story; and knowing that you liked "good" Englishmen, I ventured. He will be in Hartford about January and February; so you will have time to get settled before he comes. Mrs. Clemens will like his Countess, who is very pretty and agreeable, and not at all unlike a pleasant sort of American. The Earl is out of health I believe, and is here to get it back. He's a light of the Beef-steak Club in London, and seems to know a lot of artists and literary men. I dare say we shall meet before you see him, and then I can post you further, if I can think of anything else.

I admire your method of English history by the running foot, and predict a success for it. You had better patent or copyright it before some one else gets hold of it; I see the newspapers have exploited it.[2]

By the way, do you want to go in for a pair of grape-scissors which my father has invented? They are for gathering grapes, and enable a man to do it with one hand and convey them without bruising to the basket he carries in the other; and they have been patented.[3]

We have taken this house for a year, and you can't come to see us in it any too soon. We wish that Mrs. Clemens could come with you, and we both long to see you both.

Mrs. Howells joins me in love to all of you.

Yours ever

W. D. Howells.

---

1. William Hillier Onslow, the fourth Earl, thirty years old at the time he met Howells on the S.S. *Parisian,* was soon to become Governor of New Zealand and was eventually made Undersecretary for India. Howells's characterizing Onslow as a "good" Englishman suggests his divided feelings about the English. In Venice during the Civil War, he had been enraged by the strong pro-Southern talk and sentiment in the British colony there. His "attack" on Dickens and Thackeray in his essay on Henry James, of

November 1882, had turned many English critics sharply against his work and had aroused personal hostility in some of them. Yet he had been widely entertained and honored in England, both on his way to Italy and, more recently, on his return; and his farce, *A Letter of Introduction* (1892), deals more sharply with the reverent Anglophilia of the Bostonian characters than it does with a young visiting Englishman's enthusiastic misunderstanding of "California humor."

2. The Hartford *Courant* had published an account of the game on 24 July (p. 2). See letter 327, note 2.

3. Clemens, with his taste for inventions, eventually guaranteed William Cooper Howells against any loss in the venture of manufacturing and selling the shears (letter 327; WDH to WCH, Boston, 17 December 1883, Houghton). Charles L. Webster found a toolmaker in Newark named Peter Lowentraut who produced sixty dozen pairs of the shears, and for a time advertised them for sale (CLW to SLC, New York, 7 November, 4 December 1883, MTP).

327. CLEMENS TO HOWELLS

Elmira, Aug 22/83.

My Dear Howells —

How odd it seems, to sit down to write a letter with the feeling that you've got *time* to do it. But I'm done work, for this season, & so have got time. I've done two seasons' work in one, & haven't anything left to do, now, but revise. I've written eight or nine hundred MS pages in such a brief space of time that I mustn't name the number of days; *I* shouldn't believe it myself, & ⟨therefore⟩ of course couldn't expect you to.[1] I used to restrict myself to 4 & 5 hours a day & 5 days in the week; but this time I've wrought from breakfast till 5.15 p.m. six days in the week; & once or twice I smouched a Sunday when the boss wasn't looking. Nothing is half so good as literature hooked on Sunday on the sly.

I wrote you & Twichell on the same night; & was appalled to get a note from him saying he was going to print part of my letter, & was going to do it before I could get a chance to

4 Louisburg Square,
   Boston, Aug. 12, 1883.
My dear Clemens:
      What I've done to
you is to launch a lord
at you. The Earl of Ons-
low, now eating breakfasts
at Newport, was one of our
fellow-passengers on the Parisian, and I gave him a
letter to you, because I
liked him and he liked you.
He seemed a simple, quiet,
gentlemanly man, with a
good taste in literature which
he evinced by going about
with my books in his pockets
and talking of yours.
That is the whole story, and

Beginning of letter 326, Howells to Clemens. (For Clemens's misreading of Howells's handwriting, see letter 327.)

Elmira, July 21/85.

My Dear Howells —

You are really my only author; I am restricted to you; I wouldn't give a damn for the rest. I bored through Middlemarch during the past week, with its labored & tedious analyses of feelings & motives, its paltry & tiresome people, its unexciting & uninteresting story, & its frequent blinding flashes of single-sentence poetry, philosophy, wit, & what-not, & nearly died from the over-work. I wouldn't read another of those books for a farm. I did try to read one other ——

Beginning of letter 410, Clemens to Howells.

forbid it. I telegraphed him, but was of course too late.[2] He not only made me feel ridiculous, but he broke up & ruined a fine large plan of mine. ⟨— a several-thousand dollar plan⟩ So I wrote him a letter which was pretty much all English — & he hasn't replied yet, after all these weeks. But he didn't print any of it.[3]

If you haven't ever tried to invent an indoor historical game, *don't*.[4] I've got the thing at last so it will work, I guess, but I don't want any more tasks of that kind. When I wrote you, I thought I *had* it; whereas I was only merely entering upon the initiatory difficulties of it. I might have known it wouldn't be an easy job, or somebody would have invented a decent historical game long ago — a thing which nobody *had* done. I think I've got it in pretty fair shape — so I have *caveated* it.[5] If I fetch it out it will cost a raft of money to do it; but if I don't fetch it out, I shall wish to be counted in on the grape-scissors, for I must speculate in something, such being my nature.

Earl of Onston — is that it?[6] All right, we shall be very glad to receive them & get acquainted with them. And much obliged to you, too. There's plenty of worse people than the nobilities. I went up & spent a week with the Marquis & the Princess Louise,[7] & had as good a time as *I* want.

I'm powerful glad you are all back again; & we *will* come up there if our little tribe will give us the necessary furlough; & if we can't get it, you folks must come to us & give us an extension of time. We get home Sept. 11.

Hello, I think I see Waring[8] coming!

Good-bye — letter from Clark, which explains for him. Love to you all from the

Clemenses.

OVER[9]

No — it wasn't Waring. I wonder what the devil *has* become of that man. He was to spend to-day with us, & the day's most gone, now.

We are enjoying your story[10] with our usual unspeakableness; & I'm right glad you threw in the shipwreck & the mystery — I *like* it. Mrs. Crane thinks it's the best story you've written yet. We — but *we* ALWAYS think the last one is the best. And why shouldn't it be? Practice helps.

P.S. I thought I had sent all our loves to all of you, but Mrs. Clemens says I haven't. Damn it, a body can't think of everything; but a woman thinks you can. I better seal this, now — else there'll be more criticism.

I perceive I haven't got the love in, yet. Well, we *do* send the love of all the family to all the Howellses.

S L C

1. This euphoric burst of creative energy had gone into the writing of *Huckleberry Finn*. A month earlier Clemens had written to his mother: "I haven't had such booming working-days for many years. I am piling up manuscript in a really astonishing way. I believe I shall complete, in two months, a book which I have been fooling over for 7 years" (Elmira, 21 July 1883, MTL, p. 434).

2. Twichell had caused extracts from a letter to him from Clemens (Elmira, 20 July) to be inserted in the Hartford *Courant* of 24 July ("Mark Twain's Vacation," p. 2). A paragraph explains in somewhat greater detail the scheme of driving pegs along the driveway to mark the reigns of English kings which Clemens described to Howells in his letter of 20 July. "The reason it took me eight hours," adds the letter quoted in the *Courant,* "was because with little J[ean]'s interrupting assistance, I had to measure from the Conquest to the end of Henry VI. three times over — and besides I had to whittle out all those pegs."

3. Twichell was, however, unrepentant. "I'm glad to have such a thing set going the rounds," he wrote, "on account of the pleasant impression it will make of M.T." (Hartford, 24 July, MTP). On 8 September he was still "entirely impenitent," but said he would "write a vow never to do anything of the kind again" (Hartford, MTP).

4. In the letter which Twichell published in the *Courant,* Clemens says: "I did a full day's work and a third over, yesterday, but was full of my game after I went to bed, — trying to fit it for *in*doors. So I didn't get to sleep till pretty late; but when I did go off, I had contrived a way to play my history game with cards and a cribbage board" (24 July, p. 2). This was the "fine large plan" which Clemens believed Twichell had spoiled. He spent much time trying to devise a board with holes in it for pegs to be inserted by players who gave correct answers about dates in English history; he meant to place the game on the market. He wrote to Edward H. House on 1 October 1883 that Twichell's publication of his letter "broke up some quite extensive plans of mine, & squandered & rendered useless the material out of which I had meant to build an illustrated small book —

but that was the smallest part of the plan which he ruined" (Hartford, Barrett).

5. The caveat, as Charles L. Webster explained to Clemens (New York, 31 July 1883, MTP), "holds good for one year and no one can apply for a similar patent without your being first notified . . . you have three months still from date of notification in which to perfect your patent. The caveat can be extended after the 1st year by paying $10.00 a year." The actual patent on the game is dated 18 August 1885 (MTP).

6. Clemens's reading "Earl of Onslow" as "Earl of Onston" indicates how hard to decipher Howells's handwriting became, at certain periods, under physical and nervous pressure. As early as 1871 his wrist had weakened to the point where he changed his style of handwriting a dozen times a day, to no avail (WDH to WCH, Cambridge, 30 July, Houghton). In 1886 Howells would apologize to Henry James for sending a typewritten letter, and explain that his wrist had weakened again and his handwriting had "gone all to pieces" (Boston, 25 December, LinL, I, 386).

7. Clemens made a flying trip to Montreal early in May to secure his British copyright on *Life on the Mississippi,* returned briefly to Hartford, and went back for a stay later in the month in Government House, Ottawa, as the guest of the Marquis of Lorne, then Governor-General of Canada, and the Princess Louise, daughter of Queen Victoria. Invitations to Clemens and Mrs. Clemens for a reception and dinner on 24 May are in MTP.

8. George E. Waring. He had written from Newport on 19 August (MTP) that a pressing matter in Buffalo would make it impossible for him to stop in Elmira, but Clemens had evidently not yet received the letter.

9. This notation appears at the bottom of p. 5 of the letter, but nothing is written on the verso. The letter and postscript continue on a new sheet, recto and verso.

10. The September installment of *A Woman's Reason* in the *Century.*

328. HOWELLS TO CLEMENS

4 Louisburg Square [Boston], Sept. 18, 1883.

My dear Clemens:

Osgood gave me your MS. to read last night, and I understood from him that you wanted my opinion of it. The opening passages are the funniest you have ever done; but when I got into the story itself, it seemed to me that I was made a fellow-sufferer with the Sultan from Sheherazade's prolixity. The effect was like that of a play in which the audience is surprised along with the characters by some turn in the plot. I don't mean to say that there were not extremely killing things in it; but on the whole it was not your best or your second-best; and all the way it skirts a certain kind of fun which you can't afford to indulge in: it's a little too broad, as well as exquisitely ludicrous, at times.

You're such an impartial critic of your own work that I feel doubly brutal, and as if I were taking a mean advantage of your magnanimity when I fail to like something of yours. But I fail so seldom that I have some heart to forgive myself. At any rate I feel bound to say that I think this burlesque falls short of being amusing. Very likely, if you gave it to the public, it might be a great success; there is no telling how these things may go, and I am but one poor, fallible friend of yours.[1]

You are back in Hartford again, and I mean to see you there before long on my way to visit my father in Virginia.[2] Mallory of the Madison Sq. Theatre has asked me to meet him here on Thursday and talk play. Perhaps I shall have something to report.

You're all well enough to stand the shock of our united affection, I hope.   Yours ever

W. D. Howells.

1. Howells's tact as a friend and his taste as a critic are particularly clear in this letter. Clemens had been writing "1002d Arabian Night" (DV 353 and 353a, MTP) more or less alternately with *Huckleberry Finn,* and could not easily distinguish between his finest novel and a work DeVoto justly spoke of as "almost lethal" in its dullness (MTW, p. 60). The "certain kind of fun" to which Howells objects arises from the fact that the framework of the tale places the beautiful Scherezade in bed with King Shahriyar. Though Clemens thought of publishing "1002d" anonymously the next spring, "right after Huck," in a format that would allow it to be sold for fifteen or twenty cents (SLC to CLW, 14 April 1884, MTBM, p. 249), he soon dropped the idea of printing it in any form.

2. Howells's father bought a farm in 1884 on the James River near Richmond after renting one in Goochland County, Va., but his farming, at the age of seventy-six, proved a failure and he returned with his family to Jefferson, Ohio (LinL, I, 340).

329. CLEMENS TO HOWELLS

Hartford [September] 20th/83

Dear Howells —

While madam stops in at this house to gouge this lady out of one of her servants on the sly, I will drop you a line in my notebook to say your letter is just received last night & we — d–n the d–d expression, I've forgotten it already — Mrs. Clemens furnished it, & it was very neat — but anyway, the idea of it was, to send our love to you & Mrs. Howells & say we are desperately anxious & in a hurry to see you both; & will you come right along, now? Right away — to-morrow, next day, any day you please. (Everybody that drives by, bows to me, & it makes a most confusing procession of interruptions; so I shant try to write any more — but you get the idea of what I wanted to say, anyway, & Mrs. C will write Mrs. H, so as to have all the etiquettical requirements fulfilled).   Ys Ever

Mark.

330. HOWELLS TO CLEMENS

4 Louisburg Square, Boston, Sept. 30, 1883.

Dear Clemens:

I find that I shall not be able to stop at Hartford on my way south, but I hope to see you coming back, ten days later.

I leave here to-morrow on the 4.30 P.M. train: [1] why couldn't you meet me at the depot, if only for the few minutes it stops? Or if you had the time, run down as far [as] the next station with me? Do!   Yours ever

W. D. Howells.

1. Howells was setting out for a visit with his father in Virginia.

331. HOWELLS TO CLEMENS

4 Louisburg Square Boston, Oct. 12, 1883.

My dear Clemens:

As soon as I mentioned our plan for a play, Mrs. Howells nobly declared that she would do anything for money, and that I might go to you when I liked.[1] She will come to spend part of the time with me — the last part. She thinks the Earl of Durham business is a famous idea.[2]

I suppose I can be with you in about ten days.

Mrs. Howells joins me in love to your family.

Yours ever

W. D. Howells.

P.S. Be thinking over what proportion of the spoil you could give me if the play came to a head.

1. In March of this year Marshall H. Mallory had written to Clemens that before Howells left for Europe he had been "in negotiation with me for a play for the Madison Square Theatre," and had referred Mallory to Clemens (New York, 21 March 1883, MTP). Now that *Huckleberry Finn* and "1002d" were finished, Clemens was ready to respond to Mallory's renewed expression of interest (see letter 328). On 29 September he had asked Charles L. Webster to "get that play out of your safe — 'Colonel Sellers as a Scientist' — & express it to me" (Hartford, Webster, TS in MTP).

2. Clemens has now evidently proposed making Sellers the American claimant to an English earldom, in the manner of Jesse M. Leathers (see letter 228 and Appendix).

332. CLEMENS TO HOWELLS

Hartford, Oct 15/83.

My Dear Howells —

Your letter must have reached here Saturday, but I didn't run across it till this minute — it lay under the newspaper mail.

Good — then I will expect you at the time specified, & **Mrs. Howells** at the time which she has selected: & ye will both be welcome.

As to the apportionment of spoil, it would in most any play but this, be half & half, naturally & of course; but in this case I will smouch two-thirds if the reasons & arguments which I shall lay before you shall convince & wholly satisfy you;[1] but if they shouldn't, the apportionment will then be equal division of the swag, & no cussing.

Of course I ought to have gone to New Britain before this,[2] but I allowed one thing & then another to interfere; — the main trouble being that I don't like to travel so far without company, & I couldn't seem to get the right kind. That is all arranged now, though; for unless Providence springs a purely wanton & unnecessary wedding or funeral on us, I can have Twichell's company tomorrow. But with my prejudices, I never count any prospective chickens when I know that Providence knows where the nest is. How many an ill-assorted match has been suddenly precipitated, & the parties to it doomed to life-long unhappiness, merely that Providence might head off a preacher who had it in his mind to do a sinner a good turn — & many a person has been untimely killed by Providence with no better end in view. And how do you suppose the books are kept up there? Are the entries made with frankness, candor, squareness?

1845.
In account with John
L. Smith —

Time not properly up till May 27, 1888; knocked out with lightning, June 4, 1845, in order to provide a funeral job for his pastor, who would otherwise have gone off junketing with a person whose errand it was desirable to balk.

It is doubtable.   Ys Ever

                                                      Mark.

P.S. Tom Sawyer has been steadily climbing for years — & now at last, as per enclosed statement, has achieved second place in the list of my old books.[3] I think that this promises pretty well for Huck Finn. Although I mean to publish Huck in a volume by itself, I think I will also ⟨publish it in a⟩ ⟨combine⟩ jam it & Sawyer into a volume *together* at the same time, since Huck is in some sense a continuation of the former story.

1. Clemens means that he deserves the larger share of the royalties because Colonel Sellers, the central character, is his creation. For the same reason, he had asked Warner to release all claim to a share in the proceeds from the play *Colonel Sellers* (Elmira, 5 May 1874, MTP).

2. The occasion of Clemens's visit to New Britain — some ten miles southwest of Hartford on the main rail line to New Haven and New York — cannot now be discovered.

3. The enclosed statement of sales of Mark Twain's books, submitted by the American Publishing Co. (SLC to CLW, Hartford, 15 October 1883, MTBM, p. 223), has been lost, but a statement covering the first three months of 1883 showed that 600 copies of *Tom Sawyer* had been sold, as against 594 copies of *The Innocents Abroad*, 486 of *A Tramp Abroad*, 414 of *Roughing It*, and smaller numbers of *The Gilded Age* and *Sketches* (CLW to SLC, New York, 7 April 1883, MTP).

333. HOWELLS TO CLEMENS

Boston, Oct. 17, 1883.

My dear Clemens:

The terms are good and just: two thirds for you and one for me. I'll probably be with you about the 2d of November — I'm afraid I can't before; I have to get the family in winter running order, and pay up some bills falling due, then, and get my story [1] well started.

We must take old Sellers back to Virginia, and start him fresh in Richmond! [2] Place reviving and everything to rekindle his energies. We could get some wonderful types by simply dropping down there.

I've read every bit about Sellers in the book. [3] There's a great play in him yet. [4]   Yours ever

W. D. Howells.

1. Probably *Indian Summer*.
2. Howells had just visited Richmond on his trip to see his father.

3. *The Gilded Age.*

4. That is, despite the fact that one play had already been built around Sellers.

334. HOWELLS TO CLEMENS

4 Louisburg Square, Boston, Nov. 1, 1883.

My dear Clemens:

I expect now to go to Hartford by the 4:30 train Saturday afternoon.[1] It *may* be that I cannot get off till Monday; in that case I will telegraph you.

Osgood told me of your inspiration during sermon-time,[2] and I am very curious to see it. I have kept my own imagination in check till we meet, having only the idea that Sellers should be on the stage as much as possible.   Yours ever

W. D. Howells.

Couldn't we do some such business as Hawkins [3] always treating him in private as an Earl, and suffering from the disrespect that others showed him?

1. 3 November.

2. The inspiration (which presumably came to Clemens while his mind wandered during Joe Twichell's admittedly uninspired preaching) evidently concerned *Colonel Sellers as a Scientist,* but his report of it to Osgood was either oral or contained in a letter not now extant.

3. Washington Hawkins is a character from *The Gilded Age* introduced into *Colonel Sellers as a Scientist.*

335. CLEMENS TO HOWELLS

[Hartford] Sunday [4 November 1883].[1]

My Dear Howells —

I telegraphed last night "Come Wednesday" because Mrs. Clemens has a menagerie on her hands from now till Tuesday

Evening — the preparation & achievement of a big lunch party of old ladies to meet her mother.

Raymond strenuously objects to my terms,[2] thus far, but I have no others to offer him. Meantime I have instructed Webster to look sharp for the right actor, & when he thinks he has found him, I will go to New York & see him play. You better watch & inquire — we might strike the right man there.

Raymond is to play the old play [3] in New York after Xmas. So he *thinks* — but doubtless I'll spring quite a disorganizing surprise on him before that.   Yrs Ever

                                                                Mark

1. The date of this letter is set by Howells's proposal in his previous note to come on either Saturday (3 November) or Monday (5 November). The inference is that Howells did not take the train Saturday afternoon, but telegraphed he would come on Monday; whereupon Clemens wired back proposing Wednesday instead. On 11 November, Howells wrote his father from Hartford: "I have been here some days with Clemens, who is expecting his nephew to report upon the scissors business very shortly. . . . I think Clemens means to take hold of it . . . " (Houghton).

2. Probably $400 a week for the use of the play (SLC to CLW, 2 January 1884, MTBM, p. 231).

3. *Colonel Sellers.*

336. HOWELLS TO CLEMENS

Boston, Nov. 19, 1883.

Dear Clemens —

I enclose a scrap or two from a newspaper with valuable suggestions for Sellers inventions. I have just been talking with Mrs. Howells about when I can go to Hartford for the revision, & I have about concluded to postpone it till I can see a week clear before me. The trouble now is that I am so tired — actually brain-weary — with our work on the play already that I couldn't do anything on it that wouldn't hurt it for five or six days at any rate. Then Cable comes here to read next Monday,[1] & in decency I ought to be present. By the first of December

Arnold is to be here again with a lecture that he has several times told me he has put me into, & so I ought to be on hand to hear that.[2] I don't believe, therefore that I can get to Hartford with a solid week before me & a good conscience behind me till two weeks from to-day. But the time needn't a moment of it be lost. We are perfectly sure to make that play just what you want it & you can push on the negotiations with Raymond on that understanding. As soon as you have the type-writer copy complete, send it to me & I will doctor all the dialogue except the Sellers speeches. When we meet we can go over them together & my corrections, & decide about them.

I have been about half dead to-day from eating & laughing yesterday. I hope that having got rid of me, you got safely off from the Aldriches. That was a terrible moment yesterday when she consented to let you go to Norton's with me, & never did a wish fulfilled bring me so little joy.[3] None but the pitying angels will ever know, what Mrs. Howells said to me when she got me out of doors. She began by saying that I was always very lenient to *her* when she committed a blunder, & so she was not going to be hard on me. But I think the enormity of my crime must have grown upon her as she painted it to me. At any rate I never wish to be *spared* again.

This is done on the new type writer I told you of. You see how distinctly it writes.[4] I can use it with a fair degree of speed, & I shall give it fair trial. I have hired it for a month, paying $10 which goes as a payment on the machine if I keep it. It is only to cost $40 in all.

Mrs. Howells sends her love with mine to all your house. Pilla is very anxious to go back with me & see your girls. Tell Clara not to neglect that calf.[5]   Yours ever

W. D. Howells.

1. 26 November.

2. Matthew Arnold had lectured in Boston on 7 and 17 November, and in Hartford on the fifteenth. Howells, with the Clemenses, had attended a reception for Arnold given in Hartford by the David Clarks on the evening of the fourteenth (Hartford *Courant,* 15 November, p. 2; James D. McCallum, "The Apostle of Culture Meets America," NEQ, II, 357–381,

July 1929). In his third Boston lecture, on 1 December (Boston *Transcript*, 3 December 1883, p. 4), Arnold said: " . . . think of the turn of the good people of our race for producing a life of hideousness and immense ennui; think of that specimen of your own New England life which Mr. Howells gives us in one of his charming stories which I was reading lately; think of the life of that ragged New England farm in the *Lady of the Aroostook*; think of Deacon Blood [Deacon Latham], and Aunt Maria, and the straight-backed chairs with black horse-hair seats, and Ezra Perkins with perfect self-reliance depositing his travellers in the snow!" (*Discourses in America*, London, 1885, p. 187).

3. The social situation alluded to here is obscure, except for the indication that Clemens was in Boston on 18 November and there accompanied the Howellses in a call upon the Aldriches. Clemens had disliked Lilian Aldrich since his first meeting with her in 1868. Aldrich on that occasion brought Clemens to his home, having invited him to dinner. But Mrs. Aldrich, concluding that he was drunk because he lolled around and gestured and drawled in his usual fashion, refrained from ordering dinner to be served, and Clemens left unfed (*Crowding Memories*, Boston, 1920, pp. 128–132). He recalled in 1906 that he had conceived an aversion for her "the first time I saw her," and added, "I do not believe I could ever learn to like her except on a raft at sea with no other provisions in sight" (MTE, pp. 293, 295).

4. It used an italic script typeface with capitals and lower-case letters.

5. Clara's calf, named Jumbo, was probably the one Patrick McAleer, the coachman, had persuaded her would turn into a horse if she curried him every morning and put a saddle and bridle on him (MFMT, p. 28).

337. CLEMENS TO HOWELLS (TELEGRAM)

Hartford Conn Nov 19, 1883.

W D Howells, 4 Louisburg Square; Boston.

Please do come right along You and Mrs Howells and pilla and Save me from imminent trouble.[1] One of my Very Chiefest Commissions was to arrange this Visit and bring positive acceptance from Mrs Howells and I am having bushels of difficulty to explain why I dont seem to have accomplished it I have told thirty lies and am not out of the Woods yet; S L Clemens

1. Clemens is evidently repeating an invitation he had delivered to the Howellses during the visit in Boston from which he had just returned.

He had of course not yet received Howells's letter of the very same day.

338. HOWELLS TO CLEMENS

[Boston, 20 November 1883]

Forgot to enclose these scraps [1] last night.

Your noble telegram came just after I'd posted my letter. Sorry for *you* and grateful to Mrs. Clemens. But at present it isn't possible.   Yours

W. D. H.

Nov. 20

1. The newspaper clippings mentioned in letter 336.

339. CLEMENS TO HOWELLS

Hartford Nov 21/83

Dear Howells —

Good — & all right. Within an hour I shall be deep in an old piece of work which always interests me, any time of the year that I take it up.[1] So I will go down into that, & not appear at the surface again till the Howellses arrive here the 3d of December.[2]

I'll send you the play to-day — & while you are working at it, introduce more people on the stage, or new incidents, where they may seem *necessary*. And another turn or so of the *phonograph*.[3] And maybe Sellers with his robe of the Garter & his coronet.

You make a mighty clean proof with your type-writer. (Cable [4] is stopping with us over night. He's been training under an expert, & he's just a rattling reader now — the best amateur I ever heard; & with 2 seasons of *public* practice, I guess he'll be the best professional reader alive.) It'll *pay* the Howellses & Aldriches & their friends to go & hear him.

Of course Mrs. C instructed me to arrange about that visit

451

with Mrs. Howells, because she *said* she did; & she says that you also knew that that would be a part of my Boston business — but *I've* no recollection of it. I thought it had all been fixed before. I thought you were to come here, & Mrs. Howells & Pilla to *follow*. I am required to explain *why* I thought that. It's a hell of a thing to require of a person. But it seems to me, sometimes, that there is nothing Mrs. Clemens *won't* require of a person. Why can't a body be reasonable? — *I* can't be supposed to know everything, & do everything right, & never make any mistakes. But as soon as I see Mrs. Howells, I will apologize & ⟨expl⟩ — no, just apologize.   Ys Ever

Mark.

1. Possibly the Sandwich Islands story about Bill Ragsdale (letter 344).

2. I.e., two weeks from 19 November (the date Howells gave, letter 336).

3. One of the schemes with which Colonel Sellers was to be concerned in the play. His idea was to record profanity for use in emergencies at sea, to supplement the efforts of ships' officers in giving orders to their crews. *Colonel Sellers as a Scientist* would eventually be produced on a set filled with machines and gadgets lent by Thomas A. Edison, including a phonograph (letter 457, note 2). Although Clemens was more emphatically the frustrated Franklin, Howells shared his fascination with the gadgetry of the Gilded Age, and made a series of farces turn on the spectacle of men caught in their own machines.

4. George Washington Cable had first met Howells and then the Clemenses and Warners in the summer of 1881, and had shown Mark Twain and Osgood around New Orleans at the end of their trip down the Mississippi. He was now lecturing in New England and about to decide to settle in the North (Guy A. Cardwell, *Twins of Genius,* East Lansing, 1953, pp. 1–3).

340. HOWELLS TO CLEMENS

Boston, Dec. 3, 1883.

My dear Clemens:

After telegrafing you yesterday I hoped to have gone to Hartford to-day; but Mrs. Howells couldn't let me, in view of the pending arrival of my sister, with her two little children, and with or without her husband,[1] whose artistic nature I haven't been able to extract any information out of on that point. It's provoking; but I can't help it. I'm in the meantime reducing the work of revision on the play to a minimum. Yesterday, just before I fell asleep after dinner, I remembered the flying machine business,[2] which you invented in the old plot, and as soon as I got up, I struck out a gorgeous scene between Sellers and his wife, where he tries his wings from a chair on a table. He comes down in a lump, but he considers the experiment perfectly successful. The wings are to be used in connection with the extinguisher.[3] The scene occurs in Act III, just before the interviewer appears, and Sellers wears the wings through the rest of the act. You can imagine how delicious he will be with them, gesticulating in his final speech. I felt that the Act III needed lengthening and strengthening, and this is the very thing. We shall now have the wings, the interviewer and the éclaircissment about De Bohun[4] in it, and I think it will go with a yell. But the wings-scene needs some genuine Sellersism from you.

I hope you will keep a stiff upper lip with Raymond.[5] We've got a great play, and if he declines, we can make a new Sellers out of some one else. He should agree to put the play on at once.

Cable has had a fine success, here.[6] We gave him a little blow out.[7]

I'll write or telegraph as soon as I can come. Yours, with the family love to all of you

W. D. Howells.

1. Annie Howells Fréchette; her poet-husband Achille, of Quebec; and their children, Marie Marguerite and Howells (Frederic C. Marston, Jr., "Descendants of Thomas Howells," MS).

2. Orion Clemens was "inventing a *flying machine*" in 1873 when the Clemenses returned briefly to New York from England (MTB, p. 495).

3. A device for putting out fires which Colonel Sellers wore on his back. It had the disastrous effect of making fires burn even more furiously, because it contained "Greekfire" and operated on the "principle of vaccination."

4. Rupert de Bohun is a character in the play whom Sellers believes he has "materialized" after death. The *éclaircissement*, at the end of Act III, reveals that de Bohun is a living man, suitor for the hand of Sellers's daugh-

ter and willing to renounce his claim to the earldom of Dover in favor of Sellers, the American claimant, if Sellers will consent to the marriage.

5. Four days earlier Mark Twain had told Webster he was offering Raymond the play because he had a "sentimental right" to it, though no moral or legal right — but was offering it to him only once (Hartford, 30 November 1883, MTBM, p. 228).

6. Cable had lectured at Chickering Hall in Boston on 26 and 28 November, and would lecture again on 4 December. Howells and Holmes had "endorsed him in the newspapers" and he had been a guest at the reception for Matthew Arnold at the St. Botolph Club (Turner, *Cable,* p. 147).

7. At the Tavern Club on 27 November; it was attended by nearly a hundred guests (Turner, *Cable,* p. 147; WDH to Cable, telegram, Auburndale, Mass., n.d., Tilton, AGM TS).

341. HOWELLS TO CLEMENS (POSTCARD)

[Boston, 19 December 1883] [1]

Saw Warren [2] today, but he couldn't tell me anything. He has only a slight acquaintance with F. [3] Why not telegraph?

W. D. H.

1. The date is of the postmark.

2. William Warren (1812–1888) was a celebrated comic actor, said to have studied seven hundred roles, who had been identified with the Boston Museum for more than thirty years at the time of his retirement in May 1883 (Kate Ryan, *Old Boston Museum Days,* Boston, 1915, pp. 25–43). Both Howells and Clemens were now looking for an actor to play Sellers if Raymond would not accept their terms. Apparently they had been working hard on the play, some of the time face to face, for Howells had been in Hartford with Clemens, probably on 9 December (WDH to JRO, Boston, 6 December, Houghton, AGM TS; WDH to CDW, Boston, 27 December, Watkinson, AGM TS), and Clemens was at 4 Louisburg Square on 17 December when Howells wrote his father, "I've just askt Mark Twain, sitting on the other side of the fire, about your scissors" (Houghton, AGM TS).

3. William Jermyn Florence (the stage name of Bernard Conlin), an American comedian who excelled in dialect impersonation.